LONDON JEWS
AND
BRITISH COMMUNISM,
1935–1945

LONDON JEWS
AND
BRITISH COMMUNISM,
1935–1945

Henry Felix Srebrnik

VALLENTINE MITCHELL

First published in 1995 in Great Britain by
VALLENTINE MITCHELL & CO. LTD.
Newbury House, 900 Eastern Avenue,
Ilford, Essex IG2 7HH, England

and in the United States of America by
VALLENTINE MITCHELL
c/o International Specialized Book Services, Inc.
5804 N.E. Hassalo Street, Portland, Oregon 97213-3644

Copyright © 1995 Henry Felix Srebrnik

British Library Cataloguing in Publication Data

Srebrnik, Henry Felix
London Jews and British Communism,
1935–45
I. Title
320.532089240421
ISBN 0-85303-238-6 (cloth)
ISBN 0-85303-302-1 (paper)

Library of Congress Cataloging-in-Publication Data

Srebrnik, Henry Felix.
London Jews and British communism, 1935–1945 / Henry Felix Srebrnik.
p. cm.
Includes bibliographical references and index.
ISBN 0-85303-238-6 (cloth)   ISBN 0-85303-302-1 (paper)
1. Jews – England – London – Politics and government. 2. Jewish communists – England – London. 3. Piratin, Phil. 1907–   . 4. East End (London, England) – Politics and government. 5. London (England) – Ethnic relations.   I. Title.
DS135.E55L6654   1995
942. 1'004924 – dc20   93-34043
                                                         CIP

All rights reserved. No part of this publication may be reproduced in any form or by any means, electronic, mechanical, photocopying, recording or otherwise, without the prior permission of Vallentine Mitchell & Co. Ltd.

Typeset by Vitaset, Paddock Wood, Kent
Printed in Great Britain by
Bookcraft (Bath) Ltd, Midsomer Norton

Contents

List of Illustrations	vii
Acknowledgements	viii
Abbreviations	x
Preface	xi

1	Introduction	1
	The Jews in East London: Ethnic Cleavages and Political Grievances	4
	Jewish Communism: A Social Movement	11
2	The East London Jews within the Stepney Political System	20
	Portrait of a Community	20
	Stepney in the 1930s	27
	Ethnic Animosity in Stepney	29
3	Housing, ARP and the Blitz	38
	The Stepney Tenants' Defence League	38
	ARP and the Blitz in Stepney	42
	The Housing Issue in Wartime	49
4	Opposition to anti-Semitism, Fascism and Nazism	53
	The Campaign Against Mosley	53
	Opposition to Fascism in Wartime	57
	The Defence of the Jewish Community in Wartime	64
	The National Jewish Committee and anti-Semitism	71
	Anti-Nazism and the Second Front	76
5	Support for the Soviet Union	83
	The Nationality Policy of the USSR	83
	Pro-Soviet Activities, 1941–43	86
	The Visit of Mikhoels and Feffer and Its Aftermath	94

6	International Issues and Jewish Concerns	103
	The Spanish Civil War	103
	The 'Polish Question' in Stepney	111
	The Future of Palestine	121
7	The Communist Electoral Victories of 1945	128
	Building the Political Base, 1935–45	128
	The Demography of Stepney	132
	Ideological Hegemony in a Constituency	133
	The 1945 General Election Campaign in Mile End	138
	The Stepney Borough Elections of 1945	142
8	Conclusion	148
	Piratin's Victory: The Ethnic Dimension	148
	Why Communism? The Conjuncture of 1945	151
	The Decline of Jewish Communism	156
Notes		165
Select Bibliography		220
Index		251

List of Illustrations

between pages 26 and 27
1. The agenda for a Trade Union Conference in Shoreditch in 1928 was printed in English . . .
2. . . . and in Yiddish for the members' convenience
3. Meeting of the United Ladies' Tailors' Trade Union, London, 1 May 1939
4. Pamphlets of the period produced by Communists or Jews
5. The Jewish People's Council held a mass meeting to protest against Fascism and anti-Semitism in 1937
6. Such meetings were advertised in Yiddish as well as in English
7. By 1938 the tone of the Jewish People's Council's posters had become more urgent as examples of Fascist and Nazi oppression proliferated
8. The posters warned that Hitler's advances could not be ignored

between pages 106 and 107
9. The *Daily Worker* was drawing attention to Fascist atrocities during the Spanish Civil War
10. And at home there were the setbacks of Mosley's British Fascists to be celebrated
11. During the war the suffering of Soviet Russia was a cause that won popular support
12. In Stepney the Jews led an Aid to Russia Committee
13. Joyful headlines in the *Daily Worker* in 1945 proclaimed the end of the war and the election of a Labour government
14. Phil Piratin became the Communist member of Parliament for Mile End in the 1945 general election
15. Piratin published an article in the *Daily Worker* on the post-war future of the Jews
16. All too soon after the war the Fascists were staging a comeback

Acknowledgements

It is a pleasant task to acknowledge that in the course of researching and writing this book I have incurred a number of obligations.
I am deeply grateful to Dr Martin Kolinsky for his insightful criticisms and practical suggestions. They have provided me with a model of scholarly activity. I have also benefited from conversation with Geoffrey Alderman, Stan Beeler, Bob Brym, David Cesarani, William Fishman, Paul Hoch, Colin Holmes, Leon Jick, Tony Kushner, Henry Pelling, Shloime Perel, George Rudé, Raphael Samuel, Adrian Shubert, Elaine Smith, Victor Treschan, Harold Waller, Kenneth Waltzer and David Weinberg. Nitza Parry, Instructor of Hebrew at Dawson College, Montreal, kindly translated for me the transcript of an interview conducted in Hebrew.

For their reminiscences, and in some cases hospitality, I am grateful to the many individuals who consented to be interviewed for this book. Those who shared their knowledge with me are named in the Bibliography and in numerous Notes. I owe special thanks to the following people, who granted me access to invaluable collections of primary material: Julius Jacobs, Maurice 'Tubby' Rosen, Mrs Ray Waterman, and Mrs Ray Zaidman.

I have been assisted by the staffs and librarians of many institutions, including the University of Birmingham Library; the Board of Deputies of British Jews, London; the British Library, London; the British Library of Political and Economic Science, London School of Economics and Political Science; Congress House, Trades Union Congress, London; Goldfarb Library, Brandeis University, Waltham, Massachusetts; Institute of Contemporary History and Wiener Library, London; Institute of Historical Research, University of London; Jewish Studies (formerly Mocatta) Library, University College, University of London; Jews' College, London; Kressel Collection, Oxford Centre for Postgraduate Hebrew Studies,

Yarnton, Oxford; Labadie Collection, Harlan Hatcher Graduate Library, University of Michigan, Ann Arbor, Michigan; London Museum of Jewish Life, Sternberg Centre for Judaism, London; Marx Memorial Library, London; National Amalgamated Furnishing Trades Association, East London United Office; National Museum of Labour History, London; Newspaper Library of the British Library, London; National Union of Tailors and Garment Workers, London and Southern Divisional Office, London; Parkes Archive, University of Southampton Library; Public Record Office, Kew, London; and the Tower Hamlets Local History Library and Archives, Bancroft Library, London.

Finally, I wish to express my deepest gratitude to my wife Patricia, whose faith in the importance of this study has been essential to its completion. This book is dedicated to her.

Henry Srebrnik
Department of Political Studies
University of Prince Edward Island
Charlottetown, PEI, Canada
January 1994

Picture Credits

The author and publisher are grateful to the following for permission to reproduce illustrations: the Julius Jacobs collection; the Marx Memorial Library; McIrming; the National Union of Tailors and Garment Workers; the Lazar Zaidman collection.

Abbreviations

ARP	air raid precautions
BNP	British National Party
BUF	British Union of Fascists
CPGB	Communist Party of Great Britain
IAC	International Affairs Committee
ICOS	Organizatsye far Yiddishe Kolonizatsye in Sovyet-Rusland (Organization for Jewish Colonization in Soviet Russia)
JAFC	Jewish Anti-Fascist Committee
JCC	Jewish Cultural Club
JFSR	Jewish Fund for Soviet Russia
JPC	Jewish People's Council Against Fascism and Anti-Semitism
LCC	London County Council
LTC	London Trades Council
NAFTA	National Amalgamated Furnishing Trades Association
NCCL	National Council for Civil Liberties
NJC	National Jewish Committee of the Communist Party
NUTGW	National Union of Tailors and Garment Workers
SCPD	Stepney Council for Peace and Democracy
STC	Stepney Trades Council
STDL	Stepney Tenants' Defence League
TAC	Trades Advisory Council of the Board of Deputies of British Jews
TUC	Trades Union Congress
UCWU	United Clothing Workers' Union
UJC	United Jewish Committee
ULTTU	United Ladies Tailors' Trade Union
WJC	World Jewish Congress
YKUF	Alveltlekher Yiddisher Kultur Farband (World Jewish Cultural Union)

Preface

This study describes and explains the Jewish Communist movement in East London in the period 1935–45. In the following chapters I examine the social base of the movement, the East London Jewish working class and the political and ideological role of Jewish Communists in the political system in Stepney. I describe the strategy, tactics and organizational activities of the movement, including the social and political groups it controlled or could count upon for support as it mobilized Jews around the domestic issues of housing, ARP and the Fascist incursions of Oswald Mosley; around the struggles against Nazism in Spain, Germany and Poland; and around support for the Soviet Union and, for a time, the Jews in the Palestine Mandate. The penultimate chapter focuses upon the 1945 national and borough elections as the political high point of the movement in terms of success both within the Jewish subculture and on the wider political stage of East London. I do no more than trace the subsequent demise of Jewish Communism, however; for that is a story that requires a separate work in itself.

A NOTE ON SOURCES

All problems dealt with by social scientists have an historical dimension, and without the study of real political events it is difficult to derive satisfying conclusions. For C. Wright Mills, social science 'requires a historical scope of conception and a full use of historical materials'.[1] John Harsanyi feels that 'the main task of social science is to explain historical development';[2] David Apter believes that historical events are 'a testing ground for analytically derived propositions'.[3] As Dennis Kavanagh has noted, 'for reconstructing a past culture, content-analysis of available historical data is most suitable'.⁴

Perhaps, as Bruno Ramirez suggests, it is this lack of historical research on the part of some social scientists that may underlie the ahistorical perspective found in many ethnic studies and the 'rather problematic relationship existing between ethnic studies and working-class history'.⁵ I hope this work goes some way towards integrating these methodological solitudes.

I have made use of the traditional tools of social scientists. The methodology is that of qualitative historical analysis based on extensive primary source materials such as documents and private letters; the Jewish, Communist and East London press; and the minutes of various Communist, Jewish, and trade union organizations.

Save for the R. Palme Dutt papers housed in the British Library, the Communist Party's own archives, which were in King Street in Covent Garden, for a long time remained closed to researchers who were not members of the CPGB. Betty Reid, long the party's archivist, in the late 1970s was unable to grant me access to the papers and minutes of the National Jewish Committee of the Communist Party because some of the people concerned 'are still alive';⁶ she also informed me that much of the party's correspondence had been destroyed and that prominent Communists such as Harry Pollitt left little in the way of archival materials.⁷ However, the current archivists, George Matthews and Francis King, have announced that the library, which has now moved to Wallis Road in Hackney, will become more accessible to researchers, and that it contains papers of a number of prominent party figures, including Dutt, Pollitt, William Gallacher and Ivor Montagu.⁸ But, said Mr Matthews, 'most of our stuff relates to the party nationally, with little material on the east end'.⁹

Many records of trade unions have also disappeared; for example, the East London United branch of the National Amalgamated Furnishing Trades Association, known as NAFTA 15, lost most of its pre-war records when it moved to its offices in Kingsland Road, Hackney.¹⁰

To some extent, this shortage of records has been overcome by a wealth of pamphlet material and other published primary sources in various libraries and archives; a complete list of these will be found in the Bibliography. In addition, I was granted access to a number of private collections, including those of Julius Jacobs, Maurice 'Tubby' Rosen, and Alec Waterman.[11] Especially important was the collection of the late Lazar Zaidman; the minutes and other documents of the National Jewish Committee were among the Zaidman papers. I came across this immensely important archive, in the private possession of Mrs Ray Zaidman, in the course of my research. The collection has since been removed to Sheffield University, where it has now been catalogued and made accessible to other scholars. I have also consulted the minutes of the wartime meetings of NAFTA 15, and the minutes of the United Ladies Tailors' Trade Union (ULTTU), later the Mantle & Costume branch of the National Union of Tailors and Garment Workers (NUTGW), among others. I was able to explore the experiences of those who might not otherwise have left any written record by means of personal interviews with many of those who were involved in the Jewish Communist movement; sadly, quite a number of these people have since died. The individuals, institutions and organizations which assisted me are indicated in the Notes and in the Acknowledgements above.

All translations from the Yiddish, unless otherwise specified, are my own.

1
Introduction

In the British general election of July 1945 Phil Piratin, a Communist candidate, won a seat in Parliament for the Mile End division of Stepney, a constituency populated in large part by working-class Jews of East European origin. In addition to Piratin's seat, the Communist Party won the ten Stepney Borough seats which they contested that autumn, plus Mile End's two London County Council seats the following spring.

Contemporary observers such as George Orwell and Margaret Cole regarded the Communist victories in East London as the insignificant outcome of narrow local disputes or the chance product of political opportunism in a war-ravaged constituency.[1] In fact, the 1945 results were highly significant in terms of ethnic group politics: the Stepney Communist Party served as the vehicle for the political aspirations of a sizeable sector of Stepney's working-class Jewish population; and the party's electoral breakthroughs represented the culmination of a decade of intense political activity revolving around a number of issues both domestic and international. But because the 1945 victories proved to be the apogee of CP strength in Stepney, subsequent assessments of the period have tended to minimize their importance, and standard works relating the history of the British Communist Party have given the Stepney episode short shrift.[2]

The political problems of ethnicity have not been probed by social scientists until relatively recently,[3] and there are few studies of the formation and role of ethnic groups in Britain.[4] The British sociological tradition, writes Robert Ballard, has been relatively unconcerned with ethnicity; rarely has inequality been conceptualized under any heading other than that of class.⁵ A. H. Halsey has noted that from the time of the Industrial Revolution and the rise of an urban proletariat, British academics have been preoccupied with class.⁶ According to Joseph Rothschild, 'ethnic divisions appeared to be minimal and class and estate stratifications and gaps alone seemed to be sufficiently salient to merit and require analytical, moral and political attention'.⁷ Many social scientists have thought of ethnicity as a pre-modern phenomenon, a residue of particularism and ascription incompatible with the egalitarian ethic and universalism of modern industrial society. Marxist theoreticians in particular have analysed it as a remnant of pre-capitalist modes of production, a false consciousness masking class interests.⁸ Ethnic groups have been seen as survivals from an earlier age, vestigial forms of social life;⁹ 'the capacity of ethnic groups themselves to function as instrumental interest groups in the political arena was for long not appreciated by academics'.¹⁰ An added complication in Anglo-Jewish political behaviour is that any talk of a 'Jewish vote', that is, a tendency on the part of Jewish electors to react as a distinct block, was actively discouraged by the Board of Deputies of British Jews, the communal voice of Anglo-Jewry, and by other leading opinion makers in the community.¹¹ It is not surprising, then, that political sociologists have tended to overlook the ethnic aspect of Communist adherence in East London.¹²

In fact Anglo-Jewry tended throughout much of the late nineteenth century and well into the twentieth to give its allegiance to the Liberal Party. It was mainly the Liberals who had championed Jewish political emancipation in the 1840s and 1850s; by the late 1860s, a decade after Jews were first allowed to stand for Parliament, there were eight Jewish MPs – all Liberals. As the traditional party of individual rights, the Liberals provided an ideological home not only for Jews but also for any other group which, for reasons of nationality or ethnicity or religion, felt threatened by the otherwise permanent majority, the English (Anglicans). Though there were periods of disillusionment with the party, and some support for Tory candidates, in the main 'the Jewish masses . . . were solidly Liberal',¹³ especially after a Conservative government passed the 1905 Aliens Act limiting immigration. In the 1906 general election 16 Jews were elected, 12 of them Liberals, and in 1909 Herbert Samuel became the first Jewish cabinet minister. The party never again held power after Lloyd George's coalition government fell in 1922, and it was soon to be reduced to squabbling fragments, overshadowed by the Labour Party; yet 'qualitative evidence suggests that Jewish support for the Liberal Party persisted long after the party's post-1924 decline'.[14] Still, by 1935 it was obvious to all but the most partisan that the Liberals, with only 21 seats in the House of Commons, were a spent force;[15] and in the years 1935–45 Jews were increasingly frustrated by the party's apparent inability to take a strong stand on issues of concern to themselves, such as Fascism. For long-standing reasons of ideology and class, the Conservatives failed to win a Jewish following in the East End. Many Jews now turned to Labour. But others were uncomfortable with the 'ouvrieriste' perspective of that party, not to mention its tendency, in Stepney, to cater to the Irish. For a considerable number of Jewish electors in Stepney, then, Communism proved an attractive alternative.

The political self-image of the Stepney CP was, of course, that it was the borough branch of a national party, the Communist Party of Great Britain (CPGB), which was dedicated to the attainment of state power by the British working class and allied strata of the population and to the subsequent creation of a socialist state patterned on the Soviet Union. Officially the CP related to sympathetic Jews as members of the working class; it saw itself, following the 1945 victories, as the vanguard party in what was, after all, an historically working-class neighbourhood.

Yet the CP's own classically Marxist analysis fails to explain the plainly ethnic component of the Stepney successes. Why was there such an attraction, in one sector of the population, to a party which in most parts of the British Isles remained relatively insignificant? Why was the CP in Stepney an almost entirely Jewish phenomenon in terms of leadership and followers, if not in its official programme? Why the low level of support from other 'workers' in the borough, the Irish and native English, even though some of the party's candidates for the borough elections in 1945 were non-Jews, running for office in a futile attempt to widen the party's base? To neglect such questions is to overlook the singular situation in Stepney in 1945, where politics revolved in large measure around matters of Jewish concern, and where the CP had become the most effective voice for those concerns. The election of Piratin cannot in fact be explained as a 'working-class' victory or a local protest; rather, it was the triumph of a Jewish political sub-culture in Stepney,[16] which saw the Soviet Union as its model not only for socialism but also for the solution to the problem of anti-Semitism. Yet this ethno-ideological movement, which I shall call 'Jewish Communism', managed to ignore much of Marxist-Leninist doctrine, including its analysis of the Jews and their ultimate place in society – an analysis highly unfavourable to any long-range Jewish ethnic ambitions.

THE JEWS IN EAST LONDON: ETHNIC CLEAVAGES AND POLITICAL GRIEVANCES

Of all the groups to which men attach themselves, 'ethnic groups seem the most encompassing and enduring'.[17] By almost any criterion developed by scholars of ethnicity, the Jews of East London in the first half of the twentieth century were a distinct, highly visible, homogeneous ethnic group.[18] They shared fundamental cultural values, made up a field of communication and interaction,[19] and participated in a social system where interaction was largely defined by membership in 'culture groups'. They were a community with social solidarity and subjective self-awareness;[20] and they were perceived as such by outsiders.[21]

These Jews, who tended to be recent immigrants to London, occupied a distinct ecological niche in the social environment in terms of occupation and domicile. Since 'the set of understandings, the shared culture and language necessary for communication, is provided for the immigrant by the colony of his fellow-countrymen',[22] the area where Jewish Communism was to flourish was a large working-class area of Stepney, East London, sometimes termed a 'ghetto', where the majority of streets were inhabited by Jews. The housing was of slum or semi-slum quality; the workforce laboured in factories engaged in 'Jewish' trades such as tailoring or cabinet-making. This Jewish community was socially and politically isolated within the nation, and also in many ways at odds with their Anglo-Jewish co-religionists and with their non-Jewish neighbours in East London.

In relation to the core English society, the East London Jews were what Edward Shils would term a peripheral group outside the 'central value system',[23] with only a qualified membership status in the national society.[24] East London Jews had no input into the decision-making apparatus of the national political elite; they took no part in 'the authoritative allocation of values' by the national political system.[25] Michael Hechter has observed that a superordinate core group attempts to institutionalize an existing stratification system in order to regulate the allocation of social roles in such a way that peripherals are denied access to high-status roles and receive a limited share of societal resources; control of political power on the state level remains in core hands.[26] As the dominant group, the English were 'that collectivity within a society which has preeminent authority to function both as guardians and sustainers of the controlling value system, and as prime allocators of reward in the society'.[27]

The East London Jews, in contrast, were a minority group,[28] often subjected to prejudice and discrimination.[29] Because the attitudinal environment in East London allowed the Jews few shared historical memories and symbols that might predispose them to a positive affective and evaluative orientation towards the prevalent British political culture,[30] they did not accept that set of 'commonly shared goals and commonly accepted rules' of long historical standing which govern values, beliefs, and emotional attitudes towards the state and government.[31] And so, although many observers, then as now, would characterize British political culture as deferential,[32] this was not true in the case of the East London Jews, who in terms of Robert Dahl's criteria were rationalistic, non-cooperative, alienated and mistrustful.[33] Many of them had developed an 'oppositional culture', a tradition of overt political resistance to the dominant political system.[34]

On the national level, in the years 1935–45, these Jews came to deeply distrust the Conservative-dominated government of Britain.

They felt that this national political elite was unresponsive to their concern over the Spanish Civil War, over the future course of Polish affairs, and over the German threat to the Soviet Union – all aspects of the struggle against Hitler and Fascism. While most Jews supported the Loyalists in Spain in the late 1930s, Britain's policy of 'non-intervention' was thought to favour Franco. The Jews resented the government's readiness to recognize, during the Second World War, the Polish government-in-exile in London, which was thought to be anti-Semitic, and they suspected Churchill of delaying the Second Front in order to hinder Soviet advances in Eastern Europe, advances that these Jews strongly endorsed as a means of saving East European Jewry from the Nazis. They also accused the British government of not living up to its obligations in Mandatory Palestine and of blocking immigration to that country by desperate European Jews trying to flee a continent under German domination.

The East London Jews also clashed with those middle- and upper-class Jews who had arrived in Britain earlier, who were engaged in different occupations, and who spoke little or no Yiddish;[35] the East End Jewish community became even less socially diverse after the First World War, as more prosperous Jews began moving to other parts of London, leaving it predominantly working class.[36] These Jews were unwilling to defer to the traditional Anglo-Jewish elite, the so-called 'Cousinhood', whose power was exercised through the United Synagogue, the Chief Rabbi, the Board of Deputies of British Jews, the Jewish Board of Guardians and the Anglo-Jewish Association, among other bodies.[37] East London Jews, who brought from Europe both a socialist and a Zionist tradition, 'showed little enthusiasm for the established institutions' of Anglo-Jewry.[38] From the turn of the century to the First World War, 'the politics of deference on which the Anglo-Jewish elite had built its structured community were under attack',[39] and by the end of 1917, the *ancien régime* was under pressure from both the left, inspired by the two Russian revolutions that year, and the Zionist movement, which would benefit from the Balfour Declaration committing Britain to the establishment of a Jewish home in Palestine.

The inter-war years saw a further diminution of its authority.[40] It

INTRODUCTION

is significant, for example, that the Workers' Circle, an influential friendly society for working-class Jews, did not become a member of the Board of Deputies until some three decades after its foundation in 1909. Though there were exceptions, of course, the established Anglo-Jewish community in turn made no great effort to promote closer relations with the newcomers. Indeed, many were 'dismayed and terrified by the mass immigration' and some Jewish leaders even advocated restrictions on the entry of East Europeans into the country.[41] As George Simpson and Milton Yinger have written, 'upper-class members of a minority are able to avoid some prejudice and discrimination by sealing themselves off from contact with lower-class members of their group and insulating themselves from their struggles and problems'.[42]

Finally, in addition to being stratified vertically, the East London Jewish community was segmented along a horizontal axis. William Foltz maintains that 'an ethnic group can define itself as such only by virtue of contact and comparison with other people whom its members define as being different'.[43] In East London the Jews were neighbours to another, somewhat hostile, minority even poorer than themselves: the Irish, a group which at times proved unreceptive to Jewish attempts to bridge their differences ideologically. Irish–Jewish relations in Stepney were not those of subordinate core – subordinate periphery but rather of parallel ethnic structures not ranked hierarchically. Each community was internally stratified, with a political elite representing its interests.[44] One could call the areas of Stepney where Jews and Irish lived a plural society, that is, a society under a single common political authority at the top but composed of ethnic groups maintaining distinguishably separate ways of life.[45] Though bound together within a state framework, the collectivities are closed corporations. The individual groups have no concept of moral obligation towards each other; they do not share a normative order. Competition, interaction and conflict between the groups constitute an important ingredient in the pattern of politics found in the society.[46]

In such an ethnically segmented system, there are few cross-cutting cleavages. Though many groups and associations existed in East London, membership was drawn predominantly from particular ethnic strata; this was true even of formally secular or non-specific organizations, such as trade union or Labour Party branches.[47] Such mutually exclusive networks, although they facilitate rapid mobilization of groups, allow few countervailing mechanisms for conflict moderation.[48] 'The mutual reinforcements of social, religious and political loyalties' in such circumstances 'increase antagonism between subcultures'.[49] As David Easton has pointed out, such persisting cleavages result in group loyalty being paramount; aggrieved members of the group may lose all sense of shared identity with or support for the political system.[50] In Stepney, ethnic origins had become the basis of a system of closed status groups which constrained individuals in all spheres of activity.[51]

For a time the Labour Party in the East End attempted to overcome divisions between the Jews and the Irish by practising a version of internal consociational democracy.[52] In such a system, the leaders form an elite cartel which governs the polity, aggregates the interests of the cultural groups and distributes the benefits and costs of government among component groups.[53] The interactions of the horizontal groups remind one of the relations between states: the elites engage in diplomacy with each other. Elite accommodation in segmented societies functions well only when non-elites have acquiescent attitudes towards authority and are sufficiently depoliticized to allow elites to engage in compromise and concessions.[54] It is also important for the groups involved to be approximately equal in terms of access to power and economic resources and to engage in political reciprocity,[55] for, as William Gamson has observed, the political trust of a solidary group in its political system or government lies 'in its perception of the efficiency of the political system in achieving collective goals and its biases in handling conflicts of interest'.[56] But as M.G. Smith explains, ethnically plural societies tend to be 'defined by dissensus and pregnant with conflict';[57] Brian Barry argues that in the end many ethnic cleavages are too intense for consociational arrangements.[58]

This proved true in Stepney. Though there had been periods of Irish–Jewish political cooperation, by the 1930s the dominant Labour Party there had developed, not into an overarching political elite, but rather into an unstable alliance based more on accommodation to corruption and nepotism than on principle. In such an instance, 'people in the lowest strata of two mutually hostile communities [can] lose faith in their established leaders and become newly convinced that they are being cheated in any elite-to-elite negotiations'.[59] Then, 'ethnic solidarity provides a foundation for mobilization, the goal of which is destruction of barriers limiting social mobility',[60] and extreme ideological movements may be created as a way of rising from a fixed position within the system.[61] Ethnic grouping becomes a basis for the organization and formulation of political claims,[62] and people are mobilized along cleavage lines by parties which strengthen internal cohesion while articulating sectional interests.[63] In such circumstances, even parties that appear to be universalistic can come to represent an ethnic group in its demands upon society. For, as Donald Horowitz notes, in a plural society where ethnic affiliations permeate all spheres of life, there is a tendency, affecting parties all along the political spectrum, for 'avowedly nonethnic parties to be captured by one or another ethnic constituency'.[64]

By the late 1930s, the strong ethnic cleavages in East London were becoming increasingly apparent. The Labour Party had become dominated by the Irish. The integrative mechanisms which should have involved Jews in the political process were functioning so poorly that there was little distribution of even symbolic values to the Jews. The office of mayor came to be invariably held by an Irish member of the Stepney Council, a significant fact when we recall that, as Crawford Young has written, 'control of ritual or symbols of high standing may create its own hierarchy'.[65] The East London political system, in disequilibrium, failed to allow for the articulation of Jewish demands or for their transformation into policy outputs. Jews were concerned with poor housing, inadequate air raid precautions and Sir Oswald Mosley's Fascist incursions. But owing to corruption and other factors the Labour-dominated Council was loath to confront slum landlords; during the 1940 blitz, the Council proved itself incapable of crisis management, a fact leading to further loss of legitimacy.[66] As for the problem of Fascism, the Council was thought by Jews to be indifferent to their fears; indeed, many East End Irish, discontented with the Labour Party even though their ethnic group controlled it, became members of the British Union of Fascists (BUF). Meanwhile the Irish Labour members of the Council, who constituted a majority, differed from the Jewish population in their responses to a variety of international issues such as the Spanish Civil War. The stage was set for a conflict over the nature and outputs of local authority,[67] conflict which was all the more certain given the relatively tight social boundaries separating the communities and the low level of communal interaction.[68]

Sandor Halebsky suggests that social protest movements can form around 'the discrete interests of a particular social category seeking concrete ends that are based on legitimate remedial grievances'. Such movements may be a rational means of redress to the prevailing order, particularly if the responsiveness of the regime is low, demands remain unmet and access to political elites is limited.[69] They may be used to challenge the indifference, remoteness or negligence of party machines.[70] The Jews of the East End, ethnically distinct and working in small-scale enterprises not particularly crucial to the British economy, in conditions often approaching those of 'sweatshops', were on the margins of the core society; locally, their capacity for policy input was being sharply curtailed. But as Dale Nelson has discovered, ethnicity has a greater effect than socio-economic status on levels of political participation, and those ethnic groups that exhibit strong participant cultures 'stand to benefit politically because their members are more politically active'.[71] The East London Jews had a pre-existing ideological commitment to social change; they also had an established pattern of left-of-centre politics, expressed through various trade unions, friendly societies and, before the 1930s, the local branches of the Liberal and Labour Parties. Many of the East London Jewish garment workers had already, in the 1929–35 period, become involved with the United Clothing Workers' Union (UCWU), a Communist-controlled breakaway from the national union. This was a truly class-conscious ethnic group, a class 'for itself' and not just 'in itself',[72] an often-exploited group occupying a distinct niche in the economic system.[73] Despite their demographic and social situation and their lack of trust in the political system, the East London Jews possessed a high degree of political efficacy, 'the feeling that individual political action does have, or can have, an impact upon the political process'.[74]

A group high in political efficacy but low in trust is obviously one that will try to solve its problems by putting pressure on the authorities through a variety of means, even including violence and illegalities.[75] The East London Jewish community was ready to develop a new leadership, under the sway of neither the local Labour Party elites in Stepney nor the Jewish elite already in place nationally. Traditional British techniques of political participation would be augmented by activist modes of intervention and pressure tactics: demonstrations, strikes, occupations of buildings, and so forth.

Ioan Davies has pointed out that marginal sectors of a society not integrated into the political centre may engage in direct political action and follow 'a political religion'.[76] The East London Jews made good recruits for the specific 'political religion' which expressed their ethnic consciousness: they appropriated the existing Communist movement, which was in turn modified and shaped in such a way as to fulfil Jewish needs. This study demonstrates that the Jewish Communist movement prospered despite what seemed insurmountable ideological obstacles regarding the position of Jews in Marxist-Leninist theory because it was a rational political response, on a tactical level, to the problems confronting East London Jews in this period.

JEWISH COMMUNISM: A SOCIAL MOVEMENT

The literature on social movements provides a theoretical construct for defining the ideology, structure and limits of the Jewish Communist movement, and also for studying its role and function within the political sub-system that was the East London Jewish community.

Social movements can be described as 'noninstitutionalized group attempts' to produce social change, or as collective enterprises designed to 'introduce innovations into a social system' and establish 'a new order of life'.[77] They represent 'an effort by a large number of people to solve collectively a problem that they feel they have in common'.[78] Unlike religious sects or other-worldly cults, which call for personal transformations, social movements promote a normative vision of social change; their aim is to alter or supplant some portion of the existing culture or social order.[79] Unlike interest groups, they lack strong institutionalized linkages to political and economic elites, and they attempt to go beyond the self-interested objectives of their members.[80]

Social movements are often a function of rapid social change in a society. During such periods, subordinate groups sometimes suffer relative deprivation: the intensity of discontent may increase when 'a perceived discrepancy between men's value expectations and their value capabilities' emerges.[81] The group may feel it is not rising as rapidly as it should in the stratification hierarchy in terms of power, status or wealth.[82] The feeling of deprivation shared by the group allows for 'a sense of group identity and solidarity',[83] facilitated by communicative links and intragroup social ties. As Joseph Gusfield has observed, social movements draw their adherents from particular segments of society. This is true because discontent is not distributed at random. These are people whose experiences make them more receptive to a particular ideology and whose conditions of life facilitate communication and organization.[84] This allows for collective mobilization by a movement, coalescing around an ideology and organization.[85]

Sociological observation has taught us that ideas can be weapons, used to capture political power for one's group.[86] Ideas inspire the followers of a movement to action and give them a sense of political direction by appealing to their collective psychological and moral needs; ideas focus and interpret felt strains in order to justify the purposes of the movement.[87] Ideologies, then, are a complex mix of pragmatic, rational and emotional appeals built upon a set of core values.[88] Indeed, the formal ideology of a movement – the doctrines, beliefs, myths and values which inform its criticisms of society and demands for change – is often at variance with its social function. As Rudolf Heberle has noted, a social movement is not just a composite of its theories and ideas; it should not be evaluated strictly on the basis of its empirical or logical consistency. Rather, one must distinguish between the actual behaviour of the movement and its official doctrine if one is to comprehend the sociological basis for its successes.[89] According to Karl Mannheim, an ideology often rationalizes the socio-economic interests of a group and its quest for power: 'every point of view is particular to a social situation'.[90] Thus 'different social groups will have different affinities with . . . competing theories and will, subsequently, become "carriers" of the latter', according to Peter Berger and Thomas Luckmann. Often an ideology will be adopted if it is pragmatically superior to others on the level of its applicability to the social interests of the group that has become its 'carrier', rather than by virtue of any intrinsic qualities.[91] And, as R. S. Milne remarks, in situations of ethnic competition, even when rhetoric and terminology stress ideology and class, actions and reactions 'can often be best understood in terms of ethnicity'.[92]

The East London Jews, who shared a culture with working-class Jews of east European origin in many other countries, responded to various ideational and political currents within the global Jewish system. Many of these currents were outgrowths of the *Haskalah*, the Jewish Enlightenment which spread through Eastern Europe in the nineteenth century and was brought by Jewish immigrants to North America and Western Europe. Anarchism, socialism, Yiddishism, the ethnic and cultural programmes of the Jewish Labour Bund, the many varieties of Zionism, and finally Communism – all were responses to increasing secularization and modernization;[93] all competed for Jewish allegiance in those countries where Jewish immigrants had created 'fragments' of the Ashkenazi East European 'homeland', the Russian Pale of Settlement.[94]

Jewish Communism did not come into its own until the ten-year period leading up to 1945, when political developments within the world-wide Communist movement made such ethnic movements possible. In the summer of 1935, in an attempt to counter the growth of Fascism and Nazism, the Seventh Congress of the Comintern (the Communist or Third International), meeting in Moscow, decided to allow national Communist parties considerable leeway in their efforts to attract wider segments of the populations of their countries; one approved tactic was an appeal to minorities along openly ethnic lines. Jewish Communism would flourish as Jewish Communists were encouraged to assume political and moral leadership of a broad alliance within the Jewish community.

On paper the Jewish Communists were striving to bring socialism to the national state unit where they lived, and often they preferred to minimize or ignore the Jewish content of their movement, particularly when, as in East London, they dealt with 'non-Jewish' issues such as rent strikes or demands for air raid protection. But in practice they added ideas of Jewish renewal to Marxist-Leninist ideology, seeking, much like the Bund, to improve the Jewish condition by means of socialism. Jewish Communists differed from the Bundists, however, in having a political centre: they looked towards their old homeland, the Russian Pale of Settlement – later, of course, the USSR, the first socialist state – much as Zionists looked towards Palestine.

In East London the Jewish Communist movement, coterminous with but more broadly structured than any of its component parts, went beyond local Stepney politics and was later linked via its theoreticians on the National Jewish Committee of the CPGB not only to the national party but also to like-minded Jews in many other countries. Its ideological link with the USSR, which was via the world-wide Jewish Communist movement, was thus somewhat independent of the CPGB's own ties to Russia. Indeed, the Jewish Communist movement was an informal Comintern unto itself; it even had its own international organizations such as the YKUF, the World Jewish Cultural Union, a Yiddish-language body founded in 1937. Jewish Communists also concentrated on different aspects of Soviet socialism from other Communists, being most interested in what they saw as the solution to the 'Jewish question' and the elimination of anti-Semitism; in the regeneration of the Jewish working class; and in the construction of a Jewish socialist republic in Birobidzhan, in the Soviet Far East.

The Jewish Communists, then, thought of their movement as a positive contribution to Jewish life. They attempted to synthesize their Communist and Jewish ideas, rather than to negate or transcend Jewishness. They felt that Marxism offered the only solution to the 'Jewish question' and regarded the Communist parties as the only organizations willing to fight Fascism and anti-Semitism. Hence their ideas converged with those of the world Communist movement over an extended period. People like Lazar Zaidman, an influential East End theoretician active in the Workers' Circle and on the National Jewish Committee of the CP, 'were never alienated from their Jewish heritage; they never found Communism incompatible with being Jewish'.[95] Although classical Marxism was hostile to Jewish nationalism,[96] the Jewish Communists managed to square this with fervent support of 'non-Zionist' forms of Jewish consciousness, remaining, if sometimes covertly, left-wing Diaspora nationalists.

As a social movement of the left, Jewish Communism changed the conception of the Jewish situation from that of a misfortune to that of an injustice.[97] In advocating action to rectify social, political and especially ethnic problems in the East End, it became a focal point of conflict. It shaped and created public opinion,[98] thus contributing to the formation of political group will.[99]

Mobilization – the process by which a group becomes 'an active participant in public life' and 'assembles and invests resources for the pursuit of group goals'[100] – works best when the group is already cohesive. Recruitment follows the lines of pre-existing social relationships and other inter-group linkages; it is often based on incorporating solidarity groups which already possess a high level of common awareness and group identity. Since ethnic groups already share clusters of beliefs and values, ethnicity can always become politically salient and assist in the organization and mobilization of movements. 'A still viable network of communal relations can be the foundation and breeding ground for the rapid growth of modern associational networks'.[101] The potential power of such collectivities, then, is based as much on their availability to mobilization as on the resources at their command.[102] 'Effective agitation . . . creates turbulent interaction within a collectivity, and draws people into a growing movement. Its cumulative effect is to transform the collectivity from its unorganised, fluid state into a powerfully structured agency of directed socio-political action.'[103] This is why social movements so often 'develop in class, racial, national, or sexual struggles'.[104] These optimal conditions for social mobilization were clearly present in the Jewish working-class community of East London in 1935–45.

Social movements are admixtures of formal association and informal participation. Individuals may sometimes participate in a movement without making any formal organizational commitment.[105] Typically, however, participants are recruited, not to a movement as such but to one or more core organizations which serve as the actual components of the movement.[106] 'Some movements use political parties as the spearhead of their action in seeking political power'; they engage also 'in action at pressure group, educational or cultural levels'. A social movement may therefore encompass all or parts of political parties, pressure groups and voluntary organizations.[107] There is a division of labour between these various organizations: each attempts to implement one or more of the goals of the larger social movement,[108] thereby mobilizing different (although sometimes overlapping) sets of individuals.[109] Some of the specific organizations may be regarded with suspicion even by individuals willing to join other organizations in the movement.[110] Hence the Jewish Communists utilized an attractive array of front groups dealing with a wide range of issues in order to guarantee that there would be a specific organization available to complement every issue of importance to the East London Jewish working class.[111]

It is difficult, then, to define the exact limits of the Jewish Communist movement in East London. Certainly it encompassed the Jewish members of the Stepney CP plus a significant portion of the leadership and members of various East London Jewish organizations, including the Workers' Circle and certain local branches of the NUTGW, ULTTU, and the NAFTA. There were in addition a number of popular front groups such as the Stepney Tenants' Defence League (STDL), the Jewish People's Council Against Fascism and Anti-Semitism (JPC), the Jewish Fund for Soviet Russia (JFSR), and the Jewish Cultural Club (JCC). Much of this cohort was intertwined; there was a crossover of people in various organizations. Its leadership was basically to be found in what came to be known as the National Jewish Committee of the CPGB; these theoreticians, some of them unassimilated immigrants, did not themselves run for public office, but acted as mentors to the formally non-Jewish Stepney CP.

Though the movement was composed of a series of organized groups without a formal federal structure, it did have the essential group consciousness – a sense of a shared paradigm of symbolic experience[112] – necessary to be effective. The members were all first- or second-generation Jews of East European origin, living in East London and working in the clothing or furniture industry or in ancillary trades. A network of interpersonal relationships reinforced structural ties. Such a movement, which creates ideologically linked activities and organizations so as to form an entire world for its members,[113] exists on a continuum somewhere between a *Gemeinschaft* – an organic, ascriptive community based on a common mode of existence – and a *Gesellschaft* – a voluntary, limited association.[114] Ideological and personal loyalty are intertwined.

Social movements of these sorts are highly dynamic. They draw upon a wide variety of collective strategies for change; their adherents reject convention and are committed to new ideas.[115] The tactics of the Jewish Communists included the innovative use of existing channels of action (such as standing for borough and parliamentary office); the creation of new channels of questionable legitimacy (such as the rent strikes and tenement occupations of 1939); and wholly non-legitimate actions (such as the 'Battle of Cable Street' in 1936).[116]

The well-formulated *Weltanschauung* of the Jewish Communist movement was eloquently expressed by its prolific theoreticians, who were often unknown outside their immediate community circles. Their output was not systematically collected and 'codified' in the manner of Marxist–Leninist ideology; rather, it remains scattered throughout newspaper articles, essays, reports of speeches, and other ephemeral media.

Jewish Communism gave ideological direction to whole congeries of groups apart from the Stepney CP. Some, like the JPC, were popular fronts designed to attract wider support for the movement; others, like the Circle and the 'Jewish' trade union branches, already existed as arenas for debate, where the movement's spokesmen worked to make converts among other left-wing Jews. There were organizations such as the Stepney Tenants' Defence League, outwardly unconcerned with any ethnic dimension, whose aims were in fact congruent with those of the Jewish Communists: to win non-Jews away from Fascism and to mobilize Jews along class lines, in this case by pre-emptively attacking Jewish slum landlords while simultaneously minimizing their ethnic identity.

Different groups concentrated on various issues of concern to the Jewish population at large: the STDL dealt with local issues such as housing and air raid protection; the JPC led the struggle against Mosley; the Yiddishists of the Jewish Cultural Club and the Jewish Fund for Soviet Russia concerned themselves with international issues such as the fate of Poland and the Soviet defence against Nazi Germany. In this way the Jewish Communist leadership aggregated the interests of Jews as workers, as tenants, and as East Europeans with an interest in the fate of fellow-Jews in their countries of origin as well as in Palestine.

Jewish Communism made gains at a time when left-wing social movements were acceptable within the larger society as never before. During the years 1935–45 there was a change in societal attitudes and opinions regarding socialism, an overall shift to the left and, for many, a pro-Soviet orientation in international affairs. Thus Communism came to seem an acceptable alternative for many Jews, especially as they felt grateful to the USSR for its struggle against Hitler. A number of Labour councillors, upset with the narrowness of their party, rebelled and became sympathetic to the aims of the Jewish Communist movement: H. H. Gordon, Henry Solomons, and former mayor I. M. Vogler, all well known in Stepney politics, at various times supported the CP. Jewish Communism was a mass movement around which many left-wing and radically inclined Jews could find common ground.

This was not accomplished without some degree of compromise. 'Organizations exist in a changing environment to which they must adapt. Adaptation to the environment may itself require changes in goals and in the internal arrangements of the organization.'[117] During the war years the Stepney CP became more 'routinized' and concerned with elections. It found modes of relating to the established system, with all that this entailed in terms of strategies and goals.[118] As its base widened, the movement managed to accommodate itself to the rise of Jewish nationalist feeling, particularly after news arrived of the disaster which had befallen European Jewry. By the end of the war the East End Jewish community was thus highly amenable to political entreaties from the Jewish Communists, who had managed to concern themselves with most of the items on the Jewish agenda. The 'popular front' in Stepney had become very much a 'Jewish front' – the CP had reached so far beyond the normal class constituency of any socialist movement that a small, informal, yet politically and financially influential group of Jewish businessmen were involved in Phil Piratin's campaign.

Thus, through sustained agitation based upon the set of issues informing Jewish concerns, Jewish Communism for a brief period gained political hegemony within the East London Jewish community.[119] As a result of political developments in the international arena as well as in England, it benefited from a conjuncture whereby its platform and Jewish interests were largely congruent. In other words, the Jewish Communist movement, a constellation of officially independent groups, which in reality were under the political and ideological guidance of those Jewish members of the CPGB who themselves formed a distinct stratum within the national party, was by 1945 in a position whereby it could realistically compete for electoral office in the public arena. Indeed, the CP was able to win over sectors and organizations within the Jewish community which were officially Labour rather than Communist.

2
The East London Jews within the Stepney Political System

PORTRAIT OF A COMMUNITY

As part of a vast westward migration of over one million Jews from Eastern Europe, and despite economic, social and legal impediments, as many as 150,000 Jews immigrated to Britain between 1881 and 1914, and soon came to greatly outnumber the 'established' community of some 65,000.[1] In the decade from 1891 to 1901, nearly 50,000 Jews came to London alone.[2] Most settled in the newly formed borough of Stepney, which by 1914 had about 100,000 of London's 150,000 Jewish inhabitants.[3] Despite the cessation of large-scale immigration after 1914, at the beginning of the 1930s Stepney still contained the largest number of foreign-born residents of any borough in England – 30,032 people,[4] who constituted about one-seventh of the total population in the borough.[5]

These Jews, who for the most part came from Russia and Poland, had been 'catapulted as it were into Great Britain, with their language, standards, ideals and institutions'.[6] Though exposed to secular ideas, including radical politics, 'they retained a culture of their own, which they transferred to their new centres in British cities. It comprised a distinctive religion and language and fear of the Gentile world'.[7] Since they 'formed a society apart, with standards derived from other sources than England', they did their best to preserve themselves as an autonomous community, 'more in England than of it'.[8] As one historian has remarked, 'it was as if a piece of Jewish East Europe had been torn up and put down again in the middle of east London';[9] the east European atmosphere was commented upon by all visitors to the area, be they hostile or merely curious.[10] In the Spitalfields, Whitechapel and Mile End districts of the borough there were numerous Jewish synagogues, welfare agencies, social clubs and schools, 'an indication of the way in which the Jew has replaced the Gentile' in many parts of the East End.[11] In the late 1930s the Jewish community still retained 'a separate and active, self-contained and relatively autonomous culture';[12] the lives of most East End Jews were 'by no means typical of the British working classes'.[13] The East End could still be described by some as an 'alien city' whose streets resembled those of Warsaw or Cracow.[14] A popular magazine put it well: 'You are in High Street, Whitechapel, but it might just as easily be High Street, Poland'.[15] The older immigrants 'faithfully reproduced East European Jewish life',[16] creating a world that 'consisted mainly of Jewish people'.[17] In the words of Emanuel Litvinoff, life in Stepney was a 'journey through a small planet'.[18]

As elsewhere, the newly arrived immigrants had tended to work in small-scale industries such as clothing, boot-making and cabinet-making. As sweatshops proliferated, much of this work was done under degrading conditions.[19] The result was that Jewish workers were often shunned and derided by their English fellows: the Trades Union Congress (TUC) passed resolutions in 1892, 1894 and 1895 against the landing of 'pauper aliens',[20] remarking that the Jews 'were either sweaters or sweated'.[21] Even some socialist organizations, such as H. M. Hyndman's Social Democratic Federation, were hostile to Jews, fearing that they would bring down wages and lower the standard of living for British-born workers.[22] Hence even Jewish socialists, tied to their community, had little to do with the wider working-class movement: men such as Lewis Lyons, Morris Winchevsky and Aaron Lieberman, leaders of strikes and founders of Jewish trade unions, were almost unknown outside their milieu.[23] The unions themselves, in this early period, rose and fell rapidly, often vanishing without a trace. In 1906–7 there were over 30 Jewish trade unions in Britain; the garment industry alone had 15.[24] Only a few of these survived long enough to be amalgamated with their larger, non-Jewish counterparts, often as East London-based locals.

In the 1930s there were some 30,000 clothing workers in Stepney, employed in approximately 2,600 factories and workshops in the borough;[25] they constituted a full 25 per cent of the working population.[26] Many of these workers became members of the NUTGW, founded in January 1932 as an amalgamation of two major garment unions, themselves the result of previous fusions.[27] Although the NUTGW had its headquarters in Leeds until the war, it included some East London branches which had been separate Jewish unions. The London No. 2 (sub-divisional) branch, for instance, had about 1,400 members; sub-divisional workers, that is, tailors employed in small workshops which received work from larger West End firms, tended to be Jewish.[28]

Meanwhile, in 1929, many other Jewish workers, under the influence of Communist leaders, formed a breakaway 'dual' union, the UCWU. Only with difficulty were these workers gradually coaxed back into the newly formed NUTGW; the UCWU finally collapsed in 1935.[29] But the NUTGW itself became increasingly receptive to Communism, particularly after the ULTTU, the last independent Jewish union, joined the national organization in 1939.[30] Communists were so strongly entrenched in the leadership of the ULTTU that the parent NUTGW had no choice but to ignore its own rules, as well as those of the TUC, which made it difficult for CP members to become executives in their branches. According to Hymie Cohen, 'The national NUTGW couldn't keep us off the leadership in the east end, because we were very active, and known amongst the people in the trade.'[31] Cohen was referring not only to himself but also to other Communists such as Hymie Kanter, Mick Mindel and Sarah Wesker; Kanter and Mindel were on the union executive, Wesker was a full-time women's organizer.[32] Wesker was cheered at the annual congress of the London District Communist Party, held in Shoreditch Town Hall in June 1938, when she announced that the ULTTU's membership gains had occurred 'since the Communist Party gained great influence' in the union.[33]

Another national union with a predominantly Jewish branch in the East End was the NAFTA, which had been founded in 1902 as a union of cabinet-makers, upholsterers, woodworkers and other

THE EAST LONDON JEWS WITHIN THE STEPNEY POLITICAL SYSTEM

craftsmen in the furniture industry. The East London United, also known as NAFTA 15, had been an independent Jewish union, the Independent Jewish Cabinet Makers Association; for the benefit of its immigrant members, meetings had been conducted and minutes kept in Yiddish as well as in English. When this union joined NAFTA after the First World War, it retained the right to organize Jewish workers throughout the East End. In 1936, NAFTA 15 had about 1,000 members of whom approximately 70 per cent were Jewish.[34] Because of its 'real roots in the Jewish people', NAFTA 15 'played a big role' in the economic and political struggles that preoccupied East End Jews;[35] it was particularly active in the agitation against fascism.[36] In this union branch, also, the leadership was dominated by Communists, including Sid Fineman, Julius Jacobs, and his father Morris.[37]

The unions were not the only influential organizations in East London. Many Jews belonged to the Workers' Circle (in Yiddish, the *Arbeter Ring*), a friendly society which, in addition to concerning itself with social welfare, unemployment and sick benefits, aspired to become 'an organization of activists, of fighters for social change, for freedom and justice'.[38] Two groups had been responsible for founding the Circle: 'Russian revolutionary elements' fleeing the Tsarist empire after the unsuccessful 1905 revolution,[39] and anarchist elements already active in London.[40] By the time of its first London conference, in May 1912, the Circle had 814 members and a number of branches in the provinces.[41] After the 1917 Russian Revolution about 300 members returned to Russia; but new immigrants to England continued to join, and by 1921 there were over 1,100 members.[42] In 1925 Circle House was opened in Great Alie Street in Stepney; by 1935 the membership had grown to 2,720.[43]

During the 1935–45 period, however, the Circle had an influence far greater than these figures would seem to indicate. In this section of London which was to a large extent a 'fragment' of the Polish–Russian Jewish Diaspora, organizations such as the Workers' Circle constituted 'a real connection, a living link . . . between everything that Jewishness meant on the Continent, and what it was in London'.[44] Alf Holland, later a member of the National Jewish Comittee of the CPGB, joined the Circle in the second week after he had arrived in England from Poland in 1927. 'The Workers' Circle,' according to Holland, 'wasn't something I picked up here':

> I came to it straight away. It had a name. Don't forget, in the Jewish socialist movement – in Poland, Romania, Russia and so on – we knew who our friends were. The Workers' Circle was known in Poland, it was known throughout eastern Europe as *the* Jewish working class organization. When the Yiddish school movement in Poland needed something, money or speakers, they approached the Workers' Circle.[45]

In the Circle, 'many of the leading lights had tried to bring a little of the "old country" into their lives. They were "Bundists" from Poland, Anarchists and Libertarians from all parts, Socialists and Freethinkers. Every shade of Russian and European Labour thought and action was represented here.'[46] Each of these currents of left-wing opinion, along with various kinds of Zionists, Labour Party supporters and Communists, competed for acceptance among Circle members. Each ideological persuasion founded one or more branches; it was possible for these fairly autonomous branches to co-exist within the organization. While some branches worked on behalf of Zionism and the Jewish settlement in Palestine, others – particularly Branch 11 – supported Friends of the Soviet Union and the Birobidzhan project in the Soviet Far East. The Communist members, who were particularly active in branches 3, 9 and 10, helped the Circle to take the lead in setting up the Jewish Labour Council in August 1934 and its successsor, the Jewish People's Council Against Fascism and Anti-Semitism, in July 1936.[47] The Circle was also active on the international scene: B. A. Bagnari and Dr Noah Barou were among the British delegates to the first World Jewish Congress held in Geneva in August 1936.[48] The Circle also was represented at the World Congress Against Racialism and anti-Semitism held in Paris, September 1937.[49]

The members of the Workers' Circle were unified by their common sociological origins as East European Jews, their class position as workers or small businessmen in a few well-defined trades, and their love for Yiddish language and literature, especially if it were 'proletarian'. One Circle militant referred to the organization as a

THE EAST LONDON JEWS WITHIN THE STEPNEY POLITICAL SYSTEM

'small corner of light' where the Yiddish language, culture and social traditions were being kept alive in London.[50] In this way the members of the Circle, whether radicals or moderates, differed significantly from the older, more assimilated Anglo-Jews, who tended to look upon these newcomers with mixed feelings. 'The personal relations between native and immigrant Jews were distant, and feelings of mutual disdain were heard from both quarters.'[51] This was true not only because the newly arrived Jews were set apart geographically and economically from the established Jews, but also because the immigrants spoke the despised 'jargon', Yiddish, which was symbolic of all that the older community found 'strange and distasteful about the new English Jews'. Nothing was more devoutly desired by the native Jews than the speedy disappearance of this language.[52]

But this was not to be. Yiddish, true enough, did not achieve the significance in England that it did in the major area of East European Jewish settlement, the United States and Canada;[53] indeed, by the 1930s, some commentators were already decrying the impending death of Yiddish as a living tongue among English Jews.[54] None the less, as long as the Jews of Stepney continued to live in a compact mass and followed certain narrowly prescribed occupations in which most of their employers and co-workers were Jews, Yiddish retained its hold on much of the community. The immigrant Jews had established 'a veritable Yiddish civilization in the East End',[55] and in the decade before the war, 'Yiddish was a living language – no doubt about it'.[56] Writing in the late 1930s, the noted East End social worker Basil Henriques, warden of the Bernhard Baron St George's Jewish Settlement, observed that many immigrants 'seldom strayed beyond the East End. There was no need to learn English and few have'.[57] Because of the Stepney Jews, 'London was still a major Yiddish centre outside Eastern Europe'.[58]

Many Yiddish newspapers, most of them the vehicles of ideological and polemical debate, flourished briefly and then were extinguished in the ferment of immigrant London. Anarchists, socialists, Zionists – all shared the spotlight. A more successful venture was *Di Tsayt*, a non-political daily founded by Morris Myer in 1913, which became a flourishing concern for over three decades.[59] There was also for a time a viable world of Yiddish letters and theatre in East London. Leo Koenig wrote novels, A. N. Stencl published poetry and the playwright Itzik Manger produced his works there.[60] Two repertory companies operated in the East End before the war: the Jewish National Theatre in Adler Street and the Yiddish Folks Theatre at the Grand Palais in Commercial Road; in 1937 each had four different productions in its repertoire.[61] There was also left-wing Yiddish theatre, particularly Proltet, a Yiddish group, organized by Alf Holland and Alec Waterman, which grew out of the Yiddish Drama Group of the Workers' Circle to become part of the (non-Jewish) Workers' Theatre Movement. Its first production, *Strike!* by Mike Gold, was translated into Yiddish by Alf Holland. Another sketch was entitled *Birobijan*. Proltet functioned between 1932 and 1934.[62] In late 1935, Branch 10 of the Workers' Circle founded a new theatre which in 1938 became affiliated with the Left Book Club Theatre Guild,[63] but it did not survive the onset of war.

Many in the Yiddish literary community also became involved with the Communist-dominated YKUF, the World Jewish Cultural Union formed in Paris in 1937 by prominent Jewish intellectuals such as Gina Medem, Joseph Opatoshu and Dr Chaim Sloves. The London branch, with I. A. Lisky as secretary, the poet Moshe Oved as treasurer and Morris Myer as chairman,[64] sponsored lectures, meetings and other events in order to, as Lisky put it, 'plough up the sandy soil and make it fertile'.[65] A. M. Fuchs, Leo Koenig, L. S. Creditor, Joseph Leftwich, Alec Waterman, and A. N. Stencl, newly arrived in London, all contributed to its publication, *Yiddish London*.[66] Dr Noah Barou, the Poale Zionist and Circle activist, had long bemoaned the lack of a 'Yiddish People's University' in 'such a big Yiddish centre as London'.[67] In 1938 the YKUF approached the eminent University of London mathematician and Jewish Communist, Professor Hyman Levy, to help them to gain the university's approval for a course in Yiddish literature. The YKUF agreed to pay the £300 salary of the lecturer, Shloime Birnbaum,[68] and it was taught at the School of Slavonic and East European Studies in 1938–39.[69]

THE UNITED
Ladies' Tailors Trade Union.

Telephone; *Registered Offices;*
BIShopsgate 9293   12, Gt. Garden St., E.1

AGENDA

FOR THE FIRST

Delegates' Trade Conference

TO BE HELD AT

SHOREDITCH TOWN HALL,

(OLD ST., E.C.2)

ON

SATURDAY AND **SUNDAY**
AUGUST 18TH. AND 19TH. 1928

S. JOSEPH, Chairman.   L. COLTON, Vice-chairman
J. CAPLAN, Organiser.   J. L. FINE, Secretary.

B. WEINBERG, T.U. Printer, 138, Brick Lane, E.1.

1 The agenda for a Trade Union conference in Shoreditch in 1928 was printed in English . . .

יוניטעד ליידים טיילארס
טרייד יוניאן,

הער אפיס: 12, גרייט גארדען סטריט, א.
טעלעפאן: בישאפסגייט 9293.

אדזשענדא

פאר דעם ערשטען

טרייד קאנפערענץ

אפגעהאלטען אין

שארדיטש טאון האל,
(אלד סטריט, איסט.)

שבת און זונטאג,
18־טען און 19־טען אויגוסט 1928.

ס. דזשאזעף, טשערמאן.   ל. קאלטאן, וויים.
י. קאפלאן, ארגאנייזער.   י. ל. פיין, סעקרעטא־.

ב. ווייצבערג, ט יו. פרינטער, 138, בריק ליין, א.1.

2 . . . and in Yiddish for the members' convenience (courtesy of National Union of Tailors and Garment Workers, London and Southern Divisional Office)

3 Meeting of the United Ladies' Tailors' Trade Union, London, 1 May 1939. Left to right: J.L. Fine (secretary); A.M. Wall (speaker); W. Colton (chairman); George Bell (General Federation of Trade Unions). (Courtesy of McIrming)

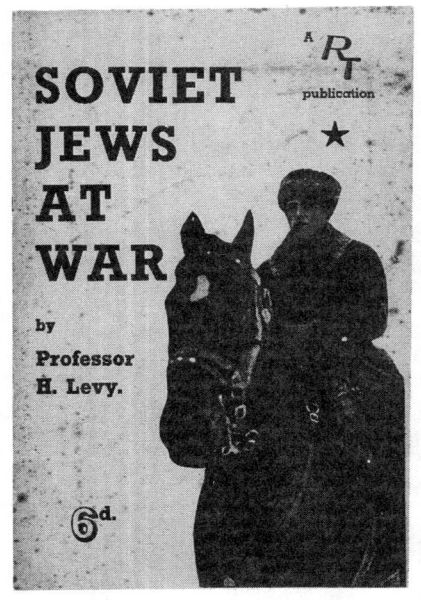
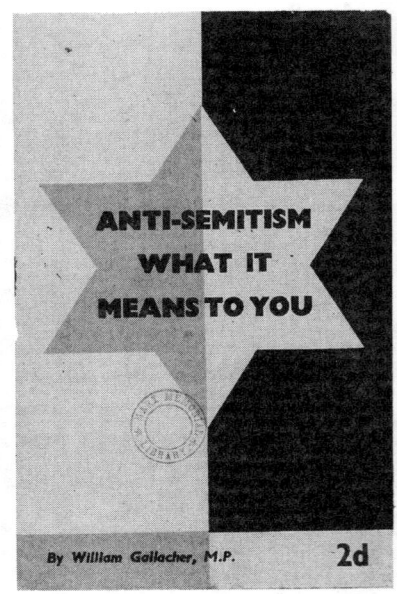

4 Pamphlets of the period produced by Communists or Jews. Top left: *Soviet Jews at War* by Professor Hyman Levy (courtesy of Lazar Zaidman collection); top right: *Anti-Semitism What it Means to You* by William Gallacher, MP (courtesy of Marx Memorial Library); left: *Russia at the Peace Conference* by Phil Piratin, MP (Lazar Zaidman collection)

CENTRAL LONDON BRANCH of the
JEWISH PEOPLE'S COUNCIL
Against Fascism and Anti-Semitism (Non-Political)

The Fight Against Fascism and Anti-Semitism

ALL THOSE WHO WISH TO AVOID
THE SUPPRESSION OF ALL DEMOCRATIC INSTITUTIONS AND MOVEMENTS;
AND OPPOSE
THE INCITEMENT TO RACIAL HATRED, AND THE PERSECUTION OF JEWS, CATHOLICS AND ALL WHO ARE AGAINST FASCISM—

COME TO THE

MASS MEETING

on WEDNESDAY, SEPTEMBER 1st 1937
AT THE
CIRCLE ROOMS, 162, New Cavendish Street,
Gt. Portland Street, W.1. at 8 p.m.

Speakers Include—
 Rev. A. D. BELDEN, Whitefields Tabernacle
 S. JOSEPH, Speaker in Yiddish
 P. VALENTINE
 P. HELLMAN
Chairman—J. D. BAILEY

● Jew-Baiting is a Trick to Destroy Your Democratic Liberties ! !

Issued and Published by the Central Office, Jewish People's Council Against Fascism and Anti-Semitism (Non-Political). 164, Commercial Road, E.1—Stepney Green 3906
Printed by B. Weinberg, Ltd. (T.U.) 73, Brick Lane, E.1

5 The Jewish People's Council organized mass meetings to protest against Fascism and anti-Semitism in the 1930s (courtesy of Julius Jacobs collection)

ייִדישער פֿאָלקס קאָונסיל
קעגן פֿאַשיזם און אַנטיסעמיטיזם.
איסט לאָנדאָן בראַנטש

די ייִדן אין רומעניע און אין ענגלאַנד

נעכטן — דייטשלאַנד און פּוילן !
היינט — רומעניע !

אַכט הונדערט טויזנט ייִדן אין רומעניע שטייען
אין געפֿאַר אויסצוּוואָרטן פֿון פֿאַשיזם. דאָ אין
ענגלאַנד פֿירט דער פֿאַשיזם אָן מיט ייִדן-העצעס
און אַטאַקעס קעגן דעמאָקראַטיע.

קומט צו

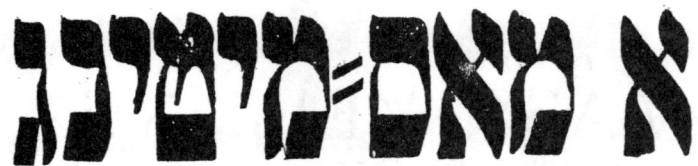
אַ מאַס=מיטינג

אין דער ליידיס טיילאַרס האָל, 12 נעריט גאָרדן סטריט.
מיטוואָך דעם 2-טן פֿעברואַר, 1938

רעדנער: י. ה. האַלל, מ. פּ. פֿאַר וויטשעפּל.
ד. גאָלדבלאַט, ליבעראַלער קאַנדידאַט פֿאַר וויטשעפּל.
מ. מייער, רעדאַקטאָר די "צייט".
י. רושייקאָבה, עקזעקוטיוו קאָמ. ייד. פֿאָלקס קאָונסיל.

פֿאָרזיצער:
י. רעננאַפּ

אָנפֿאַנג 8 אַ וויניגער פֿינקטלעך.

איינטריט פֿריי ! קומט אין מאַסן !

---

6   Such meetings were advertised in Yiddish as well as in English

EAST LONDON BRANCH of the JEWISH PEOPLE'S COUNCIL
Against Fascism and Anti-Semitism.
(NON POLITICAL)

Rumania and the Jewish People of Britain

**Yesterday—Germany and Poland!
To-day—Rumania!**

800,000 Rumanian Jews threatened by Fascism. The menace of Fascism and Anti-Semitism is increasing. Here in Britain Fascism with its filthy Jew-baiting is attacking Jewry and Democracy.

Come to the

MASS MEETING

at the

LADIES TAILORS HALL,
12, Greatorex Street (Gt. Garden Street), E.1. on
Wednesday, February 2nd, 1938
at 8 p.m.

Speakers include:

J. H. HALL, M.P. Whitechapel & St. George's.
M. MYER, Editor "Jewish Times."
D. GOLDBLATT, Liberal Candidate,
 Whitechapel & St. George's.
J. JACOBS, E. C. Jewish People's Council.
I. RENNAP, Chairman.

Jew-Baiting here and abroad is an attack upon liberty and all progress!

Issued by Jewish People's Council Against Fascism and Anti-Semitism, East London Branch
164, Commercial Road, E.1.   · Printed by the Superior Printers, Ltd. (T.U), London. E.1

7 By 1938 the tone of the Jewish People's Council's posters had become more urgent as examples of Fascist and Nazi oppression proliferated (Julius Jacobs collection)

Hitler Pays the Piper -
-What Tune does he Call?

Hitler Financed Austrian Nazis—
 ... THEY SOLD AUSTRIA TO HITLER.

Hitler Finances Czecho Slovakian Fascists—
 ... THEY PROPOSE TO SELL CZECHO SLOVAKIA TO HITLER.

Hitler provides money for Fascist propaganda in Belgium—
 ... WHY?

Hitler Financed Rumanian Fascists—
 ... TO PUT RUMANIA UNDER THE SWASTIKA FLAG?

Hitler and Mussolini assist Spanish Fascists—
 ... ARE GIBRALTAR AND THE CANARY ISLANDS THE PRICE?

British Fascists receive funds from abroad—
 ... WHAT HAVE THEY PROMISED IN RETURN?

The Fascists claim to be Patriotic—
 ... TO WHICH COUNTRY?

Such "Patriotism" is the "Last Refuge of a Scoundrel!"

● The Fascists use lying anti-Semitism in an attempt to get your support!

Remember Jew-baiting is a cloak to hide their Treachery—

● DEFEND YOUR FREEDOM ——
FIGHT FASCIST ANTI-SEMITISM!

Issued and Published by the Jewish People's Council against Fascism and anti-Semitism (Non-Political) 118, Commercial Road, E.1   Royal 4670
Printed by B. Weinberg Ltd., (T.U) 73, Brick Lane. E.1.

THE EAST LONDON JEWS WITHIN THE STEPNEY POLITICAL SYSTEM

This project, along with the YKUF branch itself, collapsed with the onset of war, but other cultural institutions continued to flourish. In 1943, the Association of Jewish Writers and Journalists opened a Folk House on Adler Street. Participants in this venture included such East London Yiddishists as Solomon Lever, Morris Myer, N. M. Seedo, I. A. Lisky, Itzhak Nathani, A. M. Kaiser and David Goldinger – most of whom were active in the Workers' Circle. One practical result of the activities sponsored by the Folk House was the creation of the London Yiddish Theatre in Adler Street in 1943, under the direction of Mark Markov, formerly with the Yiddish Folks Theatre in the Grand Palais. The London Yiddish Theatre was 'not a private but a *communal concern*';[70] N. Beitler, the theatre's secretary, explained during a showing of *Der Dybbuk* by S. Anski that 'we are trying to foster and preserve something which Hitler tried to kill'.[71] Many Yiddishists already saw themselves as trustees of a heritage which had come close to extinction and was in need of careful tending. Along with many other East European Jews in London, they saw themselves as the successors to Polish Jewry:

> We are living in an epoch when upon us has *fallen the particularly heavy burden of caring for the fate of our cultural heritage*, which has suffered so grievously in our old homelands. We, here in England, are the only free Jewish community in Europe, we alone have escaped the ordeal. Sacred is the duty we owe to the millions of our brethren who have fallen and to those who are still living. *Let us give everything within our power to help revive our spiritual life.*[72]

STEPNEY IN THE 1930s

Although not the poorest borough in London, in the 1930s Stepney was a somewhat squalid area with problems that were financially beyond the means of the local borough council.[73] Although population had been declining steadily since the turn of the century as those who became more affluent escaped to points east and north such as Ilford or Stoke Newington, Stepney remained overcrowded.[74] In 1931, when an average of 58.7 people occupied each acre in greater London, the average in Stepney was 127.5;[75] in 1936, its 1,766 acres were home to a population of over 200,000.[76]

The overcrowding was particularly evident in terms of housing. Stepney's buildings were old: of the available housing still standing in the borough in 1949, 48 per cent (378 acres) had been built before 1870, 31 per cent (247 acres) between 1870 and 1916, and only 21 per cent (168 acres) after 1916.[77] The 1931 census showed that while the average rate of occupancy in London was 0.98 people per room, the average in Stepney was 1.33 people per room, with 23.6 per cent of the inhabitants living more than two to a room.[78] Statistics for 1937 show that 6,738 families lived in overcrowded conditions in the 37,206 houses in Stepney, and that 5,949 basement rooms were illegally occupied.[79] Some 16,000 people in Stepney were actually living three to a room; the density per housing acre in the borough was 184 people in 1938.[80]

Poverty increased as tailoring and cabinet-making, industries which employed many Jews, were severely affected by the depression.[81] In the furnishing trades, the percentage of insured workers unemployed nationally varied from 9.8 per cent to 13.9 per cent in the years 1935 to 1939; for tailoring the figures were 12.6 per cent and 15.4 per cent.[82] In both industries, unemployment actually rose in the first months of the war.[83]

In Stepney, which of course had large concentrations of both industries, the overall unemployment rate at the end of December 1936 was at 10.3 per cent, compared to 6.7 per cent for London as a whole. A year later it had risen to 11.3 per cent, compared to 7.6 per cent for all London.[84] The two East End NAFTA branches, Numbers 15 and 141, reported 180 members unemployed out of a combined membership of 1,264 in January 1937;[85] by December 1939 this had risen to 295 unemployed members out of 1,626.[86] As for tailoring, conditions were so bad that J. L. Fine, secretary of the ULTTU, despaired that 'in the very near future certain manufacturers will compel our members to resolve on a General Strike as the only remedy which will alleviate the unbearable conditions in our trade'.[87] Idle workers in the industry would converge on the Settles Street Labour Exchange in Whitechapel, 'where thousands of unemployed Jewish tailors sign on daily',[88] and also at the 'slave market', a stretch of pavement near the union's offices at Greatorex Street and Whitechapel Road.[89] The depressed clothing industry did much to contribute to the high levels of poverty and unemployment in Stepney,[90] where many families had less than £2 a week to spend, and the fear of losing one's job hung 'always over the head of almost every working man and woman'.[91]

Poverty, overcrowding and all the attendant ills of slum living created health problems for the residents of Stepney.[92] The grim figures were there for all to see, in annual reports released by Dr F. R. O'Shiel, the Medical Officer of Health for Stepney; in London County Council statistics; and in the annual statistical reviews published nationally by the office of the Registrar-General for England and Wales. Stepney residents were troubled with a higher than average rate of such diseases as tuberculosis and pneumonia; infant mortality rates were usually above the national average. In terms of the standardized mortality figure – that is, a ratio of all deaths using 100 as the base figure for England and Wales – the Stepney figure was between 110 and 122 in the years from 1936 to 1939.[93]

In the words of the Reverend St John B. Groser, the East End Anglican priest who was active in the 1930s rent strikes, Stepney was 'a black spot – one of the worst in London'.[94] As Phil Piratin put it in 1948, Stepney 'was almost an entire slum. The borough had gone through a long period of decline, and a complete overhaul was called for.'[95]

ETHNIC ANIMOSITY IN STEPNEY

By the turn of the century, the East End was already sharply divided into Jewish and Irish districts, and there was mutual antagonism over work, trade and politics.[96] The Irish had 'strong concentrations in the dockland areas of East London' and in Limehouse.[97] According to Tom Rampling, an Irish Catholic who joined the Labour Party as a youth but left it for the CP in 1937, the two communities kept mainly to themselves: 'Jews didn't come into Wapping and Irish people didn't very often go into Whitechapel.'[98] Although both communities were largely working class, labourers were in different trades and belonged to different unions. Even those working in the same industries were often divided: for many years the Jewish tailors' union – the ULLTU – hesitated to join the NUTGW because they regarded the Irish leadership of that union as 'a quite alien religious and ethnic group'.[99] Some political activists have recalled separate Jewish and Irish Labour groups in the East End before the founding of a unified Stepney Central Labour Party in 1918.[100] Soon the Irish had assumed a pre-eminent role in the new Labour Party.[101] Many studies have noted 'the intense Labour proclivities of Irish immigrants';[102] in Stepney, as elsewhere, the majority of Irish gave their allegiance to the Labour Party,[103] and a large faction within the party was Irish in origin.[104]

Many Jews in the interwar period tried to remain faithful to the Liberal Party. 'The Liberal Party had had a tradition in Stepney, and particularly in Whitechapel and St. George's Division, where their main support came from the tradesmen's section and from a large proportion of the Jewish community.'[105] But already in 1919, Labour had won control of the Stepney Borough Council and Clement Attlee had become Stepney's first Labour mayor; in 1922, the enlarged Whitechapel-St George's seat was won for Labour by C. J. Matthew, an Irish Catholic. As the 1920s and 1930s progressed, it became clear that the Liberals were fading fast as a political force. None the less, in the 1931 parliamentary election in Whitechapel-St George's, Barnett Janner, then a Liberal and active in Jewish affairs, defeated J. H. Hall, the Labour candidate, who had won the seat in a by-election the previous year,[106] by emphasizing his ethnic identity. Hall was also hurt by the candidacy of Harry Pollitt, general secretary of the CPGB, who split the vote on the left.[107] Janner's campaign was criticized by both Pollitt and Herbert Morrison, London's Labour Party leader, on the grounds that it had done 'a great deal of harm'; many people charged the Jewish community with group clannishness.[108] Four years later, in what the *Jewish Chronicle* described as a 'rough' campaign,[109] Hall defeated Janner. Although Janner made a strong showing in the Jewish sections of Whitechapel, Hall, an Irish Catholic, won by virtue of his commanding lead in the Irish areas of St-George's-in-the-East.[110]

THE EAST LONDON JEWS WITHIN THE STEPNEY POLITICAL SYSTEM

With the Liberals in eclipse, many Jews felt powerless. The Tories were not considered a viable alternative, and so many Jews did turn to the Stepney Labour Party, which began to serve as a meeting point for those more moderate Jews who were willing to unite with the Irish Catholics on matters of common concern. Both groups had been the victims of 'anti-alien' and anti-immigrant actions during the First World War and feared continued discrimination and prejudicial behaviour on the part of government and society. They also made common cause over education questions, including the issue of state subsidies to denominational schools. There were also many other local 'bread and butter' issues, including an inclination on the part of some towards using political office for patronage and other minor forms of corruption.[111] As we shall see, even those Jews who joined the Labour Party felt closer in many cases to the Communists than to the Irish who dominated their own party. Meanwhile, Labour was supreme: the Stepney borough council elected in 1934 was entirely Labour; in 1937, 59 of the 60 councillors returned were Labour candidates.

Although the council was ethnically more or less equally divided between councillors of Irish Catholic, Jewish and 'English' descent, Labour supremacy increasingly meant Irish supremacy. Despite the fact that there was a Jewish caucus in the party, a group mainly from Mile End led by such figures as M. H. Davis, a member of the Stepney and London County councils, and Dan Frankel, a Stepney and LCC councillor who was elected MP for Mile End in the general election in November 1935,[112] these Jewish members became increasingly subordinate to their Irish Catholic allies, who had 'absolute domination' over the party and hence over the Stepney Council,[113] which Julius Jacobs has described as a 'Tammany Hall'.[114] The Council did elect Jewish mayors as late as 1934–35 (I. M. Vogler) and 1935–6 (Helena Roberts) – though the latter was a convert to Christianity. But commencing with the succession of Mayor John Charles Lawder in November 1936, the position was henceforth occupied by an Irish Catholic member of the party.[115]

Animosity between the Irish and the Jews tended to paralyse the Labour Party, particularly on Jewish concern over Fascism at home and abroad. Because the East London Jewish community had arrived from Eastern Europe relatively recently, they reacted very strongly to any manifestations of anti-Semitism in Britain. Mosley's Fascists, for example, seemed to them to be analogous to the East European perpetrators of pogroms and other violence. To them, Mosley loomed as an even greater threat than his actual activities may have warranted:[116] on 4th October 1936, the day of the 'Battle of Cable Street', an elderly Jewish woman told Edith Ramsay, the well-known Stepney social worker, 'Lady, lady, I have seen it all in Poland, and it is coming here'.[117]

The Labour Party as a whole, however, was relatively indifferent to such matters. One problem was that the Roman Catholic Church, which remained the focus of Irish life,[118] was more concerned with combatting Communism than with stopping Fascism. Another problem was that the primary international concern of the Irish was, of course, Ireland,[119] a country so little interested in fighting Fascism that it remained neutral in the Second World War. From 1936 onwards, tensions between the Irish and the Jews were further exacerbated by the Spanish Civil War. Nationally, the Labour Party, aware that many Catholic workers actively opposed the Spanish Republic, feared that it might lose the Catholic vote if it appeared too vigorously pro-Republican.[120] This was even more the case in Stepney. Montagu Einhorn, ward secretary of the Spitalfields East Labour Party branch during the 1930s, has recalled that two prominent Irish politicians – Morgan Phillips, secretary of the Whitechapel–St George's Labour Party, and J. J. Long, one of the Labour councillors – supported a resolution presented to the executive committee of the party which condemned the Spanish Loyalists for using the churches as posts from which to attack the Nationalist forces. 'In other words,' Einhorn remarked, 'it wasn't a resolution in support of the Republicans, it was a resolution in support of the Fascists. That was the way it was going, that was the action the Labour Party was taking!'[121] In October 1936, Long interrupted a meeting in support of the Spanish Republic organized by the Communist-front Stepney Council for Peace and Democracy, and was asked to leave by I. M. Vogler, the Jewish Labour councillor and supporter of left-wing causes;[122] Long also spoke at a gathering in opposition to Communism a few weeks later.[123] Hence many Stepney Jews, even those who were social democrats ideologically, were 'thoroughly disillusioned by the official Labour Party representation' which failed to express their deep feelings of outrage against Fascism and Nazism.[124] Some went so far as to accuse the party of harbouring anti-Semites.[125]

This impression was reinforced by the fact that, for many Irish, admiration for the doctrine of the Catholic corporate state, for Franco and for Mussolini did actually spill over into extreme anti-Communism and anti-Semitism. These Irish were ready to lend their support to Oswald Mosley's British Union of Fascists (BUF). Stuart Rawnsley has taken note of Mosley's popularity among the Irish: 'Certainly the "Irish Connection" seems to loom large in the anatomy of the BUF.'[126] According to Robert Skidelsky, 'the Irish run like a bright thread through Mosley's chequered career'.[127] He explains that the Irish sought out the BUF as 'a vehicle for their local grievances' and that the campaign in the East End – which was managed by two Irishmen, Owen Burke and E. G. 'Mick' Clarke – was run 'along ethnic lines'.[128] The BUF made a practice of 'playing the Irish off against the Jews',[129] and in his attempt to woo the Irish, Mosley aimed much of his electoral propaganda at them during the London County Council (LCC) elections in March 1937 and the borough elections that November.[130]

Catholic anti-Semitism 'continued to be a source of anxiety to Anglo-Jewry in the inter-war years',[131] and Mosley and the BUF found a staunch and highly vocal ally in the *Catholic Herald*, a popular weekly which was 'an irritant in the life of the Jewish community',[132] and which even during the war continued its attacks on Jews. In one sensationalist story, for example, it described the biggest East End air raid shelter, Tilbury, as a 'brothel' where 'the ubiquitous Jew and his family' spread disease and the 'young Jewish Communist' added 'fuel to the Red fire which East End Communists are now eagerly fanning in the shelter'.[133] The *Catholic Herald* also continued to blame Jews for the Russian Revolution,[134] suggested that reports of Nazi atrocities against Jews in occupied Europe were Russian-inspired exaggerations,[135] and defended the Polish government-in-exile in London against charges of anti-Semitism.[136]

In the face of these and other provocations, it is not surprising that Jews increasingly regarded the Communist Party as their 'only form of self-defence'.[137] Disgusted with both the Labour Party and the Irish, they turned to the only party in which they constituted an ethnic majority. Morry Lebow has recalled that the party in the East End 'was mainly Jewish';[138] Tom Rampling, in what is obviously a subjective distortion from the vantage point of a non-Jew who must have felt slightly uncomfortable at being in such a distinct minority, has said that 'more than 90 per cent' of the membership were Jewish.[139] Certainly 'the whole of the Stepney leadership was predominantly Jewish';[140] for Tubby Rosen, 'it was uncanny to notice that very few Christians were on the branch committee, or in the leading positions'.[141] By 1936, 'the ordinary impartial East Ender' could hardly help regarding the Stepney CP as 'little more than a group of young Jewish men and women, mostly of recent foreign extraction who, reasonably disgruntled with their lot, find in this movement a means of expressing their refusal to accept the inferior social status allotted to them'.[142]

They also found a means of expressing their opposition to Fascism. Phil Piratin, who became secretary of the Stepney CP in June 1937, has aptly summed up the situation:

> Only the Communist Party stood out as the forthright opponent of fascism, and of the National Government which supported and protected it. No one in East London and particularly Stepney, in those days, was unaware of this fact. A number of Labour members acknowledged this leadership of the Communist Party and regretted the weakness of their own leadership. Such 'premature' anti-fascists were condemned and in some cases expelled, by the Labour Party.[143]

Piratin was referring to a ginger group of Jewish Labour councillors who were ostracized or thrown out of the party in the late 1930s by the dominant Irish faction. One of these episodes occurred just before the borough elections in November 1937, when four Jewish councillors were suspended, including I. M. Vogler, whose pro-Loyalist stand offended some of the Irish council members.[144]

The overt hostility between Jewish and Irish councillors may

THE EAST LONDON JEWS WITHIN THE STEPNEY POLITICAL SYSTEM

have had some bearing on the CP's first electoral success in Stepney. This was Piratin's victory in the November 1937 borough elections in the Spitalfields East ward, an area in the north-west corner of the borough that included Brick Lane, Hanbury Street, and Flower and Dean Street, and that had a large Jewish population.[145] Piratin maintained during his campaign that the CP deserved the seat because it had 'been in the front line of defence against Fascism' in this 'critical period of local, national and international history'; Piratin also argued that the presence of a Communist councillor would strengthen and vitalize the Labour representation on the council.[146] Piratin's electoral manifesto, the *Communist Plan for Life in Stepney*, proposed large-scale slum clearance, the use of every available site for housing, and stronger action against slum landlords.

The CP worked hard to win the Spitalfields East seat. It also benefited from the anti-Fascist activities of many of the Jewish trade union activists who were in conflict with right-wing Labourites such as Davis, Frankel and Long,[147] as well as from the CP-dominated Jewish People's Council Against Fascism and Anti-Semitism, which had campaigned actively against the BUF in the LCC elections in March and was now doing the same in the borough elections.[148] Throughout Stepney, including Spitalfields East, JPC speakers warned of the Fascist danger and dispensed leaflets urging that 'Every Jewish elector must vote – must vote anti-Fascist!'[149] Whether by chance or design, the JPC campaign dovetailed nicely with Piratin's own. The CP also received help from a most unexpected quarter when the Tories distributed a leaflet that accused the outgoing Labour councillors of being sympathetic to Fascism because they had approved the use of Limehouse Town Hall for a Mosley meeting earlier in the year. The general secretary of the Communist Party, Harry Pollitt, feigning indignation at this Tory ploy, made use of the occasion to scold the 'disgraceful . . . action of Right-wing Labour representatives', which had thus played into the hands of 'our enemies'.[150] Piratin came third in the election, receiving 616 votes; it was enough to gain a council seat.[151]

His victory seemed to heighten the antagonism between the left-wing Jewish councillors and the Irish-dominated Labour leadership in council. On 23 February 1938, two former mayors, I. M. Vogler and Mrs Helena Roberts, were evicted from a council meeting after being ruled out of order by the incumbent mayor, J. J. Long. Their comments on the episode give some sense of the ideological and political hostility dividing these two factions within the local Labour Party. Roberts, who referred to Mayor Long as a 'Mussolini', asked, 'What can you expect from a disciple of Franco's chief lieutenant?' Vogler remarked as he was being thrown out, 'It is with pleasure that I leave this session of the Reichstag'. In a statement to the press, Roberts and Vogler elaborated on their 'deep and fundamental' complaints, criticizing the Labour majority in council for its failure to act on rent control and ARP; for its mismanagement, waste and poor treatment of council staff; and for its open hostility towards the newly elected Communist councillor, Piratin. Vogler asserted that a Labour 'oligarchy' ran the council on 'the Fuhrer Prinzep [sic]'; Roberts added that the council was dominated by an 'Axis . . . which sets its face definitely against progress'.[152]

From this time onwards the two evicted councillors sat as independent Labour members, voting with Piratin on many issues. They had little chance of prevailing against the other Labour members, even after they had been joined, late in 1938, by Councillor H. H. Gordon, who also served as chairman of the Stepney Tenants' Defence League; like Roberts and Vogler before him, Gordon was expelled from the Labour caucus.[153] In June 1938, Roberts and Vogler unsuccessfully opposed a measure that made the chalking of slogans on pavements an offence; Vogler asserted that it was 'deliberately introduced to cripple the Communist Party as revenge for their electoral victory' and demanded to know whether the council had any objection to the most frequently written slogan: 'Stop Hitler.'[154] In July, the council refused to consider a motion by Roberts concerning 'alleged batoning of Stepney citizens by police at recent Fascist meetings within the Borough'.[155] In February 1939, when Mayor Joseph Johnson ordered Piratin out of the council chambers following a dispute, Vogler protested, to no avail, 'This is not Germany. This is Stepney.'[156] A few months later Vogler, bitter against 'the steam-rolling caucus which controls

THE EAST LONDON JEWS WITHIN THE STEPNEY POLITICAL SYSTEM

the Council', complained in a letter to the *East London Advertiser* that his faction's motions were usually ruled out of order or sidetracked; sometimes they were not even given the courtesy of a reply.[157]

That winter, the Stepney CP achieved an active membership of 500; the Young Communist League branch of the party had a membership of 250.[158]

3
Housing, ARP and the Blitz

THE STEPNEY TENANTS' DEFENCE LEAGUE

Of all the local issues around which the East London Jewish Communists provoked opposition to the political system, the most important was housing. Phil Piratin mentions a short-lived group formed by the CP in Stepney to fight for better housing as early as 1934; the main focus of its activity was Fieldgate Mansions in Whitechapel East ward. Piratin was the leader of this group, while Michael Shapiro, another Jewish Communist, served as its housing expert.[1] In 1935, Shapiro, writing under the pseudonym 'Michael Best', produced *Heartbreak Homes: An Indictment of the National Government's Housing Policy*, in which he challenged the government's claims of progress in slum clearance and in the elimination of overcrowding. Shapiro warned his readers that the problem of adequate working-class housing could never be solved completely 'so long as private, speculative, ruthless profit-grabbers have the upper hand', as they did in the capitalist system. Still, Shapiro called for the implementation of a seven-point programme to clear out existing slums without compensation for condemned property, and to stimulate local authorities to construct working-class housing which would be rented at a maximum of 10s a week inclusive of rates.[2] Shapiro produced other pamphlets as the tenants' movement developed, including *The Tenants' Guide* (1938), which explained new legislation concerning rents and described how tenants could best protect their own interests.[3] By this time other Communists were publishing literature on the same subject,[4] and the groundwork was being laid for a movement of tenants who had had their fill of paying high rents for bad housing. There were sporadic rent strikes in 1935–37 at tenements such as Paragon Mansions in Mile End Centre ward. Communists had been involved in organizing the local tenants' committee at Paragon Mansions; the committee was advised by a group of architects headed by Michael Shapiro. During their strike the tenants, reinforced by 'strong-arm' men such as Tubby Rosen, managed to hold off the bailiff and police and to win a partial victory.[5] Piratin was able to use this incident, which took place in June 1937, in his own campaign to win a council seat in November. His literature included a picture of himself addressing a crowd at the tenement, 'leading the fight against the agent, wealthy Mr Benabo'.[6] Piratin also circulated an eight-point programme calling for strong action against landlords who charged excessive rents, full support for the demands of tenants' associations, an extension of rent control under the Rent Acts which were due to expire within a year, and large-scale slum clearance and rehousing schemes.[7]

The Stepney Tenants' Defence League, a federation of various tenants' committees such as that at Paragon Mansions, was established, according to Piratin, in the autumn of 1937; Shapiro was its first secretary. In addition to dealing with problems of rent and repairs, the STDL taught tenants how to organize, determine their legal rights and fight landlords in a collective, disciplined way. Not until the end of 1938, however, did the STDL come into its own, stimulated by decontrol of much of the area's housing and by the consequent attempts by landlords either to raise rents by as much as 40 per cent or to neglect their responsibilities. Tubby Rosen replaced Shapiro as secretary; he was assisted by two full-time organizers, Harry Conn and Mrs Ella Donovan. All three were Communists.[8] The more honorific positions of president and chairman were filled by the Reverend St John B. Groser, Vicar of Christ Church, Stepney,[9] and Councillor H. H. Gordon, the left-leaning socialist who had been expelled from the Labour Party caucus in November 1938.[10]

In the new year, Tubby Rosen announced that the STDL wanted rent control for all working-class houses.[11] Rent strikes took place 'in street after street in rapid succession'; many landlords capitulated and signed 'collective agreements' with their tenants.[12] By the end of January 1939 the STDL had four central offices and ten local committees, and had almost 5,000 affiliated members.[13] Rosen announced that with 2,000 tenants already refusing to pay rent, the big landlords were 'on the run'.[14] By the end of February, the STDL had recovered £10,000 in overcharged rents and had won rent reductions totalling £18,000. It had also forced landlords to carry out numerous repairs: one landlord had to increase his staff of workmen from six to 57.[15] The League had gained another 1,000 members,[16] and still more tenants were joining in the rent strikes: 1,500 were on strike on 10 March, with another 500 due to join them.[17] Michael Shapiro predicted a mass rent strike of 100,000 people throughout East London within three months if the STDL's demands for rent control were not met. Rosen, presenting a report on the League's activities, told of people who paid one-third to one-half of their weekly income for unsanitary, overcrowded accommodation in houses dripping with water and lacking lavatories and bathrooms. Rosen added that the 'wholesale bullying and intimidation of tenants' by landlords and their agents had finally been challenged.[18]

At the end of April, rent strikes were still in progress in nine different parts of Stepney; other disputes were being settled quickly, as landlords decided against confronting the STDL. To celebrate its victories, the League called a march for 30 April, to coincide with May Day activities. Columns of marchers from five centres of recent strikes converged on Stepney Green, where about 10,000 people, preceded by bands and singing League songs, settled down to hear a concert under the Clock Tower.[19]

The East End novelist Simon Blumenfeld, author of four 'proletarian' novels depicting working-class Jewish life,[20] pointed to the growth of the STDL in an article that appeared towards the end of May in the *News Chronicle*: the League was now composed of 50 defence committees, with a total of 7,000 members; it had forced landlords to refund excess rates of more than £20,000, and to reduce rents amounting to another £25,000 – even so, the STDL still charged landlords with collecting £200,000 a year in excess of the legally controlled rents.[21] By late June, when Ted Bramley,

London District CP organizer, noted that 18 rent strikes had been settled peacefully,[22] membership had grown to 7,500.[23]

So prominent had the STDL become in its fight for tenants' rights in East London that it drew national attention. An article by Hamilton Fyfe entitled 'Why Do We Pay Rent?' appeared in *Reynolds News*, the Sunday newspaper of the Co-operative movement, in February 1939.[24] The issue was taken up in the House of Commons after 70 Stepney women, STDL members, lobbied MPs on 16 May;[25] on 6 July, Sir Percy Harris, Liberal MP for Bethnal Green South-West, and J. H. Hall, Labour MP for Whitechapel-St George's, asked the Minister of Health, Walter Elliot, whether he proposed to do anything concerning the serious unrest in East London, which was due to increased rents and unsanitary conditions.[26]

By mid summer many East End residents would have been ready to agree with Father Groser that since the mass activity had commenced, 'we have beaten back the landlords who have for years sucked the lifeblood of the people of Stepney'. Groser urged STDL members to continue to support those still on strike; to contribute to the general fund; and to persuade their neighbours to join the League.[27] To celebrate its achievements, the League held a large victory parade from Brady Street to Philpot Street on 9 July; 6,000 participants heard Tubby Rosen declare that £25,000 had been refunded to tenants in lump-sum settlements for rent overcharges, and that landlords had been forced to spend another £60,000 on repairs.[28]

The coming of war brought immediate rent controls which froze rents as of 31 August 1939, thus incorporating into law the lower rents won through political action by the tenants. The work of the STDL was not at an end, however; the League shifted its attention to wartime problems such as air raid precautions, food profiteering and sudden increases in the cost of living. 'We shall fight profiteers, whether wholesale or retail, with the same tactics we used against the landlords', announced Tubby Rosen,[29] and to this end the STDL, along with the Stepney Trades Council, called a conference in Christ Church on 12 November.[30] Soon 'a new wave of rent strikes' was 'sweeping the East End', according to Rosen.[31] In June

1940, as the rent strikes continued,[32] Stephen Murray, the STDL lawyer, stated that the League's membership was up to 11,000.[33]

But the STDL was no longer the broadly based movement it had been. With the coming of the war, the Communist Party turned its back on attempts to forge popular-front unity with liberals and members of the Labour movement, substituting denunciations not only of the war but of all 'bourgeois politics'. The reverberations were felt in the STDL. Father Groser, for example, after a long struggle behind the scenes with the Communists, resigned as president of the League in February 1940.[34] Although Groser admired the work of people such as Shapiro and Rosen, he was disturbed that 'we found ourselves in different camps, as they were forced to take the "party line"' concerning the war.[35]

The CP and its fronts were not, however, to be written off, as they might have been in more middle-class neighbourhoods: according to Piratin, the Stepney CP 'met with very little hostility', even among those who disagreed with its wartime policies.[36] The CP had dealt far more effectively than the Labour-dominated local government with problems concerning housing; and their popular support would be reinforced by their activities during the blitz.

ARP AND THE BLITZ IN STEPNEY

It was becoming clear to many people in the 1930s that in the borough of Stepney, with its dense housing, few open spaces, heavy concentration of industry, and, of course, the London docks, war would bring massive destruction and a great loss of life unless the levels of government took steps towards providing adequate protection against aerial bombing. From 1937 onwards the CPGB campaigned steadily to make itself appear to be the defender of civilians against the criminal negligence of a national government more concerned with war preparations and profits than with the defence of its own population. Foremost in the ranks of CP experts on the subject was Professor J. B. S. Haldane, who in 1938 published the popular Left Book Club edition of his work advocating deep bomb-proof shelters, *A.R.P.*;[37] the deep shelter advocated by the Communists became popularly known as the 'Haldane shelter'.

In the East End, one of the organizations promoting the agitation over ARP was the Stepney Council for Peace and Democracy. In a study of ARP, the SCPD asserted that Stepney, due to its residential overcrowding and its value as a military target, was 'more vulnerable perhaps than any other area in the country'.[38] The Stepney CP itself distributed a pamphlet pointing out the obvious dangers to Stepney, where, it was said, the dilapidated dwellings *'would collapse like a pack of cards!'* during mass bombings. The Stepney CP then revealed its own proposal for 110 60-feet-deep tunnel shelters, at a total cost of about £2 million; factories and docks would have special shelter entrances to link up with the system of tunnels. But, as the same pamphlet noted, the total amount of money available for ARP under the government's scheme for Stepney was a mere 2s. 2½d. per head, as compared to 16s. 9d. per head in the City of Westminster. It was unfair to ask Stepney to meet such heavy costs as would still be needed from local rates, according to the party: the responsibility for ARP, just as for guns and battleships, should be the government's.[39] Phil Piratin, too, was calling for better shelters: speaking at Limehouse Town Hall in October 1938, he proposed a system of deep tunnels which would cost £11 6s. per head.[40]

The Stepney Borough Council, handicapped by its lack of money and authority, tried to meet some of the mounting criticism. In May 1938, after Councillor M. H. Davis became chairman of the new Committee for Air Raid Precautions, debates in the council chamber concerning protection from bombers became more frequent. One particularly lively exchange in December 1938 set the Communist councillor, Piratin, along with the two left-wing independent Labourites, I. M. Vogler and Mrs Helena Roberts, against the rest of the council members.[41] The council debated ARP again a few weeks later, but to little avail.[42] Despite rumours of corruption surrounding Davis, he was appointed Air Raid Precautions Controller of Stepney by his colleagues in May 1939, and an ARP Emergency Committee was created to assist him in the event of war.[43]

In the summer and autumn of 1939, as events moved rapidly towards war, the national government refused to budge from its position that deep shelters were impractical. In a debate with Professor Haldane at Circle House, organized by the Stepney Council for Peace and Democracy, Viscount Hinchingbrooke, late parliamentary secretary to Stanley Baldwin, summed up the feelings of the Tories when he said that bomb-proof shelters 'would disorganize industry by keeping workers underground for long periods of time'.[44]

On the day Germany invaded Poland, and even before the official British declaration of war, the Stepney Tenants' Defence League began to receive requests for help in securing air raid protection. The League decided to take up the question of ARP with all landlords who had signed agreements with them;[45] the landlords in turn pressed the borough council to proceed with plans for shelters. The League itself sent a deputation to Dan Frankel and J. H. Hall, the MPs for Mile End and Whitechapel-St George's; but nothing was accomplished.[46]

On 4 January 1940, at a special meeting of the Stepney Borough Council called to discuss ARP, councillors Vogler and Piratin both pointed out that according to a report submitted to the Home Office, Stepney lagged behind every other local authority in London in regard to ARP. Though approximately 200,000 people inhabited Stepney, only a quarter of these could be accommodated in the available Anderson (surface) shelters and reinforced basements.[47] When Councillor Davis attempted to defend himself he was interrupted from the gallery by Tubby Rosen, who asserted that the STDL would 'take measures for the protection of tenants in Stepney'. Mayor Frank Lewey had Rosen evicted from the council chambers.[48] The Stepney CP and the STDL continued to criticize Davis and press for Haldane shelters throughout the year;[49] they had planned a major campaign, including a meeting with Davis, for 7 September – the day the blitz began in earnest.[50]

When the main aerial attacks on London began, the East End was particularly hard hit; Mayor Lewey would later declare that Stepney had been 'the bull's-eye on Hitler's Luftwaffe target'.[51] The mood of the people, said one local paper, was 'magnificently grim';[52]

44

Lewey paid tribute, in a national broadcast on 5 October, to the manner in which the East End was standing up to the pounding.[53] But already there were bitter complaints concerning the government's handling of the situation: according to the STDL, the government was negligent in providing even the rudiments of transportation, food and accommodation.[54] Ritchie Calder and Kingsley Martin reported on the chaos in the *New Statesman*; a year later Calder would remark in his book, *The Lesson of London*, that Stepney along with West Ham 'proved to be the worst administered of all the boroughs' and that the poor in these areas were virtually left to fend for themselves: 'The treatment of the homeless in the first weeks of the Blitzkrieg was so deplorable that disclosures of the scandal were called in Government circles "giving comfort to the enemy".'[55] Kingsley Martin pointed out that casualties in East London were high, that the surface Anderson shelters were proving ineffective and that the whole area was suffering from 'administrative failure'.[56] The *Jewish Chronicle* commented, 'it has become plain that preparations for the homeless and the helpless have been totally inadequate' and that those who might have been expected to take charge of these preparations had instead 'muddled and argued'; organization was 'particularly bad' in Stepney.[57] Claude Cockburn, writing as 'Frank Pitcairn' in the *Daily Worker*, referred to M. H. Davis as 'Stepney's Local Dictator of ARP' and 'this Lord Boss Almighty'.[58] In fact, some residents, referring to local government as 'a washout', wanted to get rid of the borough councils entirely.[59] Herbert Morrison, who replaced Sir John Anderson as Home Secretary on 3 October, finally removed Davis as head of the borough's ARP administration; he was at first replaced by J. E. Arnold James, the town clerk, then by W. Eric Adams, another non-elected official from outside Stepney altogether.[60] Councillor I. M. Vogler, at a borough council meeting held on 22 December, said he had read with shame accounts of how civil defence in Stepney had broken down during the raids. But he added that he still considered Whitehall more to blame than the local authorities; the government, he felt, was scapegoating Stepney.[61]

The Communist Party remained active and highly visible, taking 'a prominent role in shelter committees and other *ad hoc* organizations responding to wartime problems which affected ordinary people'.[62] Even though many members and supporters had scattered, the branch committee continued to function; the local CP still had 18 street groups and 19 factory groups.[63] Ted Bramley led a deputation to No. 10 Downing Street in mid-September regarding those victims of the blitz who 'need not have died'.[64] The delegation, which included Phil Piratin, Pat Devine of the London District Committee of the CP, William Zak of NAFTA's London Management Committee and four others, met with the then Home Secretary, Sir John Anderson, who told them frankly that government policy had never been to build bomb-proof shelters, but rather shelters which could 'withstand splinters'.[65]

Of all the memories of the blitz, the most famous are those scenes of people huddling in the London Underground stations at night. It is less well known that at first the government refused to allow the people of London to use the stations for shelter, and that it was Communist-led street action in the East End which forced the government to change this policy. According to the *Daily Worker*, the first demand to open the platforms occurred at an East London clothing factory;[66] soon the Underground was occupied through sheer force of numbers. Admitting defeat, Home Secretary Anderson, in a memorandum to Prime Minister Churchill dated 23 September 1940, said that the use of the Underground for shelter, although a bad idea, was now a *fait accompli*.[67] The *Daily Worker* gloated that this was a working-class victory: 'They occupied the Tubes in the teeth of Government order to the contrary – and they have got them still.'[68] International notice was taken of the part played by the Communists in this episode: Eric Sevareid, reporting from London on CBS Radio, explained that 'The Government gave in on this issue because it had to. And this outcome represents a big victory for Britain's small Communist Party.'[69]

Another Communist activity designed to embarrass the government, point out the class-based inequities in people's chances of survival during the blitz and win friends among East Enders was the campaign to take over wealthy homes and establishments, which culminated in the attempt to occupy the Savoy Hotel, in London's West End. A leading article in the *Daily Worker* of 11 September,

'The People Must Act', prepared the groundwork by comparing the 'holes' in the East End with the Savoy, where people were 'tucked into bed by servants in a luxury bomb-proof shelter'.[70] On the night of 14 September, 40 East-Enders, led by Phil Piratin and Tubby Rosen, took shelter in the Savoy. The management called the police, and nine officers arrived to evict the intruders; but they refused to move until an air raid then in progress came to an end.[71]

The Communist press made much of the work done by Communists such as Piratin and Rosen: 'Instead of seeking for personal safety, as many Labour representatives in the area have done, they have been working day and night, going from shelter to shelter, speaking to the people and helping to organize them.'[72] The Tenants' League also remained active, publishing propaganda on ARP and shelters and opening advice centres for those who had suffered war injury or damage; the Stepney Shelters Co-ordinating Committee, formed under STDL auspices, undertook various activities to help those in need.[73] On 24 November, an ARP rally in Stepney was held under the auspices of the *Daily Worker*; the 300 people who attended heard Phil Piratin and Professor Haldane again demand the immediate opening of private shelters and the construction of Haldane shelters.[74]

The worst of the public shelters was the biggest: Tilbury Shelter, between Commercial Road and Cable Street, which on some nights may have held as many as 10,000–15,000 people, perhaps half of them Jewish.[75] There, amid a 'horrifying stench', urine lapped up against people,[76] and men and women were 'herded together like animals'.[77] The *Jewish Chronicle* wrote that the 'shocking condition' of the shelter was a scandal.[78] Ted Bramley declared that it recalled 'the horrors of London before the Great Plague' and rhetorically demanded to know who was responsible for this state of affairs in the richest city in the world; he answered his own question by assigning the blame to 'guilty men, who represent a guilty class. The landowning, bank-owning, factory-owning, capitalist class'.[79]

The police seemed to assume that Tilbury was a Communist stronghold, and the Port of London Authority forbade sales of the *Daily Worker*.[80] Despite attempts at control by the authorities,

Tilbury was, of course, rife with political activity. Issie Panner, for instance, arrested in March 1941 with Communist literature in his possession, was charged with obstructing a police officer in the execution of his duty; Panner was fined £5 plus 5 guineas in costs at the Thames Police Court.[81] Ivan Maisky, then the Soviet Ambassador to Britain, has described what took place when he visited Tilbury in the company of Admiral Sir Edward R. Evans, who was in charge of the organization of bomb shelters in the metropolis. Maisky was 'rapidly recognized' by many of the 4,000 people in the shelter at the time, and hundreds gathered round, calling for a speech, which Maisky reluctantly made. The crowd called him a friend of the British proletariat, there was loud applause and singing of the 'Internationale', and he and Evans took their leave surrounded by 'an enthusiastic crowd'.[82] Yet Tilbury was not closed down, perhaps on the advice of people like Basil Henriques, who feared that doing so would cause a riot.[83]

Fascists were also active during the blitz; as Ritchie Calder remarked, Jews served as the 'objects of transferable vengeance'.[84] Not content to claim that Jews monopolized space in the London Underground, the Fascists also implied that Jews were somehow to 'blame' for the bombing, which was said to 'follow the Jews'.[85] British fascists may have picked up this theme from Nazi propagandists in Germany, who spread the word that German bombers were fulfilling Hitler's wish to 'rain bombs on the Jews'. One German radio station referred to a 'panic-stricken rush to leave London, headed by Jews'.[86] Calder heard 'curses against the Jews' in the first days of bombing: 'It was real, it was dangerous; it was fairly widespread. But the pogrom and anti-Jewish riots which so many dreaded never materialized even in the worst situation the East End has ever had to face.'[87]

Five years later, Phil Piratin called attention in his campaign literature to the grossly inadequate provision made for air raid protection. He made much of the Labour Party's failure to act: M. H. Davies, the former leader of Stepney Borough Council, was castigated for refusing to pay heed to Piratin's proposals for deep shelters, even though such shelters 'would have saved the lives of hundreds of Stepney people';[88] '*We Remember Too*', proclaimed one leaflet, *Mile End's Member of Parliament* [Dan Frankel] 'who insulted deputations of Stepney people . . . that requested his support for safer shelters.'[89] Piratin could honestly remind the voters that he himself had taken the lead 'in the campaign for safer and better shelters'[90] and that he had helped to organize shelter committees during the blitz.[91]

THE HOUSING ISSUE IN WARTIME

With the publication in July 1943 of the *County of London Plan*, post-war reconstruction became a major political issue.[92] That October, Lewis Silkin, chairman of the LCC Town Planning Committee, opened a 'Stepney To-day and To-morrow' exhibition at the Whitechapel Art Gallery, promising residents of the borough improved housing and more open spaces after the war.[93] Dr J. J. Mallon, warden of Toynbee Hall, was made chairman of the Stepney Reconstruction Group, set up to oversee post-war planning.[94]

But when the German V-1 and V-2 rocket campaigns began in the summer of 1944, Stepney was again in the firing line; and by the end of the year the area was experiencing a severe housing crisis. W. J. Edwards, MP, Mayor of Stepney and Whitechapel, predicted that the borough would be reduced by 7,000 houses by the end of the war.[95] Phil Piratin, speaking at a 'Stepney Housing Discussion' organized by the branch CP, said that Stepney would be a pitiable sight in the coming years 'if things go on as they are at present'; according to Piratin, 35,000 of the approximately 40,000 houses in Stepney were little better than hovels, a fact which indicated the need for vast slum clearances. Only drastic solutions would suffice: the government would have to take over all the land and then lend to local authorities whatever funds were necessary to rebuild homes quickly and cheaply.[96]

Piratin's remarks were an indication that although the Stepney Tenants' Defence League had been allowed to expire following the German attack on the Soviet Union in June 1941, the Communist Party was eager in 1944–45 to take up once again the campaign for good working-class housing. The *Daily Worker* articulated the CP view that 'property rights and upper-class prejudices must not be allowed to stand in the way' of solving housing problems;[97] Michael Shapiro discussed war damage and the general chaos in East London in his pamphlet, *How to Speed Up the Repairs*;[98] and Bertha Sokoloff, Secretary of the Stepney CP, called for the immediate creation of a single government department to supervise the repair of bomb-damaged houses.[99] In a pamphlet published in the winter of 1944–45, the Stepney CP asserted that only by taking land out of private hands would Stepney be enabled to build housing for all: 'If the present Government will not do it we must get the Tories out at the very first chance – at the next election – and put in a united Labour and progressive majority strengthened by as many Communists as possible.'[100]

On 27 March 1945, not long after the appearance of this pamphlet, the last V-2 rocket to fall on London came down on Hughes Mansions, Vallance Road. A total of 130 people were killed, including 102 Jews,[101] and the area was plunged into mourning by this 'most tragic of the blows struck at Stepney in six years of war'.[102] Stepney, the last area of London to suffer death and destruction, was also the worst hit in terms of total wartime damage: by 1945, 10,800 dwellings had been destroyed and many more made uninhabitable; the population of the area was only about one-quarter of what it had been before the war.[103]

With the war at an end and a general election in the offing, Ted Bramley, the London Communist leader, warned that 'a new generation of people, the people who have withstood the "blitz" and the flying-bomb, who forged the weapons for victory and bore them in triumph across Europe are in no mood to tolerate the evils of the past'.[104] In May 1945 the Labour Research Department, which served as the party's 'think tank', published *Houses for the People*, an extensive critique of the inadequacy of proposed governmental post-war measures to reduce overcrowding and build new houses.[105] The Stepney Communists based much of their campaign on the housing issue, publishing detailed plans to solve the borough's housing shortage. An undated mimeo produced by the party 'for Speakers and Canvassers' asserted that Stepney needed

20,000 new homes; overcrowding, always a serious problem, was becoming so much worse with the return of soldiers from the war that the Ministry of Health had actually proposed the use of Tilbury, the notorious air raid shelter, to accommodate the homeless. In place of the Conservative government's clearly inadequate plans, the CP proposed speedy, workmanlike repairs to those existing structures which could be salvaged; the building of 2,500 new homes within two years, with more to follow; and controlled rents at a price workers could afford. No Tory government, it said, would implement these plans. Only a Labour and Communist majority would be able to manage it.[106]

Phil Piratin's campaign propaganda in Mile End promised a good self-contained house or flat with modern conveniences, at a reasonable rent, for every family. 'The people of Stepney have suffered too much in the blitz and in the pre-war neglect of housing to be kept waiting any longer. Tenants must not be left at the landlords' mercy.'[107] The whole of Stepney was to be reconstructed, said Piratin: 'I will not rest till Stepney people have good homes.'[108]

Piratin's *Mile End Election Special!* elaborated further on these themes, referring to the Tory reconstruction plans, which provided for large-scale payments to landlords, as a form of 'blackmail' which would cost untold millions:

> The owners of the land will hold the Borough Council up to ransom for the right to build new homes. The new homes, promised so often and so long, will be very slow in coming, rents will be high and speculators will go on ruling the roost, *unless you vote into Parliament men like Phil Piratin, who know how to stand up to them and put them in their place.*

Piratin, 'the Tenants' Champion', had fought the landlords and helped organize the Stepney Tenants' Defence League before the war; now he fought the landlords again. Dan Frankel, the Labour candidate, on the other hand, had disapproved of the League, according to the *Election Special!*[109] The *Special!* also carried an article devoted entirely to the STDL, 'When Landlords Trembled', which asserted that the STDL had proved to everyone 'that Jews and Gentiles have the same enemies', that is, landlords who aim to exploit them, and thus disproved fascist theories blaming all forms of exploitation on the Jews. Now, the Jewish–Gentile unity fostered by the STDL and carried over into the war against Nazism would win the fight for new homes and a better post-war world.[110] Other CP literature asserted that Piratin had 'helped to build the great Tenants' Movement of Stepney'[111] and that he, along with Father Groser, had stopped 'the landlords and speculators ruining the lives of families by high rent and no repairs'.[112] During the war, he had continued to concern himself with housing problems, fighting for 'speedier and better repair of houses', cutting through red tape and bureaucratic delay on behalf of people who needed homes, and urging the Borough Council to carry out 'a more vigorous policy' when building new homes.[113]

Piratin's election victory in Mile End, then, was based in no small measure on his reputation as a concerned champion for better housing in Stepney. As the *Daily Worker* declared, Piratin put forward 'with passionate earnestness' a vision of a new Stepney arising from the 'desert of slums and rubble' within five years;[114] and even the non-Communist press described him as 'one of the soundest housing experts in London'.[115]

4
Opposition to anti-Semitism, Fascism and Nazism

THE CAMPAIGN AGAINST MOSLEY

One important reason for Jewish attraction to the Communist Party in Britain was the CP's self-appointed role as a steadfast opponent to all manifestations of domestic Fascism, including the Imperial Fascist League of Arnold Leese; Henry Hamilton Beamish and the Britons; the National Socialist League founded in 1937 by William Joyce and John Beckett; the Anglo-German Fellowship; the pro-German 'Link' organization; the Right Club; the Militant Christian Patriots; and, of course, Sir Oswald Mosley's British Union of Fascists.[1] The CP was also prominent in the agitation against individual Fascists such as Captain Archibald Ramsay, a Conservative MP who was a rabid anti-Semite. In Stepney, the Jewish Communists stood for opposition to Fascism and all forms of racial prejudice; as Solly Kaye has since recalled, 'The Stepney party was *the* leadership of the Stepney people – it led the agitation, led the propaganda, led the campaigning' against Fascist incursions such as those of Mosley's BUF.[2]

Labour politicians, in contrast, were strangely quiescent concerning these matters; and the CP overlooked no opportunity to embarrass Labour by exhorting the rival party to demonstrate a zeal equal to its own in the battle against Fascism. In June 1936, for example, Joe Jacobs, who was then serving as secretary of the Stepney CP, sent to the local Labour Party branches and to Stepney's three Labour MPs – Clement Attlee, Dan Frankel and J. H. Hall – an open letter which linked the increase of BUF activities in and around Stepney with the wider Fascist threat, including Mussolini's invasion of Abyssinia, Hitler's occupation of the Rhineland and increased repression on the part of the National Government. Noting that the BUF got 'strong police protection' during its provocative marches, Jacobs asked Labour to join the CP in a united front 'to smash the Fascist menace now, when it is beginning to show itself'. Although reported in the *East London Advertiser*,[3] this appeal went unheeded. Dissatisfaction with Labour's failure to act resulted in public manifestations of hostility towards Dan Frankel, the Jewish member for Mile End: at an open-air meeting held on 7 September at Stepney Green, Frankel was heckled concerning the fact that he was soon 'going off to America in the Queen Mary' for a visit, 'leaving us here to get broken heads'.[4]

The hecklers knew whereof they spoke: the 'Battle of Cable Street' took place during Frankel's absence. Joe Jacobs wrote to the *East London Advertiser* to blame the Home Secretary, Sir John Simon, for being 'so indifferent to the fate of British civil liberties' that he had failed to act upon 'his plain duty' and prevent Mosley from marching into the East End.[5] The Communists insisted that it was not their intention to make political capital out of the problem of Fascism; rather, as one East London Communist, J. Podrushnik, explained the situation, the CP had taken over the leadership of the anti-Fascist forces only because the Labour Party, instead of mobilizing the working class and all democratic forces against the Mosley menace, was itself describing the events in East London as a contest between Communism and Fascism.[6] Frankel did nothing to help his cause when, upon his return from America, he criticized what he regarded as the 'hysteria' of the Jewish population in response to the Fascist incursions. One letter to the *East London Advertiser* described Frankel's remarks as silly, misleading, and beneficial to the BUF.[7]

The CPGB continued its attempts to shake Labour's complacency. At the 14th national Communist Party congress, held at Battersea in May 1937, the central committee of the party criticized the national Labour leadership for failing to follow up on the Cable Street action organized by the Communists: had Labour acted vigorously, the CP stated, Mosley would never have dared to show his face in the East End.[8] At the 15th party congress, held in

Birmingham in September 1938, the CP called for 'the imposition of the heaviest penalties against anti-Semitism'.[9] That same autumn, when the Communists approached the three divisional Labour parties in Stepney concerning the problem of Fascism, there was almost total indifference. Morgan Phillips, the secretary of the Whitechapel-St George's party, said that under no circumstances would he consider united action with the CP against the National Government's policies.[10] As for the Mile End party, it had already sent out, in May 1938, a letter criticizing the (Communist-influenced) Stepney Trades Council for attempting to influence the party to take action against Fascism.[11] Two months later, Councillor M. H. Davis went so far as to block an attempt by Helena Roberts to have Stepney Borough Council express concern over police actions against Jews at Fascist meetings. Such continued behaviour on the part of the Labour leadership could only benefit the local Communists.[12]

Meanwhile, the Stepney CP was divided over what its own tactics should be. Joe Jacobs argued that the party should try to 'drive Mosley out of East London', using 'the maximum force available'.[13] Others, including Sarah Wesker, Ruby Silkoff, 'Ginger' Greenblatt, Morrie and 'Chick' Segal, and Alf Finkelstein, were in opposition to Jacobs on this point;[14] their main spokesman was Phil Piratin, who argued that the party's tactics should be more politically sophisticated than mere 'Fascist baiting'. Mosley had managed to attract many ordinary working-class people: 'Do you bash ordinary people?' demanded Piratin. Clearly, it would be more effective to win people away from the Mosleyites by means of careful propaganda and patient political work which would expose the fallacies of Fascist reasoning and recruit workers to the Communist point of view. Only when the CP could help people to improve their living conditions and organize them to recognize and fight their real exploiters would the lure of the BUF fade away.[15] Following a bitter battle within the ranks, the views of Piratin's faction prevailed.[16]

One result was the creation and support of a number of popular-front organizations. The Jewish People's Council Against Fascism and Anti-Semitism, formed in July 1936 in response to widespread concern in the Jewish community over 'the failure of communal leaders to wage a real fight against the Mosleyites' activities',[17] was granted access to Communist resources. Party members supplied much of the JPC's leadership: the secretary was Jack Pearce, and the editor of *Vigilance*, the JPC's publication, was Issie Pushkin;[18] prominent Communists such as Issie Panner were also very active.[19] The JPC mobilized the Jewish community by stressing the potential dangers posed by the Fascists; one meeting held a few weeks after the 'Battle of Cable Street' compared the climate in the East End to that which preceded pogroms against Jews in Tsarist Russia.[20] The Communists contrasted the 'vigorous campaign' carried out by the JPC against the BUF with the 'passive, supine attitude' of the Board of Deputies;[21] they also criticized the Board for its hostility to the JPC.[22] Another mass organization, the Stepney Tenants' Defence League, also managed to make some headway against the Fascists, by uniting Jews and non-Jews against landlords along economic rather than racial lines. In some cases where the BUF was using the issue of Jewish slum landlords to stir up anti-Semitic feelings, the STDL defused this issue: at Paragon Mansions, for example, where two families who happened to be members of the BUF were being threatened with eviction by the Jewish landlord, it was the STDL rather than the BUF which came to their assistance.[23] The STDL devoted special attention to winning over tenants in areas where the BUF was strong: according to Piratin, 'we had the fascist areas marked in thick green on the map, and we had lists of the blocks of flats in the streets in that area where there were possibilities. And the research section had to work on them'.[24] There was, for example, the neighbourhood around Duckett Street, which in 1936–37 belonged, according to the *Jewish Chronicle*, 'to the Blackshirts';[25] under the 'reign of terror' instituted by the fascists, Jews were regularly beaten by street gangs.[26] But the Communists 'did not shirk going into Mosley ground to win people there';[27] after two years of work by Communist activists such as Sid Greenberg and A. L. 'Chirps' Steinberg, the BUF had been neutralized to the extent that some of the residents in the Duckett area were helping the STDL in a Brady Street dispute where nearly all the tenants were Jewish.[28]

'Drawn into the struggle are bishops, rabbis, mayors, Members of Parliament, as well as ordinary folk,' exclaimed the *Daily Worker*. 'The narrow bounds of party and religion have been broken.'[29] Even the *Jewish Chronicle* hoped that the BUF 'had been impressed by the common struggle of Jewish and non-Jewish tenants against landlords, whether Jewish or not'.[30] The ultimate goal of the Jewish Communists in undertaking such work was articulated in a pamphlet issued in July 1939 by the East London Branch of the JPC: 'To-day,' announced the pamphlet, 'the people of East London are faced with an enemy more dangerous and unscrupulous than any slumlord', an enemy which aimed at 'enslaving the whole of the people, destroying their rights, stealing their liberties and completely impoverishing them'. This enemy was, of course, anti-Semitism, and the JPC called for the same unity against anti-Semitism as had been displayed against the slum landlords.[31] With the coming of war, prominent members of the STDL such as Councillor H. H. Gordon had to counter charges made by Fascists that the lack of ARP in the borough was due to Jewish landlords.[32] As the Stepney CP explained in 1944, the fight against the landlords had been 'but part of the battle against the rising menace of fascism'.[33]

OPPOSITION TO FASCISM IN WARTIME

Although historians have written extensively on pre-war Fascism in Britain, it is less well known that the coming of war did nothing to diminish anti-Semitic prejudice; indeed, many observers believed that anti-Semitism was on the increase.[34] Certainly, the BUF felt no ideological reluctance to continue its attacks on Jews. Britain should 'not fight to defend Polish Jews', argued the Mosleyites; their slogan was 'No War for Warsaw'.[35] On the day Poland was attacked, a number of windows were smashed in Jewish-owned shops in Kingsland High Street, Dalston;[36] within months, this had become a regular occurrence.[37]

A leading article in the *Jewish Chronicle* castigated the Metropolitan Police Force for its failure to prevent these acts of vandalism:

'It would seem they are either asleep or indifferent.'[38] The *Chronicle*'s 'Jewish Defence Correspondent' in the East End was allowed to report some of the resentment which Jews there felt at the inaction of the official Jewish leadership on the Board of Deputies: 'What has happened to the leaders of Jewry,' asked one cabinet-maker, 'are they asleep, or have they buried their heads in the sand?'[39] As anti-Semitism intensified, various groups urged the Board of Deputies to do more 'to counteract this dangerous propaganda'.[40] Finally the Board's Defence Committee, taking note of 'the deliberate campaign to connect the Jewish Community, and indeed Jewry at large, with the war that is now being waged',[41] began to counter-attack with its own pamphlets.

With the German invasion of France and the Low Countries, the 'Phoney War' ended and the British government became more concerned with the possibility of Fascist sabotage and treason. Mosley was detained on 23 May 1940 under defence regulation 18B and sent to Brixton prison; soon about 700 members of the BUF were in gaol, its publications were banned, and the organization itself was ordered to be dissolved.[42] During the spring and summer a number of other prominent Fascists were arrested, including Captain Archibald Ramsay; John Beckett of the National Socialist League; Sir Barry Domvile and Captain Robert Gordon-Canning, both of whom had been active in the 'Link' and in the British Council for Christian Settlement in Europe, a group formed in 1939.[43] Arnold Leese of the Imperial Fascist League managed to escape arrest until November 1940.[44] Altogether, more than 1,400 people were interned under this legislation.[45]

Even as it remarked that a 'vague, amorphous anti-Jewish feeling' was still apparent in Britain, the *Jewish Chronicle*, along with the Jewish community as a whole, naturally applauded the arrests.[46] But almost from the first, there was dissatisfaction that a number of Fascists were still free and that those who were detained received what the *Daily Worker* described as 'velvet glove treatment'.[47] The *Jewish Chronicle* reported that the imprisoned Fascists were getting better food and cigarettes than were soldiers and citizens – even beer was available to them. The men held political meetings, wore the BUF insignia openly and were cocky and arrogant.[48] In December

1941, Mosley was transferred from Brixton and reunited with his wife Diana in a self-contained four-room flat at Holloway prison. Here the Mosleys, according to Diana's sister Jessica Mitford, were treated with deference and consideration, 'in the incomparable style of the Old Boy network'.[49]

On 6 December 1942, Captain Bernard Acworth, who had been in the 'Link' but had not been detained, organized a meeting at Holborn Hall which marked the beginning of a campaign for the release of the '18Bers', that is, those imprisoned under defence regulation 18B.[50] Within months, meetings such as the one at Caxton Hall, Westminster, on 17 March 1943, which drew 500 people, were organizing opposition to Churchill, Soviet Russia and the war effort; exhortations to this effect mingled with cries of 'Mosley a hero' and 'filthy Jew'.[51] The government took no action against Acworth or any others involved in these activities.

Meanwhile, the Communists were making political capital out of the resurgence of Fascist activity centred around H. W. S. Russell, the twelfth Duke of Bedford, and the British National Party. Walter Holmes launched an attack on the BNP in the *Daily Worker* on 29 October 1942, noting that the organization blamed Jews in government for the calamities that had befallen Britain. Warned Holmes, 'Anti-Semitism is not merely disgusting and contemptible. It is a danger to our country and to our cause'; the BNP propaganda, if it succeeded in directing hostility against the Jews, would weaken the national war effort. 'Action against anti-Semitic propaganda ought to be taken here as it is under the law of the Soviet Union.'[52] Soon the Political Bureau of the CPGB, taking note of increased Fascist activity in East London,[53] asked the London District Committee to be on guard 'against all pro-fascist and anti-semitic propaganda, which is especially dangerous in London';[54] and Ted Bramley, head of the London District Committee, called on Home Secretary Herbert Morrison 'to take immediate action to ensure that the fascists in our midst are tracked down and rendered harmless'.[55]

In February 1943, the *Daily Worker* published a feature article on the British National Party,[56] and the CP called an open-air meeting at Lincoln's Inn Fields to demand that the organization be banned. Among the scheduled speakers were the mayors of Stepney and Shoreditch; Maurice Orbach, an LCC councillor and member of the Board of Deputies' Trades Advisory Council; and Stepney councillor Phil Piratin.[57] Piratin warned the crowd of thousands that 'To allow Fascism again to raise its head in Britain after we had thought it was suppressed, would be to run a grave danger'. He concluded that the organization was 'trying to stab our boys in the Forces in the back', and urged that the BNP's officials be arrested.[58]

The CP campaign against the BNP seems to have had immediate results: the fascist organization tried to call a meeting of its own for 22 February, but this had to be cancelled when the group could find no proprietor willing to rent them a hall. By 25 February, over 300 organizations had expressed their agreement with the CP that the BNP should be outlawed.[59] As a result of the furore, the group disbanded in April 1943.[60] 'Thanks to the vigilance of the *Daily Worker* and the workers', wrote Willie Gallacher, after 1935 the Communist Party's only MP, the BNP had been shown to have 'connections with traitors' and to be interested only in 'Jew-baiting and a demand for a negotiated peace with Hitler'.[61]

Early in August, the Churchill government released Sir Barry Domvile and Captain Robert Gordon-Canning, two of the Fascists imprisoned since 1940.[62] Soon the Communists were warning that Sir Oswald Mosley was to be freed from his 'luxurious apartments' in Holloway prison.[63] They were thus in a position to take full political advantage of the storm which erupted when Home Secretary Herbert Morrison announced that, due to his medical problems, Mosley would be released on 20 November. The National Council for Civil Liberties criticized the government's decision in an emergency meeting called for 19 November,[64] hundreds of telegrams and petitions poured into the Home Office,[65] and mass protest meetings were held. The CP's propaganda machine ran at full speed. In the *Daily Worker* of 19 November, Douglas Hyde published a profile of 'The British Hitler';[66] Walter Holmes remarked sarcastically that while the Russians were fighting the real Hitler inch by inch, the British people were given, not a second front, but Oswald Mosley.[67] In the next day's issue of the Communist newspaper, Harry Pollitt reminded readers that Mosley had participated in the 'Battle of Cable Street' in 1936; his release, according to Pollitt, was 'a betrayal of the anti-Fascist war'.[68] The CP also rushed into print an eight-page pamphlet, *Keep Mosley in Prison*, which described some of the protest meetings that had already taken place; these, according to the pamphlet, were proof of the 'white-hot angry hatred of fascism' felt by the working class.[69]

Morrison assured the House of Commons on 23 November that although the government would continue to oppose the 'evil cancer' of Fascism, Mosley the man no longer posed 'any undue risk to national security'. His remarks did nothing to mollify Willie Gallacher, who demanded to know why, if Mosley was set free as a result of medical problems, the Indian leader Mahatma Gandhi remained in prison despite frail health.[70] Outside the House, 2,000 demonstrators from 300 war factories staged a protest, shouting 'Mosley in, Morrison out'.[71] A few days later the *Jewish Chronicle* asserted, in a leading article entitled 'Morrison's Folly', that Mosley's release raised some doubt as to whether government leaders were 'really heart and soul in the war against the monstrosity Fascism'; the *Chronicle* dismissed the medical reasons given for the decision as 'preposterous'.[72] The *Daily Worker* wrote that the government had done more to harm national unity 'than Goebbels could ever have hoped to achieve'.[73] The CP put out an update of its earlier pamphlet, now retitled *Put Mosley Back in Prison*, which noted that William 'Lord Haw-Haw' Joyce had broadcast his congratulations from Berlin upon hearing the news.[74]

Although Morrison was himself a Labour member of the coalition government, the national Labour Party was split when the House debated the matter for an entire day on 1 December. George Woods, a Labour MP from Finsbury, moved a resolution which regretted the decision to free the former BUF leader as one 'calculated to retard the war effort and lead to misunderstanding at home and abroad';[75] the resolution was seconded by Labour MP John Parker. A total of 51 Labour members voted in its favour, including Jewish members Dan Frankel, Emanuel Shinwell and Sydney Silverman; they were joined by Communist Willie Gallacher, the pro-Communist D. N. Pritt and the Independent Tom Driberg. But 64 Labour MPs supported the government; another 50 abstained or were absent, enabling the government to defeat the resolution, 327 to 62.[76] During Question Time in the House of Commons nine days later, Commander Oliver Locker-Lampson summed up the sentiments of those on the losing side when he told Morrison, 'Mosley has got off, and so will Mussolini and Hitler'.[77]

In the working-class neighbourhoods of Stepney, where Mosley's release led to widespread disapproval, the local Labour Party was unwilling to share in the 'general loss of faith' which the national party experienced as a result of the controversy.[78] On 24 November, the Stepney Borough Council became the first municipal body in Great Britain to pass a resolution protesting against the government's action; the resolution, which was moved by M. H. Davis, the leader of the council, and seconded by W. J. Edwards, who had succeeded J. H. Hall as the MP for Whitechapel-St George's, pointed out that Stepney had suffered more from the activities of the BUF than had any other part of London.[79] At the urging of Phil Piratin and J. L. Fine, a town meeting was called to demand that Oswald and Diana Mosley be re-interned and that Morrison be required to resign. Piratin, to the accompaniment of loud cheers, commended Frankel and Edwards, two of Stepney's MPs, for speaking out against Mosley's release; Davis expressed shock that Clement Attlee, the MP for Limehouse, who served also as Deputy Prime Minister in Churchill's government, had refused to receive a deputation concerning the matter. Mayor Edward O'Brien criticized Morrison, while Fine promised that 'the protest is only just beginning'.[80] Many left-wingers saw in Morrison's behaviour a continuation of attitudes and policies dating back to the 1930s, and were driven into the Communist camp.[81] Even the Irish members of the Stepney Labour Party, normally virulently anti-Communist, were pushed into an alliance with the local Communists as a result of the release of Mosley.

The National Jewish Committee of the CPGB, formed nine months earlier, saw in the Mosley imbroglio an opportunity to 'make of the Jewish people an active element of the Democratic life of the country' by encouraging them to participate in 'democratic and progressive action such as the demand for the re-internment of Mosley'.[82] Chimen Abramsky, one of the members of the NJC, castigated the Board of Deputies, in a letter to the *Jewish Chronicle*, for failing to protest against Mosley's release: 'This cowardice shames all Jews fighting heroically against Fascism. This backwardness, this lagging behind the democratic forces is a blot on our name. Let us Jews line ourselves up with all those who fight for real democracy.'[83] As if on cue, Branches 3 and 9 of the Workers' Circle took up Abramsky's challenge: when the Circle met for its eleventh convention on 25–26 December, they introduced resolutions opposing the release of 'this Fascist and Anti-Semite'.[84]

But the release of the '18Bers' – and the attendant protests – continued. Arnold Leese, a rabid anti-Semite, was freed in January 1944 for 'medical reasons'.[85] One of the last to emerge from prison, later in the same year, was Tory MP Archibald Ramsay, who in some ways personified the ties which before the war had linked some right-wing Tories with Fascism. The *Daily Worker* compared Ramsay's doctrines to 'those which terminated in the massacre [at the Maidanek concentration camp, Lublin] of more than 1,500,000 people';[86] the Communist newspaper spoke also of the 'Streicher-like obsession' of this, 'Britain's No. 1 Jew baiter'.[87] The 'Daily Worker Defence League' issued an attack in the form of a pamphlet, *The Case of Captain Ramsay*.[88] The Central Committee of the Workers' Circle dispatched to Churchill a strongly worded resolution which deplored the release of this 'self-confessed anti-semite': 'We remind the people of Britain that Captain Ramsay has been described by a High Court Judge as a man whom Hitler could call friend.'[89] The Board of Deputies, however, once again remained silent; as Lazar Zaidman wrote in an Australian Communist publication, the Board, despite 'continued agitation on this matter within the Jewish community . . . has refused to budge in taking the matter up with the government'.[90]

Soon many of the newly released Fascists formed a group, the League of ex-Servicemen and Women, which held its first meeting in Hyde Park on 5 November 1944; despite Home Secretary Morrison's stipulation that they refrain from political activity, they passed the day with anti-Semitic tirades.[91] A week later, Jeffrey Hamm, a figure well known for his Fascist activities before the war, lectured to the crowd at Hyde Park on 'Jewish financiers'.[92]

The *Jewish Chronicle* reporter covering these events wrote that 'As I listened, I thought I was back in Green Street, Bethnal Green, in the hectic Jew-baiting years between 1935 and 1940'.[93] The *Chronicle* blamed these developments on Morrison, who had been confronted a few days earlier in the House of Commons by D. N. Pritt: 'Does there, should there exist in this country,' asked Pritt, 'the right to demand the liberty to destroy liberty?'[94]

'The threatened renewal of large-scale activity by these reactionary elements is a reminder that we have a tough job ahead,' warned the National Jewish Committee of the CPGB in February 1945.[95] 'Staggering as it may seem,' wrote Douglas Hyde on the eve of victory in Europe, 'former Fascists are more active in Britain today than they have been for the last five years. They play an active part in newly-created organisations and in old ones that are being resurrected.'[96] The end of the war also brought an end to wartime restrictions on freedom of expression, including regulation 18B; and Fascist groups such as the Duke of Bedford's British National Party – now known again as the British People's Party – sprang back into life. On 10 May, in the House of Commons, D. N. Pritt, pointing to the inefficacy of peacetime laws, asked how the Fascists were to be controlled now.[97] It was a question that preoccupied many East London Jews.

THE DEFENCE OF THE JEWISH COMMUNITY IN WARTIME

Although the coming of war led to the imprisonment of hundreds of Fascists and the temporary suppression of many Fascist organizations, it also created new problems for the Jewish community. In the summer of 1940, Lord Rothermere's *Daily Mail* led a media campaign which hinted that Jews were likely to be 'Fifth Columnists'. German Jews in particular became 'objects of hate and suspicion' almost overnight;[98] but all Jewish aliens and refugees, and even some British-born Jews, were liable to be singled out. One Jew who had won the Victoria Cross, for example, was expelled from the Home Guard because his father was an alien;[99] three Jews who were Russian-born or the children of Russian-born parents were unable to persuade the Stepney Labour Exchange to send them to work in aircraft factories, even though they were British citizens.[100] Soon the mass round-ups began, and over 27,000 people were interned, including more than 7,000 who were shipped to Canada or Australia;[101] on board one ship, Jews were made to salute the German flag.[102] Most, however, were held under 'sub-human conditions' in British camps,[103] where they could be put into solitary confinement or denied razors or extra blankets.[104] Sometimes they were interned alongside Nazis;[105] at one camp in York, a number of pro-Nazi Germans were released while the Jews remained behind.[106] One Tory MP, Captain Alan Graham, representing a Cheshire seat, wanted assurances that the government would not release aliens 'whose devotion to the cause of the Communist world revolution' might prove 'a menace to the peace and institutions of this realm'.[107]

Britain's treatment of refugees did not go unnoticed. On 16 August *The Times* published a protest from nine London correspondents of newspapers in neutral countries: 'Millions of sympathizers with Britain's cause begin to doubt whether the British ideals of humanity and justice still prevail . . . the treatment of the refugees seems to be less favourable than that of prisoners of war'.[108] Penguin Books published a 'special' on the scandal.[109] Dr J. J. Mallon, warden of Toynbee Hall, asserted that the round-ups had included people who 'have occupied a single residence for half a century; men who are ailing or have ailing wives; obscure and helpless men about whom the synagogue and their neighbours know all that can be known'. Those left behind in East London were ignorant of the whereabouts of 'aged and feeble fathers or grandfathers who were whisked away from them a week or a fortnight ago' and then held incommunicado. Mallon called for an end to these policies, 'in the interests of sanity and humanity and of the national cause'.[110] The *Jewish Chronicle* said that the round-ups had 'besmirched the fair name of this humane land'.[111] The trade unions and the CP were especially active in opposing the mass internments.[112] The Workers' Circle called a special conference in July 1940 to pressure the government to release a number of internees;[113] the Mantle & Costume branch of the NUTGW supported the Committee for a Christmas to Interned Refugees, which sent packages to refugees in ten camps.[114] An article in the *Daily Worker* on 26 July 1940 described the fear and paranoia in East London's squalid back streets, where the government's policies were tearing 'husband from wife, son from mother with complete ruthlessness'; the round-ups had meant 'grief and despair, terror and humiliation' for the Jews of East London.[115] Given this evidence, it would be hard to refute the conclusions drawn by scholars almost half a century later that the internment of the aliens drew upon 'the strong strains of anti-alienism and anti-Semitism within British society',[116] as much motivated by prejudice as by the military situation; it 'was an episode that witnessed the disintegration of liberal sympathies to the refugees'.[117]

Although the worst of the round-ups were over by the autumn of 1940 and some prisoners were even being freed, the new Home Secretary, Herbert Morrison, who had replaced Sir John Anderson in October, acknowledged in the House of Commons on 3 December that 19,500 aliens were still interned.[118] Various MPs, especially Eleanor Rathbone, worked tirelessly on behalf of the internees, but their release came slowly. Why, asked the *Daily Worker*, did they continue to 'rot in concentration camps'?[119] As late as May 1942, over 2,000 refugees remained in 104 camps in Canada and Australia and on the Isle of Man.[120]

Meanwhile, anti-Semitism ran high in Britain. George Orwell recorded several manifestations of 'the current feeling against the Jews' in his diary entry for 25 October 1940.[121] Sidney Salomon, secretary of the Defence Committee of the Board of Deputies, expressed his 'disquiet' in a letter dated 19 December 1940: as he explained, Britain had been bombarded for six years with Fascist and Nazi propaganda; 'thousands of Englishmen from all classes' had visited Germany, in many cases as guests. Little wonder that 'there should be in this country now a distinct substratum of anti-semitism.'[122] In fact, anti-Semitism appeared in almost every issue of the Home Intelligence Weekly Report compiled by the Ministry of Information throughout 1940 and 1941.[123]

One of the most persistent accusations made against the Jews during this period was that they dominated the black market; indeed, this charge 'was probably the most important element of

British hostility to Jews in the war'.[124] Two left-wing Zionists – Dr Noah Barou and Maurice Orbach – were instrumental in persuading the Board of Deputies to establish in 1940 the Board's Trades Advisory Council (TAC), an autonomous unit which attempted to remove 'causes of friction in industry, trade and commerce'.[125] It was definitely an uphill battle. Early in 1942, Orbach blamed 'fifth column' elements for the propaganda connecting Jews with the black market.[126] But even in the House of Commons, these accusations were being made almost openly.[127] The *Jewish Chronicle* asserted in a leading article that many people regarded black marketeering as 'almost a Jewish monopoly'; these slanders, warned the *Chronicle*, were rotting the unity of the country and imperilling its national will to fight Hitler.[128] An anonymous letter in the same issue deplored the 'bitter, brutal, and scarcely-veiled attack' upon the Jews which had been made in Parliament by one Tory MP, Beverley Baxter: 'Over very many years of active contact with the Jewish Community I cannot recall a period when such a mood of doubt and disgust has settled over English Jewry'.[129]

By mid-July, some newspapers were claiming that not only individual Jews but even synagogues were involved in the black market.[130] Frustrated by the failure of those in authority to take any steps to counter such allegations, the *Jewish Chronicle* pointed out that in the Soviet Union, anti-Semitism was a criminal offence. But in Britain, 'Not a day passes without . . . examples of prejudice and intolerance coming to light'.[131] Writing about this period two decades later, Maurice Orbach recalled that 'While the nation was seemingly united against the common enemy . . . the unscrupulous blamed Jews for reverses and for shortages. Anti-Semitism, for which we denounced Germany, was present in our own midst.'[132]

One local official did speak out. On 22 July, John Pritchard, the mayor of Stepney, accused the press of giving more publicity to those cases of black marketeering in which the culprits were Jewish than to cases involving non-Jews. The *East London Advertiser* countered by declaring that 'a legend of a biased Press will not help to cure the trouble';[133] but Pritchard continued to defend the Jewish population of Stepney, declaring that the number of offences committed by Jewish traders was 'very small'.[134]

In January 1943, the Stepney Communist Party sponsored a mass meeting at the Grand Palais to protest against black marketeering; 500 people showed up to pass a resolution calling for prison sentences for offenders.[135] As the editor of the *Daily Worker* explained, Communists believed that the solution was not anti-Jewish propaganda but stricter surveillance on the part of the government: 'It is the job of the Government to put an end to the black market by strict control over the financial interests involved.' Instead, Jews were being blamed 'in order to cover up the vile methods of the profiteers and to sidetrack popular anger'.[136] Willie Gallacher devoted three pages in his pamphlet, *Anti-Semitism: What It Means to You*, to refuting charges that Jews controlled the black market. Gallacher pointed out that in Germany, where by 1943 the Jews were in no position to run anything, the black market continued to flourish. 'They've got rid of the Jews in Germany, but they haven't got rid of the financiers and they haven't got rid of the black market.'[137]

In February 1943, J. L. Fine and 14 other councillors called a special meeting of the Stepney Borough Council to discuss a resolution which noted that 'efforts are being made to propagate and disseminate anti-Semitism and racial hatred and prejudice on lines clearly enunciated by Nazi agents'; the resolution urged the government 'to introduce, without delay, such legislation as will recognise anti-Semitism and any other form of racial and religious discrimination as a criminal offence'.[138] Phil Piratin announced that he welcomed the resolution, 'as must everyone who is concerned about the growth of public activity by Fascist elements'.[139] During the council's debate on 2 March, Fine remarked that it was a reflection on British democracy that the British National Party was allowed to exist: 'The Fascism which exists in high places and in low must be dealt with.' When the resolution was passed, I. M. Vogler asserted that the unanimity shown at the meeting had laid the foundations 'for a deeper and lasting unity'.[140]

In the same week that the Stepney Borough Council met, an incident in nearby Bethnal Green gave rise to another demonstration of anti-Jewish feeling: at the Bethnal Green Underground station 173 people were killed and hundreds more injured when panic swept through a crowd seeking entrance to the shelter. Widely circulating rumours blamed the tragedy on panicking Jews, even after it was established that few Jews were among the victims. Sam Alexander, a prominent Workers' Circle activist and a member of the newly formed National Jewish Committee of the CPGB, wrote in the *Circle-Arbeter Ring* that the reaction to the Bethnal Green disaster was an example of the 'whispering campaigns' being conducted against Jews. Alexander, who also remarked that in certain districts 'Anti-Jewish slogans cover walls in every street', called upon the government to 'make race hatred a crime'.[141] But Home Secretary Morrison, in a message to the people of the Bethnal Green area, seemed all too sympathetic to the anti-Jewish rumours when he commented that 'after an event like this there might have been a tendency to look for somebody or something to blame'.[142]

Already, in September 1942, the government had been required to respond in the House of Lords to charges that some of its policies might be regarded as unfair to Jews. Lord Wedgwood (the former Colonel J. C. Wedgwood) had remarked that anti-Semitism was prevalent among the upper classes and among government officials; Lord Strabolgi had added that anti-Semitism was as real a danger in Britain as in Nazi-occupied Europe: 'we saw the beginning of it before the war.'[143] In the spring of 1943, the Archbishop of Canterbury, William Temple, told the Lords that he was perturbed by 'the antisemitic feeling in this country', which 'could be easily fanned into flame'.[144] Still the government took no action.

In late March, at its annual meeting, the National Council for Civil Liberties, an organization in which Communists played a very active role, called for legislation which would make the dissemination of anti-Semitic or Fascist propaganda a criminal offence. D. N. Pritt described existing legislation as 'extremely obscure and insufficient to deal with the evil as it exists at present'.[145] A few weeks later the NCCL convened a London conference, attended by 450 delegates representing 273 organizations, to plan a nation-wide campaign against anti-Semitism.[146] It was a disturbing fact, said the NCCL, that anti-Semitism should be on the increase in Britain 'at the very time when we are fighting for our national existence against Fascism, which makes the persecution of the Jews a cardinal point of its doctrines'. Julius Jacobs of the London Trades Council warned that 'anti-Semitism is a knife at the throat of Jew and non-Jew alike'.[147]

The Board of Deputies was not so eager for legislation against anti-Semitic propaganda. On 24 June 1943, representatives of the Board met with Jewish members of Parliament to discuss the idea. It was decided that such legislation would be ineffective at best; at worst, it might result in court cases which would create bad publicity for the Jewish community.[148] In December, the Board's Committee on Community Libel argued that it would be difficult to secure passage through Parliament 'of so radical an alteration of the law as would enable civil proceedings to be brought for defamation of the Jews as a community'.[149] Even so moderate a periodical as the *Jewish Chronicle* was disgusted with the Board's reasoning.[150]

The issue remained a source of friction within the Jewish community throughout 1944. B. A. Bagnari, general chairman of the Circle and one of its representatives on the Board of Deputies, repeatedly raised the issue at Board meetings, but to no avail. At a meeting of the Circle's central committee on 1 October, Lazar Zaidman moved a resolution expressing disapproval of the Board's attitude and asking that the Board reconsider, particularly in view of the release of Captain Ramsay.[151] Nathan Weiner, General Secretary of the Circle, sent a letter to A. G. Brotman, Secretary of the Board, informing him of the resolution;[152] Harry Lubbock, another of the Circle's representatives on the Board, had already submitted a motion to the same effect for consideration at the next Board meeting.[153] To the dismay of Circle members, the Board of Deputies executive refused to allow the motion to be considered.[154] Alec Waterman, Sam Alexander and Sam Dreen felt that the Circle should continue to press ahead with action to counter anti-Semitism, including further agitation at the Board. Itzhak Nathani and Sam Dreen also suggested the formation of a progressive bloc of Deputies to fight for the introduction of legislation outlawing anti-Semitism in Britain.[155]

Meanwhile the *Jewish Chronicle* was again comparing Britain unfavourably with the Soviet Union, where 'anti-Semitism is banned as something Stalin would call "cannibalistic". . . . If this country does not want to protect its Jews against slander, it surely ought to be interested in protecting itself.'[156] But such arguments fell on deaf ears: in May 1945, Home Secretary Morrison could offer no better solution to the problem of anti-Semitism than to suggest that Jewish refugees in Britain now be returned to Europe lest they become 'an explosive element in the country'.[157] His was far from being the 'searching and ruthless analysis' of anti-Semitism for which the *Jewish Chronicle*, among others, was calling.[158]

THE NATIONAL JEWISH COMMITTEE AND ANTI-SEMITISM

During the war years, the CPGB's ideological response to anti-Semitism became increasingly the domain of the Jewish Communists. In April 1942, Issie Panner, writing under the pseudonym 'I. Rennap', outlined the position of the party at that time in *Anti-Semitism and the Jewish Question*, which commenced with a short but comprehensive survey of Jewish history from antiquity to modern times. As a Communist, Panner stressed the 'universalistic' significance of what he described in one chapter heading as 'The Jewish Contribution to Human Progress'; Zionism was pronounced to be in conflict with the 'rich, revolutionary tradition' of Jewish history admired by Marx and Lenin. In his analysis of anti-Semitism, Panner was particularly concerned to absolve workers of any responsibility for this 'diversionist weapon against the progressive forces in their struggle for a better and higher order of things';[159] anti-Semitism was explained, not as a deep-rooted conflict between cultures, ethnic groups or religions, but as a deliberate tactic of Fascist politics. It followed that anti-Semitism was to be countered by appealing to the pragmatic self-interest of the workers. 'To blame the Jews for the evils and discomforts created by war conditions and to accuse them of exploiting for profit the issues that are sore problems with the people', reasoned Panner, 'is to play Hitler's game here'. It was to be understood that 'the reactionaries in this country' who sought to exploit racial or religious prejudice were 'working against the interests of the British people and of democracy and freedom everywhere'.[160]

Panner's analysis conformed with that of other, non-Jewish Communists writing at about this time, who saw anti-Semitism as a capitalist ploy to divide the working class. In *Anti-Semitism: What it Means to You*, Willie Gallacher described anti-Semitism as 'a trick by which people are persuaded to tie the rope around their own neck . . . the trap whereby people voluntarily surrender themselves into slavery'.[161] John Gollan discussed anti-Semitism, in an article in the *Labour Monthly*, in the context of a Fascist conspiracy which attacked an 'imaginary enemy' in order to distract the people from its real aim, the destruction of socialism;[162] William Rust, the editor of the *Daily Worker*, in the foreword to *13 Years of Anti-Fascist Struggle*, described anti-Semitism as 'a method of covering up foul and reactionary policies and setting the people against themselves'.[163]

But as the war progressed, the CPGB came to encourage a more explicitly Jewish campaign in the East End; Morry Lebow has recalled that this strategy was referred to as 'Jewish work'.[164] The National Jewish Committee of the Communist Party (NJC), a subcommittee of R. Palme Dutt's International Affairs Committee (IAC), was established in April 1943 to study problems specific to the Jewish community; its members included Lazar Zaidman, Chimen Abramsky, Issie Pushkin, Alec Waterman, Alf Holland, Professor Hyman Levy, Mick Mindel, Alf Silverman, Peter Valentine and Harry Lubbock. Abramsky and Zaidman, who had lived in the Soviet Union and Romania, respectively, and were fluent in a number of languages, seem to have been its chief theoreticians.[165] In 1944, Marx House published, as Leaflet No. 8 in its 'Educational Commentary' series of 'Study and Discussion Notes', *Anti-Semitism – a Nazi Weapon*. The Board of Deputies and the CP made some cautious attempts to cooperate with each other in the dissemination of pro-Jewish and anti-Fascist material, even though Sidney Salomon, secretary of the Board's Defence Committee, thought it might be going a little too far to employ speakers from Marx House, 'an organisation which is so notoriously Communist'.[166]

A weekend school for Jewish party members was held at Marx

House on 22–23 April 1944; among the tutors were Maurice Essex, who had been active in the Jewish People's Council before the war, and Professor Hyman Levy, the well-known University of London mathematician and Marxist philosopher.[167] The Jewish Communists published their programme at a conference of 450 people held on 9 May at Beaver Hall. The theme of the conference, which was organized by the East London District of the CP, was 'The Jewish Problem and the Role of the Communist Party'. In the opening address, Hyman Levy called for a Jewish Charter of Freedom in the spirit of the Atlantic Charter and the December 1943 Teheran agreements. Under such a charter, Jews would achieve equality of citizenship in every sphere of social and economic life; anti-Semitism would become a crime; and the Allied governments would take steps against racial discrimination in every country. 'Jewish progressives must serve their people', added Levy, by helping them to unite with the progressive forces everywhere. Bertha Sokoloff, who became branch secretary of the Stepney CP in the autumn of 1944, explained how 'politically proud' she was to be a Jew; another speaker, Alf Holland, urged Jewish Communists to study Jewish history, especially the role played by liberating heroes such as Bar Kochba. Asher Frucht of the Jewish Cultural Club and Alec Waterman both spoke of the need to persuade more Jews to become Communists; already, said Waterman, 'some of the best elements of Jewry have joined the CP'. The conference was concluded by a non-Jew, Willie Gallacher, who spoke on one of his favourite topics, the need for Jewish Communists to remain active in Jewish life. It was not enough, according to Gallacher, that they take part in trade union and working-class activities; they must also work as Jews so that all Jews, led by their Communist brothers, would support the working-class movement, which in turn would support freedom for the Jewish people.[168]

The party line was also made explicit in a 19-page pamphlet, *The Jewish Question: A Statement by the National Jewish Committee of the Communist Party*, which appeared in late 1944. After pointing out that 'support for progressive Parties' was widespread among the Jewish people and asserting that the CP was 'in full sympathy with the Jewish people and their desire to be free from the scourge of antiSemitism', the statement reiterated Levy's demand for a 'Declaration of Jewish Freedom' which would be part of the worldwide post-war settlement and which would legally guarantee equality of civil rights for all Jews.[169]

After being approved by the executive committee of the CPGB, the *Statement* was presented at the NJC's third annual conference of Jewish Communists on 13–14 January 1945. R. Palme Dutt, vice-chairman of the CP and head of the International Affairs Committee, opened the conference by noting that 'there has been a marked advance and development in the past year as a result of the work of the NJC and the Jewish comrades generally'. Dutt went so far as to regret that some Communists who were Jewish preferred to do general Party and trade union work, to the neglect of work in Jewish organizations. The NJC, according to Dutt, had been formed to combat this tendency without becoming too particularistic. During the discussion of 'The Jewish Question' which followed, various participants expressed the movement's intent 'to win all the most progressive, intelligent, and most active Jews to its ranks'.[170]

One result of the conference was the drafting of yet another statement by the NJC, 'The Election Campaign & the Jewish People', which asserted that 'only a Labour and Progressive Government' would eliminate the underlying economic conditions which enabled anti-Semitism to flourish. The statement urged campaign workers to promise that 'care and attention' would be paid 'to the special cultural and communal needs of Jews in largely Jewish areas': 'fight to rally the Jewish people!'[171] Another paper on 'Jews and the General Election' explained that whereas the Tories had co-existed with Mosley and with Nazism in Europe, a Labour and progressive government would implement the February 1945 Yalta agreements and cooperate with Russia. 'If this is good for the people of Britain, as a whole, it is doubly good for the Jews of Britain. In such a situation Fascism and Anti-Semitism will be throttled.'[172]

As the election drew near, the Jewish Communists insisted all the more urgently that 'only a Labour and Progressive Government will enable us to wipe out the spreaders of race hatred, the enemies of the people';[173] Lazar Zaidman wrote to a friend that the Jews, who held 'a key position in certain constituencies', would realize that it was in their own best interest to vote for the left in order to eliminate the social causes of anti-Semitism.[174] At the same time, the CP did its best to discredit the Tories. One pamphlet, entitled *Fascist Murderers: Pictures of the Concentration Camps You Must Never Forget*, interspersed gruesome stories and photographs of newly liberated camps such as Buchenwald with quotations from the Tory officials who had failed to take a strong stand against Hitler: 'When the General Election comes we must be sure that not one of these Tories who praised or appeased the fascists before the war, and so bear a responsibility for these crimes, will get back into Parliament.'[175] Another pamphlet, by R. Palme Dutt, linked the Tories with pre-war pro-German organizations such as the Anglo-German Fellowship; by means of extensive quotations, he demonstrated to his own satisfaction 'how Tories backed Hitler, Mussolini and Japan': 'Every elector must feel a sacred duty to drive these Tory friends of fascism from public life'.[176]

The *News Chronicle* noted that the election manifesto of the CP was very like that of Labour, although the Communists added two further proposals: that the voting age be lowered to 18 and that anti-Semitism be made a criminal offence.[177] In Stepney, the local CP also emphasized 'Jewish–Gentile unity' in the fight against anti-Semitism. Tom Rampling, who later became a borough councillor, wrote that 'every anti-Semite is a friend of the fascists; either as a fool or a knave he is keeping the people divided, so helping the Hitlerites and endangering the freedom of ordinary folk everywhere'.[178]

In May 1945, the *Jewish Forum* published an article on the resurgence of Fascist movements, which were said to be 'as active to-day as ever they were before': 'Behind these little men are the Big Shots, the representatives of Big Business and Monopoly who backed Mosley and put Hitler into power. They are the men who determine Tory policy.' Jews had 'a fearful responsibility' to vote out the Tories: by doing so they would help to ensure that no one would 'revive the horrors of Belsen and Buchenwald'; but if they failed, it would be no more than a few months before Mosley and his thugs were 'terror-parading the streets again with anti-Jewish banners'.[179] Opinions such as these were not limited to the Communist press. In

June 1945, *Di Tsayt* described the Tories as 'the traditional anti-alien party': 'In its ranks were to be found virulent anti-Semites. Many of its members, before the war, gave support to Hitler and Mussolini. They went to the Nazi rallies at Nuremberg, and were on intimate terms with Ribbentrop when he was the German ambassador here.'[180]

Candidate Piratin made skilful use of such themes and sentiments. In his 'Appeal to the Jewish Electors', Piratin referred to himself as 'a good son of the Jewish people'; he termed the CP 'the champion of the freedom of the Jewish people'. From the ranks of the Tories, he asserted, had come the Captain Ramsays, the Anglo-German Fellowship and the 'Link'.[181] Piratin noted elsewhere that the Tories had never repudiated Ramsay; indeed, upon his release from prison and return to Parliament, Ramsay had been allowed to make a mockery of the democratic system by introducing a motion which would have revived a thirteenth-century law requiring Jews to wear yellow badges.[182] One of Piratin's hand-outs featured the eye-catching announcement, 'British Fascists stage a return'; Piratin pledged as one of his 'immediate demands for Jewry' a law 'making anti-semitism and racial incitement illegal, as it is in Soviet Russia'.[183] His campaign literature linked the CP's opposition to Mosley and Ramsay with a long tradition of Communist agitation on behalf of 'full and equal rights for Jews'; in 1936, for example, at the 'Battle of Cable Street', while Labour and the Board of Deputies counselled passivity, the CP had 'made a stirring call to resist'.[184] In 1945, the reminder seemed a timely one to the Jews of East London.

ANTI-NAZISM AND THE SECOND FRONT

Jewish Communists were just as concerned with international Fascism as with the domestic variety, and in the 1935–45 period they led much of the opposition to Nazi Germany and were in the forefront of the campaign to save Jews from the Holocaust. During a May 1938 demonstration which began at Trafalgar Square and ended at the German embassy, for example, the Stepney CP contingent broke through security cordons and fought a battle with police on the very steps of the embassy;[185] Communists also organized a number of rallies and meetings at the time of the Munich crisis, in September 1938.[186] Their anti-German agitation was minimized during the German–Soviet non-aggression pact of 1939–41, but after Hitler attacked the Soviet Union in June of 1941, the Communists, intent on gaining the maximum possible assistance for the beleaguered Russians, combined their call for a Second Front with a very hard line indeed on Nazi Germany.

In East London and elsewhere, even those Jews who were not particularly pro-Soviet supported the Communist campaign for a Second Front, which by diverting some Nazi forces to the west would enable the Soviets to march more quickly across eastern Europe, liberating the Jews as they went. Other sectors of the British population preferred to delay the Second Front in order to force the Soviets to bear the brunt of the fighting against Hitler; this policy had the advantage of minimizing Western casualties. But because the Jews wanted as speedy a victory as possible over Hitler, their ethnic interests coincided with Communist politics.

In Stepney, there was little dissension concerning the need for a Second Front. The man in the street, remarked the *East London Observer* in October 1941, 'is disturbed as seldom before by Britain's failure . . . to help Russia by some sort of strategic diversion'.[187] In the course of the next year, Communists played heavily upon these sentiments. In February 1942, for example, the Stepney CP called for a '100 Per Cent Win the War' government.[188] In mid-May, the Communists took an advertisement in the *East London Advertiser* to argue the case for a Second Front; one week later they advertised again suggesting that Stepney citizens sign a petition calling for a town meeting on the subject.[189] Then, on 6 June, the CP sponsored its own meeting at Trinity Hall, Mile End; the chairman of this meeting was not a CP member but a well-known local Conservative, A. J. Lyons.[190]

In all their pronouncements, Stepney Communists took care to emphasize the anti-Fascist nature of the battle being fought by the Soviet Union. Alf Rockman, the then-secretary of the borough party, was in the chair at the Grand Palais on 4 October 1942, as an array of speakers helped to celebrate the sixth anniversary of the 'victory' at the 'Battle of Cable Street'. There were calls for a Second Front 'to finish the job you started in Stepney in October 1936, when you drove the Nazis from the streets of London. Now go on to drive them from the streets of the world.'[191] The local trade unions were apparently in agreement: in November 1942, a meeting of the Shop Stewards Council of the Eastern Area of the NUTGW No. 1 Branch called for the immediate opening of a Second Front.[192]

Churchill's government took a different point of view. In a speech delivered at Blackpool in May 1942, Home Secretary Herbert Morrison criticized the 'foolish and purposeless vindictiveness' of the Versailles Treaty of 1919; then he recommended a lenient peace and what he termed 'justice' for the German people.[193] Liberal, Labour and radical periodicals and newspapers such as *Tribune*, the *New Statesman*, the *Daily Herald* and the *People* also took a moderate line: rather than suggesting any collective guilt on the part of the Germans, these tended to blame the war on such abstract causes as the crisis of world capitalism, the rivalries of imperial powers, or even man's innate inclination to aggression – much to the disgust of the *Daily Worker*, which was far more hostile to Germany.[194]

The *Daily Worker* felt that its stand had been fully justified when in December 1942 all of Britain became aware of the mass genocide undertaken by the Nazis. On 14 December, the Communist paper published a number of articles on the extermination of European Jewry; Chief Rabbi J. H. Hertz was quoted to the effect that 'the silence of large sections in this country had been taken by the Nazis as an encouragement to continue their techniques of annihilation'.[195] Three days later, Foreign Secretary Anthony Eden described the Nazi extermination methods to a horrified House of Commons; Eden concluded by referring to a resolution against the mass killings which had been lodged with the German government by those members of the United Nations who were fighting against the Axis. The *Daily Worker*, unimpressed with such formal measures as these, called attention to the anti-Semites within Britain itself: 'it is precisely among us that anti-Semitism is one of Fascism's most insidious weapons.' The newspaper went on to urge that hatred against Fascism and the desire for retribution be kept at white heat: 'May that determination not fade among us!'[196]

Within weeks, the government gave the Communists – and the Jews – good reason to suspect that very little 'determination' underlay Eden's remarks in the House. Early in January, Home Secretary Morrison refused to permit the entry of 2,000 Jewish children from Vichy France, arguing that their arrival might lead to anti-Semitic outbursts in Britain. Walter Holmes, writing in the *Daily Worker*, suggested that Britain should restore its ancient tradition of asylum 'and let the British people deal with our anti-Semites as they deserve'; instead, the Home Office 'prefers to keep the doors of Britain locked against the victims'.[197]

In February, the National Jewish Committee of the CPGB passed a resolution demanding that 'the British Government give positive form' to their expressions of sympathy for European Jewry 'by undertaking at once to rescue as many of the persecuted Jews as can be rescued into Britain'.[198] The NJC did not intend that Jews should overlook the connection between their own interests and that of the Communist Party: one NJC document explained that 'We must tell the Jewish people and prove it to them that fighting against anti-Semitism and Fascism in Britain is helping also the Jews in Europe, and demanding the Second Front in Europe is bringing nearer the day of salvation for those Jews'.[199] At the end of the month, the CPGB was demanding that the government undertake at once to receive into Britain as many Jews as could be rescued; that it facilitate the transfer of Jews who managed to escape the Nazis to territories controlled by those countries which were members of the UN coalition against Hitler; and that it encourage neutral countries to receive Jews.[200] But four months after Eden's denunciation of the Nazi programme of mass murder, as the *Daily Worker* reminded its readers in April, Jews were still being killed at the rate of tens of thousands a day, while the Allies were engaged in 'preliminary exploration' of the problem. True enough, the Allies were to hold a conference in Bermuda on 19 April to discuss joint measures for saving European Jewry; but discussion, commented the newspaper, could just as easily be conducted on the telephone.[201]

In the same month, the Russia Today Society published *Soviet*

Jews at War, a pamphlet by Professor Hyman Levy, who wrote that Jews 'must be in the forefront of the fight against Fascism': 'For us in Britain it becomes an urgent necessity to see to it that the front in Europe is opened as soon as possible.' Levy remarked that 'Hitler has declared war on the Jews . . . Whosoever has a drop of Jewish blood can have no place in the so-called New Order.'[202] But his rhetoric was mild compared to that of other publications from the Communist presses. For by now, as more details emerged from Russia concerning the mass murder of civilian populations by the Nazis, the desire for revenge was intensifying. The Russian writer Ilya Ehrenburg, who in March 1943 referred to the Germans as 'repulsive marauding beasts',[203] represented that school of thought which would allow no distinction between Nazis and 'good' Germans. In 'I Cannot Remain Silent', one of several wartime articles by Ehrenburg distributed in Britain by Communist organizations, he insisted that 'these crimes were not committed by Hitler, or by the German Nazi leaders, but by ordinary German officers and men. We have in our possession diaries and letters written by German officers, and German soldiers, describing with glee how they watched the extermination of the Jews.'[204]

The Jews of East London expressed their support for views such as these in a variety of ways. In May 1943, for example, when the East London sub-district of the CP was soliciting contributions for a campaign to ban all Fascist groups and to urge the invasion of western Europe, 37 out of 50 people in one Stepney factory promptly subscribed 17s. each; other workers throughout the borough and in neighbouring Hackney responded with similar generosity.[205] At the TUC Congress at Southport in September, NAFTA, a union with many East End Jewish members, supported a resolution calling for a Second Front.[206] The Communist faction within the Workers' Circle prepared for that group's annual convention in December by drafting a resolution which declared that 'the only way to save the remnants of European Jewry from complete extermination is to win the war in the shortest possible time. This can only be accomplished by the immediate invasion of Western Europe.'[207] Jews also made their position clear by flocking to rallies and meetings called by the East London branches of the

CP. On 1 December 1943, for example, 1,300 people crowded into East London's largest theatre, the Hackney Empire, to attend a Communist rally. One month later, this attendance record was surpassed when 2,200 people were packed into the same hall for a New Year's Day rally; 153 people signed up on the spot to become party members. The East London sub-district of the CP attributed these successes partly to good organization, partly to 'the political situation', which had demonstrated that Communist demands for a Second Front and for total victory had been correct all along.[208]

Their zeal was not shared by the government. In April 1944, a leading article in the *Daily Worker* complained that, 16 months after Eden's revelations in the House of Commons, 'the indignation is cold and the promise of retribution is forgotten'. The House had become 'as passionless as ever'.[209] Indeed, neither the Conservative nor the Labour candidates had much to say about British policy towards Germany in the months leading up to the elections of July 1945.[210] But the Communists forcefully made this issue their own.

In late 1944, the Stepney CP, already preparing for the elections, again invoked the 'Battle of Cable Street': 'Today, when fascism is being pounded to the dust . . . we can take pride in the knowledge that our long years of struggle have borne fruit, that our defeat of Mosley at Cable Street was a milestone on a road which will include the handshakes that our boys will exchange with the men of the Red Army when they meet in Berlin.'[211] In February *Jewish Opinion*, the organ of the National Jewish Committee, was quoting Ilya Ehrenburg on 'sham humanitarians . . . who are sorry for butchers and traitors'; such people, commented the periodical, would only pave the way for the deaths of further millions.[212] Another article in the same issue asserted that the murderers of Maidanek 'cannot change, they cannot be improved, and must not be forgiven . . . Humanism today consists in absolute mercilessness.'[213]

Remarks such as these were gratifying to the many Jews of East London who were eager to see the Nazi war criminals get their retribution. Early in May 1945, B. A. Bagnari of the Workers' Circle met with the Board of Deputies to express the Circle's 'very definite views' concerning the need to bring all war criminals to trial; the memorandum which he submitted to the Board was to be forwarded to the government.[214] Within days, however, the *Daily Worker* was reporting that former members of the German government, such as Admiral Karl Doenitz, Hitler's successor, were still living in comfort in their own villas and were even allowed to carry arms;[215] it was not information calculated to foster Jewish confidence in the Allied governments. The *Daily Worker* alleged that Churchill's government was already hindering the efforts of anti-Fascist elements in the British zone of occupation; it was essential, therefore, that the electorate defeat the Conservative Party, upon which 'the hopes of all Nazi whisperers . . . are pinned'.[216]

In their election literature, the Communists stressed their own unflagging hostility to German Fascism: 'The Nazis and war criminals must be sternly punished, not treated as "friendly enemies". Nazism and German militarism must be wiped out once and for all.'[217] To this end, the CP advocated the destruction of the Nazi Party, the German armed forces and general staff, and all German military equipment. Industry which might be used for military production was to be eliminated or controlled. Repayment was to be 'made in kind for the destruction wrought by the Germans, and all traces of Nazi organisation, thought and influence . . . removed from German life'.[218]

The Communists urged those who might forget what Fascism had wrought to look at Dachau and Belsen, Maidanek and Treblinka – 'tragic monuments to the mass of victims'. While the Soviets had proposed guidelines for the punishment of Nazi war criminals as early as 1943, in Britain debate still floundered on the problem of defining who and what were 'war criminals' and 'war crimes'. A debate in the House of Lords on 20 March 1945 had demonstrated that there was much indecision and hesitation on the matter. '*This indecisive attitude must be altered. No softness must be shown to the Fascist beasts.*'[219]

In his own campaign literature, Phil Piratin made the same point, arguing that 'We must end the kid-glove handling of the Nazi war criminals'.[220] In the Jewish neighbourhoods of East London, he was not likely to be contradicted.

5
Support for the Soviet Union

THE NATIONALITY POLICY OF THE USSR

While it gave the same wholehearted and unquestioning support to the Soviet Union as did the CPGB, the Jewish Communist movement was particularly concerned to demonstrate how effectively the Soviet Union had solved specifically Jewish problems through the implementation of Marxist ideology. The Jewish Communists were able to draw upon a long-standing legacy of pro-Soviet feeling. Mick Mindel has recalled that for the Jewish workers he knew as a child, the Russian Revolution of 1917 was 'a tremendous event. They thought it was the end of pogroms, the end of anti-Semitism.'[1] In the 1930s, the USSR established a Jewish national region in Birobidzhan in the Soviet Far East; it emerged as the primary ideological and military opponent to Nazi Germany; and Jews increasingly came to regard it as the state most interested in bettering the condition not only of its own Jews but of Jews everywhere. As one CPGB pamphlet put it, 'The Jewish workers all over the world know the name of Lenin'.[2]

In East London, many Jews were brought into the movement by means of pro-Soviet front groups such as the Friends of the Soviet Union (later the Russia Today Society), an organization whose British section was formed in 1927;[3] two years later, Alec Waterman and Tom Bell, the prominent party intellectual, organized a Stepney branch.[4] Solly Kaye has recalled that a casual acquaintance introduced him to the activities of the Friends of the Soviet Union, who met in the same building, as did the Workers' Circle:

There were great discussions about Communism, about socialism, about anti-Semitism. There was a local schoolteacher who gave a whole series of lectures on dialectical materialism, which I attended. And there the seeds were planted, well and truly. In the search for an answer to anti-Semitism I came upon the Communist Party.[5]

CPGB propaganda, such as that to which Kaye responded so readily, emphasized the theme that the solution to the Jewish problem was 'only to be sought from within the class struggle: it is inseparable from the class struggle'.[6] Jews were warned against 'utopian' schemes such as the one calling for territorial concentration in Palestine.[7] The problem with this particular idea, as Willie Gallacher explained in a debate in 1935 with the Reverend M. L. Perlzweig at the Shoreditch Town Hall, was that the economy of Palestine was certain to be based upon the same capitalist property relationships that characterized the British Empire as a whole; and this meant that Jewish workers would inevitably be exploited in Palestine just as they were in every other capitalist country.[8]

Jewish Communists were far more impressed with the Soviet solution to the problem of Jewish nationality: the designation of Birobidzhan as a Jewish Autonomous Region and a potential fully fledged Soviet republic on 7 May 1934. Typical was the response of Issie Panner, who contrasted the 'increasing chaos of world capitalism', and its Fascist reaction and violent anti-Semitism, with the new socialist construction in Birobidzhan, which was turning *luftmenschen* into productive agricultural workers.[9] Jewish Communists were far from being the only Jews, however, to respond with enthusiasm to the creation of a refuge from Hitler's Europe.[10]

Communists and non-Communists came together in ICOS, the Yiddishist organization for Jewish colonization in Soviet Russia. ICOS had a considerable following among Circle members: Barnett Weinberg, general chairman of the Circle until 1941, was also for a time chairman of ICOS; CP members Alf Holland and Alec Waterman, its secretary from 1930 to 1933, edited the organization's bilingual journal, *New Life–Neilebn*,[11] which according to one admirer gave 'a remarkable picture of the development of real racial equality and cultural progress under socialist conditions'.[12]

SUPPORT FOR THE SOVIET UNION

Issie Pushkin and Abe Gilbert, both Communists, also appeared prominently in its work.

ICOS was extremely active. In 1935 it celebrated the first anniversary of the Birobidzhan proclamation with a mass meeting at the Whitechapel Art Gallery;[13] it also held a number of fairs in aid of the new Jewish region.[14] In the spring of 1936, when Simon Gilbert of the *Jewish Chronicle* asserted that Jews in the USSR were subjected to conditions worse than anywhere except Nazi Germany,[15] Holland and Panner, then the joint honorary secretaries of ICOS, led the counter-attack. Under the national policy of the Soviet government, they responded in the *Chronicle*, 'this once-isolated caste of economic parasites' was being 'transformed into healthy productive workers' and now occupied 'the first Jewish State since the dispersion'.[16] A few weeks later, on Birobidzhan's second anniversary, Holland and Panner contributed to the *Daily Worker* a feature article entitled 'U.S.S.R. Solves the Jewish "Problem"'; in this article, they described the rapid progress and the 'enthusiastic, constructive atmosphere' of the region where Jewish dreams were being realized. Zionist opposition to the project could now be seen as 'petty' and 'discredited': for while Birobidzhan became ever stronger, Zionist hopes for Palestine were being undermined by Jewish-Arab tensions and by a 'growing Jewish Fascist Movement', that is, the Jabotinsky Revisionist Zionists.[17] ICOS also held another mass meeting, this time in Shoreditch Town Hall, to celebrate the region's second anniversary; among the speakers were Communists and Communist supporters, including D. N. Pritt, Isabel Brown, Jack Gaster and, of course, Holland and Panner. Gaster was the son of Rabbi Dr Moses Gaster, the prominent Jewish religious figure and Zionist, and the former *Haham* or spiritual leader of the Sephardic community, but this did not prevent him from denouncing British imperialism in Palestine; Panner asserted that in the USSR, Jews were now the equals of all other nationalities.[18]

During the war, Jewish Communists continued to make much of the Soviet analysis of the national question. In his 1942 treatise on *Anti-Semitism and the Jewish Question*, for example, Issie Panner praised the Soviet Union for establishing the Jewish Autonomous

Region and for strictly enforcing Article 123 of the Soviet Constitution, which guaranteed equal rights to all religious and ethnic groups. By these means, asserted Panner, the USSR had solved 'the Jewish Question'.[19] Professor Hyman Levy, speaking at Maccabi House, London, in April 1944, was as impressed as Panner by the provisions of the Soviet Constitution; Levy went on to hint that after the war, Stalin would apply the same Marxist principles to 'multi-national' problems concerning Jews outside the Soviet Union.[20]

By late 1944, even the *Jewish Chronicle* was quoting Stalin with approval: it noted that in 1931 the Russian leader had termed anti-Semitism 'an extreme form of racial chauvinism', the 'lightning rod which helps capitalism ward off the blow of the working people'.[21] The favourable attitude of the *Chronicle* is evidence that among Jews, a pro-Soviet feeling had developed.

PRO-SOVIET ACTIVITIES 1941–43

As a result of the German invasion of Russia in June 1941, the Soviet Union became the main hope of the Allies in terms of military victory, and the political consciousness of large segments of the British public was almost totally transformed. 'Enthusiasm for the Soviet Union is sweeping like a great wave through the masses in this country,' wrote Victor Gollancz, the publisher, 'nothing must be done to cause a reaction.'[22] Jews in particular were keenly aware that Russia was the ally closest to Poland, Hungary and the Baltic States – that part of Europe where the endangered Jews lived; Jacob Sonntag, founding editor of the *Jewish Quarterly*, recalled that Jews 'looked at the Soviet Union as the great redeemer'.[23] In July 1941, for example, A. N. Stencl published a special issue of his Yiddish magazine, *London–Veitchepl*, entitled *Sovyet–Rusland*;[24] from this time onwards, the magazine was full of essays, poems and stories glorifying the Soviet struggle against Nazi Germany.

The Soviets moved quickly to ensure that they would reap the full benefit of Jewish goodwill: in August 1941, the most prominent members of Soviet Jewry were summoned to a conference in Moscow. Among the speakers were authors such as Peretz Markish, David Bergelson and Ilya Ehrenburg; Shloime Mikhoels, the actor; Sergei Eisenstein, the film maker; and Shakhno Epstein, who was to become secretary of the Jewish Anti-Fascist Committee (JAFC) which emerged from this conference. The group also issued an appeal on behalf of 'Our Red Army', addressed 'To Our Jewish Brothers All Over the World'. Henceforth all propaganda and other communications to the West concerning Soviet Jewry were to come through the JAFC.[25]

The Jews of East London were highly receptive to the appeals of the JAFC; on 27 September 27, the *East London Advertiser* reported that 'enthusiasm for the Russian war effort is widespread in Stepney'.[26] Much of the actual organizing was done by the Jewish socialist and trade union groups, who even before the war had been favourably disposed towards the USSR. The Mantle & Costume Branch of the NUTGW, for example, arranged for a meeting to be held at Toynbee Hall which was to launch a 'vigorous' campaign to aid 'our great Ally, Soviet Russia'. Among those involved in the meeting were East London MPs C. R. Attlee and J. H. Hall; Stepney councillor M. H. Davis; the prominent social worker, Basil Henriques, JP; Morris Myer of *Di Tsayt*; Mick Mindel of the NUTGW; Nathan Weiner, the general secretary of the Workers' Circle; and Barnett Janner, chairman of the Zionist Federation and president of the Association of Jewish Friendly Societies. Dr J. J. Mallon, the warden of Toynbee Hall, said at the meeting that helping Russia would be a good thing for Stepney. J. L. Fine added that he had already been in contact with the Foreign Office, which was to relay to the Soviets his desire to know what kind of help was most needed.[27] Another group active on behalf of the USSR was the Workers' Circle, which had already, in a meeting of the central committee on 6 July 1941, put aside its internal disputes regarding the relative merits of socialism, Labour Zionism and Communism in order to express 'its warmest sympathy with the peoples of the USSR in the unprovoked attack by Nazi Germany'.[28] On 5 October, the Workers' Circle reaffirmed its complete support of the USSR in a resolution sent to the Soviet embassy.[29] At a November meeting,

Dr Noah Barou, a prominent member of Poale Zion, expressed the hope that close cooperation would ensue with Russian Jews in the struggle against Nazism; A. L. Easterman, representing the British Section of the World Jewish Congress (WJC), called for 'full, complete, and immediate whole-hearted cooperation' with the USSR.[30]

Meanwhile, the Stepney Aid to Russia Committee was officially launched at Toynbee Hall on 10 October. Dr Mallon presided over the meeting, which brought together such local notables as Mayor George Chamberlain; councillors Frank Lewey and Phil Piratin; Ben Tillett, the trade unionist; Mick Mindel and J. L. Fine of the NUTGW; Basil Henriques; and Barnett Janner. J. H. Hall, although unable to attend, promised all possible support. Dr Mallon was unanimously elected chairman of the committee, with Fine as secretary, Chamberlain as honorary president and Janner as honorary secretary. A British Red Cross representative 'welcomed Stepney's special effort on behalf of Russia'; the committee was also to help stimulate interest in the Stepney Red Cross Penny-a-Week Fund.[31] Stepney had more collectors than any other London borough for this and other funds aiding Soviet Russia, and the residents of the borough were giving an 'excellent response', according to the *East London Advertiser*.[32] In the course of 1942, for example, the Workers' Circle collected over £1,150 for the TUC's Russian relief fund;[33] Morris Millet Lodge No. 126 of the Grand Order of Israel and Shield of David Friendly Society, which was headed by Barnett Janner, raised £400 for Mrs Churchill's Red Cross Aid-to-Russia Fund.[34]

The various fund-raising campaigns were punctuated by numerous pro-Soviet events and festivities. In March 1942, Alf Silverman, a member of the National Jewish Committee of the CPGB who also served as president of the Stepney Trades Council, announced that a 'Salute to the Soviet Trade Unionists' would be held at Toynbee Hall in honour of 'the brave and heroic efforts of our Russian Allies'.[35] Mick Mindel chaired the meeting; the speakers included Victor Feather, organizing secretary of the TUC, and Mayor John Pritchard, who remarked that 'The people of Stepney must show Russia that they were 100 per cent in the war'.[36] Soviet

SUPPORT FOR THE SOVIET UNION

Ambassador Maisky sent the trades council a letter expressing his appreciation for what it was doing 'in the cause of Anglo-Soviet unity, which I regard as a valuable contribution towards ensuring a speedy victory over our common enemy'.[37] Soon Maisky sent Stepney another message, praising an 'Aid to Russia Week' which was to be opened on 20 June by Clement Attlee, the Deputy Prime Minister, and which included a colourful procession through the borough led by the band of the Grenadier Guards.[38] Addressing a crowd at the People's Palace, Dan Frankel, the Mile End MP, admitted that his political views conflicted with those of the Russians, but informed his listeners that he had 'always favoured friendship between the people of this country and Russia'.[39]

In the same month, Simon Blumenfeld, the left-wing novelist, announced the formation of another pro-Soviet fund-raising group, the Jewish 1942 Committee, which was intended to represent 'every class of Jews': its membership included artists and scholars such as Dr Cecil Roth, Jacob Epstein, Moshe Oved, Professor Hyman Levy and Professor Norman Bentwich; Communists and fellow-travellers such as A. M. Fuchs, Alf Holland, Leo Koenig, Mick Mindel and Alec Waterman; and trade unionists such as A. R. Rollin, J. L. Fine and Noah Barou. The point was to demonstrate to the Soviets that English Jews, 'whatever their political opinions, are behind them to a man'.[40] Blumenfeld became the organizing secretary, with Percy Phillips as treasurer and Jacob Sonntag as joint honorary secretary. On 24 June, at its inaugural meeting, the Committee drew up a Declaration of Aims which was sent to Ambassador Maisky.[41] That week, in an editorial entitled 'Our Russian Allies', the *Jewish Chronicle* endorsed the 1942 Committee. The Soviet Union, said the *Chronicle*, had a claim to Jewish support as the only country in which anti-Semitism was a crime; if the USSR were to be defeated, 'then indeed would the lamps go out not only over Jewry but throughout the world'.[42]

On 1 July, Leo Koenig and Professor Levy spoke in Stepney at a meeting held under the auspices of the Association of Jewish Writers and Journalists;[43] a few days later, at the Grand Palais, Commercial Road, Morris Myer presided over a meeting at which Blumenfeld and Levy gave speeches publicizing the work of the

1942 Committee.⁴⁴ A delegation visited Ambassador Maisky on 7 July, and was impressed with his knowledge of various aspects of Jewish communal life. 'The news of the formation of your Committee will be welcomed in my country,' he told them.⁴⁵ Two days later, Blumenfeld, Myer, Oved and I. A. Lisky met with Selig Brodetsky, the president of the Board of Deputies, on behalf of the 1942 Committee; Myer explained that the Committee was 'anxious to raise aid for Russia from the Jews of this country as a specific Jewish effort'. The response was lukewarm: Brodetsky felt that a specifically Jewish endeavour would be politically unwise and would fail to receive the general support of the community.⁴⁶

Despite Brodetsky's disapproval, the committee, which in August 1942 was enlarged and incorporated as the United Jewish Committee (UJC), did manage to win support in a number of influential quarters; the Zionist Federation of Great Britain, for example, sent a letter 'expressing Zionist sympathy with Russia in her heroic struggle'.⁴⁷ Blumenfeld was writing to various Anglo-Jewish organizations, societies and synagogues, asking them to send delegates to a national conference to be held on 30 August at the People's Palace, Mile End Road. The Russian allies had requested help, said Blumenfeld, and this conference 'must shine as an historic symbol of Jewish Unity'.⁴⁸ Delegates representing 90 organizations attended the meeting, which passed a resolution calling for the immediate launching of a fund to aid the Soviet Union; Morris Myer suggested that the United Jewish Committee set up local committees throughout the country to coordinate the raising of funds.⁴⁹ Selig Brodetsky took no part in the conference: in his response to Blumenthal's letter he explained that 'doctor's orders' prevented him from being present.⁵⁰

By this time the Yiddish author and translator Joseph Leftwich had become secretary of the committee and was editing for it a booklet entitled *Jews Must Answer!*. In October, Leftwich appealed to all the Jews of Britain, be they religious or secular, Zionist or non-Zionist, to support the Russian cause; upon the Soviet struggle against Hitler, wrote Leftwich, depended 'the whole future of civilization . . . They are fighting our battle.'⁵¹ Leftwich's attitude was shared by many other Yiddishists in East London, and particularly by those who were active either in the YKUF or in another influential organization dominated by Communists: the Jewish Cultural Club (JCC).

The JCC, which in Yiddish was known as *Der Yiddisher Arbeter Kultur Farband*, had its origins in a group of East European Jews who had come to Britain from Belgium and France after the fall of France.[52] Chimen Abramsky has recalled that 'many of them were Communists';[53] according to Jacob Sonntag, 'they met regularly, and when the war with Russia broke out, they initiated a group to do something, to help Russia'.[54] The JCC reprinted appeals from the Jewish Anti-Fascist Committee, often adding its own urgent commentary.[55] It also published works of its own, such as *Yidn In'm Kamf Kegn Hitlerism [Jews in the Struggle Against Hitlerism]*.[56] In November 1942, the JCC commemorated the Russian Revolution of 1917 by publishing *25 Yor Sovyetn Farband [25 Years of the Soviet Union]*, a pamphlet which included contributions by A. N. Stencl, Alec Waterman, Jacob Sonntag, Professor Levy, Chimen Abramsky, A. M. Fuchs, Moshe Oved and Leo Koenig, as well as reprints of articles by Shakno Epstein and Itzik Feffer, two members of the Jewish Anti-Fascist Committee.[57] The JCC also circulated appeals for aid to the USSR and announcements of conferences, such as the one held in March 1943 to celebrate the twenty-fifth anniversary of the Red Army. At this conference, which was chaired by Alec Waterman, tribute was paid 'to a form of government that for the first time in history treats Jews as equals'; messages were received from Ambassador Maisky, Britain's Chief Rabbi J. H. Hertz, Professor Harold Laski and the Communist MP Willie Gallacher.[58]

During the same period, the United Jewish Committee continued to expand. The East London branch, with I. A. Lisky as its secretary, held an inaugural meeting on 11 October 1942; two Stepney MPs, Dan Frankel and W. J. Edwards, made speeches.[59] But the committee was about to be transformed beyond recognition, as the Anglo-Jewish establishment finally joined the pro-Soviet bandwagon. In October 1942, Brodetsky met with Leftwich, who agreed that the UJC should be reconstituted as part of a general fund which would then receive the official blessing of the Board of Deputies.[60] While the reorganization was being arranged, the soon-to-be-defunct UJC sponsored a meeting, on 5 November, at which Chief Rabbi Hertz fulsomely praised the Soviet Union for outlawing anti-Semitism; Hertz reminded his audience that 'the lives of millions of our Jewish brethren depend on a Russian victory'. Another speaker, Mrs Israel M. Sieff, wife of one of the owners of Marks & Spencer Ltd, asserted that the polity of the Soviet Union was based upon moral values propounded 2,000 years earlier by the great Jewish prophets.[61]

By mid-December, the UJC disappeared into the Jewish Fund for Soviet Russia (JFSR), a charity authorized to collect contributions for Mrs Churchill's Red Cross Aid-to-Russia fund; it was promised that medical units purchased with Jewish funds 'shall bear an inscription that they are subscribed by the Jews of Britain'. The JFSR was also authorized 'to establish and maintain contacts of a Jewish cultural character with the Jews of Soviet Russia'. Dr Redcliffe Salaman, FRS, served as the organization's president; Lord Nathan of Churt was chairman of the Appeal Committee. The list of patrons included such other notables as Brodetsky, Chief Rabbi Hertz, Mrs Israel Zangwill, Mrs I. M. Sieff, Berl Locker, Leonard J. Stein, Barnett Janner and Dr Simon Rawidowicz.[62] Sydney Silverman, MP, was on the group's executive; Leftwich was its secretary. But as Jacob Sonntag has recalled, 'The actual motivators and movers were people connected with the National Jewish Committee; they did the work'.[63] Maurice Essex, for example, was chairman, and Harry Ibbetson treasurer, of the London Area Committee of the JFSR; Alf Holland was chairman of the East London branch.[64] In February 1943, the Jewish Communists called for the formation of additional JFSR branches throughout Britain: 'The work in connection with the JFSR becomes more and more important.'[65] A few weeks later, Ben Bradley, who was one of R. Palme Dutt's chief aides, met with the National Jewish Committee to discuss the JFSR, which he described as 'vital for establishing strong bonds between the Jews of Britain and the people of the Soviet Union'.[66] Even Ambassador Maisky conveyed 'sincere thanks to all those who have organised this effort in aid of the Jewish Fund for Soviet Russia'.[67]

Meanwhile the Nazi army, defeated at Stalingrad, was being

pushed back by the Soviets, who quickly uncovered evidence of Nazi war crimes. The mass murder of civilian populations and the genocide of the Jews were described in a number of books and articles; one of the first of these to appear, early in 1943, was *New Soviet Documents on Nazi Atrocities*, a work issued by the Press Department of the Soviet embassy in London.[68] These revelations gave increased impetus to the stream of pro-Soviet pamphlets and articles which already came from the printing presses of front or support groups such as the Russia Today Society and the JFSR. The JFSR was able to include an appeal from Chief Rabbi Hertz in its January 1943 pamphlet, *Jews of Britain! Soviet Russia Needs **Your** Help!*.[69] Another JFSR publication, *Calling All Jews to Action!*, edited by Chimen Abramsky and which appeared in May 1943, contained an emotional appeal from Soviet Jewry: 'Fellow Jews of Great Britain, America and the other countries, if you want to prevent Hitler from exterminating us, if you want to save your own lives . . . Help the great heroic Red Army.'[70] Another passage in this pamphlet appealed to British Jews even on the level of family ties: 'It may have been your own kin or your own family whom you left behind in Russia whom the Nazis have murdered. How will you avenge them? We Soviet Jews are doing our duty; we shall come to the day of trial as a fighting people and we shall ask what you have done to help us.'[71] In the Foreword, Redcliffe Salaman urged British Jews to 'show our obligation' to the country which, by bearing the brunt of the fighting against 'the Nazi hordes', had saved not only Britain but also 'the Jewish National Home in Palestine' from 'the horrors of Nazi invasion . . . the ordeal which Russia herself has suffered'.[72]

Rhetoric such as this explains why even Zionist organizations were willing to give the Soviets the benefit of the doubt after June 1941. Messages of support were sent to Moscow by various groups;[73] and British Communists defending the USSR were given access to Zionist platforms.[74] Poale Zionists such as Noah Barou, Schneier Levenberg, Sydney Silverman and Berl Locker, a Palestinian Jewish intellectual who, during the war, was in London on behalf of the Jewish Agency and the *Histadrut*, the Jewish trade union movement in Palestine, were key links in this growing *rapprochement*.[75] Locker, on behalf of the *Histadrut*, handed Soviet Ambassador Maisky a cheque for £10,000 in August 1942 'as a small token of friendship and admiration' from the Jewish workers of Palestine;[76] Poale Zion in February 1943 began donating funds to the JFSR.[77] At the Workers' Circle convention in December 1943, Branch 15, predominantly Poale Zion, sent greetings to the JAFC in Moscow as well as to the *Histadrut*.[78] The pages of the *Zionist Review*, edited by Levenberg, now contained pro-Soviet articles. The issue of 13 August 1943, for example, included an article by Ilya Ehrenburg, 'Let the Blood of the Children Call to the Conscience of the World!' which appealed to all Jews outside the Soviet Union 'to help us, and fight with us, to the utmost of your strength!'[79] One month later, another article in the *Review* explained that Soviet Jews were fighting hard for Russia because there they enjoyed equality of citizenship: 'All doors have been opened wide to them. There is nothing which Soviet Russia has left undone to eradicate anti-Semitism.'[80]

Soon after this article appeared, pro-Soviet enthusiasm reached its peak during the visit to Britain of two famous Russian Jews: Shloime Mikhoels and Itzik Feffer.

THE VISIT OF MIKHOELS AND FEFFER AND ITS AFTERMATH

In December 1942, Itzik Feffer's poem 'Ich Bin a Yid' ['I am a Jew'] was published in *Einigkeit [Unity]*, the organ of the Jewish Anti-Fascist Committee. Soon the poem, with its powerful and emotive imagery, was being republished around the world, in both the original Yiddish and in an English translation, becoming for many Jews an expression of defiance against Hitler. In Britain, the JFSR included 'Ich Bin a Yid' in its January 1943 publication, *Jews of Britain! Soviet Russia Needs **Your** Help*.[81] Feffer, who was also a colonel in the Red Army, visited Canada, the United States and Mexico on behalf of the JAFC in the summer of 1943, along with another Soviet Yiddishist of equal fame, Shloime Mikhoels, Director of the Moscow Yiddish State Theatre. By April, the newly formed National Jewish Committee of the CPGB was arranging, through the JFSR, that Mikhoels and Feffer should spend three weeks in London, Glasgow and Manchester on their way back to the Soviet Union,[82] and JFSR activists began to arrange support for the visit in the East End.[83] Joseph Leftwich had also organized a National Reception Committee supported by 28 organizations, many of them non-Jewish, and including prominent individuals from the world of theatre, music, art, literature and academia.[84]

Their arrival was eagerly anticipated. In his regular *Daily Worker* column, 'A Worker's Notebook', Walter Holmes emphasized the artistic accomplishments of the two men, especially Mikhoels, whom he described as one of the USSR's leading Shakespeareans; Holmes asserted that Mikhoels had made the Moscow Yiddish State Theatre 'a part of the Soviet struggle against Fascism'.[85] A. N. Stencl remarked in the September 1943 issue of *London–Veitchepl* that it was particularly gratifying to receive these visitors from 'the only country where our language [Yiddish] is officially recognized'.[86] The October issue of *London–Veitchepl*, which was devoted to the theme of 'Yiddish–Sovyetish-Shafn' ['Soviet Yiddish Creativity'] contained four poems by Feffer; the issue for November, devoted to 'Yiddish Teater' ['Yiddish Theatre'], included two articles honouring Mikhoels, another highlighting his and Feffer's visit, and a poem by Stencl dedicated to the heroic Russian Jews.[87]

Meanwhile, as newspaper reports of the North American tour of Mikhoels and Feffer added to the groundswell of expectation, their arrival was preceded by two mass meetings. The first of these was held in the People's Palace in Stepney on 10 October; according to the *East London Advertiser*, 'Jewish men and women from all parts of East London' flocked to the meeting 'to pay tribute to the Red Army, and to their brethren in the USSR'.[88] Although there was room for more than 2,000 people, hundreds had to be turned away. The mayor of Stepney, H. C. Roeder, served as chairman of the meeting; speakers included Dr J. J. Mallon of Toynbee Hall and Professor Brodetsky of the Board of Deputies, who told the overflow audience that 'In Russia the Jew is something . . . Stalin is proud of the Jews . . . May Russia be an example to other countries.'[89] One week later, at a meeting in the Stoll Theatre, Chief Rabbi Hertz remarked that the USSR had saved 'the men, women and children of Palestine', and that 'If Russia had not made her immortal stand, Jews in this country would by now have been led off in "death trains"'.[90]

Mikhoels and Feffer arrived on 30 October. At their first press conference, in London, they announced the purpose of their visit: to develop comradeship between British and Soviet Jews and to assist the war effort against Fascism.[91] On the next day they travelled to Manchester, where Joseph Leftwich introduced them to a crowd of 4,500 at Belle Vue.[92] After a visit to Glasgow they returned to London, where on 7 November they were the guests of honour at two official functions: a meeting at Caxton Hall sponsored by the JFSR, where the speakers included Morris Myer, Professor Levy, J. L. Fine and other Jewish labour leaders;[93] and a celebration at the Stoll Theatre of the October 1917 Revolution, presided over by Hewlett Johnson, the Dean of Canterbury, and attended by such notables as J. B. Priestley and the new Soviet ambassador, Feodor Gusev.[94]

Their first East London rally was held a week later, at the People's Palace. Miriam Moses, warden of the Brady Girls' Club, opened the meeting to 'scenes of amazing enthusiasm' on the part of the crowd; Mick Mindel, who had become chairman of the Stepney Trades Council, was the first to speak, followed by Barnett Janner. 'Loud and prolonged applause' then greeted the two Russians, who, of course, spoke in Yiddish. Mikhoels, 'a short, stocky figure with a grizzled, kindly face', announced that 5 million Jews were fighting in the Red Army and that 10,000 had been decorated.[95] After describing the Nazi barbarities at Kiev, which had just been discovered during the Soviet recapture of that city, he asserted that 56,000 Jews had been massacred there; all told, the Germans had by now killed 4 million Jews in Europe. 'That is what you must realize. It is not only a Russian affair. It is an all-Jewish affair, and we have come here . . . to transform your feelings of hatred and indignation into bullets and into shells and into bayonets to plunge into the heart of the enemy.' Mikhoels concluded with the Hebrew words, '*Am Yisroel Chai*' ['The people Israel lives']. Then Feffer spoke, telling the crowd that 'I have been through the streets of Whitechapel, and I have seen the ruins, and they reminded me of . . . the ruins in Stalingrad'. Feffer went on to express his pride in all the Jews who were fighting back, in the Red Army, in the Allied armies, in the ghettos, and with the partisans in Poland and Russia. 'We are proud,' he said, 'of the Jews of Palestine who are fighting.'[96] Not only were the visitors given a 'terrific welcome', noted the *Daily Worker*, but £427 was raised for the JFSR.[97]

Mikhoels and Feffer also received a particularly warm reception at a gathering sponsored by the Workers' Circle. Chimen Abramsky has recalled that 'To this party came many people, not only Communists, but Jews who were active in the unions, especially in the tailors unions that many Jews belonged to'.[98] Alf Holland recited a few of Feffer's poems, including 'Ich Bin A Yid'.[99] It was announced that £1,600 had been collected for the JFRS by means of a voluntary levy upon Circle members; a month later it would be announced that this money was being used to purchase a mobile X-ray unit for the Red Army.[100]

On another evening during their visit, Mikhoels and Feffer had a long meeting with Hertz, Janner and Brodetsky; then, from midnight until 3 a.m., they met Lazar Zaidman, Chimen Abramsky, Hyman Levy, Jacob Sonntag and Alec Waterman – all members of the National Jewish Committee of the CPGB – in order to urge the NJC to work for the JFSR and for Mrs Churchill's fund.[101]

On 21 November, the day before their departure, the two guests attended three different events. In the morning, they spoke to a conference of the Federation of Jewish Relief Organizations, and heard Chief Rabbi Hertz state that during their visit to Britain they had expressed sentiments to which no Jew, no matter how pious, could take exception; in response, Feffer told Hertz he 'would be given a great welcome' if he visited Moscow.[102] Mikhoels and Feffer were then officially welcomed at a full meeting of the Board of Deputies later that day. Brodetsky introduced them as representatives of Russia, adding, 'we express our admiration and love for that great Army and people'. Mikhoels thanked the Board for its participation in the work of the JFSR, and hoped that, following the visit, Soviet and British Jews would establish closer ties. Feffer added that Hitler had tried to do 'what Mussolini's forebears did to us in Palestine two thousand years ago', but the Soviet Jews were fighting back. In a calculated taunt at the British government, which had just released Oswald Mosley from detention, Feffer remarked that 'if we catch a Fascist in our country we do not let him go'.[103] That evening the two Russians made their farewell appearance in a public meeting at the Stoll Theatre sponsored by the JFSR. Again it was noted, this time by Chief Rabbi Hertz, that anti-Semitism was a crime in the Soviet Union. Rabbi Hertz read aloud 'Ich Bin a Yid'; then he cried.[104]

Long after the departure of Mikhoels and Feffer, the political repercussions of their visit were still to be felt. Mick Mindel has explained that because the Jewish workers were deeply attached to Yiddish, they 'were tremendously proud' of 'these great artists'.[105] According to Mrs Ray Waterman, another witness, Mikhoels and Feffer had an 'electrifying' effect, 'everyone was delighted to find out how Yiddish they were'.[106] Sentiments like these translated readily into pro-Soviet enthusiasm; even organizations such as the Federation of Synagogues, representing mainly East End Orthodox Jews, extolled the virtues of Soviet Jewry.[107] J. W. Bentley, who before the war had been chairman of the Jewish People's Council Against Fascism and Anti-Semitism, has said that 'Mikhoels and Feffer created a sensation in the East End of London. They were loved, they were respected, and great hopes were generated in favour of the Soviet Union in consequence of their coming.'[108] The two Russian Jews had even met with Chaim Weizmann and other Zionist leaders; the *Zionist Review* declared that Anglo-Jewry would now be 'vitally interested' in cooperating with Soviet Jewry in the work of Jewish redemption in Palestine.[109]

In late December, the Workers' Circle, meeting for its eleventh convention, articulated some of these feelings in a resolution which sent 'greetings to the Soviet Union and its heroic Red Army' and pledged the Circle's 'utmost support against those forces who are carrying on an open or concealed struggle against it'; the resolution declared that 'the fate of European Jewry depends upon the strength of the Soviet Union'.[110] Throughout 1944, A. N. Stencl's periodical, *London–Veitchepl*, was pervaded by the theme that

Russia was the only hope of the Jews. Stencl published poems with such titles as 'Unzere Brider in Sovyet Rusland' ['Our Brothers in Soviet Russia'] and 'Vilna Yerushalayim d'Lita' ['Vilna, the Jerusalem of Lithuania']; for the November 1944 issue, which was dedicated to the twenty-seventh anniversary of the Soviet Union, Stencl himself wrote a poem 'Tsu der Roiter Fon' ['To the Red Flag'].[111] Communists such as Zaidman and Abramsky were allowed to contribute articles concerning Soviet life;[112] Alec Waterman, too, became a regular contributor, writing on such subjects as Soviet Yiddish poetry and the tenth anniversary of Birobidzhan.[113] Many East London trade unions also, of course, remained loyal to the Soviet cause: in October 1944, for example, Morry Jacobs, the chairman of NAFTA 15, praised 'the magnificent way Marshal Stalin and the Soviet government . . . are helping to bring about happiness to the whole of mankind'.[114]

But pro-Soviet feeling was not limited to Yiddishists or socialists or East End immigrants; indeed, given the fact that every important Jewish organization in Britain had officially supported the mission of Mikhoels and Feffer, it was by this time impolitic to express anti-Soviet sentiments. On 11 June 1944, a conference sponsored by the JFSR at Beaver Hall, London, brought together 94 representatives of 60 different organizations, including cultural organizations, synagogues and Zionist groups; many of these had not been even remotely favourable to the Soviet Union before the war. Barnett Janner, who was at this time serving not only as chairman of the Zionist Federation but also as head of the Stepney Aid to Russia Committee, told the audience that Russia had rescued 1,800,000 Jews; the lives of millions of others depended on a Soviet victory in Europe. Janner put forward a resolution thanking the Soviets for their sacrifices on behalf of the Jews, and calling on British Jews to continue to provide financial support for Russian medical services.[115] His exhortations did not sound so very different from those of the Communists on the National Jewish Committee of the CPGB, who during 1944 continued to urge that 'every support and assistance' be given the JFSR as a means of expressing goodwill towards the Soviet Union; only through such support, according to the NJC, could 'democratic advance be achieved' and the Jewish people be encouraged in their hopes for a better post-war life.[116] The *Jewish Chronicle* participated in the euphoria by reprinting in totally uncritical fashion the press releases that emanated from the Jewish Anti-Fascist Committee via the JFSR; the *Chronicle* also praised Stalin's government in a number of editorials. One of these, which appeared in November 1944, explained that the Soviet Union was deepening its ties with all freedom-loving countries, and that Jews could 'contribute valuably' to the establishment of the new order of peace 'by cultivating brotherly contacts with their Russian fellows and thus helping strengthen the ties of which Marshal Stalin speaks'.[117] On Red Army Day, in February 1945, the *Chronicle* expressed its confidence that 'Jews will joyfully celebrate this 27th birthday of the Soviet fighting forces'.[118] Chief Rabbi Hertz, too, continued to remind the Jewish community of its 'gratitude to Soviet Russia, which had saved not only the remnants of European Jewry from Nazi extermination, but the Jews of England and the world . . .'[119]

With the war in Europe coming to an end, the JFSR wound up its affairs; Mrs Churchill announced that the overall total collected had come to £42,077 11s. 7d.[120] The Jews of Britain had responded positively to the many appeals put to them on behalf of the Soviet cause.

Jewish Communists were keenly aware of the political value of this pro-Soviet sympathy. In December 1943 the National Jewish Committee had suggested that one of the tasks of the party should be 'to foster and develop the friendship of the Jewish people for the peoples of the Soviet Union in general and for the Soviet Jews in particular: to strengthen their knowledge and appreciation of the achievements of Socialism and of the flourishing Jewish life and culture in the Soviet Union'.[121] An internal communication of 1944 indicates that this goal was already close to being achieved: 'The Soviet Union is admired and respected amongst the broad masses of the Jews. . . . The national policy of the Soviet Union, particularly as it affects the Jews of that country . . . is widely appreciated and is looked upon as an example for emulation.'[122]

Later in the year, the National Jewish Committee remarked, in its publication entitled *The Jewish Question*, that 'The deep and

SUPPORT FOR THE SOVIET UNION

widespread regard for the Soviet Union, which has saved millions of the Jews of Europe, and realisation of its role as prime guarantor of a better world after the war, should find practical and tangible expression amongst British Jewry'.[123] Clearly, the Jewish Communists were prepared to make good use of the 'Russia card' in the forthcoming elections.

In the early months of 1945, a favourite theme of the Jewish Communists was that unity between the Jews of the West and the Jews of the Soviet Union would help to defeat Fascism and to promote the spread of progressive ideas in the post-war world. The *Jewish Clarion* explained to its readers that since all of European Jewry outside the USSR had been destroyed, Soviet Jews would exercise a greater gravitational pull than ever before on British Jews; fortunately, the Soviet Jews were 'citizens of the most progressive nation in the world'.[124] 'There is no better friend of persecuted Jewry than the mighty Soviet Union,' announced *Jewish Opinion*.[125] Thanks to Russia, added the *Jewish Forum*, the Jews are saved:

> *Where the Red Army stands, there Fascism will be pulled out by the roots. There the foundations of anti-Semitism, too, will be destroyed...*
> *It is the duty of Jews everywhere to support the Soviet people in their struggle for genuine peace. It is not only a question of gratitude to the power which saved the Jews of Europe from complete annihilation. It is in the vital interests of the Jews themselves, for only in the complete victory of the Soviet Union in the field of international co-operation is guaranteed the regeneration and further progress of all the Jewish people.*[126]

Non-Jewish Communist publications also took part in the campaign: *Russia Today* asserted that 'Only under the Soviet system has the Jewish people become equal amongst equals, received access to useful and productive labour, and has built up its own State'.[127]

Bill Carver, who was Phil Piratin's election agent in 1945, has since described the atmosphere of that time: 'In certain areas, there was emotional admiration for the Soviet Union – many people were themselves from Russia, or were old socialists. There was definitely a feeling towards the Communists in that election, in our area, anyway.'[128] Piratin's campaign literature played upon these emotions, urging all Jews to 'vote for the most progressive candidate in your constituency' – a Communist wherever possible, a Labour candidate in areas where no Communist ran. A Labour government with Communist support, promised Piratin, would work towards 'amicable relationships with Soviet Russia and all the newly formed progressive governments of Europe'.[129] Another campaign leaflet explained that 'It is from the ranks of the Tories that come today the whisperings of mad plans for war with the Soviet Union, the great champion of Jewish as well as all other freedoms'.[130] But Piratin, the Communist candidate, understood that 'Closest friendship with Soviet Russia is the guarantee of future peace. . . . *When you vote Communist you vote for friendship with Russia.*'[131]

Piratin's electoral supporters in Mile End were told to stress his pledge to fight for a law outlawing anti-Semitism, and to point out that his position was based on the best of models: the Soviet Union. Speakers and canvassers were also told to say that 'Jewish culture and development' were specifically encouraged in the USSR. As examples they were to mention Mikhoels's Moscow Yiddish State Theatre; the Jewish Anti-Fascist Committee; and Birobidzhan, with its universities, newspaper and administration 'entirely in Yiddish'. All this, as Piratin's campaign literature pointed out, had been accomplished in a country where 'the worst pogroms were carried out less than thirty years ago'.[132] Piratin's campaign urged the Jewish electors of Mile End to express their desire for a similar, Communist transformation of British society.

6
International Issues and Jewish Concerns

At times during the 1935–45 period, Jewish Communists thought, talked and behaved more like left-wing Jewish nationalists than like Marxist internationalists. They were as interested as other Jews in the fate of the Jewish people world-wide; they hoped to assume the leadership of the working-class Jewish community by addressing the most pressing items of Jewish concern. These motivations lay behind their work on behalf of the Spanish Republicans; their desire to see the 'new' Poland reborn as a centre of Jewish life and culture at the close of the Second World War; and their interest in the well-being of the Jewish *Yishuv* in the Palestine Mandate.

THE SPANISH CIVIL WAR

When the Spanish Civil War broke out in July 1936, most Jews in England perceived the struggle as part of a wider European conflict between left and right. The forces led by Generals Francisco Franco and Emilio Mola represented the threat of Fascist ascendancy on the Continent, and hence an increase in anti-Semitism. Though Spain itself had very few Jews, the victory of those political groupings supported by Hitler's Germany and Mussolini's Italy would, by definition, bode ill for Jews everywhere, including those in Britain. 'Spain had a big impact in the east end,' explained Morry Lebow, who was for a time secretary of the Stepney CP, 'because it went from macrocosm to microcosm. Hitler equalled Spain, as Mosley equalled the Battle of Cable Street.'[1]

The Jewish Communists analysed the conflict as part of the age-old saga of Spanish reaction, which included intolerance towards Jews. Julius Jacobs, a Jewish Communist active on the London Trades Council, announced that the Fascists had vowed to turn the clock back to 1492, the year of the Jewish expulsion from Spain.[2] This attitude was prevalent among those Communists involved in Jewish working-class organizations such as the East London trade unions and the Workers' Circle.

Sam Alexander, a member of the Circle's central committee, warned the membership in October 1936 that a rebel triumph in Spain would affect all Jews: 'Already the Spanish Fascists are extolling the year 1492, in which the Jews were expelled.' He went on to link the battle in Spain with the 'reign of terror' being conducted at the time against the Jews of East London by Britain's own Mosley-led Blackshirts.[3] Alec Waterman, chairman of Branch 3 of the Circle, also described the Spanish struggle within a Jewish framework. In an article published in *Yiddish London*, he referred to Franco and the Falangists as the contemporary manifestation of a long tradition of anti-Semitism in Spain. Hence 'the Jewish heroes from the Polish cities and towns, from Belgium, France, Hungary, Czechoslovakia, and from the kibbutzim in Palestine, from America and Canada' who fought for the Republic in the International Brigades were working 'to stop a return to the Middle Ages, to the autos-da-fe. . . . In the Spanish fields they took revenge for the time of the Inquisition. . . . They are our modern Bar Kochbas, our Hasmoneans, in our day and generation.'[4]

Sentiments such as these compelled an increasing number of Jews of all nationalities to take part in the fighting in Spain. Many of those who came from England naturally fought in the British Battalion of the XV International Brigade, making up at least 3 per cent and perhaps as many as 10 per cent of the total – impressive figures, considering that Jews comprised less than 1 per cent of the British population.[5]

The working-class Jews who remained at home in East London, keenly aware of the implications of a Fascist victory, worked hard to raise money for the Republican cause and to express opposition to the British government's policy of 'non-intervention'; and myriad organizations, some of them independent, some attached to the

Labour or Communist parties, sprang up to serve these ends. A number of the groups, including the Spanish Relief Committee (Jewish Section) and an Aid to Spain committee affiliated to the CP-sponsored National Joint Committee for Spanish Relief, had their offices in Circle House; many of their officials, including Sam Alexander, Abe Gilbert, Julius Pilchik, Alf Holland and Alec Waterman, were members of both the Circle and the Communist Party.[6]

In the summer of 1936, the Circle itself created the Jewish People's Council, an organization which, as Julius Jacobs stated at a meeting held that September in the ULTTU Hall, was buying 'pills with plenty of lead in them' for use by the Republicans;[7] Jacobs, whose younger brother had volunteered to fight, would soon afterwards visit Spain and on his return speak on behalf of the Republic at JPC rallies.[8] In the same month, B. A. Bagnari, then president of the Circle, criticized the paltry support being given to the Spanish Loyalists by various British trade unions in a speech made at the annual meeting of the Trades Union Congress.[9] Circle members were setting a better example: by October they had raised £400 which was donated to a Spanish Relief Fund set up by the TUC;[10] the minutes of the October meeting of the Circle's central committee record that a grant of an additional £25 was made to the same Fund to 'help the Spanish workers in their fight against Fascism'.[11] In its 1937 May Day appeal, the Circle called on its membership to collect a further £1,000 over the following three months in order to provide an ambulance for those of its members fighting in Spain.[12] Meanwhile, some branches of the Circle – particularly the Communist-oriented branches 9 and 10 – were contributing independently to various Aid Spain funds and to the East London Spanish Medical Aid Committee.[13] I. M. Vogler, honorary secretary of the medical aid committee, expressed thanks at one of its conferences 'for the invaluable assistance' rendered by the Circle, which was 'playing its part nobly in helping all phases of Spanish relief work'.[14]

In contrast to the national trade unions singled out for criticism by Bagnari, the East End unions were working hard on behalf of the Spanish Republic. NAFTA 15 (the East London United Branch) sent numerous messages to the TUC and to the National Council of

Labour calling for military aid to the legitimate Spanish government. In Julius Jacobs, a member of the branch, NAFTA 15 had a voice on the London Trades Council, itself a CP-influenced body which raised money and organized demonstrations on behalf of the Loyalists.[15] Jacobs was a sharp critic of the TUC's initial support for a 'non-intervention' policy; and in September 1936, the Council passed a resolution condemning this stand.[16] A few months later, Jacobs asked how Britons would feel if a popular front government including the TUC faced an armed revolt led by Sir Oswald Mosley and assisted by foreign troops.[17] NAFTA 15 also raised money: in March 1937, NAFTA's general secretary complimented the branch's members for having collected over £200 for Spain.[18] The branch wanted to buy an ambulance, and appealed to other NAFTA locals for help.[19] Seven members of NAFTA 15, including Alf Silverman, a Communist who later became head of the Stepney Trades Council, joined the volunteers in Spain;[20] and on May Day, 1938, the branch sent greetings 'to our members fighting in Spain for democracy'.[21]

The tailors' unions were equally zealous on behalf of the Loyalists; indeed, the very first Britons to fight in Spain had been two tailors from Stepney, Nat Cohen and Sam Masters, who together organized the Tom Mann Centuria. Cohen was wounded in Spain and returned to England; Masters was killed at Brunete in July 1937.[22] In April 1938, the London No. 2 (sub-divisional) branch of the NUTGW, an East End local group that was almost entirely Jewish, and which had counted Masters among its members, held a joint rally with the ULTTU at the Shoreditch Town Hall. A. R. Rollin, organizing secretary of the branch, and J. L. Fine, secretary of the ULTTU, suggested the gift of an ambulance to Spain.[23] Dedicated to the memory of Sam Masters and of Harry Gross, another member of the No. 2 branch who had just died in Spain, the ambulance was sent on its way by 5,000 garment workers gathered at High Beech, near Epping Forest, in July 1938. Professor J. B. S. Haldane, the noted geneticist and Communist propagandist, was one of the speakers.[24] Branch 2 even sent food to Spain.[25] The ULTTU, which like the Circle and the NUTGW had members of its own fighting in Spain, was also raising money which it contributed to the TUC's

THE DAILY WORKER

| How They Got Cancer (See Page 4) | WORKERS OF ALL LANDS UNITE | Sportsmen Tell Of Revolt (See Page 6) |

THURSDAY, JULY 30, 1936 — One Penny

Fascists Bomb Spanish Workers From Foreign Plane

PEOPLE ACT TO MAINTAIN ORDER

Britons With Militia

"D.W." CORRESPONDENT IN RAID NEAR SARAGOSSA

Republican Columns Hemming In Enemy At Strategic Centre

Marching with the Republican forces on the road to Saragossa, our Special Correspondent was involved in a Fascist air raid from which he only narrowly escaped. Here is his thrilling story.

STIRRING SCENES WITH WORKERS ON MARCH

Builders' Tribute To Gallant Fight Of Spanish Workers

(From Our Special Correspondent)

SPANISH SITUATION ANALYSED

From Our Own Correspondent, FRANK PITCAIRN

Eden Tackled On Refusing Oil To Spain

FIFTEEN THOUSAND PROTEST

---

9 The *Daily Worker* was drawing attention to Fascist atrocities during the Spanish Civil War

| HOW FRENCH WAITERS WON (See Page 5) | # THE DAILY WORKER WORKERS OF ALL LANDS UNITE | JARROW MARCH: SPECIAL FEATURE (See Page 4) |

No. 2097   MONDAY, OCTOBER 5, 1936   One Penny

MOSLEY DID NOT PASS: EAST LONDON ROUTS THE FASCISTS

Barricades Raised In Stepney Streets
Police Forced To Ban March

REBEL ADVANCE STOPPED

Franco Harried On All Sides

"Daily Worker" Special Reporters

SIR OSWALD MOSLEY'S challenge to East London yesterday resulted in the most humiliating rout of the Blackshirts. The trumpeted march through Whitechapel never took place—and never looked as if it could possibly take place. Instead, the Blackshirt marchers were escorted by thousands of police from Royal Mint Street at 4 o'clock—two hours after their scheduled time of departure—away from Whitechapel, westwards, not eastwards.

'Labour Faces A New 1914' —POLLITT'S WARNING

HARRY POLLITT

---

10 And at home there were the setbacks of Mosley's British Fascists to be celebrated

| PASS THIS ON TO A FRIEND— | **Daily Worker** No. 3431 | LATE EDITION | —TEN READERS FOR EVERY COPY! |

MONDAY, SEPTEMBER 7, 1942

STALINGRAD BEATS OFF ANOTHER MASS GERMAN ASSAULT
Von Bock's South-West Drive Fails

VON BOCK'S SECOND AND GREATEST MASS ONSLAUGHT AGAINST THE HEROIC CITY OF STALINGRAD HAS BEEN SMASHED AND THE RESISTANCE OF THE DEFENDERS IS STIFFENING, ACCORDING TO A DESPATCH FROM MOSCOW LATE LAST NIGHT.

Though the situation must remain grave while 50 German divisions with thousands of tanks and planes are ceaselessly battering at the gates of the city, the drive from the south-west has failed, cables Reuter's special correspondent, that was confirmed by the Moscow communique yesterday:—

"All German attempts to break through to the city are meeting with staunch resistance from Soviet troops," it was reported. "During the past 24 hours the Germans have made four attempts to attack one fortified sector, all of which were unsuccessful."

From JOHN GIBBONS Daily Worker Special Correspondent
MOSCOW, Sunday night.

THE great Stalingrad battle rages with undiminishing intensity. With first grey streaks of dawn German Junkers and Messerschmitts come over in their hundreds trying to bomb and machine-gunning to pulverise Soviet defences.

"Yesterday's fighting was characterised by several heavy tank attacks launched simultaneously from different directions.

At one point south-west of the city, Germans made supported by a hundred tanks delivered seven successive but fruitless attacks against Soviet positions.

Two there was a period when it seemed that the enemy had been successful. That was when his battering ram of tanks made a breach in the defence and the Germans mobile units began to stream through.

Danger was averted by a shifted Red Army move. The advancing enemy infantry were attacked from either wing, while the tanks were caught in a concentrated fire from Red Army Mortars.

Many of the panzers were put out of commission, and the mobile infantry, cut off from their tank support and having lost heavily, were forced to retreat.

In the Caucasus two major battles are raging which may decide the fate of the great naval base of Novorossisk and the oil-fields of Grozny.

Novorossisk is being fought among advancing from the north-west and north-east.

While the Germans claimed yesterday that his German forces from the Crimea which landed on the Taman Peninsula north-west of Novorossisk had now mopped up the whole of the western tip of the Caucasus, the Soviet communique spoke of defensive engagements against strong enemy forces.

RIVER FORCED
Fifty-five miles from the Grozny oilfields the Germans have forced a passage of the Terek River at Mozdok, but a battle of annihilation is going on at the bridgehead.

Soviet Tank Unit Struck At Full Speed

From HAROLD KING Reuter's Special Correspondent
MOSCOW, Sunday night.

It is known to-night that one of the most tremendous tank assaults ever staged in modern warfare has been beaten at the south-western outskirts of Stalingrad by a Soviet tank unit which drove at full speed into the flank of the panzers and its empetus has been irresistible.

Now for the second time the German armoured infantry has been checked.

The climax of this second battle came after wave on wave of Luftwaffe planes had bombed the Soviet lines unmercifully for two hours. Then hundreds of tanks raced forward, vainly outnumbering the Russian force.

Wheeling suddenly and outmanoeuvring their tank force let loose with their cannon and machine guns against the oncoming motor vehicles, crushing lorry after lorry, crashing in a heap of twisted and blazing metal.

The Germans tried in turn to meet the new menace but by that time the remainder of the German motorised infantry had fled, leaving their tanks to be plastered by Soviet anti-tank guns and anti-tank rifles.

The defeat of this attack enabled Soviet troops in neighbouring sectors to recapture several strong holds.

HOLD FIRM
North-east of the city the Russians' lines are also holding firm despite repeated German attempts to drive on Stalingrad along the right bank of the Volga.

But evidently Von Bock still has enormous reserves at his disposal. German troops are still pouring in a deep echelon along many miles behind the front line, ready, levelled battalions.

Some "super" divisions have started the offensive a week ago have now been reduced to 50 or 30, but new tanks are arriving in a steady stream.

Zhukov Presses On West of Moscow

On the Moscow front General Zhukov continues to storm the German-held town of Rzhev, and it is officially announced in Moscow that several more populated places have been taken, including the Germans big losses in man power and equipment.

Harry Pollitt's Appeal

I APPEAL on behalf of the Central Committee of the Communist Party to every member and Party organisation to carry out the example in the way we all work for the success of the Daily Worker.

The Daily Worker is our fighting lead. We are all going to place we know how to use it. How to apply it to every job we can see. It is a tool that every worker, skilled and unskilled, man or woman, can use.

It can be used by every man and woman, because I feel it is the people's paper fighting in the people's war in the people's victory and a people's peace.

How to Win the War
DAILY WORKER'S POLICY

The following declaration of the aims of the Daily Worker has been adopted by the Editorial Board:

ON this historic day of re-publication the Daily Worker thanks all those in the Labour, trade union, co-operative and democratic movements whose magnificent support not only succeeded in removing the nineteen months' ban, but also very considerably strengthened the unity of the people in the fight for victory over Fascism.

The Daily Worker, which belongs to you who made its rebirth possible, solemnly pledges to repay all you have done by the service it will give in the struggle to destroy the Hitlerite enemy.

We shall speak for Britain, for a virile national unity, firmly buttressed by a united working class.

We shall speak for the millions of ordinary folk, the men and women in industry and the services, whose toil and courage and sacrifice will bring victory and the new world of security.

The people want the truth: we shall give it to them.

Increasing Output
They want the selfish exposed, the pro - Fascists hounded from office, the vested interests vanquished: we shall be fearless and without mercy in attacking those obstacles to Britain's victory.

The Daily Worker pledges itself to make its editorial concern a mighty increase in the production of all war materials essential for victory.

It will stimulate output competition between factory and factory throughout Britain's industries and fight to remove every obstacle to increased production, no matter from which quarter it arises.

The Daily Worker will support the work of the democratic Governments and uphold the principles of trade unionism.

The Second Front
The people want to know how to win the war within this fourth year: we shall tell them. This is our policy.

RATION all commodities at fixed prices within reach of the lowest paid workers. Penal servitude, instead of fines, for Black Marketeers. Abolish all inequalities in the distribution of food.

INCREASE pay for men in armed forces to 5s. a day basic rate, from which 2s. can be allotted to dependants. Proportional increases for women in the services. INCREASE allowances for serving men's wives to £2 a week, with 15s. for each child under 14 and 10s. for every child between 14 and 16 still at school.

PROMOTE men from the ranks. Remove barriers standing in the way...

| Malta Gunners Greet Us | CABLE AND WIRELESS |

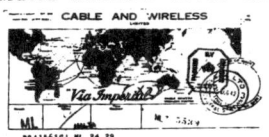

CHARLES CAYTON STREET LONDON EC2
COMRADES ON SUCCESS GREETINGS
FROM MEMBERS OF MALTA BEST WISHES FOR FUTURE
BT ... AS AGAINST FASCISM - ARUNDELL G

Drive Rommel Back From Our Minefields

ROMMEL'S Afrika Corps has now been pushed back across our minefield by the Eighth Army battlefront through which first advanced a week ago.

Two panzer divisions and other German and Italian units took part in the battle, yesterday said:—

"My impression is that the battle has started in his latest attempt to smash through to the Nile Valley. Since the Axis troops began their retreat, Allied land and air forces have hammered them ceaselessly by day and night."

Mr. Wendell Willkie, after touring the Egyptian front yesterday said:—

Mr. F. P. Roland, Reuter's Special Correspondent in Cairo, says:—
"Pursued without rest by the Eighth Army's mobile columns, Rommel is to-night back where he was taken over the Fund blow from Violet Lansbury. We are very, very sorry to say good-bye to our Violet, but her command of the Russian language has called her away for vital service elsewhere.

"The battlefield," I have seen the nazis..."

£50,000
26,354 19s. 7d. in ten days! This is the record sum into our Fighting Fund since the lifting of the ban.

A grand response—but, we need every penny. The Daily Worker has got to run for six weeks without income against an expenditure running into thousands of pounds.

On top of this we must complete the purchase of our presses which replaces our Cayton Street works destroyed by the nazis.

We need £25,000 to give the Daily Worker a firm start.

The Fund letters make wonderful reading. What enthusiasm and energy! Thanks for all the amounts, large and small. Many shop stewards are organising for collections and setting target figures. As example to follow.

All supporters of the Daily Worker know George Allison and the ban job he has done in the fight against the ban. In the Fighting Fund, Beeston House, 294, Grays Inn Road, W.C.

Hungry Blacks Out Following the Russian air-raid on Hungary, the Hungarian Minister has ordered a black-out throughout the country, says Reuter

---

11 During the war the suffering of Soviet Russia was a cause that won popular support

STEPNEY AID FOR RUSSIA COMMITTEE

STEPNEY is calling for help

To aid the people of Soviet Russia.

Every day counts and everyone must help.

Play YOUR part !

No sacrifice is too big, no contribution too small.

Enrol as helper,

You are urgently needed.

Send your contribution or collections to the Hon. Treasurer Mr. B. JANNER, B.A., 200, High Holborn, W.C.1. All enquiries at Toynbee Hall or at 12, Greatorex Street, E.1. Telephone : BiShopsgate 4417.

This Appeal is made on behalf of the War Organisation of the British Red Cross Society and the Order of St. John of Jerusalem (registered under the War Charities Act, 1940).

SUPERIOR PRINTERS, LTD. (T.U.), 13, New Road, E.1.

2. In Stepney the Jews led an Aid to Russia Committee (Lazar Zaidman collection)

Daily Worker
No. 4230 WEDNESDAY, MAY 9, 1945 4 A.M. EDITION

FINAL SURRENDER IN BERLIN
Tedder, Zhukov and Keitel Sign: Nazis Give Up in Prague

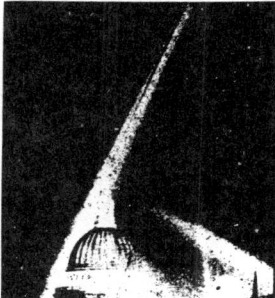

CO-OPERATE TO WIN THE PEACE
—EISENHOWER

MOSCOW RADIO THIS MORNING BROADCAST A SPECIAL ORDER OF THE DAY ANNOUNCING THAT TODAY WILL BE VICTORY DAY IN THE SOVIET UNION. THE FINAL ACT OF MILITARY CAPITULATION HAS BEEN SIGNED BY KEITEL, FRIEDEBURG, STUMPF, FOR THE GERMAN HIGH COMMAND, IN THE PRESENCE OF MARSHAL ZHUKOV AND AIR CHIEF MARSHAL TEDDER.

The surrender took place in Berlin yesterday. This is the first announcement from Moscow of Germany's unconditional surrender.

The German High Command will immediately issue orders to all their forces on sea, land and in the air to cease military operations at 11.01 p.m. Moscow time, the radio added.

The instrument of capitulation reads:—
(1) We, the undersigned, acting on behalf of the German High Command, agree to the unconditional surrender of all our armed forces, on land, sea and in the air, and also all forces which at present are under the German command and to the Supreme Command of the Red Army and simultaneously to the Supreme Command of the Allied Expeditionary Force.
(2) The German High Command will immediately issue orders to all German commanders of land, sea and air forces and to all forces under the German Command to cease

'WINNIE' SPOKE TO CHEERING THOUSANDS
Daily Worker Reporter
MR CHURCHILL appeared for the second time last night on the balcony of the Ministry of Health in a blaze of floodlights.
A crowd of over 30,000 people had gathered in victory mood to

"OUR common problems of the future can best be solved in the same conception of co-operation and devotion to the cause of human freedom so have made this Expeditionary Force such a mighty engine of righteous destruction," declared General Eisenhower last night.

In an Order of the Day to men and women of the Allied Expeditionary Force, General Eisenhower said they had taken in their stride "military tasks so difficult as to be classed by many doubters as impossible."

"You have confused, defeated and destroyed your savagely fighting foe," he declared.

"Every man, every woman, of every nation here represented has served according to his or her ability, and the efforts of each have contributed to the outcome."

ALLIED TEAM
Field-Marshal Montgomery told all ranks in the 21st Army Group: "Let us never forget what we owe to our Russian and American Allies. This great Allied team has achieved much in war; may it achieve more in peace."

CADBURY means QUALITY

WEATHER
Light, variable winds, fair, rather warm.

Daily Worker
No. 4756 FRIDAY, JULY 27, 1945 LATE EDITION

Churchill Resigns: Labour Forming Government

ATTLEE: 'BRITAIN IS FACING NEW ERA'
Big Majority Over All Other Parties: Tories Are Routed

Mr. Attlee was last night asked by the King to form a new Government after Mr. Churchill had tendered his resignation.

IN THE MOST SENSATIONAL ELECTION IN BRITAIN'S WHOLE HISTORY, THE PEOPLE HAVE SWEPT LABOUR TO GOVERNMENTAL POWER WITH A CLEAR MAJORITY OVER ALL OTHER PARTIES.

After more than five years of battle against Fascism in Europe, the British people have turned their attention to the Tories and routed them at the polls.

THE PEOPLE'S OPPORTUNITY
By Harry Pollitt

"We are facing a new era and I believe that the voting at this election has shown that the people of Britain are facing the new era with the same courage as they faced the long years of war." Mr. Attlee told a Press conference last night.

"I am confident that British democracy can make a tremendous contribution to the building of world peace and prosperity on firm foundations."

Labour, he said, went into this election on a carefully thought-out programme based on very definite principles. In foreign affairs they had a long tradition dating back for many years.

"We have never swerved," he continued, "from our position of the need for a new world order for the prevention of war. Equally we have a world economic policy which is based on an endeavour to raise the standards of life of the masses all over the world."

Victory in Figures
With only two results to come in, the state of the parties late last night was:—
Labour 389
Tory, Lib. Nat. and Nat. ... 209
Liberal 11
Communist 2
Common Wealth 1
I.L.P. and Independents ... 13
Thirteen other results will be declared in a few days' time.

Two Communists In the New House
Daily Worker Reporter
PHIL PIRATIN is going from Mile End to join William Gallacher in the next Parliament.

---

13 Joyful headlines in the *Daily Worker* in 1945 proclaimed the end of the war and the election of a Labour government

14 Phil Piratin became the Communist member of Parliament for Mile End in the 1945 general election (Lazar Zaidman collection)

What Future for the Jews of Europe?

ONE of the outstanding tragedies of the war, and for that matter of the years leading up to the war, has been the fate of the Jews in Europe.

It is estimated that nearly six million Jews have been killed, and there are now about one-and-a-half million scattered over Europe.

There are some 80,000 Jewish displaced persons in the various camps in Germany, Austria and Italy.

★

WHAT is the future of European Jewry?

Undoubtedly Nazism will have left its legacy, but in the countries of Europe, and particularly those of Central and Eastern Europe, where the greater number of Jews live, new democracies are growing up that aim at the elimination of all oppressions and persecution.

Reports of the revival of democracy in these countries, together with the economic changes that make for greater freedom and contentment, lay a firm foundation for Jewish welfare in the future.

It is vital that Jewish people, who have been fighting reaction for centuries and Fascism since its inception, should now equally devote their energies to the building of democratic anti-Fascist countries in which they have an honoured place.

Eighty thousand displaced Jews have so far not found their way back to their respective countries.

No figures have been published of the nationalities of these Jews, though it is reckoned that many are German and Austrian, some Polish and others from the Baltic and Balkan countries.

★

INSTEAD of the utmost consideration being given to their special problem and measures being taken to secure their speedy recovery and rehabilitation, the military authorities responsible (British and American) have treated them with an utter lack of sympathy and vision.

I have received reliable reports that in Germany today it is a commonplace in conversation that Hitler did one good thing for Germany in getting rid of the Jews, and no positive propaganda whatever is being done to answer this.

There are instances of German Jews being dismissed and Nazis engaged by the British Military Government.

There was even the case of a U.S. Government court intervening to reverse a decision of a local authority, which evicted an S.S. man's family from a flat to let it to a Jewish family released from a concentration camp.

Anti-Jewish demonstrations were organised by Nazis in this region following this incident.

Such actions have only emboldened the Fascists still in Germany.

★

THE Governments of the countries whence the displaced Jews come, occupied in rebuilding their new societies, have not found it possible to devote personnel and effort to winning their confidence to go back to their respective countries.

about 60,000 desire to go to Palestine.

It is not difficult to believe that a number of Jewish displaced persons, after their terrible experiences and memories, would not wish to go back to their own countries; though with the process of rehabilitation and an understanding of the new possibilities in their native lands, many of them would review their attitude.

Our ultimate aim should be to ensure the utmost support for the new democracies of Central and Eastern Europe so that the Jewish nationals of these countries can take their full share

by

PHIL PIRATIN
Communist M.P. for Mile End

in a rapidly developing free society.

The Zionists, in discarding such possibilities for the future of Jewry and focussing attention only on Palestine as the solution to the problem, are strengthening the hands of those who would stem the democratic development of these countries.

Our immediate concern should be to ensure assistance and opportunities for rehabilitation for all displaced Jews who at this stage are not physically or mentally fit to determine their future.

★

WHILE this stage of rehabilitation is proceeding, arrangements can be made for their subsequent immigration to such countries as are prepared to receive them, it being recognised that there will undoubtedly be a number of Jews who will in no circumstances return to the scenes of their former persecution.

In some cases they will prefer to go to Palestine rather than any other country, perhaps because they have relatives there, or 'perhaps because they have more confidence in their security among people of their own race.

Or they may be political Zionists who see an opportunity of realising their aspirations.

It is this section around which the most vigorous propaganda is now proceeding, relating to the whole future of Palestine and the Jews.

The Zionists, who represent the viewpoint of only a section of the Jewish people, are making the utmost use of the general sympathy for these displaced Jews in aiming to achieve the objective of a Jewish State in Palestine.

If seen, however, in the light of my earlier remarks, it is obvious that the two questions should be treated separately.

The Zionist insistence that the solution to the immediate problem of the displaced Jews can only be resolved in a solution of the whole Palestine problem may in the long run solve neither.

The question of immigration into Palestine should be settled democratically on the basis of agreement with the popu-

bound up with the whole problem of the Middle East, will have to be settled by the United Nations. To force this issue now by the one-sided demand for 100,000 certificates for the entry of Jews into Palestine is to injure the cause of assisting the displaced Jews.

★

THE solution to these problems would appear to be along these lines:—

1. Hand over the responsibility for the displaced Jews in Europe, now in the hands of the British and American military authorities, to special civilian authorities that will include representatives of Jewish organisations in Great Britain and other democratic countries.

These civilian authorities would be supplied with financial resources, possibly from Unrra, so that they could ensure the comfort and welfare of these people, while at the same time providing education, training and general rehabilitation.

If it is felt that the places where these displaced persons are at present located would not suit these purposes, the authorities should allocate other suitable accommodation.

2. British citizens who have relatives among the displaced Jews and other refugees in Europe, should be given permission to bring them into this country for a period of rehabilitation.

3. The process of rehabilitation should have as one of its objectives the education and encouragement of those Jews to return to their respective countries.

I am confident that once they realise the truth of events as they are now developing in their respective countries, many would return to their original homes.

4. After the period of rehabilitation for those still unwilling to return to their native countries, steps should be taken to ensure asylum and favourable conditions in the democratic countries.

For those who then desire to go to Palestine, every effort should be made to secure the agreement of the communities in Palestine on humanitarian grounds to accept their immigration to that country.

5. The Government should take urgent steps to bring Jews and Arabs together, if necessary consulting directly with the Jews and Arabs in Palestine, and in co-operation with the other United Nations work out the future state in which both peoples could work and thrive.

LET HIM THAT IS WITHOUT

A GREAT IRIS

HOW was it that the orange, white and green never streamed in the breeze among the battle flags of the United Nations—of that greatest brotherhood ever known of peoples,

lative wit, this volume builds up to a tremendous panorama the impressionistic stuff of history.

Here are Larkin and Connolly (the latter treated somewhat critically), the Citizen Army and

BRITISH FASCISTS STAGE A RETURN

" Star " 27-6-45

AFTER six years of war against Fascism ; after the sacrifice of 300,000 casualties ; after the murderous death of 5 million Jews in Europe, a London newspaper has to report that British Fascists are staging a return.

Is this the reward for the hardship and sacrifice that the Jewish people, alongside other British citizens, have made during these six years of war ?

Was this a war only against German Fascism, or against Fascism everywhere ?

We have no doubt about your answer.

The Fascists are preparing a comeback, hoping for the return of a Conservative majority, which, under cover of so-called free speech, would allow them, once more, to resume their monstrous activities. Divide the people in order to rule them has always been the Tory game.

In Mile End you have the opportunity, in the coming General Election, of returning Phil Piratin to Parliament—a Communist and a Jew who will fight, as he has done before, in the interests of the whole nation—Jew and Gentile alike. You can depend on him to fight against all provocation, as he has done time and again in the past, when he led the people of East London against Mosley.

PHIL PIRATIN SAYS that the answer to anti-semitism is :—

(1) To make sure that all people have a good standard of life, and thus remove the causes of the discontent upon which Fascism breeds.

(2) To introduce legislation prohibiting anti-racialism and anti-semitism.

All too soon after the war the Fascists were staging a comeback fund, to the British Battalion, and to various Aid Spain committees influenced by the CP.[26] The ULTTU took a special interest in a group of orphaned Basque children who were allowed into England in May 1937, sponsoring a concert on their behalf which was held in the union hall in Greatorex Street.[27] As late as 24 January 1939, the ULTTU participated in a rally held at Caxton Hall in a vain, last-ditch attempt to persuade the British government to reverse its policy of 'non-intervention' in the Spanish Civil War.[28]

The British Communist Party concentrated its attention on the British Battalion, supplying it with recruits and money and disseminating propaganda in England on its behalf. But in Stepney, many of the Yiddish-speakers born in Russia, Poland or Romania took a greater interest in the fate of the East European Jews who comprised the Botwin Company.

The Botwin Company, which fought as the second company of the Palafox Battalion of the XIII (Dombrowski) Brigade, was named after Naftali Botwin, a Polish Jewish Communist. When founded on 12 December 1937, with Yiddish as its official language, it had 20 men; soon this number grew to 175, most of them Polish Jews.[29] They suffered many casualties, in some of the heaviest fighting of the war, at Teruel, on the Aragon front, and elsewhere.

Stepney's Jews supported the company through the London Botwin Aid Committee, which had its headquarters, as did so many other pro-Loyalist groups, at Circle House. On 3 July 1938, at a special conference called to set up its own Aid Spain committee, the Workers' Circle noted with pride 'the fearless record of these Jewish volunteers' and assumed the patronage of the Botwinists, sending them money and cigarettes.[30] In an article published in the August issue of the *Circle-Arbeter Ring*, Alf Holland praised the mettle of these brave and disciplined soldiers, who were fighting hard against Fascism and anti-Semitism.[31]

The Circle's commitment to the Botwinists reflected a difference in ideological emphasis between Jewish and non-Jewish Communists: whereas the non-Jewish Communists tended to think of the Spanish Nationalists led by Franco and Mola as just one more movement in the aggressive international advance of Fascism, Jewish Communists were more likely to stress the implications for their own ethnic group. For example, the American Communist Gina Medem, who went to Spain as a correspondent for the New York Yiddish newspaper *Morgn Freiheit* and who frequently visited London to give first-hand accounts of the Spanish conflict to members of the Circle, described the activities of the Botwinists as 'a glorious page' in the history of the specifically Jewish labour movement.[32] As for the Botwinists themselves, although a large percentage were Communists, they fought not just as 'proletarian internationalists' but also as Jews: they were keenly aware of being in a country that had expelled their own people four centuries earlier; and unlike the many Jews who fought with other units in the International Brigades and whose primary identification was with their countries of origin, the Botwinists wished to be seen as an independent national entity. In other words, they wanted to represent the Jewish people as a whole in the battle against Fascism.[33]

The fighting came to an end for all the International Brigades in late 1938, when they were sent home by the Spanish government. Many Stepney men had fought for Spain; eight had been killed there.[34] Throughout East London, returning volunteers were welcomed with great enthusiasm. In the first week of December a 'Grand Carnival Dance' was held in honour of the returning members of NAFTA 15;[35] a few days later Dan Frankel, the MP for Mile End, conveyed the appreciation of the Labour Party to a gathering of veterans of the Spanish war.[36] In February 1939, 63 British volunteers taken prisoner in Spain were released from Franco's jails. Those from Stepney were treated as heroes in the East End,[37] where the Stepney CP sponsored a welcome-home dance.[38]

The end of the war did not mean an end to fund-raising. After Mick Mindel and Sarah Wesker had urged the ULTTU to establish a fund for those members who had returned home 'maimed and destitute' and 'without means of subsistence', a special aid committee under the chairmanship of Hymie Angel was set up for this purpose.[39] The Workers' Circle was equally zealous on behalf of the Botwinists. On 2 March 1939, the Circle's Aid Spain committee sent out a letter appealing for aid for the demobilized members of the Botwin Company and, even more important, for those of the

Botwinists still interned in the 'appalling' and 'terrible' concentration camps along the Spanish frontier.[40] Soon £60 was sent to the Botwin aid committee in Paris;[41] in all, the Aid Spain committee raised more than £600 for its Spanish relief work.[42] The Workers' Circle called a conference for 21 May to discuss the problems of the demobilized Botwinists. In the same month's issue of the *Circle-Arbeter Ring*, Alec Waterman praised the Botwinists as 'our best sons' who had demonstrated that with gun in hand Jews could stand up to Italian and German Fascists and 'fight back against all the insults and violence suffered by our people';[43] Julius Pilchik, general chairman of the central committee, asserted that it was the duty of all Circle members to help these soldiers who had 'fought our fight, in fact, the fight for all Jewish people'.[44]

The CPGB recognized full well that the issue of the Spanish Civil War could be used to attract Jews to its ranks. Jews supported the Republic; so did the CP, and occasionally the national party included items in its propaganda that would drive this point home. In 1937, for example, the *Daily Worker* gave prominence to a statement by the Spanish Ambassador to Holland, who asserted that under the Republic, Jews had 'full equality of rights'.[45]

It was the local Stepney CP, however, which did all it could to tap this source of sympathy. In January 1938, the Stepney party organized a memorial meeting at the People's Palace for those East Londoners who had fallen in Spain; the speakers were A. R. Rollin of the NUTGW and Morry Jacobs, chairman of NAFTA 15 and father of Julius Jacobs.[46] The organization of such a meeting was only one of the many ways in which the Communists sought to make themselves seem a viable political alternative; and it worked. Over 200 members of the local party, along with their friends, attended the annual supper and dance of the Stepney CP held on New Year's Eve, 1938; there they were addressed by Phil Piratin, the branch secretary; Pat Devine, the East London organizer; and D. F. Springhall, who had been secretary of the London District Committee of the party before going to Spain as a political commissar. The *East London Advertiser*, which was by no stretch of the imagination a left-wing paper, termed this function 'a great success'.[47]

Phil Piratin has since remarked that 'the greatest impact on the minds of Stepney people was caused by the events from 1936 onward';[48] Solly Kaye, the East London Communist who would later be elected a Stepney councillor, has agreed that 'Spain had a very big ideological effect' among East End Jews.[49] At the Workers' Circle convention of 1943, the Spanish Civil War was referred to as 'the first defence line of World Democracy';[50] Nathan Weiner, general secretary of the Circle, asserted that the war had been a harbinger of the larger conflict to come, a conflict in which millions of Jews were being murdered.[51]

Professor Hyman Levy, writing in 1945, recapitulated the analysis of those Jewish Communists who traced the historical antecedents of the Spanish Civil War all the way back to the expulsion of the Jews in 1492 and the subsequent exploitation of the Spanish people by its aristocracy and the Roman Catholic Church: 'The sequel to that struggle was seen nearly 340 years later in the formation of a Popular Front Government in the Spain of our own time, in the Fascist uprising under Franco with the assistance of Hitler and Mussolini and the so-called non-intervention policy of the British and French governments.'[52] Levy's last point was well taken, for the failure of the Western democracies to take a stand against Spanish fascism rankled in many quarters. In 1939, for example, Morris Myer, who was not a Communist, had blamed France and England for the defeat of the Republican forces: these governments, charged Myer, had preferred to close their eyes to Franco, Hitler's ally, rather than to assist the Soviet Union indirectly by helping the Spanish Republicans, who were allied with the USSR.[53] In June 1945, *Di Tsayt*, the daily London Yiddish newspaper which Myer edited, published an editorial opposing the British Conservative party; the paper warned that many Tories 'are at the moment supporters of Franco'.[54] On this point, *Di Tsayt* was in complete agreement with the National Jewish Committee of the CPGB, which during the elections spread the word that Churchill had 'spoken warmly in support of Franco only recently'.[55]

Candidate Piratin was able to make particularly effective use of these themes. One piece of campaign literature reminded voters that Piratin had 'Fought for Aid to Spain against the Government's

INTERNATIONAL ISSUES AND JEWISH CONCERNS

"Appeasement" policy' and 'Worked steadily for better understanding with Soviet Russia and a military agreement against Fascism that could have prevented the war'.[56] 'Fascism must be destroyed everywhere, not just in Germany,' declared Piratin;[57] and he asked voters to remember, as they chose between himself and his Conservative and Labour opponents, 'when 500 Communists lost their lives in Spain' in 'the first clash against Fascism'.[58] It was not an appeal that Stepney voters were prepared to dismiss lightly.

THE 'POLISH QUESTION' IN STEPNEY

Even before the outbreak of the Second World War, Anglo-Jewry took a deep, often personal and familial interest in the fate of European Jewry generally, and in Polish Jewry in particular. The *Jewish Chronicle* gave extensive coverage to the 'desperate plight' of the Polish Jews, reduced to 'squalid poverty and harrowing misery'.[59] Their despair was like 'some grim scene in Hades', according to the *Chronicle*: 'We, here in England, can have no conception of the depths of poverty and suffering to which our Polish brethren have sunk'.[60] Noah Barou of the Workers' Circle, writing in the *Circle-Arbeter Ring* on 'The Economic and Social Position of Polish Jewry', painted an equally stark picture, asserting that millions of Polish Jews lived 'in conditions of indescribable wretchedness and misery under the starvation line'.[61]

The Workers' Circle had a 'long and firm association with Polish Jewry';[62] Polish Jews came to lecture and to solicit funds at Circle House, and many of the Circle's activists took an interest in promoting socialist activities and welfare charities in that country.[63] Members of the Circle were prominent in the numerous committees and funds set up by East London Jews to aid Polish Jews: Barnett Weinberg, for example, was chairman of the London Committee of the Medem Sanatorium for tubercular Jewish children in Poland,[64] while B. A. Bagnari served as chairman and Sam Dreen as honorary secretary of the United Jewish Workers' Committee for the Relief of the Jewish Children in Poland. At a conference called by the Circle in January 1937, Bagnari stated that

64,000 children faced starvation; Morris Myer castigated 'our wealthy English Jews' for their 'indifference . . . towards the sufferings of Polish Jewry'.[65] The Committee pleaded with East London Jewry to give aid to 'the unfortunate and helpless Jewish children in Poland, and strengthen the hearts of the parents in the struggle for civil rights'.[66] At a follow-up meeting held a year later, Morris Myer told the delegates that 'any help given to their Polish brethren would be help given to themselves'; reference was also made to the lackadaisical attitude of the official leaders of Anglo-Jewry concerning assistance for the Polish Jews.[67] A few months later, the Committee decided to disaffiliate from one of the prime offenders in this regard, the London Federation of Jewish Relief Organizations.[68]

Meanwhile, Circle members were active in the Jewish Protest Committee, which held a conference at Adler Hall on 21 July 1937 'in connection with the terrible position of the Jews in Poland'; the Committee requested financial contributions and called for a day of mourning and protest to draw attention to 'the outrages against our brethren in Poland'.[69] As conditions in Poland deteriorated, the protest rallies grew larger; a number of mass demonstrations against the persecution of Polish Jewry were organized by the Workers' Circle. The advertisement in the *Daily Worker* for one of these, to be held on 17 February 1938 at Kingsway Hall, appeared under the caption 'Four Million Jews Threatened in Eastern Europe'.[70]

In 1939, Poland fell before Hitler's armies. Most Jews who managed to escape fled eastwards into the Soviet Union. Those who fled west went first to France and Belgium, then on to England; in March 1940, the *Jewish Chronicle* estimated that there were 5,000 'Polish citizens of the Jewish faith' in Great Britain.[71] These were exiles rather than immigrants, and their own natural pre-occupation with Polish affairs made the East End more of a 'little Poland' than ever before. They had not left all their problems behind them: the Polish government and army-in-exile, including many right-wing anti-Semites, also took refuge in Britain. These so-called 'London Poles' set up their own mini-state, complete with president, prime minister, cabinet members and ambassadors; many of their troops were billeted in camps in Scotland. The Polish National Council, which served as a government-in-exile, included two Jewish members, the Zionist Ignacy Schwartzbart and the Bundist Shmuel Zygielbojm. Although technically in England only as members of the Polish government, Zygielbojm and Schwartzbart participated fully in the political quarrels and activities of the local Jewish community; they also carried diplomatic messages back and forth between Anglo-Jewry and the Polish government.

Their efforts did not prevent the 'London Poles' from becoming, almost from the day of their arrival, a provocation to the East End Jews of Polish descent or origin, an embarrassment to the Anglo-Jewish establishment and a political boon to the Communists. By August 1940, the *Jewish Chronicle* was taking note of the anti-Semitic activities and publications of two factions on the Polish National Council with a long history of anti-Semitic agitation in Poland itself, the 'Endeks' (National Democrats) and the 'Naras' (National Radicals). The *Chronicle* was particularly angry with a newspaper, *Jestem Polakiem* [*I Am a Pole*], which was being published in London by the Endeks,[72] and Willie Gallacher, the Communist MP who represented a Scottish constituency, raised the matter in the House of Commons;[73] but the newspaper continued to appear.

By this time the Polish government-in-exile had begun its lengthy tug-of-war with the Soviets over control of the Polish territories which the Russians had captured in 1939, and which they would eventually claim as their own by virtue of ethnic and historical rights. The stage was set for a final confrontation between the 'London Poles' and the Soviets; the occasion for this came, in April 1943, with the German announcement of the discovery of the bodies of more than 20,000 Poles, including almost 5,000 senior army officers, in the Katyn forests near Smolensk. The 'London Poles' believed that the Russians had committed these murders during their occupation of eastern Poland in 1940, and diplomatic relations were broken. The Soviets set about forming the nucleus of a rival Polish regime, the Union of Polish Patriots, which would be installed in power when the Russians crossed back into Poland.

The Soviet–Polish split caused great confusion in the British Labour Party, which was reluctant to side with either party in the quarrel; the *Daily Herald* remarked that 'the only beneficiaries are our enemies'.[74] But for the CPGB, and particularly for the Jewish Communists, who drew much of their support from East European Jewish immigrants, these developments were a political windfall. Not long after the decision was made in Russia that the Polish government-in-exile was to be discredited and rendered harmless, the British Communists began to make fresh charges of anti-Semitism and other crimes against the 'London Poles'. On 3 May 1943, the *Daily Worker*, in a story on anti-Semitism in the Polish army, claimed that many Polish officers were telling their troops that 'if we are to have peace, we must exterminate all Jews [after the war]'. Another story on the same page noted that 50 Polish Jewish refugees meeting under the auspices of the Jewish Cultural Club had passed a resolution condemning the Polish government's anti-Soviet activities and calling on the two Jewish members of the Polish National Council to resign at once; yet a third article reported that the Russia Today Society, a Communist-run organization, had called a meeting to denounce the 'London Poles'.[75]

Late in December, a group of Polish Jewish soldiers stationed with the Polish forces in Scotland decided to take matters into their hands. A delegation called on A. L. Easterman at the offices of the World Jewish Congress (British Section), 'complaining bitterly of anti-Semitic agitation' in the Polish army, as Easterman explained in a letter to Selig Brodetsky of the Board of Deputies.[76] The Jewish soldiers also enlisted the support of the CP and of sympathetic MPs such as Tom Driberg, a former Communist who was at this time the Independent member for the Maldon constituency in Essex.[77] Then, in January, a group of 68 Jewish soldiers deserted from the Polish forces; they were followed in February by a second contingent of 134 men.[78] At first both the Poles and the British were willing to let them transfer to British units. But when 30 more deserted in March, it was decided that enough was enough. Polish authorities arrested this last group and set about court-martialling them.[79]

At this point Tom Driberg, the National Council for Civil Liberties and the CPGB began their campaign to have the arrested men released and admitted into the British army. Tom Driberg has recalled that 'we pressed the Government hard, in questions and debate' in the House;[80] and on 5 April, Foreign Secretary Anthony Eden assured Driberg that he would look into the matter.[81] On the next day, however, a junior minister announced that the 'deserters' were to be left to the Polish authorities.[82] The 30 men were duly tried and given prison terms varying from one to two years.[83]

A storm of protest followed. Branches 4, 9 and 10 of the Workers' Circle, asserting that 'the fears of the Jewish community for the fate of the Polish Jewish soldiers [have] proven not to have been unfounded', called upon the Board of Deputies to demand the immediate abrogation of the sentences meted out to the 'thirty Jewish heroes... our Polish Jewish brothers'.[84] In a widely circulated resolution dated 16 April, Branch 9 of the Circle expressed its concern that 'the Jewish Representatives in the Polish National Council and the leadership of the Jewish Communal bodies in this country' had not dealt earlier with the problem of anti-Semitism in the Polish forces.[85] The *Daily Worker* regaled its readers with a stream of anecdotes designed to illustrate the 'terror' felt by Jews in the Polish army; one such story asserted that some Polish officers had been seen to give the *Heil Hitler* salute.[86]

Though the leaders of Anglo-Jewry, anxious to demonstrate their patriotism, were reluctant to embarrass a British ally,[87] the Board of Deputies finally could see no alternative but to take action. Selig Brodetsky met with Polish Prime Minister Stanislaw Mikolajczyk[88] and with George Hall, the British Parliamentary Under-secretary for Foreign Affairs.[89] The World Jewish Congress also informed the Poles that it was looking into the sentences.[90] But under the terms of the Allied Forces Act passed in 1940 by the British Parliament, the Polish government had the right to operate its own armed forces on British soil, with full sovereignty and internal control; and so, on 10 May, Foreign Secretary Eden told Driberg in the House that the British could not dictate policy to the Poles.[91]

The Jews of East London responded with renewed determination. After numerous protests from Jewish workers,[92] J. L. Fine, in conjunction with the Workers' Circle, organized a meeting held on 11 May at the Shoreditch Town Hall; approximately 1,000 people attended. Tom Driberg read aloud a letter from the imprisoned Jewish soldiers: 'We appeal to you to help us. Should they force us to go back to our units there will be nothing left except for us to commit suicide. This is no empty threat. We see no other way out.'[93] Three evenings later another gathering, under the auspices of the NCCL, was held at the Stoll Theatre, Kingsway. The speakers included Driberg; three other MPs well known for their concern with Jewish affairs – Eleanor Rathbone, D. N. Pritt and G. R. Strauss; and a young left-wing journalist named Michael Foot.[94] By this time, however, the matter had been settled: on 12 May 1944, Wladyslaw Raczkiewicz, the Polish president, suddenly signed amnesty papers freeing the court-martialled soldiers.

The Communists were quick to take credit for the release of the men. The *Daily Worker* asserted that the British people had been 'shocked beyond measure' at the idea that sentences were to be imposed on the victims of anti-Semitism. Rather than being sent back to 'the anti-Semitic dunghills of the Polish Army', argued the CP, the Polish Jewish soldiers should be allowed to join either the British army or 'their own countrymen on the Eastern front, where a powerful Polish force is fighting side by side with the Red Army';[95] the CP was referring, of course, to the pro-Communist army commanded by Colonel Zygmunt Berling, which became the nucleus of the Polish Committee of National Liberation, the so-called 'Lublin Poles'. On 7 June, Branch 9 of the Workers' Circle expressed its 'whole-hearted appreciation' of the success achieved by 'the recent campaign';[96] the National Jewish Committee was equally self-satisfied, remarking that 'A whole number of Jewish organisations and large numbers of Jewish people were drawn into the first-class political activity, and the whole Jewish community was stirred and enlivened as it has seldom been moved before, striking a blow for democracy and against reaction.'[97]

Meanwhile, East London Jews took an intense interest in the fate of the Jews in the European war zone. A. M. Kaiser, secretary of the Polish Jewish Refugee Fund, described in the *Jewish Chronicle* the starvation, brutalization and mass killings befalling the Jews 'in the Hell of Nazi-Poland'.[98] Pictures of the Warsaw ghetto were published in the *Chronicle*.[99] A. R. Rollin, writing in the *Circle-Arbeter Ring*, lamented 'The tens of thousands of victims . . . of our very flesh and blood': 'Hundreds of towns and districts which are overrun and devastated by the brutal invaders are particularly near and dear to us, members of the Workers' Circle, who mostly come from these areas.'[100] The Federation of Polish Jews in Great Britain issued a report on the atrocities entitled *Stop Them Now. German Mass Murder of Jews in Poland*.[101] News of the Warsaw ghetto uprising of April 1943 both inspired the Jews of London and made them all the more fearful on behalf of the Polish Jewish community. At the eleventh convention of the Workers' Circle, held on 25–26 December, B. A. Bagnari paid tribute to the heroes of the uprising, who almost without arms had fought off the Nazis like Lions of Judah: 'They indeed held high the courage, the fortitude and the sublimeness of their race. May they, in the days to come, be an inspiration and example to us in our own struggles.'[102] On the first anniversary of the uprising, the Federation of Polish Jews in Great Britain organized a day of mourning and issued a pamphlet describing in detail the last days of the Warsaw ghetto;[103] a year later the Workers' Circle commemorated the uprising at a public meeting in the Grand Palais.[104]

A. N. Stencl's Yiddish magazine, *London–Veitchepl*, gave extensive coverage to the situation of Polish Jewry. In May 1944 it commemorated the first anniversary of the Warsaw ghetto uprising. There were two articles – one by Stencl and one by Morris Mindel – on Shmuel Zygielbojm, the Jewish member of the Polish National Council who had committed suicide in London as a means of protesting against the indifference of the Allies to the fate of the uprising. Zygielbojm's suicide note was reprinted in its entirety.[105] The February 1945 issue of *London–Veitchepl*, devoted to 'Dos Bafrayte Poyln' ['Liberated Poland'], was more optimistic. There was an article, translated from the Polish, by Wanda Wasilewska, who was a prominent member of the pro-Soviet Polish Committee of National Liberation; Stencl himself predicted a new era of harmony and cooperation between Poles and Polish Jews, both of whom had suffered at the hands of the Nazis. 'We lived on the Polish soil for a thousand years, and we helped form it, and it us!' wrote Stencl; 'The Jew was tied to the Polish earth and with the people of the Polish earth.'[106] The subsequent issue included a poem by Josef Hillel Levy, 'Zay Gebentsht Du Marshal Stalin'

['Bless You Marshal Stalin'], which thanked the Red Army for liberating Warsaw and Cracow.[107]

Yiddishists were not the only ones unable to face the full horror of the Holocaust and recognize that Jewish life in its pre-war vitality would never again exist in Poland. In a private handwritten note of 9 March 1944, Lazar Zaidman predicted that the Jewish communities of the United States, the Soviet Union, Palestine and Eastern Europe would be 'the four great bulwarks of Jewish life that will aid our people in maintaining its existence and safeguarding its future';[108] as Communists, Zaidman and his colleagues on the National Jewish Committee were particularly interested in the socialist experiment which they assumed was about to provide the remnants of Polish Jewry with a better life than they had ever known. Indeed, it seemed to the NJC that to emphasize the recreation of an East European Jewish community would be a means of 'striking a note of confidence and positive outlook' and 'fighting against the evil outlook of pessimism and despair'.[109] And so the Communists, acting in all good faith, played heavily upon such optimistic feelings as those expressed in *London–Veitchepl*. In January 1945, in an article published in *World News and Views*, Zaidman explained that the victories of the Red Army over the formerly fascist East European countries had laid the basis of a renewed Jewish life there; Jews would now be able 'to play their full part, side by side with the rest of the citizens of the countries in which they live, in rebuilding and creating better conditions of life'.[110]

At the same time, the Communists continued their attacks on the Polish government-in-exile, doing their best to connect the British Conservative Party with the 'London Poles'. In October 1944, at the seventeenth national congress of the CPGB, Harry Pollitt prepared for the imminent election – which he termed 'the most decisive election of our lifetime' – by asserting that the Tories were 'the champions of the renegade and discredited Polish Government in London in their efforts to prevent firm relations with the Soviet Union'.[111]

The Communist propaganda campaign went into higher gear following the Yalta Conference of February 1945, at which the other Allies decided to accept the 'Curzon Line' proposed by Stalin as the boundary between Poland and the USSR. In a printed letter to all members of the party dated 21 February 1945, the CPGB explained that it was essential to defend the Yalta agreements against those elements in Britain – primarily the Tories – who would do everything in their power to have the agreements reversed.[112] A Communist pamphlet published in the same month asserted that the Polish government-in-exile, which objected to the Polish boundaries established at Yalta, was 'carrying the torch for German fascism. . . . They want Soviet land, but refuse German. . . . Strange behaviour of people professing friendship for the Soviet Union and Britain!' But then, gloated the pamphlet, the Yalta agreements had also recognized the new, provisional, pro-Soviet government established in Poland. The 'London Poles', who were 'neither a legal nor a democratic Government', had 'conducted the most outrageous political, racial and religious persecution amongst their soldiers on British soil'; but the new Polish government would 'make war on that anti-semitism which was so evil a thing in pre-war Poland' by guaranteeing to the Jews complete legal, social and economic equality.[113]

Jewish Opinion, the publication of the National Jewish Committee, also participated in the February 1945 offensive. That month's issue of the magazine reprinted a Soviet article which promised that 'we shall not forget the anti-Semitic activity' of the former Polish leadership;[114] another article reported that the new government in Poland had just awarded a high decoration for 'special services in the reconstruction of the Polish State' to Dr Emil Sommerstein, a Zionist who also served as chairman of the Central Committee of Polish Jews established under the new regime.[115] In April, in an article entitled 'Polish Jewry Rebuilds', the *Jewish Clarion* assured its readers that the prospect of a bright new future was emerging from the ruins of Poland. Dr Sommerstein's committee, which had 'already achieved remarkable successes in restoring Jewish cultural institutions', was developing 'cordial relations' with 'the democratic Poles' as all worked together 'in a common effort to re-build the country'. Yiddish radio was on the air in Lublin; Jews were being provided with work. Those who despaired of the future need only look to 'the courage and determination' of Polish Jewry in order to gain inspiration.[116] The same issue of the *Clarion* included a transcript of a radio broadcast from Poland by Adolph Berman, a Poale Zionist active in the Jewish underground and in the 1943 ghetto uprisings; according to Berman, the Polish Communists had assisted the underground 'with all means at their disposal'. Berman concluded his broadcast with a tribute to the USSR and the Red Army, which had been the 'only hope of liberation' for Jews in occupied Poland.[117]

In May, it was the turn of the *Jewish Forum* to announce that in Poland and the other 'new democracies' of Eastern Europe, 'The Jewish inhabitants and communities are again playing their part in the progressive developments'. War criminals in Poland were being executed; Jewish communal bodies, synagogues and schools were being restored; and individual Jews were being employed as state officials and bureaucrats. 'We are confident,' hinted the *Forum* somewhat broadly, 'that the Jewish electors in Great Britain will use their vote in the coming general election to make sure that a government is elected which can be relied on to give every assistance and encouragement to this development in Europe.'[118]

The Jewish Communists were already doing their best to ensure this. In February 1945, for example, the National Jewish Committee had encouraged the Jewish Cultural Club in its plans to sponsor a meeting that would welcome the establishment of the new Polish government and raise funds for clothing to be sent to the Jews of Poland; the NJC remarked that activities such as these would generate positive political results.[119] On 26 April, at a meeting of the London Jewish Committee of the NJC, it was agreed that 'unless the comrades assisted in such campaigns as "clothing for liberated Jewry" etc., Jewish people would not be convinced of the sincerity of the party, and that would have an effect at the elections'.[120] The horror of what had transpired in Poland was also kept fresh in people's minds: *The Yellow Star*, a play about the Holocaust written by Ted Willis, then active in the Young Communist League, was produced by the Unity Theatre in April and May 1945. It was widely publicized by the NJC, Branch 9 of the Workers' Circle and the London District Committee of the CP,[121] and was well attended

INTERNATIONAL ISSUES AND JEWISH CONCERNS

by East London Jews.[122] A few weeks later Willis shared an election platform with Phil Piratin in Mile End.[123]

The linchpin of the CP's election strategy, however, was to attack the inadequacies of Tory foreign policy regarding Poland. During the war, according to one Communist publication in June 1945, these policies had 'brought Britain to the brink of disaster'; now, with the war ended, the Tories were among those 'trying to restore the rule of reactionary feudal elements in countries of Eastern Europe which have been liberated from the Nazis'.[124] The *Jewish Forum* charged the members of Churchill's caretaker cabinet with supporting the claims of the Polish government-in-exile;[125] the *Daily Worker* did its part by asserting that the Tories were plotting to keep the 'London Poles' a going concern.[126]

In Mile End, Phil Piratin, the Communist candidate, accused the Conservatives of allowing 'the Polish emigrés to spend endless sums of British taxpayers' money on poisonous anti-Semitic literature'.[127] As was true in the case of so many other Jewish concerns, the struggle between the Soviets and the West had assumed great importance in the East End of London: the 'Polish Question', as it related to the Jews, was being played out in microcosm within the confines of Stepney.

THE FUTURE OF PALESTINE

Most Zionists had shown themselves ready to support the Soviet Union during the war; the converse, too, was true. Jewish Communists grew more sympathetic towards the Zionist project in the Palestine Mandate, and more insistent that Britain live up to its commitments as outlined in the Balfour Declaration and elsewhere. They came to oppose the British government's policy, set out in the White Paper of May 1939, of severely limiting Jewish immigration to Palestine and thus making very unlikely the future creation of a Jewish state. Hence the growing strength of Zionism among Anglo-Jewry, especially after the Zionist 'capture' of the Board of Deputies in May 1943,[128] did not necessarily diminish support for the Jewish Communists.

Much of the pre-war propaganda concerning the creation of a Jewish republic in Birobidzhan had echoed Zionist themes, but the CP remained steadfastly anti-Zionist.[129] 'Who are the real friends of the Jews,' asked the *Daily Worker* in 1936, 'the Zionists or the Communists, who fight race oppression everywhere?'[130] *Discussion*, the CP's 'Journal for Political Controversy', provided a forum for an ongoing debate between Communists, both Jewish and non-Jewish, and socialist-Zionists, regarding the relative merits of Birobidzhan and Palestine as potential Jewish national homelands. While the Jewish Communists occasionally had to 'correct some errors' by extremely anti-Zionist contributors like Reginald Bridgeman, secretary of the League Against Imperialism, and Sylvia Townsend Warner, the novelist, their main thrust was to demonstrate that Zionism 'as a whole is a pillar of imperialist domination'.[131] As Chimen Abramsky has stated, 'the British Communist Party was deeply involved [in] conducting a campaign against Zionism and immigration to Palestine'.[132]

After 1941, however, Jewish Communists came increasingly to view the growth of the Jewish *Yishuv* in Palestine as a positive development in its own right, especially since Palestinian Jewry – unlike its Arab counterpart – was overwhelmingly supportive of the Allied war effort, hence also receptive to pro-Soviet entreaties. The Palestine Communist Party split into Arab and Jewish wings in 1943; the latter, which became almost indistinguishable from left-wing Zionist parties, criticized the Arab Communists for their opposition to Jewish immigration and also accused them of condoning the pro-Fascist political inclinations of many Arab leaders, including Haj Amin el-Husseini, the Mufti of Jerusalem. The Soviets were placed in the position of supporting the Jewish Communists in Palestine, a position that could not be overlooked by the National Jewish Committee or by the Jewish Communists in the East End. When Soviet Ambassador Maisky's tour of duty in Britain came to a close in autumn 1943, he visited Palestine, touring Jewish *kibbutzim* and speaking with Zionist leaders such as David Ben-Gurion. Maisky apparently discussed 'the possibilities of a solution to the Jewish problem'[133] and 'showed much interest in the absorptive capacity of Palestine for new immigrants', leading

Joseph Leftwich, for one, to assume that the Ambassador would support increased Jewish immigration after the war.[134] Maisky continued on to Moscow, where he took up the post of deputy commissar of foreign affairs, and delivered a comprehensive report on Palestinian Jewry to his superiors; he pronounced himself 'impressed with their achievements and potentialities'.[135] By September 1944 a leading article in the *Jewish Chronicle* confidently asserted that 'Russia today has no desire to embarrass or interfere with the Jewish National Movement in Palestine';[136] in February 1945 the newspaper wondered whether the Soviets were on the verge of recognizing the legitimacy of Zionism.[137]

Chimen Abramsky has stated that during the latter part of the war the question of Palestine 'became a burning issue' for the NJC, which 'was involved in international negotiations' and 'formulated a lot of CPSU [Soviet Communist Party] policy on Palestine, as [the Soviets] themselves didn't know too much about it. [R. Palme] Dutt was mainly responsible for this'.[138] Lazar Zaidman reported to an Australian Jewish colleague that any NJC statement of policy on Palestine would become the basis of 'a programme of action. . . . It should be realised that London is the place where all of the various interests and views with regard to Palestine (and the Middle East) meet and are decided upon.'[139]

At its very first meeting on 9 April 1943, the NJC agreed that 'a re-evaluation of the whole question of Zionism and Palestine' was in order. Were the half-million Palestinian Jews a nation, in the Marxist sense? To what degree were their claims compatible with the interests of the Arabs?[140] Discussions continued throughout the year, and by 9 December Peter Valentine had prepared a draft document which stated that Jewish Communists had been countering Zionism in a 'negative and unsympathetic way'; the document suggested that it might prove beneficial 'to examine anew our estimation of the problem of Palestine and of related questions . . . in light of the need for greatest unity in the fight against fascism. . . .'[141]

This softer line began to take shape in 1944. Writing on 'The Middle East' in the January issue of R. Palme Dutt's journal, *Labour Monthly*, Issie Panner began to hope for a 'common ground' between 'responsible' Arab and Zionist leaders; this might result in Palestinian Jewry playing 'a vitally important part in Arab progressive advance and development'.[142] The 'Statement on the Jewish Question' drafted by the NJC later that year pointed out that the *Yishuv* was now an established community 'playing a progressive role in the economic and social development of Palestine and the Middle East'; it was also taking part 'in a most positive fashion' in the struggle against Fascism and giving 'powerful expression' to its solidarity with the Soviet Union. Pro-Soviet movements such as the left-Zionist *Hashomer Hatzair* were especially worthy of support.[143]

Sympathy for Zionism was endemic by late 1944 not only in the Jewish community but also among many on the left of the political spectrum. On 5 November the Board of Deputies issued a statement not only condemning the 1939 White Paper but also stressing that Palestine should in due course become a Jewish state.[144] One month later, the Labour Party's annual conference called for unlimited Jewish immigration to Palestine and even suggested that Arabs be encouraged to move out of the country.[145] This was the climate in which the NJC on 13–14 January 1945 convened a meeting of Jewish Communists from communities throughout Britain to discuss the final draft of their policy statement, which would include the Communist position on Palestine. As good Marxist-Leninists, the participants agreed on the 'reactionary character' of Zionist ideology; but a 'sympathetic understanding' of the problems that faced Palestinian Jewry was clearly required.[146] As the NJC pointed out in an information document dated 16 March 1945, the leadership of the Arab community in Palestine, unlike in other colonial countries, 'has remained in the hands of the reactionary Arabs. The progressive forces have not yet managed to come to the fore and wrest the leadership'. Their 'uncompromising attitude' towards the 500,000 Jews in Palestine had led them to consider Palestinian Jewry, rather than Hitler's Germany, as 'the main enemy of the Arab world'. Britain and the United States, more concerned with their oil interests in the Middle East than with the fate of Jews, were supporting these reactionary forces, so it was not surprising that Jews felt insecure and that 'some feel a longing for some sort of National Home'.

The NJC went on to note the favourable attitudes towards the *Yishuv* shown by Jewish Communists in France, South Africa, the United States and, most importantly, the USSR: Shakhno Epstein, secretary of the JAFC, had announced 'the Jews in Palestine have a right to *self-government*', while the New York Communist daily *Morgn Freiheit* was campaigning for renewed Jewish immigration to Palestine. Recognizing the 'positive role' of Palestinian Jewry as 'the most progressive force in the Middle East', the NJC recommended that Palestine be opened to Jewish immigration and that the 1939 White Paper be denounced 'by all sections of Jewry as a wrong policy'.[147] A statement produced one month later declared that 'Jews – everywhere – may aspire to Palestine as a homeland'; immigration was 'a Jewish right'. The time had come for the Jews in Palestine, as a firmly established community entitled to self-rule, to 'restore many of the glories of which the Jewish people are only aware from their Bible stories'.[148]

Even the Board of Deputies was now seen in a more positive light. Harry Ibbetson told an NJC meeting in April that the Board, no longer controlled by the grandees of the community, was more representative of Anglo-Jewry than ever before. Though under Zionist control, it was 'definitely progressive' and 'inclined to support Labour policies'; 'our comrades were able to unite with them on some issues affecting the welfare of the Jewish Population,' he announced. It was agreed that Jewish Communists should be prepared 'to unite' with the Zionists 'in the interests of Jewry. People like Brodetsky should not be attacked for their Zionist ideas, but rather supported on his more positive and progressive points of view.'[149]

The CPGB itself was more careful in its approach to Arab–Jewish relations in Palestine. On the same day that the NJC met, Dutt's IAC released its own information document on Palestine. Dutt called the leadership of both the Arab and Jewish Communist groups 'immature and sectarian', with 'no common policy on the national question and the question of the Jewish Home'. He refused to abandon the idea of a democratic bi-national state and suggested that the CP 'use our influence to bring progressive sections of the two communities . . . together' and help them see 'the need for concessions and compromise on both sides'.[150]

Communist propaganda aimed at Jews in the 1945 election tended to elide Dutt's reservations regarding a Jewish state in Palestine. A statement released by the NJC called for 'revision of the Palestine White Paper of 1939';[151] campaign workers were told to emphasize the following:

> The C.P. sees Palestine as playing a progressive role in the Middle East — development of collective farms, Co-ops, Trade Union movement and so on. It recognises the existence and rights of 500,000 Jews there, and the fine effort they have made in the fight against fascism.
> It also recognises the aspirations of many Jews to go to Palestine, especially from Europe, where some, who have survived, desire to go to Palestine, away from the memories of the horrors of German occupation.
> It supports the rights of the Jews in Palestine to develop their economy and culture.
> Therefore the C.P. opposes the Government White Paper which restricts immigration and prevents Jews in Palestine acquiring land.
> At the same time, in common with many Zionists, it does not see Zionism as being THE solution to the Jewish problem.[152]

Branch 9 of the Workers' Circle allowed Phil Piratin to express his views on Conservative foreign policy in their periodical, the *Jewish Forum*; he observed that in Palestine 'they play off Jews against Arabs according to what suits them at a given time'.[153] In his 'Appeal to the Jewish Electors' of Mile End, he attacked the Tories as the party most opposed to Jewish aspirations in Palestine; the Palestinian Jews, he declared, 'are entitled to demand the fullest support in their efforts to rebuild the Jewish national Home. . . .'[154] Another election pamphlet described him as 'a Communist and a Jew' who would fight to open Palestine to Jews.[155]

By 1945, many Jews were thoroughly upset by British policy on the Palestine Mandate and hence antagonistic to the Churchill coalition government. The Soviet Union, on the other hand, seemed favourably disposed towards the socialist-Zionist project in Palestine and to Jewish national aspirations in general. Many of the Jews voting for Piratin were thus as sympathetic to Zionism as to the Jewish Communist agenda; these feelings were not considered contradictory in 1945 but rather were regarded as complementary expressions of Jewish identity.

7
The Communist Electoral Victories of 1945

BUILDING THE POLITICAL BASE, 1935–45

East London Jews in the period 1935–45 were very much a self-contained group within British society. They had their own Yiddish newspapers, theatre and other cultural forums. Their local trade unions, including the ULTTU and the East London branches of the NUTGW and NAFTA, were largely distinct from those of the non-Jewish working class. The Workers' Circle was typical of their social and political organizations: despite its name, this was a group of largely Yiddish-speaking Jews, for the most part foreign-born, who had significant vestigial ties with Poland.

Relations between the East London community and the more established sectors of Anglo-Jewry were distant and mutually wary. On the other hand, the East London Jews were highly receptive to the ideological, political and emotional currents circulating in the larger world of East European Jewry, from Russia to New York. In the Workers' Circle and elsewhere, Communism, Bundism, Zionism and other international ideologies gained adherents and were the subject of debate. The East London Jews had produced a political culture that was peripheral to the concerns of the larger British polity.

Locally, tension between this Jewish community and their Irish neighbours had resulted in the increasing fragility of consociationalism and of the brokerage politics practised in Stepney by the Labour Party. The Jews and the Irish were in conflict over the domestic growth of Fascism; they differed concerning related international matters such as the Spanish Civil War. Some sections

THE COMMUNIST ELECTORAL VICTORIES OF 1945

of the Catholic press engaged in anti-Semitic attacks and slurs. In 1937, the Irish faction succeeded in suspending a number of Jewish councillors from the Labour caucus of the Stepney Council. By this time, polarization was evident in each camp; moderates were being derided and bypassed. Some groups of Jews and Irish attempted to overthrow the larger East London political system via ideological mobilization into integrative 'flanking' parties such as the British Union of Fascists and the Communist Party.

As we have seen, much of the Stepney CP was itself but one section of a larger and indeed international Jewish Communist movement which did not have an official 'address' in Britain until the creation in April 1943 of the National Jewish Committee of the CP, a sub-committee of the International Affairs Committee. From the mid-1930s, however, East End Jewish Communists were active in various groups such as the local trade union branches, the Workers' Circle and, of course, the Stepney CP itself. The front groups which they controlled produced an unending stream of pamphlets and broadsheets. They also controlled a number of periodicals, including *Jewish Opinion*, the *Jewish Clarion* and the *Jewish Forum* which was produced by the Communist-dominated Branch 9 of the Workers' Circle. They published extensively in other journals of left-wing Jewish thought such as the *Circle-Arbeter Ring* and A. N. Stencl's Yiddish magazine *London–Veitchepl* [*London–Whitechapel*], as well as in the regular Communist press, which included R. Palme Dutt's *Labour Monthly* and the *International Press Correspondence* (later the *World News and Views*). Occasionally they appeared in the regular Jewish press, such as the English-language *Jewish Chronicle* and the Yiddish *Di Tsayt*. Thus, they were able to disseminate and propagate a comprehensive world-view within the Jewish community.

Through various overlapping groups, including some that were ostensibly non-Jewish, the East London Communists addressed local economic problems such as poverty, unemployment, overcrowded housing, and inadequate health care; they were active in the agitation for better ARP. Jewish Communists naturally placed greater emphasis on anti-Semitism than did their non-Jewish comrades. They held public meetings to promote the CPGB line on anti-Semitism; they called for a Jewish Charter of Freedom and for laws which would make anti-Semitism a criminal offence. The circle of theoreticians who were to comprise the National Jewish Committee were involved in the publication of numerous pamphlets and essays on the subject, including Issie Panner's *Anti-Semitism and the Jewish Question* (1942). From 1941 onwards they took a hard line on Nazi Germany, demanding the immediate opening of a second front in Europe and war crimes trials for Nazi leaders after the cessation of hostilities. Jewish Communists took the lead in combatting local Fascism and other manifestations of anti-Jewish feeling in Britain. They spoke out vociferously against the charges of black marketeering made against the Jewish community during the war; they protested against the round-up of aliens in 1940. The Stepney Tenants' Defence League and the Jewish People's Council Against Fascism and Anti-Semitism, among others, led the campaign against Oswald Mosley. Jewish Communists within the Workers' Circle, the National Council for Civil Liberties, the Jewish Cultural Club and the Russia Today Society exposed anti-Semitism in the armed forces of the 'London Poles' stationed in Britain.

Jewish Communist ideology was also characterized by a marked pro-Soviet orientation, based in large part on the belief that in Marxist terms, the USSR had solved the 'national question'. It was assumed that Soviet Jews, no longer an oppressed people, had taken their rightful place side by side with the other Soviet peoples as a free and equal nationality. Jewish Communists pointed to the ostensible prohibition against anti-Semitism in the Soviet Constitution and to the creation in Birobidzhan of a Jewish Autonomous Region destined to become a fully fledged republic. During the war, as the USSR came to be seen as the main bulwark against Nazi Germany, pro-Soviet enthusiasm knew no bounds. Jewish Communists were involved with larger organizations such as the Russia Today Society; they created their own specifically Jewish groups such as the ICOS, which was involved in publicizing the Birobidzhan experiment. The Jewish Fund for Soviet Russia, one of the most important front groups, took part in liaison work with the Jewish Anti-Fascist Committee in Moscow; the high point of its activities

THE COMMUNIST ELECTORAL VICTORIES OF 1945

came when it sponsored the 1943 visit to England of Itzik Feffer and Shloime Mikhoels. In Stepney itself, the Aid to Russia Committee was another major conduit of pro-Soviet sentiment. By the end of the war, the, large segments of the Anglo-Jewish world were favourably inclined towards Russia; this was especially true of the Yiddishist intelligentsia and other East London working-class Jewish socialists.

As left-wing nationalists, the Jewish Communists concerned themselves ideologically with the struggle of the 'Jewish masses' against Fascism and towards the creation of socialism wherever it might take place. Because they viewed the Spanish Civil War as a Jewish concern they were deeply involved through the Workers' Circle, the trade union branches and many other organizations in providing financial and other assistance to the Spanish Loyalists and to the Jewish fighters who went to their aid. After the war, Jewish Communists were deeply concerned with the fate of the Holocaust survivors in the new 'people's democracies' which sprang up in the wake of the Soviet advance across Europe in 1943. They took a particular interest in the welfare of surviving Jews in what was now to be a socialist, hence no longer anti-Semitic, Poland; the Jewish Cultural Club and the Workers' Circle engaged in relief work among the remnants of Polish Jewry. As the Second World War came to an end and the horrors of the Holocaust were fully revealed, the Jewish Communist theoreticians on the NJC effectively abandoned classical Marxist theory opposing Zionism and grew increasingly sympathetic towards Jewish political aspirations in Palestine.

These were issues of vital concern to the Stepney Jewish community; and each would play a part in the electoral prominence of the Stepney CP in the July 1945 general election in Mile End and in the borough elections that autumn. The Jewish Communist movement had managed to mobilize so wide a section of the population that Piratin would draw support not only from many of the leaders and members of Jewish working class organizations but even from an influential group of Jewish businessmen working on his behalf. His victory was the culmination of a decade of activity and mobilization.

THE DEMOGRAPHY OF STEPNEY

The British Census does not ask the religious affiliation of respondents, so it is difficult to estimate the number of Jews living in Stepney in 1935–45. George Lansbury, writing in 1936, believed that Jews constituted a majority in the East End, though other estimates were lower.[1] The widespread devastation during 1940–45 caused a severe reduction in population, but this seems to have affected Jews and non-Jews equally. In 1945, the National Jewish Committee of the CPGB listed Stepney as one of the areas of Britain 'where there are large concentrations of Jewish people and where the Jewish vote is of no little importance'.[2] Such research as has been done indicates that in 1945 there were probably some 25,000–30,000 Jews left in the borough; thus, they still constituted slightly less than half of the population of Stepney.[3]

Of the three electoral divisions within Stepney, the Jewish Communists were most interested in Mile End, an unusually small constituency which in 1945 had fewer than a third of the number of voters in an average constituency. As was true in all parts of Stepney, at least half of the population of Mile End was away in war industries or had been bombed out; thus the pre-war electorate, which amounted to 36,294 voters in 1935, had been reduced to 16,177.[4] Mile End included such densely Jewish neighbourhoods as Stepney Green, Jamaica Street, Philpot Street and New Road, not to mention such tenements as Hughes Mansions and Brady Street Mansions; and my own examination of the electoral register compiled for the constituency in 1945 suggests that Jews constituted between 40 per cent and 50 per cent of the electorate.[5] Those residents of Mile End who were not Jewish tended, in Tom Rampling's words, to be 'ordinary English' rather than Irish and Catholic.[6] As far as the Communists were concerned, it was an auspicious mix: both Rampling and Piratin have since remarked that it would have been more difficult to win votes either in Whitechapel-St George's, which was more evenly split between the Jews and the Irish, or in Limehouse, which had a high percentage of Catholic voters.[7]

132

IDEOLOGICAL HEGEMONY IN A CONSTITUENCY

With the exception of the two-year period of the Hitler–Stalin pact, support for the CPGB and its programme increased steadily during the war years. The Communists were aware of the demand for reform that emerged during this period and which was also to benefit the Labour Party. This was particularly true in East London, where CP membership increased from 807 in late 1941 to 2,450 in January 1943.[8] According to Douglas Hyde, then the news editor and chief anti-Fascist correspondent of the *Daily Worker*, the Stepney CP had over 1,000 members by November 1943[9] – double its pre-war strength. By the spring of 1945, the Communists were ready to translate their popularity into electoral successes; as the *East London Advertiser* remarked, they had been 'almost as active in these last years as in the peace'.[10]

The Communists were not, however, so intent on the advancement of their own party as to put it ahead of their goal of unity for the entire progressive movement, and for years they attempted to persuade the Labour Party to agree to some kind of alliance with them. In 1943, the Communists asked to become an affiliate of the Labour Party; but this proposal was rejected by a vote of 1,951,000 to 712,000 at the Labour Party conference of June 1943.[11] The CP continued to urge unity: in September 1944, for example, Harry Pollitt noted that Britain was the only country in Europe without an understanding between Communists and Socialists;[12] one month later, at the seventeenth Party Congress, Pollitt asserted that Labour need not fear a strong CP, for the stronger the Communists, the stronger the entire movement.[13] The Congress accordingly passed a resolution calling for the establishment of unity within the Labour movement, the strengthening of the CP and the co-operation of all Labour and progressive organizations.[14]

Given the failure of their attempts to affiliate with the Labour Party, however, the Communists were by this time making plans to put forward their own list of candidates in the forthcoming parliamentary elections. At first they intended to propose as many as 52 candidates, but by February 1945 they had decided to 'intensify our campaign for electoral unity'[15] by standing only in those areas where there was little or no danger that a split vote would result in the return of a 'reactionary';[16] as Julius Jacobs, who had been elected secretary of the London Trades Council, explained at a May Day 1945 rally, 'The issue closest to the heart of the people of London is unity in the fight against the Tories'.[17] Eventually it was decided that in order to build the widest possible progressive front, the CP would propose only 21 candidates; 13 of the seats to be contested by the Communists were occupied by Conservatives.[18]

Meanwhile, in November 1944, the London Committee of the NJC was preparing for a campaign in Mile End; if a Communist MP were to be elected there, it was said, he 'would be a voice in the lining up of the progressive forces and Jews'.[19] Already Bertha Sokoloff, the secretary of the Stepney CP, had attempted to persuade leaders of the local trade unions and of the Stepney Labour Party to consider the possibility of formulating a common electoral platform, and perhaps even proposing a common candidate in the forthcoming election; cooperation of this sort, explained Sokoloff in the *East London Advertiser*, would have a 'powerful effect' in ensuring the success of progressive policies.[20]

Labour, however, preferred to go its own way, renominating Dan Frankel to represent Mile End. It was not the wisest possible choice. As the incumbent during a period when the demand for reform was widespread, Frankel was handicapped by the fact that many voters viewed him as a representative of the corruption which was generally presumed to be characteristic of the Stepney Labour Party 'fixers' and 'bosses': the party's image had suffered a further setback when Councillor M. H. Davis was caught on a train with an out-of-date ticket, tried unsuccessfully to bribe his way out of the situation, and was sentenced to six months in prison as a result.[21] So the Labour Party was not, as Bertha Sokoloff has since recalled, 'in good odour'. Nor did Frankel enjoy a high level of personal popularity, for he 'had not been very visible to the local people'[22] during the years when they were grappling with such problems as Fascist threats, poor housing and inadequate air raid protection. The local Labour Party may have assumed that even Frankel would stand successfully against the Tory candidate,

Squadron Leader Vernon Motion, an engineer and stockbroker whose family had business interests in Mile End.[23] But the race developed into a straight battle between Labour and the CP when in December 1944 it was announced that Phil Piratin would also contest the seat.[24] Soon the London District Committee of the CP was circulating campaign literature which emphasized Piratin's high level of popularity and his effectiveness as a borough councillor. 'The market porters, clothing workers and small shopkeepers of Spitalfields knew they had picked a winner when they voted burly irrepressible Phil to the Stepney Borough Council', where he won respect and was followed with 'growing pride' as he fought slum landlords and Fascists, making Stepney 'a by-word for courage and advanced views'.[25]

Other campaign literature directly tackled the question of whether the Communists were actually hurting the progressive cause by proposing their own candidate in an electoral division which already belonged to Labour. One pamphlet, entitled 'Is the Communist Party Splitting the Working-Class Vote?', explained that the blame should be assigned to the Labour Party, which had refused to work together with the Communists. In Whitechapel-St George's and Limehouse, the two other electoral constituencies of Stepney, the Communists were supporting Labour candidates W. J. Edwards and Clement Attlee; why had it proved impossible for Labour to cooperate with the Communists in Mile End, where a common candidate might have been nominated?[26] Another appeal, addressed 'To the Labour Man and Woman', insisted that the Communists, by means of their membership in trade unions and other working-class organizations, were themselves 'members of the Labour Party'; yet they were excluded from that party's political hierarchy. A vote for Piratin, who was described as 'a great fighter for unity', would help to eliminate this 'old-fashioned ban', a relic of pre-war squabbling. After all, 'everyone – including prominent leaders of the Labour Movement – agrees that Piratin is the better representative of Labour in Mile End'.[27] Piratin himself was arguing that 'In Mile End . . . you have the choice of voting for the man you think will best represent Labour and the people as a whole. Communists are part annd parcel of the Labour Movement.'[28]

To the many Jews of Stepney who perceived the Communist Party within the context of international politics, thinking of it not as a fringe movement but as a participant in the world-wide alliance of workers' parties led by the USSR, these arguments seemed reasonable enough; and as I. A. Lisky has recalled, the Jewish Communists had 'big influence among their friends, in the Workers' Circle, and the Jewish unions'.[29] As early as June 1944, Branch 9 of the Workers' Circle had decided to contribute to the CP's election fund;[30] in March 1945, the Circle called on all its members to strive towards working-class unity so that 'the Socialist idea' might become 'more and more a practical reality in the near future'.[31] An election pamphlet prepared by the Circle called not only for the defeat of the Tories and the return of a Labour government but also for the election of 'those candidates fighting for a progressive Britain'.[32]

As for the Communist-dominated local branches of unions such as NAFTA and the NUTGW, Chimen Abramsky has recalled that the National Jewish Committee could mobilize these 'mighty battalions . . . at a glance',[33] even when the national unions were already committed to Labour. The Mantle & Costume branch of the NUTGW, for example, was controlled by Communist officials such as Mick Mindel and Hymie Kanter, who also occupied other positions: Kanter was a member of the national executive board of the NUTGW, while Mindel was chairman of the Stepney Trades Council. Some time in the spring of 1945, both men signed a declaration of the STC which not only endorsed Piratin, but also made clear the Council's disenchantment with the Labour candidate: 'At no time has the Stepney Trades Council, which has affiliated to it the most important of the Trade Unions of Stepney, given its support to Mr Frankel.'[34] It was an act of insubordination which the national union could hardly overlook; and on 6 June, Andrew Conley, general secretary of the NUTGW, wrote to J. L. Fine, the secretary of the branch, to point out that the NUTGW had pledged its support to Labour candidates, including Frankel. When Fine produced Conley's letter at a meeting of the branch committee held on 12 June, he also reported that Frankel's campaign agent had asked him to chair a public meeting at which Ernest

THE COMMUNIST ELECTORAL VICTORIES OF 1945

Bevin would be speaking on Frankel's behalf. After much discussion it was decided that if Communists such as Mindel and Kanter were to be prevented from supporting Piratin in their capacity as trade union leaders, then Fine – a member of the Labour Party – could chair Frankel's meeting only as a private individual.[35] Mindel, however, continued to chair meetings for Piratin in his capacity as chairman of the STC.[36]

So widespread was Jewish sympathy for the CP[37] that Piratin was even able to gather support from a group of wealthy Jewish businessmen organized in Stepney under the party's tutelage. Although this group seems to have left no written record of its activities, it is well remembered by various Communists active during and immediately after the war. Morry Lebow believed that the group had its origins in the period when the CP seemed to be the only party willing to fight Mosley's Fascists;[38] Tom Rampling agreed that the Jewish businessmen 'were with us largely, I suppose, on the basis of the struggle against fascism and anti-Semitism'.[39] J. W. Bentley, chairman of the Jewish People's Council during the 1930s, has recalled that the group was formed during the war by wealthy Jews whose 'ideas were very left' and who were 'very much concerned and disturbed by the events on the Continent';[40] Bill Carver remembered 'even the garment manufacturers . . . coming around and getting all emotional, all sentimental about the Soviet Union'.[41] According to Piratin, the group included small businessmen, master tailors, and even factory owners who lived in Stepney in rooms above their businesses: 'They would also have had parents, perhaps, who had been in socialist organizations in Russia and Poland.' One of the individuals remembered by Piratin was Issie Pushkin, who despite his business success remained active also in the Workers' Circle, becoming that group's general secretary in 1947.[42] Another wealthy member, recalled by Mick Mindel, was Harry Ibbetson.[43] The chief organizers of the businessmen's group seem to have been Jack Perry, who was in the clothing trade;[44] and Maurice Essex, a wealthy shop proprietor who became a party member after working on the Jewish People's Council. Both were members of the NJC.[45] It is unlikely that men such as these would have been allowed to become involved in Communist activities in earlier years. But during the war, when 'unity' seemed more important than ideological hairsplitting, they were welcome recruits; and in November 1944, the London section of the NJC sent Essex and Perry into Stepney 'for the purpose of rallying the Party there to Jewish work'.[46] Their actual mission, of course, was to raise money and prepare in other ways for the 1945 elections.

THE 1945 GENERAL ELECTION CAMPAIGN IN MILE END

The CPGB, and especially the London District party, poured massive amounts of energy and resources into the Mile End campaign. At an East London Area Conference held at Holborn Hall on 15 April 1945 it was announced that Communist supporters and volunteers were to be transferred from Whitechapel to work in the Mile End constituency; Bertha Sokoloff, the secretary of the Stepney CP, explained to the assembled delegates that 'our aim by the end of June is to have 7,500 listed supporters, because if we mean business and are going to win the election, this is the minimum of what we can do'.[47]

Soon the CP election machine was in top gear. Maurice Essex became campaign manager, with Bill Carver as Piratin's election agent; in June, the *East London Advertiser* added to the campaign's credibility by noting that Carver had been connected with 'the Labour movement in the Borough for over twenty years'.[48] In addition to the main CP committee room in Whitechapel Road, there were seven back-street committee rooms.[49]

Those involved in the campaign invariably recall how tightly organized it was. Bill Carver has called attention to 'the number of canvasses we did – every house was seen not once, but two or three times';[50] Alf Holland has remarked that the Tory and Labour candidates, in contrast, 'didn't do door-to-door canvassing; they relied on their national repute'.[51] As late as mid-June, Piratin was still enlisting volunteers: in a letter sent to selected London area Communists, he explained that because his election would raise the standing of the CP throughout London, 'there is . . . no more important work to do during this election than working in Mile End

138

(as your most convenient constituency) for my return'. Piratin invited his fellow party members to a special meeting where they would be assigned specific tasks.[52]

It was not forgotten that Jewish voters were the key to electoral success or failure. The Communist Party in general and Piratin in particular were associated with the struggle against Fascism: Hymie Fagan, then the national election agent of the CP, has recalled that Jews were keenly aware of Piratin's 'tremendous fight in the East End' against the forces led by Oswald Mosley;[53] Mick Mindel has remarked that Piratin, as the Communist candidate, benefited also from the intensely pro-Soviet feeling within the Jewish community.[54] During the campaign, some attempt was made to suggest that all Communists, as a result of their ideology and regardless of their personal ethnic origins, were friends of the Jews: Piratin asserted that no progressive politician or newspaper had been known to make anti-Semitic statements or to propagate race hatred;[55] his campaign workers were told to refer to the Scottish MP Willie Gallacher as a great fighter on behalf of the Jewish people. But the same set of instructions urged campaign workers to emphasize that Piratin, a Jew himself, 'knows the Jewish people and their problems well';[56] and nearly all of the Communists who helped out in Mile End were Jewish.[57] Hetty Donnelly, who had been active in the STDL in the 1930s, has recalled that this was a matter of deliberate policy: 'Piratin had a wonderful team of Jewish boys working with him. He had a few Gentiles as well – he needed them to visit the [non-Jewish] parts of the area – but most were Jews.'[58] Piratin also issued an 'Appeal to the Jewish Electors' which promised that, if elected, he would work for legislation against anti-Semitism in Britain; for a world-wide charter of Jewish rights; and for simplified naturalization procedures for Jews in Britain who were not yet legal citizens.[59]

Piratin was spending much of his time electioneering; Hymie Fagan was particularly impressed by Piratin's numerous street-corner meetings.[60] On 6 June, Piratin spoke at Queen Mary College, where he justified the Communist decision to contest Mile End and a selected number of other constituencies: 'Communists are now taking their part in the Government of all the liberated countries of

Europe. They have, by their hard work and devotion to the interests of the people, earned the right to representation in Parliament in Britain also.'[61]

At an open-air meeting held in the same week and chaired by Mick Mindel, Piratin attacked the incumbent Tory government, calling attention to its failure to address many domestic issues, such as the need for better housing: 'I know the housing conditions in Stepney, but even I was appalled at some of the cases I recently had to deal with.' Piratin also rebuked the *Evening Standard*, which was owned by Lord Beaverbrook, for claiming that Beaverbrook and Churchill had opened the London Underground stations to the people in 1940. 'The story is nonsense,' asserted Piratin:

> Stepney people know the truth about how the Tube shelters came to be used. After months and years of messing about – just like the messing about on housing now – the people were left with inadequate protection when the blitz arrived. Londoners stormed the Tubes and took charge. The Tubes were not given to the people.[62]

At a Piratin rally held at the Old King's Hall in Commercial Road on 22 June Professor J. B. S. Haldane did his part to discredit the Tories by recalling that in 1940, the year of shame, the Tory government had 'left us without arms and without allies'.[63]

Piratin's team was equally concerned to exploit the unpopularity of Dan Frankel, the incumbent Labour MP. 'We Remember,' asserted one piece of literature, 'Mile End's Member of Parliament',

> Who was never to be found when needed
> Who insulted deputations of Stepney people [requesting] his support for safer shelters
> Who never really spoke up for the people in the House of Commons
> Who scorned the Tenants' Defence League
> Who advised the people to ignore Mosley
> Who, by his behaviour and actions, has lost the support of Trade Unionists of Mile End
> Who is unworthy to act as Mile End's representative. . . .
>
> Remembering all this
> Mile End Will Vote for Piratin.[64]

THE COMMUNIST ELECTORAL VICTORIES OF 1945

By 24 June, George Orwell was predicting in the *Observer* that it would be 'a close finish between Mr Dan Frankel, the Labour candidate, and the very energetic and popular Communist candidate, Mr Phil Piratin, in Mile End'.[65] The Communists themselves seem to have been more confident of the coming victory, scheduling two separate eve-of-poll rallies, at the Old King's Hall and on Stepney Green, where Professor Hyman Levy shared the platform with Piratin. On election day, 5 July, the *Daily Worker* reported that 'All Mile End seemed to be at Stepney Green last night. . . . They covered the Green and spread into every side street. They cheered every reference by the chairman to Mr Phil Piratin's past work in Mile End and sang: "We'll be voting for Piratin on the day".'[66]

Many of Piratin's supporters were brought to the polling stations in a fleet of about 30 cars supplied by the wealthy businessmen who were working in the campaign; Hetty Donnelly has recalled that the Communists 'had more cars than the Labour party and the Tories'.[67] According to the account in the *Daily Worker*, 'Groups of people stood around the polling station and lined the streets watching the stream of Piratin cars bringing the dockers, clothing workers, servicemen, housewives and others to the booths. It seems a strong possibility that Mile End has given East London its first Communist M.P.'[68]

The results were made known on 26 July. Nationally, Labour had gained a sweeping victory, taking 393 of the 640 seats in the House of Commons. The 21 candidates fielded by the CP had polled 102,780 votes, averaging 12.7 per cent in each of the constituencies contested.[69] Although the CP did well in its traditional strongholds in East London, South Wales and Fifeshire,[70] only two Communist candidates won election: Willie Gallacher, who held on to his seat in West Fife with 42.1 per cent of the vote, and Phil Piratin, who made the only Communist breakthrough, taking Mile End with 47.6 per cent.[71] Piratin had received 5,075 votes to 3,861 for Frankel and 1,722 for Motion.[72] His margin of victory would have been greater than this had not the military vote gone heavily to Labour; but then, as Bill Carver has remarked, 'the soldiers . . . had been overseas . . . what did they know about Piratin?'[73]

According to the *East London Advertiser*, Piratin's election 'caused the greatest sensation',[74] and his supporters celebrated for weeks.[75] An article in the *Daily Worker* of 28 June predicted that Piratin, 'the "Controlled Whirlwind"', would demonstrate in Parliament 'the same verve with which he led the East End people in their fight against Mosley' and 'smashed the police cordon to get the shelterers into the tubes'.[76] One month later, the *Daily Worker* reported that Piratin, taking to Parliament 'like a duck to water', was well received by the Labour backbenchers.[77]

Piratin has since explained his victory by pointing to the intense desire for change which was widespread in post-war Britain,[78] and has continued to believe that 'it wasn't just an ethnic vote'.[79] But as Tubby Rosen has remarked, 'Mile End was a special area; it wasn't just Britain, by no means'.[80] The majority of British voters, in fact, expressed their desire for change by voting Labour in 1945, whereas Mile End behaved more like those demographically similar Jewish neighbourhoods in the United States, Canada, South Africa and elsewhere, which also voted Communist in the immediate post-war period. Even Piratin has acknowledged that 'the mood of Stepney was much more sharp than, say, in Camden Town. The Jews had more to lose. . . . Without a doubt, Jewish people felt more deeply about [the issues involved] than did others.'[81] Bill Carver has agreed that 'the Jews were more emotionally involved . . . and carried it over to the Party'; according to Carver, Piratin's victory would have been impossible 'without Jewish support'.[82] Four months after Piratin's election, the same Jewish support proved equally important in the election of no fewer than ten Communists to the Stepney Borough Council.

THE STEPNEY BOROUGH ELECTIONS OF 1945

At its meeting of November 1944, a full year before the borough elections in East London, the NJC's London Jewish Committee asserted that 'It was very important that votes in the forthcoming municipal elections be cast in the right direction' and that 'work by Jewish comrades was essential . . . in order to assure this'.[83] Jewish

Communists were ready to respond, then, when in the summer of 1945, R. Palme Dutt called on party members to follow up the Labour victory in the general election by increasing their efforts on behalf of Labour and progressive candidates in municipal elections; Dutt expressed the hope that Labour majorities would be achieved in all major cities, 'together with an increase of Communist representation'.[84] A few weeks later, at a meeting of the executive committee of the CP, Ted Bramley, the secretary of the London District Committee, also stressed the importance of electing left-wing candidates who would implement Labour's national programme at the local level.[85]

The Communists were in an excellent position to achieve this goal in Stepney. The most recent borough elections, which had taken place before the war, had resulted in a near-total victory for the local Labour party, which took 59 of the 60 council seats. The sixtieth seat had gone to Piratin, whose record, according to the *Daily Worker*, provided an example 'of what a Communist councillor can do. He gave continuous, painstaking attention to the daily interests of the people. . . . He served the people well and they sent him to Westminster to carry on the good work in a new sphere.'[86] Now, in 1945, the local Communists were a force to be reckoned with.

Stepney was divided into 20 wards which elected three councillors each. The Communists were confident that in certain wards, such as Spitalfields East and Mile End West, they were strong enough to win every one of the three seats if they chose to put forward that many candidates. But in order to demonstrate their interest in working together with Labour, the Communists decided to concentrate on five wards, contesting only two seats of three in each of these. The ten candidates were to be Phil Piratin and Tom Rampling in Spitalfields East; Edward Kirby and Michael Shapiro in St George's North-West; Max Levitas and Queenie Weinberg in Whitechapel East; Bill Carver and Fannie Goldberg in Mile End North; and Bertha Sokoloff and Tubby Rosen in Mile End West.[87] Mile End North, Mile End West and Whitechapel East were within the Mile End constituency which had just sent Piratin to the House of Commons; Spitalfields East and St George's North-

West were in the adjacent parliamentary constituency, Whitechapel-St George's. In Mile End North, where Dan Frankel was one of the Labour candidates, the Tories were proposing three candidates under the banner of the Stepney Municipal Alliance;[88] in the other four wards, it was a two-way battle between the Communists and Labour.[89]

The Communists knew that they would benefit from the unsavoury reputation of the local Labour Party. As Phil Piratin has remarked, 'The record of Labour on the Stepney Borough Council was, to say the least, a very dismal one. Corruption and inefficiency were their chief qualities.'[90] According to Solly Kaye, the Communists won many votes by promising to 'clean up the Council';[91] one of their slogans was 'Stepney needs honest and able Councillors'.[92] Still, the Communists had no wish to present themselves as the antithesis of Labour. One advertisement in the *East London Advertiser* explained that the goal of the CP was actually to complement and reinvigorate the Labour majority:

> The ten Communists will put new life into the Council and will help the best of the 50 Labour Councillors that will be selected. . . . Just as the majority of the Labour voters in Mile End recognised that Phil Piratin was the best man of the Labour movement and voted for him in the General Election, so – it is expected – will the majority of voters – especially Labour voters – vote for the Communist candidates on November 1 wherever they are standing.[93]

In his maiden speech in the House of Commons on 17 August Piratin had concentrated on what was to become a major issue in the borough elections: the need for more and better working-class housing. The present housing crisis, explained Piratin, had been caused not only by the blitz but also by capitalist irresponsibility and neglect. The Stepney Borough Council planned to build 1,200 houses within the next two years; but more houses than this would be necessary, and so Piratin called on the government to requisition uninhabited houses and unused land.[94]

As the municipal campaigns got under way, those Communist candidates who had been active in the STDL pressed hard on this theme. Michael Shapiro, recalling the pre-war struggle for lower rents and better repairs, told voters that he felt like starting the fight all over again: 'We want to build a Stepney that people can be proud of, not one to run away from.' Accompanied by Tubby Rosen, Shapiro met with slum landlords who were exhorted to remember 'the fighting spirit of the Stepney people';[95] at an election meeting held in St. George's North-West on 21 October, Shapiro warned landlords against speculating in property in Stepney.[96] Bill Carver joined in the chorus by describing some of the housing in the borough as 'simply appalling'; Tom Rampling asserted that the currently 'explosive' situation would become even more alarming as the demobilized soldiers returned home.[97] Bertha Sokoloff asked the Stepney Borough Council to take steps against such illegal practices as requiring 'key money' or charging higher rents than were allowed under the law; in a letter to the *East London Advertiser* she explained that in a seller's market such as that which Stepney was experiencing, it was important to prevent the growth of a 'black market' in housing.[98]

In the weeks leading up to the municipal elections, Communist candidates undoubtedly also benefited from national and international developments which served to remind Stepney residents of the prominent role that the CP had always played in fighting Fascism wherever it might be found. In September 1945, for example, William ('Lord Haw-Haw') Joyce was sentenced to death; but this was not enough to satisfy the *Daily Worker*, which reminded its readers that Oswald Mosley, who had nurtured Joyce in the BUF, remained a free man.[99] In October the CP was expressing concern over the treatment meted out to the 80,000 or so displaced Jews wandering about Germany; Piratin, in a *Daily Worker* article which was reprinted in pamphlet form, stated that these Jews were being treated 'with an utter lack of sympathy and vision' and that the Allies were doing nothing to prevent the circulation in Germany of anti-Semitic propaganda.[100] Meanwhile, in the British zone of occupied Germany, Josef Kramer, commandant of the Belsen concentration camp, was being tried for war crimes along with 44 members of his staff; the *Daily Worker* sent its own correspondent, Ivor Montagu, to cover the trial, and was rewarded with a stream of stories describing the atrocities which had taken place in Belsen.[101]

In October, Major Thomas Winwood, who was representing Kramer, made derogatory statements concerning the survivors of Belsen; his comments triggered protests in both Germany and Britain.[102] British officers, asserted the *Daily Worker*, were 'acting as mouthpieces of Nazi propaganda'.[103]

One week later, voters went to the municipal polls; when the results were announced it was evident that, again, Labour had done very well. In the case of nine London councils, including six councils in East London, not a single Tory was elected.[104] But if much of London could be described as a deep shade of pink, there were patches of red: the CP managed to win three council seats in Westminster, one in Finsbury, one in Hackney and all ten of those contested in Stepney. Tom Rampling has since asserted that in Stepney – where 49 Labour candidates and one independent Labourite were also elected – the Communists could easily have taken 10 to 15 more seats than this.[105] Certainly they could have picked up additional seats in the five wards where they did run: for although in 1937, Piratin – the single Communist candidate – was placed third to win his seat in Spitalfields East, he and all the other Communist candidates were well ahead of Labour in 1945. In Whitechapel East, for example, J. L. Fine, the highly regarded secretary of the Mantle & Costume branch of the NUTGW, was so far behind the two Communists that it is reasonable to assume that he would have lost his seat had there been a full Communist roster of three. In Mile End North, Dan Frankel was fifth, behind both Communists (Carver and Goldberg), the single successful Labour candidate (A. Kershaw), and even one of the three unsuccessful Tories.[106]

Even though seven of the ten newly elected Communist councillors were Jewish and all had won their seats in predominantly Jewish neighbourhoods, Communist officials were careful to avoid any reference to an ethnic vote. The *Daily Worker*, hailing a 'nationwide move to the Left in which the Communists are playing an important part', would go no further than to remark that 'the emergence of the Communist Party as a force in local politics' was 'most strikingly shown in Stepney, where a strong team of Communist administrators and local government experts has been

THE COMMUNIST ELECTORAL VICTORIES OF 1945

returned'.[107] Others, however, such as J. C. Lawder, the Stepney Labour leader representing Limehouse North, were able to provide a more perspicacious analysis: the Communist wins in Stepney, said Lawder, had come 'in that part of the borough where people of alien origin predominate and where regard for the hoary institutions of British traditionalism is weak'.[108]

8
Conclusion

PIRATIN'S VICTORY: THE ETHNIC DIMENSION

It has long been acknowledged that 'voting is essentially a group experience. People who work or live or play together are highly likely to vote for the same candidate'.[1] Groups such as these communicate their shared values, not only through formal channels like newspapers or political rallies but also in the course of day-to-day contact. Jean Blondel writes that 'The flow of ideas takes place to a very large extent through private forms of communication' and that such exchanges 'appear to shape the ideology of individuals more profoundly' than do public forms of communication.[2] People develop opinions, attitudes and beliefs in reference to their groups; the interaction of group members leads to the expression of similar values and opinions.[3] In turn the groups, acting through political parties and movements, perform the input function of interest articulation and compete for the rewards to be distributed by the political system.[4] According to David Truman, groups exist 'at the heart of the process of government'.[5] We have already seen that Stepney, with its high population density and intense communal life, was in 1935–45 an area highly conducive to this form of group political behaviour.

Because 'national origins continue to be a salient dimension in many people's perception of themselves and others',[6] ethnicity is a prime although not the sole factor in group identification; Robin Williams points out that ethnicity is one among several social formations 'through which the assembling and mobilization of collective interests in political struggle may be carried out'. Ethnic

CONCLUSION

groups, as interest groups, can become effective foci in group mobilization for concrete political ends.[7] This is particularly true when the members see themselves as outsiders excluded from the rewards of the political system.[8] Politicized ethnicity can then become an effective instrument in the competition for power, status and wealth in the society; where there are structured inequalities involving ethnicity, social solidarity on the part of the group perceiving discrimination may result in politicization.[9] The Jews of East London were such a group, and they were able to utilize their ethnic consciousness in order to advance their political and economic goals in British society.

It is difficult to disentangle ethnicity from class as a factor in the formation and cohesiveness of groups. Michael Hechter says, 'if a given group is both materially disadvantaged, that is, a proletariat, and subject to cultural discrimination as well, its political demands might be expressed either in class or in ethnic terms'.[10] Where ethnicity is reinforced by class cleavage, confrontation will be particularly intense and all-encompassing.[11] Using a term coined by Milton Gordon, we might regard the working-class Jews of Stepney as an 'ethclass'.[12] But I would argue, along with other theoreticians, that ethnicity 'tends to be . . . more permanent and . . . more basic' than does class.[13] As A. W. Wright correctly notes, the impact of class in the modern world has operated upon social formations already rooted in such basic units as family, religion and ethnicity. 'These units gained strength from their primacy and it was to be expected that social changes would be mediated through them.'[14] Because ethnicity is ascribed at birth, it has temporal priority over other allegiances; furthermore, the 'concatenation of residential and occupational segregation gives a decisive advantage to the development of ethnic rather than class solidarity'.[15] Ethnicity is more salient than class, according to Daniel Bell, 'because it can combine an interest with an affective tie'.[16] Hence, although alternative lines of cleavage are available, 'there nevertheless exists a propensity for them to be displaced into ethnic ones'.[17] At the core of ethnic solidarity is 'the synergism between interest and affect, between the drive to meet material aspirations and the desire for identity within community'.[18]

In an article which appeared shortly after the general election of 1945, Lazar Zaidman asserted that Piratin's victory was due 'in no small measure' to his having stood for office in 'one of the most thickly populated Jewish areas in London'.[19] Zaidman wrote to a friend that 'it can, therefore, truly be said that the Jewish Electorate were to a very large extent responsible for sending him into Parliament, and we can claim with justification that the Jews give support to the Communist Party'.[20]

Because the general election results were not broken down by polling district, there is no accurate record of how many votes Piratin won in each ward. We can get some idea of Jewish support for Communist candidates, however, by looking at the results of the borough elections in November 1945. The Mile End constituency – the seat won by Piratin in July 1945 – was subdivided into seven polling districts corresponding to five wards in the Stepney Borough, with two polls each in the Mile End North and Mile End South wards. According to calculations based on the electoral register, Jews constituted at least 78 per cent of the voters in the Mile End West polling district, 43 per cent in Whitechapel East, and 42 per cent in that part of Mile End South situated west of Wellesley Street and East Arbor Street; in the two polls included in Mile End North, the percentage of Jews was as little as 28 per cent. The CP chose not to stand in Mile End South in November 1945. In Whitechapel East the two Communist candidates did substantially better than the Labour candidates; in Mile End West, where the percentage of Jewish voters was extremely high, the two Communist candidates won nearly twice as many votes as did the Labour candidates. In Mile End North, however, where the percentage of Jewish voters was relatively low, the two Communist candidates, although they won their seats, did so only by a narrow margin. If we assume that those who voted Communist in the borough elections are likely to have voted also for Piratin four months earlier, it seems apparent that he probably fared better in areas more densely populated by Jews, and that his victory was indeed due in large part to their support.[21]

The British Communist Party naturally attributed its electoral successes to socio-economic rather than to ethnic factors. This

CONCLUSION

study has demonstrated, however, that ethnicity was the main factor in determining party preference in Stepney in the period 1935–45, and that the ethnic appeals made by these officially non-ethnic political parties determined in large part the content of political debate. Because the CP was able to appeal successfully to the powerful group consciousness of the Jewish population, a consciousness owing more to ethnicity than to class, the Party for a brief time gained political hegemony in the Jewish community.[22]

WHY COMMUNISM? THE CONJUNCTURE OF 1945

Ofira Seliktar has written that the Jewish predilection for liberal and radical politics 'is often explained in terms of status-discrepancy, whereby the low status of the group undermines the high status of the individuals, causing the partial elimination of economic motivation in political choice, making it a part of a more general phenomenon of minority group voting'.[23] In other words, Jews face the problem of 'status incongruity': even when they advance economically, their normative situation as a low-status ethnic group remains a problem.[24] Jews in England, and in the East End of London in particular, desired a liberal-secular society in which they would be allowed to improve their status; they were wary of the Conservative Party, which was suspected of cultural prejudice against Jews and of accommodating itself in 1935–45 to the forces of Fascism on the Continent.

The traditional political choice of English Jews had been the Liberal Party. By the 1930s, however, the Liberals were in eclipse. Jews were alarmed when in 1936 David Lloyd George, the grand old man of the party, paid a visit to Nazi Germany and seemed to have come away impressed;[25] in 1938, Oswald Mosley was allowed to state his case at the National Liberal Club.[26] By 1945, an editorial in the *Jewish Chronicle* was expressing the hope that 'the Liberal tradition of pure freedom' might be carried on by some other party.[27]

Many Jewish voters turned to Labour, even though that party's social democratic, working-class politics were somewhat less to their taste than was the bourgeois radicalism of the Liberals. Selig Brodetsky, who became president of the Board of Deputies in 1939, switched his allegiance from the Liberals to Labour.[28] Barnett Janner, Liberal MP for Whitechapel-St George's from 1931 until his defeat in 1935 by the Labour candidate – who was, significantly enough, Irish – resigned from the Liberal Party, joined Labour,[29] and won the Leicester West constituency in 1945; Janner was one of 26 Jews elected as Labour members to that Parliament.[30] With the exception of Mile End, all the East London constituencies with large Jewish populations returned Labour MPs.[31] None the less, many Jews in Stepney, where the Irish predominated in the Labour Party, perceived Labour as being intensely parochial and mired in corruption.[32] These voters, who were unwilling to allow the Labour leadership to bargain and compromise on their behalf at the level of the local elites, sought a party committed to creating a new normative order.

During the same period, the East End Jewish community proved highly receptive to the blend of Jewish nationalism and socialist internationalism propounded by the Jewish left-wing subculture. By 1945 the main organizational expression of this type of Jewish left-wing politics was the Jewish Communist movement, operating through trade unions, fraternal organizations and local community groups. The various front groups, ranging from the STDL to the JFSR, had served the East London Jewish community for over a decade, engaging in social and communal work and elaborating new norms and belief systems; they had been instrumental in helping the community to overcome its social isolation.[33] A large section of the Jewish population was also impressed by the Communist platform, with its vague yet powerful promise of ethnic and class equality in a socialist England where Jews would be free from Fascism, anti-Semitism and poverty.

The Communist Party in East London also managed, despite its clearly ethnic base, to portray itself as an integral part of the Labour movement, and indeed even as the 'conscience' of the Labour Party. We have seen that, particularly after 1941, the national climate of opinion favoured the position taken by the Jewish left-wing on various issues such as Spain, the USSR, Poland, and

CONCLUSION

Palestine, issues which had been at the centre of controversy in Stepney before the war. The polarization that had characterized much Irish–Jewish political interaction before 1939 was greatly diminished: the BUF disappeared; even the Labour Party was reluctant to seem too critical of the CP. The Irish and their Jewish allies within the East London Labour Party were put on the defensive as Jewish Communists became the beneficiaries of extensive public sympathy; men like M. H. Davis, Dan Frankel and W. J. Edwards, for example, had no choice during the war but to mouth pro-Soviet platitudes, even though in earlier years they had been anti-Communist for reasons both historical and religious. Many Jews took advantage of this blurring of party lines: it began to appear as though voting Communist, far from entailing any break with the larger Labour Party, actually served as a spur to reform Labour and thus make it more attractive to Jewish voters in the long run.

Jews had some difficulty, of course, in giving their support to a political movement – Communism – which officially believed that Jews should assimilate, and which viewed their ethnic communalism as a transitory phenomenon that in the meantime delayed their ultimate liberation. Even as news of the Holocaust became known during the war, the CP refused to recognize the specific cultural and theoretical problems posed by anti-Semitism; it continued to argue that Fascism, as a tool of capitalist reaction, attacked the Jews in order to drive a wedge into working-class unity. But in practice, the CP's desire to integrate and eventually assimilate the Jews led it to assume the role of protector of Jewish citizens and workers. In the popular-front period of 1935–45, as the CP proved itself willing to defend Jews against manifestations of anti-Semitism and Fascism in England, its theoretical lines became so blurred as to be overlooked or at least countenanced. Political activities rather than ideological positions impressed the Jewish community in East London.

It is also true that the CP's ideological opposition to ethnic differentiation, when viewed from certain angles, was actually an asset to a group intent on rising in the larger society. At the end of the war the East London Jews wanted what the CP seemed to advocate: an end to ethnically based constraints which maintained the boundaries in an ascriptive social hierarchy. In order to achieve upward social mobility, the Jews required a means of overcoming vertical stratification in the core English society. They were, then, in search of 'a new symbolic framework' within which to react to political problems.[34]

Communism set forth an ideology which would eliminate the cultural categories defining Jews as marginal. The Communist programme, intent on going beyond the formalisms of civil integration, promised to eliminate many of the cultural, historical and religious symbols that excluded Jews from the larger society. Complementarity between Jews and the nation would then come to be based upon shared characteristics such as 'class'.[35] As Raphael Samuel has observed, 'for my mother's generation Communism, though not intended as such, was a way of being English, a bridge by which the children of the ghetto entered the national culture'.[36] The Jews would then have equal opportunity for meritocratic advancement and for the improvement of income, employment rates, quality of housing and the like.

There were also practical, strategic reasons for endorsing the Communist approach to such problems. Michael Lipsky has argued that 'the essence of political protest consists in activating third parties to participate in controversy in ways favorable to protest goals'.[37] Groups that require outside support will often resort to the dimension of values and ideologies;[38] if they succeed in couching their demands in terms that appear to be consistent with broader goals, third-party support and even coalition partners may become available.[39] The Jews, seeking to alter their place in the social system, needed to mobilize in such a way as to squeeze more resources out of the host society.[40] If their objectives were interpreted as too parochial or their leadership perceived as too alien, they may have difficulty winning sympathy outside their immediate group. Thus they required an ideology that would 'serve as a vehicle not for denying ethnic identity altogether but for subsuming it under a universal movement not limited by ethnic criteria'.[41] Such a reform movement, by 'universalizing' specific demands, minimizes the difficulty of obtaining assistance from

CONCLUSION

outside the group.[42] Thus it made more sense for the Jews to support a movement that was officially part of the CPGB than a more explicitly Jewish movement, and may help explain the more limited appeal of Zionism during much of this period.[43] It was a source of political power for the Jewish Communists that they could make claims upon their fellow-Communists and upon much of the wider left-wing in their struggles against anti-Semitism.

On the local level, Jewish adherence to Communism was also a means of limiting ethnic conflict with the Irish. Although the Jews wished to rise vertically, they had no desire for cross-cultural assimilation or acculturation to the local Irish community; indeed, this was one reason for their diminished allegiance to the Labour Party. Locally the Jews retained their ethnic sub-system; the political model remained one of horizontal segmentation. But because the Jewish Communists were part of a universalistic party, they could also include – or pretend to include – the Irish in their quest for better conditions.

On paper the Stepney CP was just another constituency party composed of working-class members of the British public; a standard Marxist account would undoubtedly describe its successes in 1945 as working-class victories.[44] But these successes could not have occurred without the ethnic dimension provided by the Jewish Communist movement: analysis of voting patterns shows a significant correlation between percentages of Jewish population and support for the Communist candidates. Jewish ethnicity was the determinative social category, the salient factor accounting for the particular political cleavages to be found in Stepney at the time. It was as a result of Jewish allegiance to the CP that, as one former Jewish Communist put it, 'The whole country went left, and Stepney went lefter'.[45] Today, although a working-class population remains in the East End, the Jews are gone – and so is the strength of the Communist Party.

In summary, it was the Communist Party which, in Stepney in 1945, embodied the desire for a liberal, achievement-oriented society. By calling for a state based on rationalistic, universal criteria of membership and participation, the CP expressed ethnic discontent with the British political establishment; and the Jews voted

Communist in disproportionate numbers in order to send this message to the larger society.

In 1936, the Communist writer Robert Turner bemoaned 'this peculiarly English fact, the Liberal tradition' as 'the most important obstacle' to the achievement of socialism.[46] Nine years later, R. Palme Dutt could almost be forgiven his ideological exuberance when he announced that, given the total eclipse of the Liberal Party, 'the final battle is between Toryism and Marxism'.[47] He does not seem to have realized that in areas such as Jewish Mile End, the Communist bottle was full of the old Liberal wine.

THE DECLINE OF JEWISH COMMUNISM

'The failure in class solidarity between workers of different race or ethnic groups runs contrary to the expectations Communist Parties would derive, and did in fact derive, from classical Marxist theory.'[48] In Britain, Communists dealt with this problem at various times in two contradictory ways.

The CPGB naturally continued to emphasize economic factors as the primary determinant of political change and to treat ethnic divisions as an epiphenomenon of class conflict. But even if one insists on arguing that 'ethnic symbols are merely the facade for economic grievances', the fact remains that such symbols 'often structure the political situation and thus affect the outcome'[49] – a lesson which the Stepney CP learned well. In Stepney, the Jewish Communists accepted the independent significance of ethnicity and strove to incorporate it into the Marxist theory of revolutionary change. Rarely, however, does politicized ethnicity provide the follow-through for major social revolutions;[50] and the CP was attempting the impossible when it set out to mobilize Jews ethnically in order to pursue long-range goals incompatible with Jewish needs.

In his discussion of the types of support available to political systems, David Easton distinguishes between 'diffuse' and 'specific' support. Whereas 'diffuse' support is based on ideological commitment and is more likely to be long-standing, 'specific' support is

CONCLUSION

contingent upon the performance of the system, that is, its policy outputs, and hence can vary significantly over short periods of time.[51] The ideologically committed cadres of the Jewish Communist movement denied the legitimacy of the British political system for fundamental, theoretical reasons.[52] Their movement drew many of its followers, however, from the ranks of those who, ignoring the normative dimensions of their grievances, were attracted merely by the short-term political goals of Jewish Communism.[53] These 'specific' supporters recognized that, if the Communists were not always on the side of the angels, they were certainly ranged against all the proper devils, from bad housing to Hitler.

Even the Hitler–Stalin Pact period of 1939–41 did little to dispel this impression. Although the Pact would be used against the CP in the post-war period, its actual duration was brief, and the average working-class Jew was more immediately concerned with inadequate air raid precautions and with the anti-Jewish paranoia of 1940 – problems which the Jewish Communist movement addressed forcefully.[54] Later, the movement benefited from the pro-Soviet euphoria and the general political swing to the left throughout Britain which culminated in the Labour victory in 1945.

After the war, the Communist movement attempted to maintain its hegemony in the East End. It was active in the campaign to clear out slums and replace them with better working-class housing. Ted Bramley, Jack Gaster and Tubby Rosen, among others, were involved in the London squatters' movement in 1946, and there was even an attempt to revive the Stepney Tenants' Defence League in 1948. The Communists also agitated against what they regarded as a resurgence of Fascism in the area. Mosley and his followers were attempting a post-war comeback; in August 1947, there were major anti-Semitic disturbances in London and other cities. The Home Secretary, James Chuter Ede, was criticized for not taking this threat more seriously. Also during this period the CP favoured the partition of Palestine into Arab and Jewish states and blamed Foreign Secretary Ernest Bevin's opposition to Jewish statehood on anti-Semitism. The party continued to promote Soviet Jewish life, especially in Birobidzhan, through periodicals such as

New Life, established by Jacob Sonntag in January 1947. These efforts paid off when in March 1946 two Communist candidates — Jack Gaster and Ted Bramley — were elected to the London County Council from Mile End;[55] in 1947 and 1948, two more Communists, Alan Blatt and A. L. 'Chirps' Steinberg, managed to win by-elections to the Stepney Borough Council from Spitalfields, raising the number of Communists to 12 on Stepney Borough Council.[56]

Yet within a decade, Jewish Communism was all but extinct, in Stepney as well as elsewhere, as the whole delicate synchronization that had allowed it to flourish within the Jewish community fell apart. For one thing, the Communist programme for social change in East London became increasingly less relevant. The Attlee government introduced major reforms in education, medical care, town planning and unemployment benefits, ushering in the modern welfare state; the social impact of unemployment, poverty and ill health declined with the passage of such landmark legislation as the National Insurance, National Health Service and Rent Acts.[57] Also, Jews now increasingly achieved their goal of upward mobility and emigrated out of the East End to new centres in north-west London. They had begun to move out of Stepney even before the war, usually along a north-west 'corridor' via Stamford Hill and Hackney towards Golders Green or further east into areas like Ilford in Essex. During the war, 'Hitler's Luftwaffe opened wide the old walls of the ghetto',[58] leading to an exodus not only of population but also of the large clothing manufacturers.[59] The Communist movement itself had, of course, done much to facilitate social mobility by making the East End Jews more politically aware of economic injustice and by articulating their grievances. But as Mannheim has noted, 'philosophical systems change if the vital system in which one lives undergoes a shift'; when the social system changes, 'the system of norms to which it had previously given birth ceases to be in harmony with it'.[60] For reasons of class alone it would have been difficult for the movement to replicate its successes in newer areas of Jewish settlement in London,[61] but there were also to be powerful ideological reasons for its decline among Jews in the post-war period. As for the new, non-Jewish residents who were moving into Stepney, they were unfamiliar with the borough's politics and with its Communist 'traditions', and the CP had difficulty in winning their allegiance.[62] By 1950 the Jewish sub-system of the area would shrink to about 25,000 people.[63] The strength of the Communist movement diminished along with it.[64]

The problem, however, went beyond the exodus of East End Jews, as Jewish Communism lost its appeal within the larger Jewish sub-system itself. After 1945, international developments put an end to many of the policy debates which had fuelled pro-Communist sentiment. By the end of the war, Spain was lost; Hitler was defeated; Polish Jewry had disappeared into the Holocaust. The full horror of that tragedy was beginning to permeate the consciousness of British Jews; its effect would be 'potent and long-lasting'.[65] As their knowledge of the nature and scope of the Holocaust increased, many Jews came to regard Marxist-Leninist theories concerning the purely capitalistic causes of anti-Semitism as so much simplistic reductionism, and there was less interest in class politics and more in Zionism, especially after the formation of a sovereign Jewish state in 1948. The Communist Party did its best to keep Jews interested in the USSR and in the new 'people's democracies'. But the old equation of Soviet Communism versus German Nazism was fast fading into historical memory. Even many ideologically committed Jewish Communists found it difficult to substitute a supposedly fascistic United States for Hitler's Third Reich.

Partly as the result of an overall loss in population, Stepney's parliamentary and London County Council seats were redistributed. In 1948 the old two-member LCC seats for Mile End, Whitechapel-St George's and Limehouse were replaced by one three-person Stepney seat. Three Communists – Jack Gaster, Ted Bramley, and Michael Shapiro – stood in the LCC elections in April 1949; each one of them lost. One month later, elections to the Stepney Borough Council took place. The CP contested 59 out of the 60 seats on the council; they managed to take only nine.[66]

Before the general election in 1950, Piratin's parliamentary seat was eliminated by being merged with those of Limehouse and of Whitechapel-St George's in order to form a single, much larger Stepney seat. In the election of 23 February 1950, Piratin was forced to stand against Whitechapel Labour MP W. J. Edwards. He received

5,991 votes (12.5 per cent of the total polled) and finished behind even the Tory candidate, who received 6,238; the votes for Edwards totalled 33,475.[67] Some of Piratin's supporters attributed his defeat to outright gerrymandering.[68] Piratin himself felt that while the three old Stepney seats were clearly too small, two new seats rather than one should have been created.[69]

But the problem was not merely that Piratin could no longer stand in a small, largely Jewish constituency. His campaign was also crippled by the fact that the Stepney of 1950 was very different from that of 1945. During those five years, many Jews who had given 'specific' support to the CP became aware of the conflict between Communist ideology and their long-term goals as an ethnicity. Jewish Communists and sympathizers had been overjoyed when in 1947–48 the Soviet Union pledged its support to the fledgling Jewish state, and for a time they tried to identify with two national centres – the USSR and Israel. In the late 1940s, however, the rift between the two countries had already become apparent; soon the Soviet Union would be providing almost uncritical support – and arms – to the Arab states. Jews were also alarmed by the reports of anti-Semitism within the Soviet Union that began circulating in 1948, despite attempts by Jewish Communists to deny these charges.[70] Jewish support for the USSR 'went rapidly downhill; there was no way of stopping it'.[71] As Julius Jacobs has explained, this conflict between Zionism and Communism was a major factor in Piratin's defeat: 'The battle between Communists and Zionists was at its height. . . . Phil was a centre of the opposition, and he lost his seat.'[72] The Cold War also took its toll. By 1950 the division between the USSR and the Western allies had become very wide: the 'Iron Curtain' cut Europe into two and Britain had become a signatory to the North Atlantic Treaty, leading the British CP to embark on a political strategy which included the wholesale denunciation of the Labour government. This resulted in a further decline in Communist credibility.[73] Edwards had refused even to debate with Piratin during the election campaign, citing political and religious oppression in Communist Eastern Europe,[74] and pleas for Jewish support from Sam Alexander, Jack Gaster, Jack Perry and other Communists had fallen on deaf ears.[75] Soon after the

CONCLUSION

general election of 1950 Phil Piratin declared personal bankruptcy. His financial problems resulted from his losing a lawsuit for slander brought against him on the basis of statements he was said to have made at a meeting in October 1949.[76] The short-lived period of Communist electoral success was at an end: in the May 1953 elections, the Communists lost every one of the nine Stepney Borough Council seats that they had won in 1949.[77] Only the most 'diffuse' believers remained faithful to the CP – and they were in for further disappointments.

In February 1956, at the twentieth Soviet Communist Party Congress, Nikita Khrushchev caused a crisis in the world's Communist movement by describing the brutal criminality of Stalin's regime. These revelations were particularly disturbing to Jews as they included a long list of anti-Semitic acts such as the wholesale purges of Jewish party leaders in the East European countries; the general shutdown of Jewish cultural institutions in the Soviet Union after 1948; the murder in August 1952 of leading Soviet Jewish writers and intellectuals, many of whom had been prominent in the wartime JAFC; and the so-called 'Doctors' Plot' of 1953, in which Stalin accused a group of mainly Jewish physicians of plotting to murder him on behalf of 'Zionism' and 'western imperialism'. The outbreak of the Hungarian Revolution in October 1956 also shook the faith of many.

In England, this led to much soul-searching and to an admission on the part of the NJC that it had not taken seriously the possibility of anti-Semitism in the Soviet Union. There were numerous debates and heated arguments between people who had been comrades for decades. A few leading Jewish Communists remained steadfastly loyal to the party. Lazar Zaidman, for example, died in the faith; he continued to defend the USSR against charges of anti-Semitism which, he wrote, 'has been used as a stick to beat the Soviet Union and to besmirch the tremendous record of achievements and advances gained by the Soviet peoples, including its Jewish citizens'.[78] Michael Shapiro went even further, ideologically and geographically: during the war he had become a member of the London District Committee of the CP and after 1945 a leader of the Communist group on Stepney Borough Council. But after losing his seat in 1949, he travelled to North Korea with Jack Gaster and then accepted a position as a translator and journalist in Communist China. Though a confirmed Maoist by the 1960s, he was arrested during the Cultural Revolution and spent five years in a Chinese prison.[79]

Others, such as Mick Mindel and Sarah Wesker, attempted, somewhat awkwardly, to occupy two camps: although they continued to regard themselves as Communists, the Jewish aspect of their commitment proved in the end more important. They remained for ever on their guard when it came to Jewish issues, including Israel, even though this effectively made them 'Zionists' from the official Soviet point of view.[80] Alec Waterman, who was editor of the *Jewish Clarion* from 1953 to 1956, was 'too loyal' to contemplate quitting the party, according to his widow.[81] None the less, he became increasingly critical of Soviet attitudes: he published an article 'On the Jewish Question' in *Marxism Today* in 1959 which charged the USSR with responsibility for the 'unjust and illegal acts involving the complete elimination of all Yiddish cultural activities' after 1948.[82] Just before his death in April 1966, he completed a critical memorandum on Soviet Jewry, which the CP's executive committee attempted to conceal.[83]

One particularly sad case was that of Hyman Levy, who wanted to remain in the party but also felt compelled to criticize publicly the Soviet position on the Jews. As a well-regarded professor of mathematics at the Imperial College of Science and Technology, University of London, and a Marxist philosopher,[84] Levy was 'a very important feather in the party's cap'.[85] He had managed to overcome his doubts about the Soviets during the 1939–41 period,[86] and even at the time of the 'Doctors' Plot',[87] but the events of 1956 proved a shattering blow. He was even more disturbed at the manner in which Dutt seemed to discount Khrushchev's announcement of Stalin's crimes as being of no great concern. Levy reminded the party's chief theoretician that 'The last thing that Jewish Socialists have expected in the country of Socialism is the arousing of national bitterness, and the extermination of the cream of Jewish intellectuals'. He called David Bergelson, Itzik Feffer, Peretz Markish, and the other executed writers '*martyrs who have died for the cause of Socialism*'.[88] Levy travelled to the Soviet Union that

CONCLUSION

autumn and conducted his own first-hand investigation; in April 1957, he told the twenty-fifth (special) CPGB congress that he had heard things 'that shook me to my foundations – I got my belly full, enough to last me my life'. His criticism was passed off as that of a 'backboneless and spineless' intellectual,[89] prompting him in turn to denounce Pollitt, Dutt and the rest of the leadership.[90]

That summer Levy visited Israel for the first time, and came away impressed with the country. Back in England, he debated with Dutt and Itzhak Nathani, the socialist Zionist, on the future of the Jewish state. While Dutt attacked Zionism, Levy agreed with Nathani that the Soviet attitude was based on an incorrect analysis.[91] The dispute escalated beyond the point of no return in 1958, when Levy published *Jews and the National Question*, in which he defended Israel, Jewish culture and peoplehood, and again criticized the Soviet Union: 'Are Jews once again, as under Czarism, being reduced to the level of second class citizens?'[92] The Zionist periodical *Labour Israel* congratulated Levy on his 'short but brilliant' work.[93] The *Jewish Chronicle* called it 'the most outspoken indictment yet that any Communist has dared to bring against the Kremlin', but predicted his imminent expulsion from the party.[94] Indeed, R. Palme Dutt soon denounced the book as a 'half-hearted apologia for the ideas of Jewish Nationalism' and called the charges against the USSR 'calumnies'. 'With this book,' announced Dutt, 'Levy finally parts company with Marxism.'[95] On 30 March Levy was expelled;[96] he still insisted that the CP was making a mistake and 'is literally going down the drain'.[97] Levy had loyally defended the USSR for almost three decades, and the events of 1956–58 'brought him to the verge of complete mental breakdown'.[98] In 1959, in a letter to Lazar Zaidman, he wrote that his break with the party 'hurt me terribly – more than I have ever disclosed to anyone'.[99]

For many other veteran party members, the required level of cognitive dissonance had risen beyond the point of psychological toleration,[100] and Jewish Communism had become an impossibility ideologically as well as politically. Like Levy, they experienced extreme psychological difficulties in leaving the movement. Maurice Essex remained 'bitter about the Soviet Union' and expressed anger that the CPGB had been unable to recognize that 'things were going wrong there'.[101] Tubby Rosen had left the party after the 1953 'Doctors' Plot', no longer able to rationalize Soviet actions, yet ever afterwards feeling 'like a fish out of water. It becomes your whole life.'[102] Bertha Sokoloff, who quit after the April 1957 party congress, remembered it as a 'very traumatic' period; 'I lost many good friends'.[103] Their dedication had been as intense as in a religious belief-system.[104] It is not surprising that some of those who left, such as Chimen Abramsky, became equally fervent anti-Communists.[105]

A whole segment of the Jewish world had by now lost faith in the ideals of Communism as represented by the Soviet Union. Most of those who identified with the Jewish community had left the CPGB. The infrastructure of Jewish Communism, including its periodicals, largely disappeared: the NJC's monthly *Jewish Clarion*, for instance, ceased publication in March 1957.[106] By the late 1950s, Jewish Communism could no longer be regarded as a movement of any significance in Jewish life.

Notes

PREFACE
1. C. Wright Mills, *The Sociological Imagination* (New York: Oxford University Press, 1959; Harmondsworth: Penguin, 1978), p. 162.
2. John C. Harsanyi, 'Explanation and Comparative Dynamics in Social Science', *Behavioral Science* 5 (April 1960): 139.
3. David E. Apter, 'Radicalization and Embourgeoisement: Hypotheses for a Comparative Study of History', in David E. Apter, *Political Change: Collected Essays* (London: Frank Cass, 1973), p. 23.
4. Dennis Kavanagh, *Political Culture* (London: Macmillan, 1972), p. 52.
5. Bruno Ramirez, 'Ethnic Studies and Working-Class History', *Labour/Le Travail: Journal of Canadian Labour Studies* 19 (spring 1987): 45–6.
6. Telephone conversation with Betty Reid, London, 1 Nov. 1978.
7. Letter to the author from Betty Reid, London, 7 June 1978.
8. Francis King and George Matthews, 'The Communist Party Library', *Labour History Review* 56 (winter 1991): 2–3. See also Betty Reid, 'Communist Party Archive', *Our History Journal* 12 (Jan. 1988): 11–13.
9. Interview, George Matthews, London, 22 Aug. 1991.
10. Interview, Sid Sorrin, former secretary of the branch, London, 24 Nov. 1978.
11. Alec Waterman's papers have since gone missing, and may have been inadvertently thrown out by a porter, according to his widow. Interview, Mrs Ray Waterman, London, 5 Aug. 1991.

CHAPTER 1
1. George Orwell, 'The British General Election', *Commentary* 1 (Nov. 1945): 66; and Margaret Cole, *The General Election 1945 and After*, Fabian Research Series, No. 102 (London: Gollancz, Oct. 1945), p.5.
2. Henry Pelling, for example, in *The British Communist Party: A Historical Profile* (London: A. & C. Black, 2nd ed., 1975), refers to the Jewish East London Communists three times; in the second of these passages he remarks that Piratin ousted 'a Labour M.P. of indifferent quality' (pp. 56, 82–3, 131–2). Even left-of-centre Marxists have minimized the victory. Sam Bornstein and Al Richardson, in their study *Two Steps Back: Communists and the Wider Labour Movement, 1939–1945: A Study in the Relations Between 'Vanguard' and Class* (Ilford, Essex: Socialist Platform, [1982]), begrudge Piratin his victory, noting in passing that he stood 'for an East End constituency with an exceptionally small electorate' (p. 135). The recently published book by the Communist historian Willie Thompson, *The Good Old Cause: British Communism 1920–1991* (London: Pluto Press, 1992) ignores completely the Jewish Communists of East London; even Piratin's victory is barely mentioned.
3. Political scientists in particular have paid relatively little attention to ethnic politics, according to Lawrence G. Flood, 'Ethnic Politics and Political Science: A Survey of Leading Journals', *Ethnicity* 7 (March 1980): 99.

4. Colin Holmes, 'Introduction: Immigrants and Minorities in Britain', in Colin Holmes (ed.), *Immigrants and Minorities in British Society* (London: George Allen & Unwin, 1978), p. 13; and Ernest Krausz, *Ethnic Minorities in Britain* (London: MacGibbon & Kee, 1971), pp. 9-10.
5. Roger Ballard, 'Ethnicity: Theory and Experience (A Review Article)', *New Community* 5 (autumn 1976): 200.
6. A. H. Halsey, 'Ethnicity: A Primordial Social Bond?', *Ethnic and Racial Studies* 1 (Jan. 1978): 125.
7. Joseph Rothschild, *Ethnopolitics: A Conceptual Framework* (New York: Columbia University Press, 1981), pp. 20–1; see also pp. 67–9.
8. Leo Kuper, 'On Theories of Race Relations', in Wendell Bell and Walter E. Freeman (eds.), *Ethnicity and Nation-Building: Comparative, International, and Historical Perspectives* (Beverly Hills, CA: Sage, 1974), p. 19; Pierre L. van den Berghe, *The Ethnic Phenomenon* (New York: Elsevier, 1981), p. 17; Michael Hechter, *Internal Colonialism: The Celtic Fringe in British National Development, 1536–1966* (Berkeley: University of California Press, 1975), pp. 312–14.
9. Nathan Glazer and Daniel P. Moynihan, 'Introduction', in Nathan Glazer and Daniel P. Moynihan (eds), *Ethnicity: Theory and Experience* (Cambridge, MA: Harvard University Press, 1975), p. 4.
10. Rothschild, *Ethnopolitics*, p. 23. Of course, care must be taken not to go too far in the other direction. David Montgomery reminds us 'to deal with ethnicity without ignoring the dimension of class'. David Montgomery, 'To Study the People: The American Working Class', *Labor History* (fall 1980): 507.
11. Geoffrey Alderman, *The Jewish Community in British Politics* (Oxford: Clarendon Press, 1983), pp. vii-ix, 150; David Cesarani, 'Introduction' to David Cesarani (ed.), *The Making of Modern Anglo-Jewry* (Oxford: Basil Blackwell, 1990), p. 10; Tony Kushner, *The Persistence of Prejudice: Antisemitism in British Society During the Second World War* (Manchester: Manchester University Press, 1989), p. 164. Geoffrey Alderman has posited the reluctance on the part of the established sectors of the community to acknowledge, much less harness, this electoral force during the 1920s and 1930s as a factor in the grass-roots growth of Communism in East London; *London Jewry and London Politics 1889–1986* (London: Routledge, 1989), p. 143. This attitude persisted to some extent even after Alderman had published his own studies in the 1980s and 1990s on Anglo-Jewish political behaviour. His new study, *Modern British Jewry* (Oxford: Clarendon Press, 1992), appeared after this book was completed. See also the critique of the Cesarani anthology by Max Beloff, 'Anglo-Jewry Revisited', *Jewish Journal of Sociology* 33 (June 1991): 36–40; Beloff takes issue with some of the contributors for their emphasis on ethnicity rather than religion as a defining concept for Jews.
12. Kenneth Newton has devoted some space to this subject in *The Sociology of British Communism* (London: Allen Lane/Penguin, 1969), pp. 78-83.
13. Peter Y. Medding, 'Towards a General Theory of Jewish Political Interests and Behaviour', *Jewish Journal of Sociology* 19 (Dec. 1977): 132; see also Geoffrey Alderman, 'Not Quite British: The Political Attitudes of Anglo-Jewry', in Ivor Crewe (ed.), *British Political Sociology Yearbook*, vol. 2: *The Politics of Race* (London: Croom Helm, 1975), p. 189.
14. Alderman, 'Not Quite British', p. 194. The only seat the Liberals held in London after 1935 was Bethnal Green South-West, represented by Sir Percy Harris, a Jew.
15. In 1935, of the 16 Jews elected to the House of Commons, only two were Liberals. The election in 1935 also saw the defeat of Sir Herbert Samuel, the first High Com-

NOTES TO CHAPTER 1

missioner of the Palestine Mandate, 1920–25, and a Lloyd George loyalist. *Jewish Chronicle*, 22 Nov. 1935, p. 12.
16. For more on the concept of a Jewish radical sub-culture, see Arthur Liebman, *Jews and the Left* (New York: Wiley, 1979), pp. 26–33. Also, see the perceptive essay by Stephen J. Whitefield, 'After Strange Gods: Radical Jews in Modern America', *Forum* 56 (summer 1985): 17–41.
17. Cynthia H. Enloe, *Ethnic Conflict and Political Development* (Boston: Little, Brown, 1973), p. 15.
18. For some basic definitions of the term 'ethnic group', see R. A. Schermerhorn, *Comparative Ethnic Relations: A Framework for Theory and Research* (New York: Random House, 1970), p. 12; and Anthony D. Smith, *The Ethnic Revival* (Cambridge: Cambridge University Press, 1981), p. 66.
19. Ethnic group membership consists of wide complementarity of social communication, according to Karl Deutsch, *Nationalism and Social Communication: An Inquiry into the Foundations of Nationality* (Cambridge, MA: MIT Press, 2nd ed., 1966), pp. 96–100.
20. See Smith, *The Ethnic Revival*, pp. 68–9; Nelson Kasfir, 'Explaining Ethnic Political Participation', *World Politics* 31 (April 1979): 373–4; and James McKay and Frank Lewins, 'Ethnicity and the Ethnic Group: A Conceptual Analysis and Reformulation', *Ethnic and Racial Studies* 1 (Oct. 1978): 412–27.
21. See Jeffrey C. Alexander, 'Core Solidarity, Ethnic Outgroup, and Social Differentiation: A Multidimensional Model of Inclusion in Modern Societies', in Jacques Dofny and Akinsola Akiwowo (eds), *National and Ethnic Movements*, Sage Studies in International Sociology No. 19 (Beverly Hills, CA: Sage Publications, 1980), pp. 10–11; and Abner Cohen, 'The Lesson of Ethnicity', in Abner Cohen (ed.), *Urban Ethnicity* (London: Tavistock Publications, 1974), p. xi.
22. John Rex, *Race, Colonialism and the City* (London: Routledge & Kegan Paul, 1973), p. 11; see also John Rex, 'The Sociology of a Zone of Transition', in R. E. Pahl (ed.), *Readings in Urban Sociology* (Oxford: Pergamon, 1968), pp. 211–31.
23. See Edward Shils, 'Center and Periphery', in *Center and Periphery: Essays in Macrosociology* (Chicago: University of Chicago Press, 1975), pp. 3–16.
24. See E. K. Francis, *Interethnic Relations: An Essay in Sociological Theory* (New York: Elsevier, 1976), p. 296.
25. See David Easton, *The Political System: An Inquiry into the State of Political Science* (New York: Knopf, 1953), p. 134. Harold Lasswell has defined a ruling elite as those who get a preponderant share of deference, income and safety; see Harold Lasswell, *Politics: Who Gets What, When, How* (New York: McGraw-Hill, 1936), p. 3. Then as always, 'the political elite has remained rather firmly wedded to the upper strata of British Society', according to W. L. Guttsman, *The British Political Elite* (London: MacGibbon & Kee, 1963), p. 319.
26. See Michael Hechter, 'Towards a Theory of Ethnic Change', *Politics and Society* 2 (fall 1971): 42–5.
27. Schermerhorn, *Comparative Ethnic Relations*, pp. 12–13.
28. For further elaboration on the concept of minority groups, see R. A. Schermerhorn, 'Toward a General Theory of Minority Groups', *Phylon* 25 (fall 1964): 238–46.
29. Arnold M. Rose and Caroline B. Rose, 'Introduction: Some Definitions', in Arnold M. Rose and Caroline B. Rose (eds), *Minority Problems* (New York: Harper & Row, 1965; 2nd ed., 1972), p. 3. E. K. Francis, *Interethnic Relations*, p. 268, defines prejudice and discrimination as the illegitimate categorization of people under the aspect of ethnic descent. On prejudice and discrimination as weapons in group conflict, see also George E. Simpson and J. Milton Yinger, *Racial and Cultural Minorities: An Analysis*

of *Prejudice and Discrimination* (New York: Harper, 1953; 4th ed., 1972), esp. pp. 24–30, 103–11.
30. For a discussion of the concept of political culture, see Dennis Kavanagh, *Political Culture*, pp. 10–11.
31. Roy Macridis, 'Interest Groups in Comparative Analysis', *Journal of Politics* 23 (Feb. 1961): 40.
32. Gabriel A. Almond and Sidney Verba, *The Civic Culture: Political Attitudes and Democracy in Five Nations* (Princeton, NJ: Princeton University Press, 1963), p. 7; see also Bob Jessop, *Traditionalism, Conservatism and British Political Culture* (London: George Allen & Unwin, 1974), and Eric A. Nordlinger, *The Working Class Tories* (London: MacGibbon & Kee, 1967).
33. Robert A. Dahl, 'Some Explanations', in Robert A. Dahl (ed.), *Political Oppositions in Western Democracies* (New Haven, CT: Yale University Press, 1966), pp. 352–5.
34. Stuart Macintyre refers to this concept in his study of Communist strength in a number of isolated Welsh and Scottish towns between the wars. See his *Little Moscows: Communism and Working-class Militancy in Inter-war Britain* (London: Croom Helm, 1980), pp. 168–9, 176–7.
35. The behaviour of established Anglo-Jewry was not unusual; Norman Birnbaum, in *The Crisis of Industrial Society* (New York: Oxford University Press, 1969), p. 138, says that 'in no society have cultural and class divisions been so neatly matched' as in Britain.
36. David Cesarani, 'The East London of Simon Blumenfeld's *Jew Boy*', *London Journal* 13 (1987–88): 46, and Elaine R. Smith, 'Jews and Politics in the East End of London, 1918–1939', in David Cesarani (ed.), *The Making of Modern Anglo-Jewry*, pp. 141–2.
37. See Chaim Bermant, *The Cousinhood: The Anglo-Jewish Gentry* (London: Eyre & Spottiswoode, 1971), and Todd M. Endelman, 'Communal Solidarity Among the Jewish Elite of Victorian London', *Victorian Studies* 28 (spring 1985): 491–526.
38. Geoffrey Alderman, 'Not Quite British', p. 192. On this point see also David Feldman, 'Jews in London, 1880–1914', in Raphael Samuel (ed.), *Patriotism: The Making and Unmaking of British National Identity*, Vol. II: *Minorities and Outsiders* (London: Routledge, 1989), p. 224.
39. Eugene C. Black, *The Social Politics of Anglo-Jewry 1880–1920* (Oxford: Basil Blackwell, 1988), p. 304. See also pp. 194–221 for examples of East End Jewry's confrontations with the 'establishment'. The political interests of the two groups so often diverged: the immigrants from eastern Europe, for instance, had taken a very different position regarding military service in the First World War than had the Anglo-Jewish elite. See further Alderman, *London Jewry and London Politics 1889–1986*, pp. 61–3, and V. D. Lipman, *A History of the Jews in Britain Since 1858* (Leicester: Leicester University Press, 1990), pp. 143–8, 215–16.
40. See Geoffrey Alderman, *The Jewish Community in British Politics*, pp. 98–102; David Cesarani, 'The Transformation of Communal Authority in Anglo-Jewry, 1914–1940', in David Cesarani (ed.), *The Making of Modern Anglo-Jewry*, pp. 117, 137–40; and Stuart A. Cohen, *English Zionists and British Jews: The Communal Politics of Anglo-Jewry, 1895-1920* (Princeton, NJ: Princeton University Press, 1982), pp. 124–8, 322–3. The Balfour Declaration 'sent a thrill of excitement through the East End tenements', while among the Anglo-Jewish grandees, it produced an almost 'hysterical' anti-Zionist reaction. Geoffrey Alderman, 'The Political Impact of Zionism in the East End of London Before 1940', *London Journal* 9 (summer 1983): 36.
41. Alderman, *The Jewish Community in British Politics*, p. 52.
42. Simpson and Yinger, *Racial and Cultural Minorities*, p. 209.
43. William J. Foltz, 'Ethnicity, Status, and Conflict', in Wendell Bell and Walter E.

NOTES TO CHAPTER 1

Freeman (eds), *Ethnicity and Nation-Building*, p. 104. See also Fredrik Barth, 'Introduction', in Fredrik Barth (ed.), *Ethnic Groups and Boundaries: The Social Organization of Cultural Differences* (Boston: Little, Brown, 1969), p. 15; Barth believes that the socially constructed boundaries which divide groups within the same social system are the most important aspect of ethnicity.

44. Donald L. Horowitz, 'Three Dimensions of Ethnic Politics', *World Politics* 23 (Jan. 1971): 234–5; Rothschild, *Ethnopolitics*, pp. 80–2.
45. The concept of plural society has been most fully developed in M. G. Smith, 'Social and Cultural Pluralism', *Annals of the New York Academy of Sciences* 83 (20 Jan. 1960): 763–77. See also Leo Kuper, 'Political Change in Plural Societies: Problems in Racial Pluralism', in Leo Kuper, *Race, Class and Power: Ideology and Revolutionary Change in Plural Societies* (London: Duckworth, 1974), p. 243.
46. John Rex, *Social Conflict: A Conceptual and Theoretical Analysis* (London: Longman, 1981), pp. 85–6; Crawford Young, *The Politics of Cultural Pluralism* (Madison, WI: University of Wisconsin Press, 1976), pp. 12, 17.
47. A social, political or cultural organization is segmented rather than functional when it is organized along lines of ethnic or religious cleavage; see Val R. Lorwin, 'Segmented Pluralism: Ideological Cleavages and Political Cohesion in the Smaller European Democracies', *Comparative Politics* 3 (Jan. 1971): 141.
48. See Joseph R. Gusfield, 'Mass Society and Extremist Politics', *American Sociological Review* 27 (Feb. 1962): 29.
49. Kavanagh, *Political Culture*, p. 24.
50. David Easton, *A Systems Analysis of Political Life* (New York: Wiley, 1965), pp. 241–2.
51. See Barth, 'Introduction', *Ethnic Groups and Boundaries*, p. 17. This type of structure is described by David E. Apter, *Choice and the Politics of Allocation: A Developmental Theory* (New Haven, CT: Yale University Press, 1971), pp. 29, 51.
52. An immense amount has been written about this concept, initially developed by Arend Lijphart in 'Consociational Democracy', *World Politics* 21 (Jan. 1969): 207–25, and in *Democracy in Plural Societies: A Comparative Exploration* (New Haven, CT: Yale University Press, 1977). See also Kenneth McRae (ed.), *Consociational Democracy: Political Accommodation in Segmented Societies* (Toronto: McClelland & Stewart, 1974); and Ian Lustick, 'Stability in Deeply Divided Societies: Consociationalism versus Control', *World Politics* 31 (April 1979): 325–44. Consociationalism, being more flexible than federalism, can exist even within formally unitary states with majoritarian electoral systems, such as Britain. See the various articles on this subject in Daniel J. Elazar (ed.), 'Federalism and Consociationalism: A Symposium', *Publius: The Journal of Federalism* 15 (spring 1985).
53. Milton J. Esman, 'Introduction', in Milton J. Esman (ed.), *Ethnic Conflict in the Western World* (Ithaca, NY: Cornell University Press, 1977), p. 14.
54. See Eric A. Nordlinger, *Conflict Regulation in Divided Societies*, Occasional Papers in International Affairs No. 29 (Cambridge, MA: Center for International Affairs, Harvard University, Jan. 1972), pp. 26–30.
55. Van den Berghe, *The Ethnic Phenomenon*, pp. 185–93.
56. William A. Gamson, *Power and Discontent* (Homewood, IL: Dorsey, 1968), p. 53.
57. M. G. Smith, *The Plural Society in the British West Indies* (Berkeley: University of California Press, 1965), p. xiii.
58. Brian Barry, 'Political Accommodation and Consociational Democracy', *British Journal of Political Science* 5 (Oct. 1975): 502–5.
59. Enloe, *Ethnic Conflict and Political Development*, pp. 212–13.
60. Ibid., p. 266. See also Krausz, *Ethnic Minorities in Britain*, p. 124.

61. George De Vos, Ethnic Pluralism: Conflict and Accommodation', in George De Vos and Lola Romanucci-Ross (eds), *Ethnic Identity: Cultural Continuities and Change* (Palo Alto, CA: Mayfield, 1975), p. 6.
62. Halsey, 'Ethnicity', p. 127. 'In societies where ethnicity suffuses organizational life, virtually all political events have ethnic consequences.' Donald L. Horowitz, *Ethnic Groups in Conflict* (Berkeley, CA: University of California Press, 1985), p. 12.
63. J. P. Nettl, *Political Mobilization: A Sociological Analysis of Methods and Concepts* (London: Faber & Faber, 1967), pp. 123–4.
64. Horowitz, *Ethnic Groups in Conflict*, p. 9. This would especially hold true when one party – in this case, Labour – had already, so to speak, marked out the consociational, multi-ethnic terrain. In such a situation, 'all the electoral opportunities are located on the ethnic flanks', since the compromise politics of the multi-ethnic party causes resentment. The result is the formation of 'flanking' parties, in large part responsive to one or another ethnic group. See ibid., pp. 410–16. As we shall see, in Stepney the Communists and the British Union of Fascists to a large extent served this purpose for the Jews and the Irish.
65. Young, *The Politics of Cultural Pluralism*, p. 99.
66. David Easton writes that basic divisions within a community can cause systemic stress, especially when too many demands have been made on the system, a situation he terms 'demand input overload'; see *A Systems Analysis of Political Life*, p. 58.
67. Lewis A. Coser, *The Functions of Social Conflict* (Glencoe, IL: Free Press, 1956), p. 232; Ted Robert Gurr and Raymond D. Duvall, 'Introduction to a Formal Theory of Political Conflict', in Lewis A. Coser and Otto N. Larsen (eds), *The Uses of Controversy in Sociology* (New York: Free Press, 1976), pp. 140–1; and Walter E. Freeman, 'Functions of Ethnic Conflict and Their Contributions to National Growth', in Wendell Bell and Walter E. Freeman (eds), *Ethnicity and Nation-Building*, pp. 179–81. For more on ethnic group conflict see Robert A. LeVine and Donald T. Campbell, *Ethnocentrism: Theories of Conflict, Ethnic Attitudes, and Group Behavior* (New York: Wiley, 1972).
68. Louis Kriesberg, *The Sociology of Social Conflicts* (Englewood Cliffs, NJ: Prentice-Hall, 1973), pp. 12–14; and William A. Gamson, 'Rancorous Conflict in Community Politics', *American Sociological Review* 31 (Feb. 1966): 71–81.
69. Sandor Halebsky, *Mass Society and Political Conflict: Toward a Reconstruction of Theory* (Cambridge: Cambridge University Press, 1976), pp. 121, 179. See also William A. Gamson, *The Strategy of Social Protest* (Homewood, IL: Dorsey, 1975), pp. 136–43, for the view that social protest can be a rational form of 'resource management' by a group.
70. Tom Bottomore, *Political Sociology* (New York: Harper & Row, 1979), p. 49.
71. Dale C. Nelson, 'Ethnicity and Socioeconomic Status as Sources of Participation: The Case for Ethnic Political Culture', *American Political Science Review* 73 (Dec. 1979): 1037.
72. These terms, referring to the level of 'class consciousness' of a group, are from Karl Marx; see *The Poverty of Philosophy: a Translation of the Misère de la Philosophie (A Reply to 'La Philosophie de la Misère' of M. Proudhon)*, trans. H[arry] Quelch (many editions; the author has used Chicago: Kerr, 1910), pp. 188–9.
73. See Rex, *Social Conflict*, pp. 87–101, 117.
74. Angus Campbell, Gerald E. Gurin and Warren E. Miller, *The Voter Decides* (Evanston, IL: Row, Peterson, 1954), p. 187. See also, on the concept of political efficacy, Lester W. Milbrath, *Political Participation: How and Why Do People Get Involved in Politics?* (Chicago: Rand McNally, 1965).

NOTES TO CHAPTER 1

75. Nelson, 'Ethnicity and Socioeconomic Status as Sources of Participation', pp. 1024–7; Gamson, *Power and Discontent*, p. 155.
76. Ioan Davies, *Social Mobility and Political Change* (New York: Praeger, 1970), pp. 59–60. Seymour Martin Lipset says in *Political Man: The Social Bases of Politics* (Garden City, NY: Doubleday, 1960), p. 78, that a crisis of legitimacy may develop in a political system which denies new groups their demands or any access to power; at such points, 'extremist' movements arise.
77. J. A. Banks, *The Sociology of Social Movements* (London: Macmillan, 1972), p. 17; Herbert Blumer, 'Collective Behavior', in Alfred M. Lee (ed.), *Principles of Sociology* (New York: Barnes & Noble, 1951), p. 199; and Gary T. Marx and James L. Wood, 'Strands of Theory and Research in Collective Behavior', in Alex Inkeles (ed.), *Annual Review of Sociology* 1 (Palo Alto, CA: Annual Reviews, 1975), p. 376.
78. Hans Toch, *The Social Psychology of Social Movements* (Indianapolis: Bobbs-Merrill, 1965), p. 5.
79. William B. Cameron, *Modern Social Movements: A Sociological Outline* (New York: Random House, 1966), p. 7.
80. J. Craig Jenkins, 'Sociopolitical Movements', in Samuel L. Long (ed.), *The Handbook of Political Behavior*, 5 vols (New York: Plenum Press, 1981), Vol. IV, p. 84. See also Maurice Duverger, *Party Politics and Pressure Groups: A Comparative Introduction*, trans. David Wagoner (New York: Crowell, 1972), p. 1; John Wilson, *Introduction to Social Movements* (New York: Basic Books, 1973), p. 10.
81. Ted Robert Gurr, *Why Men Rebel* (Princeton, NJ: Princeton University Press, 1970), p. 13.
82. Robert H. Lauer, 'Introduction: Social Movements and Social Change: The Interrelationships', in Robert H. Lauer (ed.), *Social Movements and Social Change* (Carbondale, IL: Southern Illinois University Press, 1976), p. xvi.
83. Rudolf Heberle, *Social Movements: An Introduction to Political Sociology* (New York: Appleton-Century-Crofts, 1951), p. 7.
84. Joseph R. Gusfield, 'Introduction: A Definition of the Subject', in Joseph R. Gusfield (ed.), *Protest, Reform and Revolt: A Reader in Social Movements* (New York: Wiley, 1970), pp. 10–11.
85. Theda Skocpol, 'Explaining Revolutions: In Quest of a Social-Structural Approach', in Lewis A. Coser and Otto N. Larsen (eds), *The Uses of Controversy in Sociology*, p. 168.
86. Clifford Geertz, 'After the Revolution: The Fate of Nationalism in the New States', in Clifford Geertz, *The Interpretation of Cultures: Selected Essays* (New York: Basic Books, 1973), pp. 201–2.
87. Marx and Wood, 'Strands of Theory and Research in Collective Behavior', p. 382.
88. Feliks Gross, 'Dynamics of a Political Party', in Feliks Gross, *The Revolutionary Party: Essays in the Sociology of Politics*, Contributions in Sociology No. 12 (Westport, CT: Greenwood Press, 1974), pp. 85–6. 'Without an ideology a social movement would grope along in an uncertain fashion and could scarcely maintain itself in the face of pointed opposition from outside groups', according to Herbert Blumer, 'Social Movements', in R. Serge Denisoff (ed.), *The Sociology of Dissent* (New York: Harcourt Brace Jovanovich, 1974), pp. 12–13. For more on the integration, legitimation, structuring and control functions of ideology, see [Martin Kolinsky], 'Introduction' to Martin Kolinsky and William E. Paterson (eds), *Social and Political Movements in Western Europe* (New York: St Martin's Press, 1976), pp. 21–2.
89. See Heberle, *Social Movements*, pp. 1–11. Robert K. Merton has examined the discrepancy between the behaviour of a movement and its declared goals in terms of 'latent' and 'manifest' functions; see *Social Theory and Social Structure* (Glencoe, IL:

Free Press, 1949; revised and enlarged ed., 1957), pp. 71–2.
90. Karl Mannheim, *Ideology and Utopia: An Introduction to the Sociology of Knowledge*, trans. Louis Wirth and Edward Shils (New York: Harcourt, Brace, 1936; reprint ed., Harvest Books, 1955?), p. 85. According to Mannheim, people do not confront the world abstractly. Rather, they act in groups in order to change the world, and their collective activity 'produces the guiding thread for the emergence of their problems, their concepts, and their forms of thought' (p. 4).
91. Peter L. Berger and Thomas Luckmann, *The Social Construction of Reality: A Treatise in the Sociology of Knowledge* (Garden City, NY: Doubleday, 1966; Anchor Books, 1967), pp. 120–1. Berger and Luckmann define an ideology as 'a particular definition of reality' which has become attached to 'a concrete power interest' (p. 123). Hence, as Norman Birnbaum points out, the social consciousness of a group, far from being exhausted by ideology, may include an historically rooted social psychology distinct from that ideology; see Birnbaum, *Toward a Critical Sociology* (New York: Oxford University Press, 1971), p. 49.
92. R. S. Milne, *Politics in Ethnically Bipolar States: Guyana, Malaysia, Fiji* (Vancouver: University of British Columbia Press, 1981), p. 105.
93. For descriptions of these ideologies see Basil J. Vlavianos and Feliks Gross (eds), *Struggle for Tomorrow: Modern Political Ideologies of the Jewish People* (New York: Arts, Inc., 1954). A succinct summary is provided by Ben Halpern and Jehuda Reinhartz in 'Nationalism and Jewish Socialism: The Early Years', *Modern Judaism* 8 (Oct. 1988): 217–48.
94. Louis Hartz has popularized the notion of new settlements as fragments of the mother-country which faithfully reproduce the political and ideological stage reached by the mother-country at the time of emigration; see Hartz, *The Liberal Tradition in America: An Interpretation of American Political Thought Since the Revolution* (New York: Harcourt, Brace & World, 1955), and Hartz (ed.), *The Founding of New Societies: Studies in the History of the United States, Latin America, South Africa, Canada and Australia* (New York: Harcourt, Brace & World, 1964). If one regards the Pale of Settlement as the 'mother-country' of East London Jews, it is to be expected that the political culture that they reproduced in England would include a strong admixture of radical politics.
95. Interview, Jacob Sonntag, London, 15 May 1980. Mick Mindel, the trade unionist and Communist activist, put it succinctly: 'To me being Jewish and being a socialist was a natural thing.' Mick Mindel, 'Socialist Eastenders', *Jewish Socialist* 6/7 (summer/ autumn 1986): 26. The Jewish Communists in the East End of London and other immigrant neighbourhoods were very different from such assimilationist Jews as the film maker and writer Ivor Montagu, grandson of Sir Samuel Montagu, a prominent member of the 'Cousinhood', who were active in the CPGB at the national level. See Ivor Montagu, *The Youngest Son: Autobiographical Sketches* (London: Lawrence & Wishart, 1970), pp. 20, 115–18, 338.
96. The literature on this subject is enormous. See, for example, Robert S. Wistrich, 'Marxism and Jewish Nationalism: the Theoretical Roots of Confrontation', in Robert S. Wistrich (ed.), *The Left Against Zion: Communism, Israel and the Middle East* (London: Vallentine Mitchell, 1979); Robert Wistrich, *Revolutionary Jews from Marx to Trotsky* (London: Harrap, 1976); Shlomo Avineri, 'Marx and Jewish Emancipation', *Journal of the History of Ideas* 25 (July–Sept. 1964): 445–50; Nira Yuval-Davis, 'Marxism and Jewish Nationalism', *History Workshop* 24 (autumn 1987): 82–110; Norman Levine, 'Lenin on Jewish Nationalism', *Wiener Library Bulletin* 31 New Series (1980): 42–55; and Julius Carlebach, *Karl Marx and the Radical Critique of*

NOTES TO CHAPTER 1

Judaism (London: Routledge & Kegan Paul, 1978).
97. See Ralph H. Turner, 'The Theme of Contemporary Social Movements', *British Journal of Sociology* 20 (Dec. 1969): 391.
98. Gusfield, 'Introduction' to *Protest, Reform and Revolt*, pp. 3, 6. Duverger says that such social organizations 'create opinion as much as they represent it'; see Maurice Duverger, *Political Parties: Their Organization and Activity in the Modern State*, trans. Barbara North and Robert North (New York: Wiley, 1954; 3rd ed., 1965), p. 422. They are referred to as 'organised opinion' by James Jupp, *Political Parties* (London: Routledge & Kegan Paul, 1968), p. 29.
99. Heberle, *Social Movements*, pp. 417–18.
100. Charles Tilly, *From Mobilization to Revolution* (Reading, MA: Addison-Wesley, 1978), p. 69; Anthony Oberschall, *Social Conflict and Social Movements* (Englewood Cliffs, NJ: Prentice-Hall, 1973), p. 28. Karl Deutsch says that social mobilization breaks prior social, economic and psychological commitments, thus rendering people 'available for new patterns of socialization and behaviour'; see Deutsch, 'Social Mobilization and Political Development', *American Political Science Review* 55 (Sept. 1961): 493–514.
101. Oberschall, *Social Conflict and Social Movements*, pp. 123–9.
102. Amitai Etzioni, 'Toward a Theory of Societal Guidance', *American Journal of Sociology* 73 (Sept. 1967): 186.
103. [Kolinsky], 'Introduction', p. 18.
104. Ron E. Roberts and Robert Marsh Kloss, *Social Movements: Between the Balcony and the Barricade* (St Louis: Mosby, 1974), p. 11. For some of the determinants affecting the rate of mobilization into social movements, see Oberschall, *Social Conflict and Social Movements*, pp. 118–19; Nettl, *Political Mobilization*, pp. 32–3; and Neil J. Smelser, *Theory of Collective Behavior* (New York: Free Press, 1962), pp. 12–22.
105. Heberle, *Social Movements*, pp. 279–80; Jenkins, 'Sociopolitical Movements', p. 83.
106. Luther P. Gerlach and Virginia H. Hine, *People, Power, Change: Movements of Social Transformation* (Indianapolis: Bobbs-Merrill, 1970), p. 95; Roberta Ash, *Social Movements in America* (Chicago: Markham, 1972), p. 7.
107. Paul Wilkinson, *Social Movement* (London: Pall Mall, 1971), pp. 29, 31.
108. John D. McCarthy and Mayer N. Zald, 'Resource Mobilization and Social Movements: A Partial Theory', *American Journal of Sociology* 82 (May 1977): 1218.
109. Mayer N. Zald and John D. McCarthy, 'Introduction', in Mayer N. Zald and John D. McCarthy (eds), *The Dynamics of Social Movements: Resource Mobilization, Social Control, and Tactics* (Cambridge, MA: Winthrop, 1979), p. 3.
110. Mayer N. Zald and Roberta Ash, 'Social Movement Organizations: Growth, Decay and Change', *Social Forces* 44 (March 1966): 330.
111. These groups, ostensibly independent mass organizations, are easily identifiable as fronts: key positions at all organizational levels were filled by party members, while well-known but ineffectual people with honorific titles but no power served as ceremonial heads. See Duverger, *Party Politics and Pressure Groups*, p. 118.
112. Gertrude Jaeger and Philip Selznick, 'A Normative Theory of Culture', *American Sociological Review* 29 (Oct. 1964): 663.
113. See Sigmund Neumann, *Modern Political Parties: Approaches to Comparative Politics* (Chicago: University of Chicago Press, 1956), pp. 403–5.
114. See Jean Blondel, *Political Parties: A Genuine Case for Discontent?* (London: Wildwood House, 1978), pp. 58–9. These terms were, of course, coined by Ferdinand Tonnies.
115. Banks, *The Sociology of Social Movements*, pp. 13, 33.
116. For this typology see Ash, *Social Movements in America*, pp. 1, 3.

117. Zald and Ash, 'Social Movement Organizations', p. 328; see also Cameron, *Modern Social Movements*, p. 8.
118. [Kolinsky], 'Introduction', p. 16.
119. For Gramsci, hegemony is a political widening of the interests of one class and its representative party, a widening which enables it to achieve political and intellectual dominance over other social groups; see Antonio Gramsci, *Selections from the Prison Notebooks*, trans. and ed. by Quintin Hoare and G. Nowell Smith (London: Lawrence & Wishart, 1971), pp. 180–3.

CHAPTER 2

1. V. D. Lipman, *A History of the Jews in Britain Since 1858*, pp. 45, 49.
2. William J. Fishman, *East End Jewish Radicals 1875–1914* (London: Duckworth, 1975), p. 206. Before the start of the mass migration from eastern Europe, London had some 45,000 Jews; by 1900, about 135,000. Alderman, *London Jewry and London Politics 1889–1986*, p. 12.
3. Lipman, *A History of the Jews in Britain Since 1858*, pp. 50, 55.
4. Robert Benewick, *The Fascist Movement in Britain* (London: Allen Lane, 1972), p. 218.
5. *East London Advertiser*, 9 March 1935, p. 7. Of Stepney's total population in 1931 of 225,000, some 85,000 were Jewish – about 40 per cent of London's total Jewish population at the time. Lipman, *A History of the Jews in Britain Since 1858*, p. 207. Foreign-born Jews constituted at least one-third of the Jewish population in Stepney.
6. Cecil Roth, 'The Anglo-Jewish Community in the Context of World Jewry', in Julius Gold and Shaul Esh (eds), *Jewish Life in Modern Britain* (London: Routledge & Kegan Paul, 1964), p. 95.
7. Harold Pollins, *Economic History of the Jews in England* (Rutherford, NJ: Fairleigh Dickinson Press, 1982), p. 240.
8. Lloyd Gartner, *The Jewish Immigrant in England, 1870–1914* (London: George Allen & Unwin, 1960; 2nd ed., Simon Publications, 1973), pp. 166, 280. For a detailed account of Jewish life in the East End at this time, see Jerry White, *Rothschild Buildings: Life in an East End Tenement Block 1887–1920* (London: Routledge & Kegan Paul, 1980). The Rothschild Buildings were in Flower and Dean Street, Spitalfields.
9. Robert Skidelsky, *Oswald Mosley* (London: Macmillan, 1975), p. 393.
10. Nicholas Deakin, 'The Vitality of a Tradition', in Colin Holmes (ed.), *Immigrants and Minorities in British Society*, p. 161. Major William Eden Evans-Gordon, a turn-of-the-century MP, called the area east of Aldgate 'a foreign town' where the Jews had created another Wilna or Lodz; see Evans-Gordon, *The Alien Immigrant* (London: Heinemann, 1903), pp. 10–11.
11. *Stepney: The Associations and Features of this Interesting Borough [Metropolitan Borough of Stepney, Official Guide]* (London: Stepney Borough Council, 1934), p. 102.
12. Ken Worpole, *Dockers and Detectives. Popular Reading: Popular Writing* (London: Verso, 1983), p. 96.
13. Robert Wilcher, *Understanding Arnold Wesker* (Columbia, SC: University of South Carolina Press, 1991), p. 31.
14. Harold P. Clunn, *The Face of London: The Record of a Century's Changes and Development* (London: Simpkin Marshall, 1937), p. 251.
15. William Cameron, 'Whitechapel', *Picture Post* 1 (15 Oct. 1938): 24.
16. A. V. Sherman, 'Epitaph for the East End', *Commentary* 30 (Nov. 1960): 391.
17. Bernard Kops, *The World is a Wedding* (London: MacGibbon & Kee, 1963), p. 15.
18. This is the title of Emanuel Litvinoff's account of his East London childhood (London:

NOTES TO CHAPTER 2

Michael Joseph, 1972).
19. In 1901, 40 per cent of the east European Jews in London were tailors, 12.5 per cent were in boot-making, and 10 per cent in furniture-making; see Lipman, *A History of the Jews in Britain Since 1858*, pp. 57–8.
20. J. A. Garrard, 'Trade Unionism and the Jewish Immigrant', *Wiener Library Bulletin* 24 New Series (1970): 28.
21. Gartner, *The Jewish Immigrant in England*, p. 65.
22. Ibid., p. 127. See also Edmund Silberner, 'British Socialism and the Jews', *Historica Judaica* 14 (April 1952): 27–52. For more on the reaction of the host society, see Bernard Gainer, *The Alien Invasion: The Origins of the Aliens Act of 1905* (London: Heinemann, 1972) and John A. Garrard, *The English and Immigration, 1880-1910: A Comparative Study of the Jewish Influx* (London: Oxford University Press, 1971). The 'tradition' of 'racial exclusionism' in East End politics, which long pre-dated the rise of Fascist movements, is described by Christopher T. Husbands, 'East End Racism 1900–1980: Geographical Continuities in Vigilantist and Extreme Right-wing Political Behaviour', *London Journal* 8 (summer 1982): 3–26.
23. These men were, instead, really part of a wider Jewish labour movement extending across Europe and North America. See also Chimen Abramsky, 'The Jewish Labour Movement: Some Historiographical Problems', *Soviet Jewish Affairs* 1 (June 1971): 45–51. For a sympathetic treatment of these people and the events in which they were involved, such as the tailors' strike of 1889, see William Fishman's *East End Jewish Radicals 1875-1914*.
24. J. L. Fine, 'The Jewish Trade Unions', *Jewish Vanguard* No. 123 (31 July 1953), p. 3. See also Anne J. Kershen, *Trade Unionism Amongst the Jewish Tailoring Workers of London 1872-1915* (London: London Museum of Jewish Life, 1991), and Harold Pollins, *Economic History of the Jews in England*, pp. 152–64.
25. *Industries of Stepney* (London: Stepney Borough Council, 1946), p. 13. Mick Mindel maintains that 'a large proportion of those must have been Jews'; Interview, Mick Mindel, London, 5 Nov. 1978. But the numbers of Jews entering the industry had even then already begun to decline; see Lipman, *A History of Jews in Britain Since 1858*, pp. 210–11.
26. Stepney Reconstruction Group, Toynbee Hall, *Living in Stepney: Past Present and Future* (London: Pilot Press, 1945), p. 35.
27. For the entire sequence of trade union amalgamations leading up to the formation of the NUTGW, see Shirley W. Lerner, *Breakaway Unions and the Small Trade Union* (London: George Allen & Unwin, 1961), p. 91.
28. Letter from J. L. Fine, secretary, United Ladies Tailors' Trade Union, to A. G. Brotman, secretary, Board of Deputies of British Jews, London, 25 Nov. 1936, file E2/150, Board of Deputies Archives; Lerner, *Breakaway Unions and the Small Trade Union*, p. 87; and A. R. Rollin, 'A Jewish Trade Union Jubilee October, 1893–October, 1943', *Garment Worker* 12 (Oct. 1943): 197.
29. For the history of the UCWU see Roderick Martin, *Communism and the British Trade Unions 1924–1933: A Study of the National Minority Movement* (Oxford: Clarendon Press, 1969), pp. 136–41; and Lerner, *Breakaway Unions and the Small Trade Union*, pp. 99–101, 142–3. There is also a brief account in Elaine R. Smith, 'East End Tailors, 1918–1939: An Aspect of the Jewish Workers Struggle,' *Jewish Quarterly* 34 (summer 1987): 27–8, and 'Jews and Politics in the East End of London, 1918–1939', pp. 160–1. Communist organizer Sarah Wesker later thought that the breakaway union was a mistake. See her comments in R. A. Leeson, *Strike: A Live History 1887–1971* (London: George Allen & Unwin, 1973), p. 119.

30. See J. L. Fine, 'Anniversaries', *Garment Worker* 11 (June 1942): 108 for Fine's recollections of the founding of the ULTTU; Fine had been secretary of the ULTTU since its formation.
31. Interview, Hymie Cohen, London, 12 Nov. 1978.
32. Wesker was especially valuable because, at a time when most of the ULTTU's membership was Yiddish-speaking, she could speak the language. Interview, Mick Mindel, London, 5 Nov. 1978.
33. *Daily Worker*, 13 June 1938, p. 4.
34. J. L. Fine to A. G. Brotman, London, 25 Nov. 1936, file E2/150, Board of Deputies Archives. While Jewish involvement in the tailoring trades was declining in the 1930s, this was not the case in furniture-manufacturing. See Lipman, *A History of the Jews in Britain Since 1858*, p. 211.
35. Interview, Morry Lebow, London, 21 Nov. 1978. Lebow, a Communist, was secretary of the branch from 1947 to 1966.
36. See the *Jewish Chronicle*, 24 Sept. 1937, p. 13 for a report on a London Trades Council meeting at which members of NAFTA 15 urged anti-Fascist action.
37. Interview, Morry Lebow, London, 21 Nov. 1978.
38. M[orris] Mindel, 'Voo'hin Gayt Der Arbeter Ring?' ['Where is the Workers' Circle Heading?'], the *Circle-Arbeter Ring* 1 (June 1934): 5 [Yiddish section].
39. Nathan Weiner, 'Survey 1909–1933', the *Circle-Arbeter Ring* 1 (April 1934): 3 [English section]. These revolutionaries, who were members of the Jewish Labour Bund, remained an 'elite intellectual group' within the Circle for many years; interview, Mick Mindel, London, 5 Nov. 1978.
40. Branch 1 of the Circle was founded by cabinet-makers who were members of the union which later became NAFTA 15, according to A. R. Rollin, 'Jewish Labour Notes', the *Circle-Arbeter Ring* 9 (Jan. 1942): 2 (English section), and interview with Julius Jacobs, Leigh-on-Sea, Essex, 20 May 1978. According to Alf Holland, Branch 1 had an anarchist 'undercurrent' when it was founded; interview, London, 16 June 1978.
41. Rudolf Rocker, *The London Years*, trans. Joseph Leftwich (London: Anscombe & Co., 1956), p. 218.
42. Fishman, *East End Jewish Radicals 1875–1914*, p. 213; Nathan Weiner, 'Survey 1909–1933' p. 3 [English section].
43. [Nathan Weiner], 'General Secretary's Report', the *Circle-Arbeter Ring* 2 (Feb. 1935): 2 [English section].
44. N. M. Seedo, *In the Beginning Was Fear* (London: Narod Press, 1964), p. 312.
45. Interview, Alf Holland, London, 16 June 1978.
46. Joe Jacobs, *Out of the Ghetto: My Youth in the East End. Communism and Fascism 1913–1939* (London: Janet Simon, 1978), p. 38.
47. Alec Waterman, chairman of Branch 3, was very active in this work. The *Circle-Arbeter Ring* 1 (June 1934): 8 [English section]; 1 (Aug. 1934): 3 [English section]. For the formation of the JPC, see the *Jewish Chronicle*, 31 July 1936, p. 22.
48. 'General Secretary's Report', the *Circle-Arbeter Ring* 3 (Oct. 1936): 7 [English section].
49. *Jewish Chronicle*, 10 Sept. 1937, p. 20.
50. S. Joseph, 'Kampf Un Kultur' ['Battle and Culture'], in I. A. Lisky, N. M. Seedo and A. N. Stencl (eds), *Yiddish London*, 2 vols (London: YKUF [Society for Yiddish Culture], 1938–1939), Vol. 2, p. 67. The Workers' Circle ran a Yiddish school in the 1930s. Itzhak Nathani, who also edited the *Circle-Arbeter Ring*, was the teacher; see 'Yiddishe Weltleche Shule', the *Circle-Arbeter Ring* 6 (May 1939): 4 [English section].

NOTES TO CHAPTER 2

51. Gartner, *The Jewish Immigrant in England*, p. 273.
52. Ibid., p. 252. For the attitude of the Anglo-Jewish establishment, see Stanley Kaplan, 'The Anglicization of the East European Jewish Immigrant as seen by the London *Jewish Chronicle*, 1870–1897', *YIVO Annual of Jewish Social Science* 10 (1955): 267–78.
53. Jacob Sonntag, along with many other Yiddishists, felt that Yiddish failed to achieve the same significance in England as in North America because English society was less pluralistic; interview, Jacob Sonntag, London, 15 May 1980.
54. See I. N. Steinberg, 'Which Way? For Young Members of the Workers' Circle', the *Circle-Arbeter Ring* 1 (Oct. 1934): 2 [English section].
55. Harold Soref, 'Portrait of Anglo-Jewry', *Menorah Journal* 41 (spring 1953): 65–6.
56. Interview, Dr Yaacov Maitlis, London, 14 Nov. 1978.
57. Basil L.Q. Henriques, *The Indiscretions of a Warden* (London, Methuen, 1937), p. 92.
58. Jacob Sonntag, 'The Revival of Yiddish?' *Jewish Chronicle*, 22 Feb. 1980, p. 11.
59. Leonard Prager, 'A Bibliography of Yiddish Periodicals in Great Britain (1867–1967)', *Studies in Bibliography and Booklore* 9 (1969–1971): 23; Fishman, *East End Jewish Radicals 1875–1914*, p. 261.
60. L. S. Creditor, 'Yiddishe Literatur in London Biz 1948' ['Yiddish Literature in London Up to 1948'], *Fraye Yiddishe Tribune [Free Jewish Tribune]* No. 6 (Jan.–March 1948), p. 2. Stencl, who came to England in 1936, after living in Poland, Holland and Germany, 'met Whitechapel Yiddish in the door, as it were. He was coming in as Yiddish was going out.' S. J. Goldsmith, 'Yiddish Laureate of Whitechapel', *Jewish Observer and Middle East Review* 21 (2 June 1972): 17. Joseph Leftwich has noted that Whitechapel became Stencl's 'passion' and 'obsession'. Joseph Leftwich, 'Abram Stenzel', *East London Papers* 1 (Oct. 1958): 25. Stencl remarked that 'even during the war, I never left Whitechapel'. Interview, A. N. Stencl, London, 8 Aug. 1978. See also S. S. Prawer, *A. N. Stencl: Poet of Whitechapel* (Oxford: Oxford Centre for Postgraduate Hebrew Studies, 1984).
61. *Jewish Chronicle*, 15 Jan. 1937, p. 43; see also the review of the Yiddish theatre in London in 1937–38 in the *Jewish Chronicle*, 23 Sept. 1938, p. 89.
62. Ray Waterman, 'Prolet: The Yiddish-speaking Group of the Workers' Theatre Movement', *History Workshop* 5 (spring 1978): 174–8; Ray Waterman, 'Memories of Proltet', in Raphael Samuel, Ewan MacColl and Stuart Cosgrove (eds.), *Theatres of the Left 1880–1935: Workers' Theatre Movements in Britain and America* (London: Routledge and Kegan Paul, 1985), pp. 149–55. The Proltet group had to respond to criticisms from others in the Workers' Theatre Movement for performing in Yiddish rather than in English. But Holland and Waterman, who would later also be major proponents of Yiddish within the CP's National Jewish Committee, championed the language. Interview, Mrs N. M. Seedo, London, 10 Aug. 1978; Kathleen McCreery, 'Proltet: Yiddish Theatre in the 1930s', *Race & Class* 20 (winter 1979): 300.
63. Mark Clifford, 'Workers' Circle Theatre', the *Circle-Arbeter Ring* 5 (Nov. 1938): 8–9 [English section].
64. Letter from I. A. Lisky to J. L. Fine, London, 13 Dec. 1937 [in Yiddish], in the NUTGW papers, London and Southern Divisional Office, Charles Square, London; interview, I. A. Lisky, London, 10 Aug. 1978.
65. I. A. Lisky, 'A Yor YKUF Arbet in London', ['A Year of YKUF Work in London'], in I. A. Lisky *et al.* (eds), *Yiddish London*, Vol. 2, pp. 124–5.
66. See 'The Unity of Jewish Progressive Cultural Forces', *Jewish News Letter* 1 (8 Aug. 1939), pp. 4–5; TS in the Lazar Zaidman Collection.
67. N. Barou, 'Di Arbet fun Propaganda Komitet', ['The Work of the Propaganda Committee'], the *Circle-Arbeter Ring* 1 (Oct. 1934): 8 [Yiddish section].

68. The ULTTU executive committee minutes of 22 Sept. 1938 note that YKUF had sent a letter soliciting funds for the course. NUTGW papers, London.
69. *Jewish Chronicle*, 7 Oct. 1938, p. 32; 14 Oct. 1938, p. 34.
70. 'The London Jewish Theatre', in *Cultural Topics: Review of the Activities of the Folk House and Jewish Cultural Centre-Kultur Yidies. Fun Folks-Hoyz Un Yiddishn-Kultur-Tsenter* (London: Folk House (Beth Am), summer 1944), p. 6 [English section].
71. *East London Advertiser*, 12 Oct. 1945, p. 4.
72. 'The Jewish Cultural Centre', in *Cultural Topics*, p. 2 [English section].
73. In 1936 the ratable value of buildings in Stepney was £1,733,116, or £8.30 per head of population, as compared to an average figure for London as a whole of £14.70 per head. Because the buildings on which rates were levied were less valuable than their counterparts in other parts of London, they had to be taxed at a higher level to enable the local government to provide equivalent services. Hence Stepney's rates were the fourth highest in London; see London County Council, *Statistics of Metropolitan Boroughs 1936–37 (Eighth Year of Issue)*, London, Oct. 1937, p. 7; and Stepney Reconstruction Group, Toynbee Hall, *Living in Stepney: Past Present and Future*, p. 48.
74. There were only 49 acres of open space in the borough in 1938, or a quarter of an acre per 1,000 people, according to the Stepney Reconstruction Group, Toynbee Hall, *Living in Stepney: Past Present and Future*, p. 66.
75. London County Council, *Statistics of Metropolitan Boroughs 1936–37*, p. 3.
76. Ibid.
77. London County Council, *London Statistics* 1 New Series: *1945–1954* (London: London County Council, 1957), Table 128, p. 161.
78. *Census of England and Wales 1931, County of London* (London: His Majesty's Stationery Office, 1932), Table IX, p. xx.
79. London County Council, *London Statistics* 41: *1936–38* (London: London County Council, June 1939), Table 3, pp. 86–7.
80. Stepney Reconstruction Group, Toynbee Hall, *Living in Stepney: Present and Future*, p. 66; this study also pointed out that 60 per cent of all families shared houses and that 90 per cent had no indoor toilet facilities (pp. 31, 41).
81. Henrietta Adler, 'Jewish Life and Labour in East London', in London School of Economics and Political Science, Sir Hubert Llewellyn Smith, director, *The New Survey of London Life and Labour*, Vol. VI: *Survey of Social Conditions (2) The Western Area (Text)* (London: P. S. King & Son Ltd, 1934), pp. 287–8.
82. Department of Employment and Productivity, *British Labour Statistics: Historical Abstracts 1886–1968* (London: Her Majesty's Stationery Office, 1971), Table 164, p. 315.
83. *Daily Worker*, 6 Aug. 1940, p. 1.
84. London County Council, *London Statistics* 40: *1935–37* (London: London County Council, Dec. 1937), p. 79; London County Council, *London Statistics* 41: *1936–38*, p. 79.
85. *National Amalgamated Furnishing Trades Association Monthly Report* 36 New Series (Jan. 1937): 6.
86. *National Amalgamated Furnishing Trades Association Monthly Report* 38 New Series (Dec. 1939): 6–7.
87. United Ladies Tailors' Trade Union, *Twenty-Eighth Annual Balance Sheet and Report for 12 Months ended 31st December, 1935* [English and Yiddish], pp. 8–9 [English section]; NUTGW papers, London.
88. A. L. Cohen, 'The Memorable Sunday – October 4th', the *Circle-Arbeter Ring* 3

NOTES TO CHAPTER 2

89. (Oct. 1936): 2 [English section].
    William Cameron, 'Whitechapel', p. 28; *A Stepney to be Proud of: Plan and Proposals* (London: Stepney Communist Party, [winter 1944–45]), p.[3]. Ray Waterman describes the queues at Settles Street and outside the ULTTU offices in her novel, *A Family of Shopkeepers* (London: W. H. Allen, 1973), p. 240; Bernard Kops, in *The World is a Wedding*, pp. 28–9, indicates the radicalism of the workers involved: while waiting in line, the unemployed would argue the relative merits of Lenin, Stalin, and Trotsky!
90. For statistics concerning the number of people on relief, see the London County Council, *London Statistics 1935–37*, p. 65, and *London Statistics 1936–38*, p. 67. On Jewish poverty and unemployment, see Pollins, *Economic History of the Jews in England*, pp. 185–6.
91. Phil Piratin, *Communist Plan for Life in Stepney* (London: Stepney Communist Party, [1937]), p. 2.
92. George Collins, 'Stepney's Rotten Homes Breed Ill-Health. Poverty Kills Our Mothers and Children', *Voice of East London*, 1 May 1939, p. 3. Collins noted that Stepney, with its population of over 200,000, could afford only 22 sanitary inspectors to see that healthy housing conditions were maintained.
93. See the statistics in *The Registrar General's Statistical Review of England and Wales* for the years 1936 to 1939, *Text* (London: His Majesty's Stationery Office, 1938, 1940, 1947): Table IV, p. 12 in the volume for 1936; Table VIII, p. 21 in the volume for 1937; Table IV, p. 11 in the volume for 1938 and 1939.
94. St John B. Groser, *Politics and Persons* (London: SCM Press, 1949), p. 68.
95. Phil Piratin, *Our Flag Stays Red* (London: Thames Publications, 1948), p. 11.
96. Kevin O'Connor, *The Irish in Britain* (Dublin: Torc Books, 1974), p. 26. For an overview of Irish and Jewish immigration, see also Catherine Jones, *Immigration and Social Policy in Britain* (London: Tavistock Publications, 1977), pp. 43–117. For political activity and party support, see Paul Thompson, *Socialists, Liberals and Labour: The Struggle for London* (London: Routledge & Kegan Paul, 1967), pp. 25–31.
97. Krausz, *Ethnic Minorities in Britain*, p. 39.
98. Interview, Tom Rampling, Banbury, Oxfordshire, 20 Jan. 1979.
99. Margaret Stewart and Leslie Hunter, *The Needle is Threaded: The History of an Industry* (London: Heinemann/Newman Neame, 1964), p. 181.
100. The Irish grouping, which had been a front for Sinn Fein, the Irish republican movement, was 'handed over' after the granting of Irish independence to Catholic Action, a lay group dedicated to fostering close ties between the Irish and their church. Interviews, Tom Rampling, Banbury, Oxfordshire, 20 Jan. 1979; Montagu Einhorn, London, 10 Dec. 1978. Bertha Sokoloff, later a Communist borough councillor, has observed that 'the Catholic clergy took an active interest in local politics, which were Labour politics'; Bertha Sokoloff, *Edith and Stepney: The Life of Edith Ramsay* (London: Stepney Books, 1987), p. 69. The backbone of Jewish support for Labour was the socialist-Zionist Poale Zion movement, with branches established in the East End in 1903. Many of its members belonged to the Workers' Circle. It formally affiliated with the Labour Party after the First World War. See Gideon Shimoni, 'Poale Zion: A Zionist Transplant in Britain (1905–1945)', in Peter Y. Medding (ed.), *Studies in Contemporary Jewry*, Vol. II (Bloomington, IN: Indiana University Press, 1986), pp. 227–41.
101. Chaim Bermant, *Point of Arrival: A Study of London's East End* (London: Eyre Methuen, 1975), p. 71. For more on Irish political activity, see John A. Jackson, 'The Irish in East London', *East London Papers* 6 (Dec. 1963): 105–19. See also references

to the Irish throughout Colin Holmes, *John Bull's Island: Immigration and British Society, 1871–1971* (London: Macmillan, 1988). Like the Jews, the Irish community also switched its allegiance from the Liberal party to the Labour party after the First World'War (p. 133).
102. Geoffrey Alderman, *British Elections: Myth and Reality* (London: B. T. Batsford, 1978), p. 187.
103. John A. Jackson, *The Irish in Britain* (London: Routledge & Kegan Paul, 1963), refers to the 'strongly organised' Irish vote. See pp. 123–4.
104. Deakin, 'The Vitality of a Tradition', p. 173.
105. Piratin, *Our Flag Stays Red*, p. 13. See also Elaine R. Smith, 'Jews and Politics in the East End of London, 1918–1939', pp. 146–9, and Kenneth Lunn, 'Parliamentary Politics and the "Jewish Vote" in Whitechapel, 1906–1914', in Aubrey Newman (ed.), *The Jewish East End 1840–1939*. Proceedings of the Conference held on 22 October 1980 jointly by the Jewish Historical Society of England and the Jewish East End Project of the Association for Jewish Youth. (London: Jewish Historical Society of England, 1981), pp. 255–65, for evidence of Liberal strength among East End Jews. Whitechapel had been represented in the House of Commons by the Jewish banker Sir Samuel Montagu (later Lord Swaythling), a Liberal, from 1885 to 1900. He was succeeded by his nephew, Stuart Samuel, who held the seat until 1916. The Mile End seat was won for the first time by a Jewish Liberal (Bertram Straus) in 1906 but he lost it to the Conservatives in 1910.
106. Details can be found in Joseph Gorny, *The British Labour Movement and Zionism 1917–1948* (London: Frank Cass, 1983), pp. 91–6, and Gideon Shimoni, 'Poale Zion', pp. 241–5.
107. The combined Labour–Communist vote was 1,509 more than Janner's total of 11,013. John Mahon, *Harry Pollitt: A Biography* (London: Lawrence & Wishart, 1976), p. 166. Alderman, *The Jewish Community in British Politics*, p. 196, fn. 50, has estimated that half of Pollitt's 2,658 votes came from Jews.
108. Colin Holmes, 'East End Anti-Semitism, 1936', *Bulletin of the Society for the Study of Labour History* 32 (spring 1976): 32.
109. *Jewish Chronicle*, 22 Nov. 1935, p. 12.
110. *East London Advertiser*, 9 Nov. 1935, p. 3; 16 Nov. 1935, p. 5. This time Hall was endorsed by the Communists, who were by now anxious to cooperate with Labour in a 'popular front' against the right. Janner lost by more than 2,000 votes.
111. On the early history of the Stepney Labour Party, including sketches of personalities such as Alfred Kershaw, Oscar Tobin, Israel Shafran, J. J. Long, I. M. Vogler, Dan Frankel, and M. H. Davis, see Geoffrey Alderman, *London Jewry and London Politics 1889–1986*, pp. 77–84; Geoffrey Alderman, 'M. H. Davis: The Rise and Fall of a Communal Upstart', in *Jewish Historical Studies: Transactions of the Jewish Historical Society of England* 31 (1988–1990): 249–53; and Elaine R. Smith, 'Jews and Politics in the East End of London, 1918–1939', pp. 150–4. Such studies make it clear that the Jews clearly carried more weight in the party in the 1920s than they did in the 1930s and 1940s.
112. Frankel, who beat the Conservative incumbent Dr W. J. O'Donovan, was also endorsed by the Communists. See the *Jewish Chronicle*, 22 Nov. 1935, p. 12.
113. Joe Jacobs, *Out of the Ghetto*, p. 71. Davis, who was Labour leader of the council from 1935 to 1944, and J. J. Long formed 'a holy – or unholy – alliance', according to Morry Lebow, who was at the time ward secretary of the Spitalfields East CP; Interview, London, 10 Dec. 1978. Dora Einhorn, a Stepney CP member after 1936, added that 'Morry Davis was one of the tame Jews and they [the Irish councillors] let him fill

NOTES TO CHAPTER 2

his pockets until he eventually got caught'. Interview, Dora Einhorn, London, 10 Dec. 1978. In *London Jewry and London Politics, 1889–1986*, Geoffrey Alderman suggests that Davis was at first more of a political ally than a subordinate of Irish Catholic Labour leaders such as Long. However, as criticism of his politics increased among the Jewish community, he was forced to rely on his Irish allies, which in turn distanced him still further from Jewish voters (pp. 84, 97). Elaine Smith called Davis a 'power broker *par excellence*' who used 'dubious methods' to attain his ends. 'Jews and Politics in the East End of London, 1918–1939', p. 154.

114. Interview, Julius Jacobs, Leigh-on-Sea, Essex, 20 May 1978.
115. Indeed, in October 1936, two prominent Jewish councillors were asked not to have their names placed in nomination for the office. Alderman, *London Jewry and London Politics 1889–1986*, p. 94.
116. Skidelsky quotes Dan Frankel, the Mile End MP, to make this point; see Skidelsky, *Oswald Mosley*, p. 398.
117. This incident was recounted by Miss Ramsay on a BBC 2 television programme; see the report in the *Hackney Gazette & North London Advertiser*, 16 Jan. 1970, p. 8.
118. See John A. Jackson, 'The Irish', in Ruth Glass *et al.* (eds), for the Centre for Urban Studies, *London: Aspects of Change* (London: MacGibbon & Kee, 1964), pp. 305–6; Jackson, *The Irish in Britain*, pp. 116, 135–51; and Bermant, *Point of Arrival*, pp. 53–68, 71–4.
119. The Stepney Branch of the Anti-Partition of Ireland League, for example, held a meeting on 25 May 1939 at St George's Town Hall, where one of the speakers, Labour councillor J. J. Long, denied 'that the League was mixed up with the I.R.A.'; see the *East London Advertiser*, 3 June 1939, p. 6.
120. See Tom Buchanan, *The Spanish Civil War and the British Labour Movement* (Cambridge: Cambridge University Press, 1991), pp. 141, 169; Jim Fyrth, *The Signal Was Spain: The Aid Spain Movement in Britain, 1936–39* (London: Lawrence & Wishart, 1986), p. 282.
121. Interview, Montagu Einhorn, London, 10 Dec. 1978.
122. *East London Advertiser*, 17 Oct. 1936, p. 5, and 24 Oct. 1936, p. 3. Communists Mick Mindel and Ruby Silkoff were vice-presidents of the Council for Peace; the honorary secretary, Eric Hartley, was a member of the Stepney CP; left-wing Labour borough councillors I. M. Vogler and Henry Solomons also took part in its activities, the latter serving as chairman. *East London Advertiser*, 19 Sept. 1936, p. 8, and 17 Oct. 1936, pp. 5, 6. As an opponent of nepotism in council hiring policies, Solomons also incurred the wrath of Councillor Davis. See the *East London Advertiser*, 12 Dec. 1936, p. 5.
123. *East London Advertiser*, 7 Nov. 1936, p. 7.
124. Interview, Maurice Goldsmith, London, 31 May 1978.
125. *Jewish Chronicle*, 16 April 1937, p. 17.
126. Stuart Rawnsley, 'The Membership of the British Union of Fascists', in Kenneth Lunn and Richard C. Thurlow (eds), *British Fascism: Essays on the Radical Right in Inter-War Britain* (London: Croom Helm, 1980), p. 162. According to Rawnsley, BUF membership lists are not available (p. 153). Still, G. C. Webber, in *The Ideology of the British Right 1918–1939* (London: Croom Helm, 1986), p. 44, and Richard Thurlow, in *Fascism in Britain: A History, 1918–1985* (Oxford: Basil Blackwell, 1987), p. 124, estimate that after 1935 half the membership was concentrated in the East London boroughs of Stepney, Shoreditch and Bethnal Green. Mosley himself maintained that his 'personal relations were close and warm' with East London's non-Jewish working class. John D. Brewer, 'The British Union of Fascists: Some Tentative

Conclusions on its Membership', in Stein Ugelvik Larsen et al. (eds), *Who Were the Fascists: Social Roots of European Fascism* (Bergen, Norway: Universitetsforlaget, 1980), p. 545. See also G. C. Webber, 'Patterns of Membership and Support for the British Union of Fascists', *Journal of Contemporary History* 19 (Oct. 1984): 575–606.
127. Skidelsky, *Oswald Mosley*, p. 513.
128. Ibid., pp. 106, 327, 393–6. See also Colin Cross, *The Fascists in Britain* (London: Barrie and Rockliff, 1961), pp. 142, 151.
129. Benewick, *The Fascist Movement in Britain*, p. 280. Certainly the BUF was 'loud in support of Franco', as were various Roman Catholic organizations in Britain. See Fyrth, *The Signal Was Spain*, pp. 192–7.
130. Colin Holmes suggests that 'there were deliberate attempts to capture the Catholic vote'; see his *Anti-Semitism in British Society 1876–1939* (London: Edward Arnold, 1979), p. 194; the prospect of Labour losses was certainly a worry for Herbert Morrison, then secretary of the London Labour Party. Buchanan, *The Spanish Civil War and the British Labour Movement*, p. 175. The BUF won 17.8 per cent of the votes in the three East London LCC constituencies that they contested; see Benewick, *The Fascist Movement in Britain*, p. 282. Even Communists admitted that the 'overwhelming' majority of these voters were working class, according to a report in the *Jewish Chronicle*, 16 April 1937, p. 17.
131. Colin Holmes, *A Tolerant Country? Immigrants, Refugees and Minorities in Britain* (London: Faber & Faber, 1991), p. 33.
132. Holmes, *Anti-Semitism in British Society*, p. 212.
133. *Catholic Herald*, 25 Oct. 1940, p. 8.
134. Tony Kushner, *The Persistence of Prejudice*, p. 80.
135. Tony Kushner, 'The British and the Shoah', *Patterns of Prejudice* 23 (autumn 1989): 10.
136. R[euben] Ainsztein, 'The Enemy Within: Antisemitism among Polish Soldiers in War-Time Britain', *Wiener Library Bulletin* 13 (1959): 58; Andrew Sharf, *The British Press and Jews Under Nazi Rule* (London: Oxford University Press, 1964), p. 119. For other examples of the *Herald*'s anti-Semitic tone, see Sharf, pp. 18–19, 88, 94 and 136; for instances of anti-Semitism in another London weekly, the *Catholic Times*, see Sharf, pp. 66, 91–2, and Holmes, *Anti-Semitism in British Society*, pp. 201, 212–13.
137. *Jewish Chronicle*, 15 Jan. 1937, p. 17.
138. Interview, Morry Lebow, London, 21 Nov. 1978.
139. Interview, Tom Rampling, Banbury, Oxfordshire, 20 Jan. 1979. According to Rampling, 'The number of non-Jewish people was comparatively low; they were mainly the militants that were leading the dock workers, and one or two odd people like myself'.
140. Interview, Mick Mindel, London, 5 Nov. 1978.
141. Interview, Maurice 'Tubby' Rosen, London, 13 Nov. 1978.
142. Harry Roberts, 'Jew and Blackshirt in the East End', *New Statesman and Nation* 12 (7 Nov. 1936): 698; see also J. J. Mallon, 'Fascist Provocation in East London', *Daily Telegraph*, 28 Oct. 1936, p. 16.
143. Piratin, *Our Flag Stays Red*, p. 17.
144. *East London Advertiser*, 11 Sept. 1937, p. 5; and letter to the editor from J[oe] Emden, *East London Advertiser*, 25 Sept. 1937, p. 6.
145. 'By 1900, large parts of Spitalfields were 95–100 per cent Jewish', according to K[enneth] Leech, 'The Decay of Spitalfields', *East London Papers* 7 (Dec. 1964): 60–1. Spitalfields East was the more Jewish section.
146. Letter to the editor from Phil Piratin, *East London Advertiser*, 2 Oct. 1937, p. 5.

NOTES TO CHAPTER 3

147. Long was refused endorsement by the left-dominated Stepney Trades Council in the 1937 borough elections. *East London Advertiser*, 16 Oct. 1937, p. 1.
148. *Jewish Chronicle*, 8 Oct. 1937, p. 12; and 22 Oct. 1937, p. 24.
149. *Jewish Chronicle*, 5 Nov. 1937, p. 24; and *The Jewish People and the Borough Council Elections* (London: Jewish People's Council Against Fascism & Anti-Semitism, [1937]), a pamphlet in the Zaidman Collection.
150. *Daily Worker*, 4 Nov. 1937, p. 4. One of the four Jewish Labour councillors voting in favour of the motion had been M. H. Davis; another was J. L. Fine. I. M. Vogler was particularly incensed. *Jewish Chronicle*, 26 Feb. 1937, p. 17; *East London Advertiser*, 27 Feb. 1937, p. 1. Alderman, in *London Jewry and London Politics 1889–1986*, p. 85, wonders whether the four voted this way 'in deference to Irish pressures'. Davis and Fine claimed the *Jewish Chronicle* had libelled them and sued the paper, which was forced to issue an apology. *Jewish Chronicle*, 11 Feb. 1938, p. 21.
151. According to the *East London Advertiser*, 6 Nov. 1937, p. 1, the results were:

    Dr M. Barst (Labour)   851
    Mrs A. Taylor (Labour)   732
    P. Piratin (Communist)   616
    B. Purdy (Labour)   582
    S. Cohen (Conservative)   132
    E. Feiner (Conservative)   120
    B. Silverstein (Ind.)   89

    Spitalfields East was one of twenty Stepney wards; each ward elected three councillors at large.
152. This entire sequence of events is described fully in the *East London Advertiser*, 26 Feb. 1938, p. 1.
153. *East London Advertiser*, 26 Nov. 1938, p. 1. Vogler, too, was a supporter of the STDL. Gordon died the following year. *Jewish Chronicle*, 15 Dec. 1939, p. 22.
154. *East London Advertiser*, 4 June 1938, p. 3.
155. *Jewish Chronicle*, 8 July 1938, p. 40.
156. *East London Advertiser*, 25 Feb. 1939, p. 1.
157. Letter to the editor from I. M. Vogler, *East London Advertiser*, 10 June 1939, p. 5. Bertha Sokoloff, probably recollecting many such episodes, has recalled that 'there were, and had been for years, a number of Labour Party councillors who were not particularly friendly to Jews – indeed one sometimes felt sorry for some Jewish Labour councillors who knew of this and experienced it themselves'. Sokoloff, *Edith and Stepney*, p. 14. For evidence that such animosity towards Jews on the borough council preceded the rise of Fascism in the East End, see Elaine R. Smith, 'Jewish Responses to Political Antisemitism and Fascism in the East End of London, 1920–1939', in Tony Kushner and Kenneth Lunn (eds), *Traditions of Intolerance: Historical Perspectives on Fascism and Race Discourse in Britain* (Manchester: Manchester University Press, 1989), pp. 54–5.
158. Piratin, *Our Flag Stays Red*, p. 49; and Interview, Phil Piratin, London, 3 Aug. 1976.

CHAPTER 3

1. Phil Piratin, *Our Flag Stays Red*, p. 33.
2. Michael Shapiro ['Michael Best'], *Heartbreak Homes: An Indictment of the National Government's Housing Policy* (London: CPGB, [1935]), pp. 6, 8–13.
3. Michael Shapiro ['Michael Best'], *The Tenants' Guide* (London: Labour Research

Department, [1938]).
4. Ted Bramley, for example, wrote *New London* (London: Workers' Bookshop, 1936), in which he called for workers' flats in London to be built on the model of those in Vienna and Amsterdam.
5. Piratin, *Our Flag Stays Red*, pp. 28–32.
6. *Communist Plan for Life in Stepney*, p. 15.
7. Ibid., p. 5.
8. Piratin, *Our Flag Stays Red*, pp. 38, 48.
9. 'Enough of All This', *Picture Post* 2 (1 April 1939): 48. Groser first became involved in the tenants' movement in 1939, when he made room in his vicarage for young solicitors and law students to interview and advise tenants in difficulties. 'The scheme caught on and soon the tenants sought his help in establishing the organisation of which he became President,' according to Kenneth Brill, 'The World His Parish', in Kenneth Brill (ed.), *John Groser, East London Priest* (London: Mowbrays, 1971), p. 101.
10. *East London Advertiser*, 22 July 1939, p. 10.
11. *Daily Worker*, 12 Jan. 1939, p. 8.
12. Noreen Branson and Margot Heinemann, *Britain in the Nineteen Thirties* (London: Weidenfeld and Nicolson, 1971; reprint ed., St Albans, Herts: Panther, 1973), p. 219.
13. *Daily Worker*, 25 Jan. 1939, p. 5.
14. *Daily Worker*, 4 Feb. 1939, p. 6.
15. *Reynolds News*, 26 Feb. 1939, p. 3; *Daily Worker*, 28 Feb. 1939, p. 5.
16. *Daily Worker*, 4 March 1939, p. 7.
17. *Daily Worker*, 10 March 1939, p. 8. The day before, Stepney housewives had picketed shoppers in the West End as a means of calling attention to conditions in the slums.
18. *Reynolds News*, 19 March 1939, p. 7; *Daily Worker*, 20 March 1939, p. 5.
19. *Daily Worker*, 29 April 1939, p. 4; *Voice of East London*, 1 May 1939, p. 1.
20. The most successful of these, *Jew Boy* (London: Jonathan Cape, 1935), was reprinted in 1986 by Lawrence & Wishart. He also published *Phineas Kahn, Portrait of an Immigrant* (London: Jonathan Cape, 1937); *Doctor of the Lost* (London: Jonathan Cape, 1938); and *They Won't Let You Live* (London: Nicholson and Watson, 1939). A review of *Jew Boy* by N. Gorty in the *Circle-Arbeter Ring* 2 (Oct. 1935): 6–7 [English section] noted that Blumenfeld was a member of Branch 10.
21. *News Chronicle*, 24 May 1939, p. 10; not all flats in Stepney were decontrolled, even after 1938.
22. *Daily Worker*, 28 June 1939, p. 1.
23. Piratin calculated that the STDL had 7,500 members by this time; see Piratin, *Our Flag Stays Red*, p. 44.
24. *Reynolds News*, 12 Feb. 1939, p. 6.
25. *Daily Worker*, 18 May 1939, p. 8; the women were demanding a new Rent Act.
26. *Parliamentary Debates (Hansard) House of Commons*, Fifth Series, Vol. 349, 6 July 1939, cols 1492–4.
27. Brill, 'The World His Parish', p. 101.
28. *East London Observer*, 8 July 1939, p. 1; *Daily Worker*, 10 July 1939, p. 1.
29. *Jewish Chronicle*, 29 Sept. 1939, p. 15.
30. *Daily Worker*, 11 Nov. 1939, p. 6.
31. *Daily Worker*, 2 Dec. 1939, p. 2.
32. *Daily Worker*, 27 June 1940, p. 8. The STDL rent strike play, *Tenants in Revolt*, was being performed at the Workers' Circle Theatre in Great Alie Street in 1940; see the *Daily Worker*, 27 Jan. 1940, p. 5.

NOTES TO CHAPTER 3

33. *East London Advertiser*, 29 June 1940, p. 1.
34. Brill, 'The World His Parish', pp. 103–4.
35. St John B. Groser, *Politics and Persons*, p. 71. Tubby Rosen recalled this episode with more humour: Father Groser, according to Rosen, 'always used to come over to my place and resign, every time he heard the Soviets broadcasting about the tenants' movement'; interview, Maurice 'Tubby' Rosen, London, 13 Nov. 1978.
36. Piratin, *Our Flag Stays Red*, pp. 68–9.
37. J. B. S. Haldane, *A.R.P.* (London: Gollancz, 1938). Three separate printings of the CPGB's pamphlet, *ARP Act Now!*, also appeared in 1938. The last of the three printings, which appeared during the Munich crisis, attempted to connect Chamberlain's failure to provide ARP with his appeasement policies; see *ARP Act Now!* (London: CPGB, Sept. 1938), p. 2.
38. *East London Advertiser*, 14 May 1938, p. 2. Borough Councillor J. C. Lawder, an Irish member of the Labour Party, had a quarrel with the Council because he believed that ARP agitation should not be part of the Council's peace work. *East London Advertiser*, 30 July 1938, p. 8.
39. *Prepare Now! Prevent Panic Later. Air Raid Precautions for Stepney* (London: Stepney Communist Party, Oct. 1938), pp. 4, 9–11, 14.
40. *East London Advertiser*, 29 Oct. 1938, p. 3; see also Piratin's letter to the editor of the *East London Advertiser*, 2 April 1938, p. 8.
41. *East London Advertiser*, 31 Dec. 1938, pp. 2, 10.
42. *East London Advertiser*, 28 Jan. 1939, p. 1.
43. *East London Advertiser*, 13 May 1939, p. 1. See also Denys Munby, 'The Social Order', in Kenneth Brill (ed.), *John Groser, East London Priest*, pp. 151–3.
44. *East London Advertiser*, 22 July 1939, p. 2.
45. *Daily Worker*, 4 Oct. 1939, p. 1, and 10 Oct. 1939, p. 1.
46. *Jewish Chronicle*, 22 Dec. 1939, p. 18.
47. For details of the Kerr Report, see the *Daily Worker*, 23 Dec. 1939, p. 6.
48. *East London Advertiser*, 6 Jan. 1940, p. 5.
49. See *Daily Worker*, 27 June 1940, p. 8, asking for his removal.
50. *Daily Worker*, 6 Sept. 1940, p. 7.
51. Frank R. Lewey, 'Front-Line London Closes Ranks Again', *Jewish Bulletin* 37 (1944): [2].
52. *East London Advertiser*, 14 Sept. 1940, p. 1.
53. *East London Advertiser*, 12 Oct. 1940, p. 5.
54. *Daily Worker*, 14 Sept. 1940, p. 8.
55. Ritchie Calder, *The Lesson of London*, Searchlight Book No. 3 (London: Secker & Warburg, 1941), pp. 29, 35; see also Ritchie Calder, 'The War in East London', *New Statesman and Nation* 20 (21 Sept. 1940): 276–8.
56. Kingsley Martin, 'Report on East London', *New Statesman and Nation* 20 (5 Oct. 1940): 324–6.
57. *Jewish Chronicle*, 27 Sept. 1940, p. 1.
58. *Daily Worker*, 5 Oct. 1940, p. 1.
59. Negley Farson, *Bomber's Moon* (London: Gollancz, 1941), pp. 100, 103.
60. *East London Advertiser*, 12 Oct. 1940, p. 1; 20 Dec. 1940, p. 5; Frank R. Lewey, *Cockney Campaign* (London: Stanley Paul & Co., [1944]), p. 44. The *Daily Worker*, while claiming that Whitehall was now treating Stepney as 'some outpost of the Empire', agreed that Davis had become 'notoriously unapproachable'. *Daily Worker*, 7 Oct. 1940, p. 4.
61. *East London Advertiser*, 28 Dec. 1940, p. 1.

62. Angus Calder, *The Myth of the Blitz* (London: Jonathan Cape, 1991), pp. 84–5.
63. Piratin, *Our Flag Stays Red*, pp. 75–6.
64. *Daily Worker*, 13 Sept. 1940, p. 1.
65. *Daily Worker*, 16 Sept. 1940, p. 2.
66. *Daily Worker*, 10 Sept. 1940, p. 1.
67. Public Record Office, HO45/18540/704198/45. *Daily Worker*, 20 Sept. 1940, p. 1.
68. *Daily Worker*, 23 Sept. 1940, p. 4.
69. Sevareid's broadcast was reported in the *Daily Worker*, 14 Oct. 1940, p. 2.
70. *Daily Worker*, 11 Sept. 1940, p. 4.
71. *Daily Worker*, 16 Sept. 1940, p. 1. This incident, also, was reported in the United States by CBS and other American correspondents.
72. Ted Bramley, 'London's People and the Air War', *Labour Monthly* 22 (Oct. 1940): 537. Many years later, Margaret Cohen, a member of the CP's London District Committee, remembered 'following Solly Kaye', later a Stepney Borough Councillor, 'down into the underground shelters carrying bundles of blankets'. In John Attfield and Stephen Williams (eds), *1939: The Communist Party of Great Britain and the War. Proceedings of a Conference Held on 21 April 1979, Organised by the Communist Party History Group* (London: Lawrence & Wishart, 1984), p. 123.
73. *Daily Worker*, 3 Jan. 1941, p. 7.
74. *Daily Worker*, 26 Nov. 1940, p. 8.
75. There are various estimates as to the number of people sheltered at Tilbury. According to Angus Calder, *The People's War: Britain 1939–45* (London: Jonathan Cape, 1969; reprint ed., Panther, 1971), pp. 210–11, an average of 3,000 people were there every night; according to Tom Harrisson, *Living Through the Blitz* (London: Collins, 1976; reprint ed., Harmondsworth: Penguin, 1978), p. 117, the figure was closer to 10,000. Farson says in *Bomber's Moon*, p. 88, that Tilbury sheltered approximately 8,000 every night, although the figure at times grew to 15,000.
76. Martin, 'Report on East London', p. 324.
77. *Daily Worker*, 20 Sept. 1940, p. 4.
78. *Jewish Chronicle*, 18 Oct. 1940, p. 1.
79. Ted Bramley, *Bombers Over London* (London: CPGB, Oct. 1940), p. 7.
80. Harrisson, *Living Through the Blitz*, p. 118.
81. *East London Advertiser*, 8 March 1941, p. 1. Joanna Mack and Steve Humphries, in *The Making of Modern London 1939–1945: London at War* (London: Sidgwick and Jackson, 1985), p. 84, describe an incident when a delegation from the shelter, demanding better conditions, was charged by mounted policemen.
82. Ivan M. Maisky, *Memoirs of a Soviet Ambassador. The War: 1939–43*, trans. Andrew Rothstein (New York: Scribner's, 1968), pp. 119–20. The date of Maisky's visit to Tilbury was 11 Oct. 1940, according to W. P. Coates and Zelda Coates, *A History of Anglo-Soviet Relations* (London: Lawrence & Wishart/the Pilot Press, 1944), p. 647; these authors, who were fellow-travellers, remark that the 'tremendous cheers' accorded Maisky were indicative of the sympathy felt by 'the ordinary folks in London' towards the USSR.
83. L. L. Loewe, *Basil Henriques A Portrait: Based on His Diaries, Letters and Speeches as Collected by His Widow, Rose Henriques* (London: Routledge & Kegan Paul, 1976), p. 104.
84. Calder, *The Lesson of London*, p. 72.
85. *Jewish Chronicle*, 11 Oct. 1940, p. 15.
86. *Jewish Chronicle*, 27 Sept. 1940, p. 7.
87. Calder, *The Lesson of London*, pp. 72, 75. Frank Lewey, the Stepney mayor,

suggested that the Nazis chose to bomb the East End in the hope that the demoralized population would blame their plight on the Jews. But 'Catholics and Jews helped each other cordially with clothing and food supplies, though they had long been a byword in Stepney as mortal opponents'. Frank R. Lewey, *Cockney Campaign*, pp. 15, 76.
88. 'Points for Chairman at Outdoor Meetings'; mimeo in the Zaidman Collection.
89. *Mile End Has a Memory*; the Zaidman Collection.
90. *Mile End Election Special! Vote Piratin*, p. [1]; the Zaidman Collection.
91. *Piratin, Communist Candidate for Mile End. Popular Stepney Fighter and Leader*; the Zaidman Collection.
92. J. H. Forshaw and Patrick Abercrombie, for the London County Council, *County of London Plan* (London: Macmillan, 1943).
93. *East London Advertiser*, 15 Oct. 1943, p. 1.
94. *East London Advertiser*, 22 Oct. 1943, p. 2.
95. *East London Advertiser*, 17 Nov. 1944, p. 6.
96. *East London Advertiser*, 24 Nov. 1944, p. 4. J. J. Mallon had already stated in December 1941 that some 32,000 dwellings in Stepney 'have been damaged more or less'. Asa Briggs and Anne Macartney, *Toynbee Hall: The First Hundred Years* (London: Routledge & Kegan Paul, 1984), p. 127.
97. *Daily Worker*, 16 Sept. 1944, p. 1.
98. Michael Shapiro, *How to Speed Up the Repairs* (London: CPGB, [1944]).
99. Letter to the editor from Bertha Sokoloff, *East London Advertiser*, 17 Nov. 1944, p. 4.
100. *A Stepney to be Proud Of: Plan and Proposals*, pp. [8–9].
101. *Jewish Chronicle*, 4 May 1945, p. 6. Some accounts of the number of Jews killed were even higher; see A. B. Levy, *East End Story* (London: Constellation Books, 1951), p. 63.
102. *East London Advertiser*, 4 May 1945, pp. 1, 5; see also the *News Chronicle* of 27 April 1945, p. 3. Thirty children were among the dead.
103. D. L. Munby, for the Stepney Reconstruction Group, Toynbee Hall, *Industry and Planning in Stepney* (London: Oxford University Press, 1951), p. 85.
104. Ted Bramley, *The Battle for Homes*, Light on London Series No. 1 (Watford: Farleigh Press, [1945]), p. 64.
105. *Houses for the People* (London: Labour Research Department, [May 1945]), p. 1.
106. 'Notes on Housing for Speakers and Canvassers', undated mimeo, pp. 1–3; the Zaidman Collection.
107. *General Election – July 5, 1945. Parliamentary Division of Mile End. Election Address. A Personal Letter from the Communist Candidate Phil Piratin*, p. [2]; the Zaidman Collection.
108. *Piratin, Communist Candidate for Mile End*.
109. *Mile End Election Special! Vote Piratin*, p. [1]. Piratin even managed to work in some pro-Soviet propaganda, telling his constituents that Russia, with even greater difficulties than Britain, 'built thousands of new houses right through the war. Why not here?'
110. Ibid., p. [2].
111. *Piratin, Communist Candidate for Mile End*.
112. *Mile End Has A Memory*.
113. 'Points for Chairman at Outdoor Meetings'. See also the *Daily Worker*, 2 July 1945, p. 3, for a picture of Councillor Piratin inspecting a leaking roof in one of the homes in his constituency.
114. *Daily Worker*, 28 July 1945, p. 4.

LONDON JEWS AND BRITISH COMMUNISM

115. Ian Mackay, 'New Personalities in the New House', *News Chronicle*, 27 July 1945, p. 2.

CHAPTER 4

1. There is a great deal of literature on the various British Fascist movements, including Robert Benewick, *The Fascist Movement in Britain*; Colin Cross, *The Fascists in Britain*; Richard Griffiths, *Fellow Travellers of the Right: British Enthusiasts for Nazi Germany 1933–39* (London: Constable, 1980); Colin Holmes, *Anti-Semitism in British Society 1876–1939*; Tony Kushner, *The Persistence of Prejudice: Antisemitism in British Society During the Second World War*; Tony Kushner and Kenneth Lunn (eds), *The Politics of Marginality: Race, the Radical Right and Minorities in Twentieth Century Britain* (London: Frank Cass, 1990); Tony Kushner and Kenneth Lunn (eds), *Traditions of Intolerance: Historical Perspectives on Fascism and Race Discourse in Britain*; Gisela C. Lebzelter, *Political Anti-Semitism in England 1918–1939* (London: Macmillan, 1978); D. S. Lewis, *Illusions of Grandeur: Mosley, Fascism and British Society, 1931–81* (Manchester: Manchester University Press, 1987); Kenneth Lunn and Richard C. Thurlow (eds), *British Fascism: Essays on the Radical Right in Inter-War Britain*; W. F. Mandle, *Anti-Semitism and the British Union of Fascists* (London: Longmans, Green & Co., 1968); Richard Thurlow, *Fascism in Britain: A History, 1918–1985*; and G. C. Webber, *The Ideology of the British Right 1918–1939*. For brief overviews, see Stuart A. Cohen, 'Anglo-Jewish Responses to Antisemitism: Suggestions for a Framework of Analysis', in Jehuda Reinharz (ed.), *Living With Antisemitism: Modern Jewish Responses* (Hanover, NH: University Press of New England), pp. 84–103; and Geoffrey G. Field, 'Anti-Semitism with the Boots Off: Recent Research on England', *Wiener Library Bulletin*, Special Issue [1983]: 25–46.
2. Interview, Solly Kaye, London, 31 Oct. 1978. For other evidence of Communist-Fascist conflict during this period, see the various memos and other documents in file E3/245, Board of Deputies archives.
3. *East London Advertiser*, 13 June 1936, p. 7. Joe Jacobs was the Stepney party secretary from the spring of 1935 to the spring of 1937.
4. *East London Advertiser*, 12 Sept. 1936, p. 8. For more on Frankel's unpopularity as a result of his 'seemingly uncaring attitude', see Elaine Smith, 'Jewish Responses to Antisemitism and Fascism in the East End of London, 1920–1939', pp. 59–60.
5. *East London Advertiser*, 24 Oct. 1936, p. 2. There is now an extensive literature on the events surrounding the 'Battle of Cable Street'. For two of the more recent analyses, see Noreen Branson, *History of the Communist Party of Great Britain 1927–1941* (London: Lawrence & Wishart, 1985), pp. 159–68; and William J. Fishman, 'A People's Journée: The Battle of Cable Street (October 4th 1936)', in Frederick Krantz (ed.), *History From Below: Studies in Popular Protest and Popular Ideology in Honour of George Rudé* (Montreal: Concordia University Press, 1985), pp. 384–94.
6. *Daily Worker*, 3 Nov. 1936, p. 5.
7. Letter to the editor from E. A. Dickinson, *East London Advertiser*, 14 Nov. 1936, p. 2.
8. *Report of the Central Committee to the 14th National Congress, Communist Party of Great Britain* (London: CPGB, 1937), pp. 7–8.
9. *Labour Monthly* 20 (Dec. 1938): 764.
10. Piratin, *Our Flag Stays Red*, p. 62.
11. Letter from the Mile End Divisional Labour Party to all organizations affiliated to the Stepney Trades Council and Borough Labour Party, May 1938, signed by E. G. Woollon, chairman, O. R. Wright, treasurer, and I[srael] Shafran, secretary; included in the NUTGW Papers, London.

NOTES TO CHAPTER 4

12. See the *East London Observer*, 2 July 1938, pp. 1, 7; *Jewish Chronicle*, 8 July 1938, p. 40.
13. Joe Jacobs, *Out of the Ghetto*, p. 205.
14. Ibid., pp. 164, 222, 263–5, 272–4, 276–7, 285.
15. Piratin, *Our Flag Stays Red*, pp. 17–18, 27; interview, Phil Piratin, London, 30 Nov. 1978.
16. Joe Jacobs was suspended from the Stepney CP in the spring of 1937. He was succeeded as secretary by Sam Masters, a veteran of the International Brigades, whose term was a short one; Phil Piratin became secretary in June 1937. Colin Holmes credits Piratin with the decision to 'remove the bait' which attracted poor East Enders to the BUF; see Holmes, *Anti-Semitism in British Society 1876–1939*, pp. 198–9. See also Lewis, *Delusions of Grandeur*, pp. 123–6.
17. Leon Samuels, 'The Jewish Labour Movement', *Jewish Quarterly* 3 (winter 1956): 35.
18. Interview, Alf Holland, London, 16 June 1978; the *Circle-Arbeter Ring* 13 (Jan. 1949): 11.
19. *Jewish Chronicle*, 31 July 1936, p. 22.
20. *Daily Worker*, 3 Nov. 1936, p. 5.
21. Piratin, *Our Flag Stays Red*, p. 19. For the JPC's 'Statement of Policy' and a list of organizations involved in its creation, see file 15/13, Parkes archive; alongside friendly societies, Jewish trade union branches, and Zionist groups such as the Federation of Zionist Youth were Communist-inspired organizations such as ICOS, the Organization for Jewish Colonization in Soviet Russia. The JPC is mentioned in the following works: Gerald D. Anderson, *Fascists, Communists, and the National Government: Civil Liberties in Great Britain, 1931–1937* (Columbia, MO: University of Missouri Press, 1983), pp. 160–62, 176, 183; Colin Holmes, *Anti-Semitism in British Society 1876–1939*, pp. 193, 200; Tony Kushner, *The Persistence of Prejudice*, pp. 166–7; Gisela C. Lebzelter, *Political Anti-Semitism in England 1918–1939*, pp. 139–43, 152–3, 166–7; David Rosenberg, *Facing up to Antisemitism: How Jews in Britain Countered the Threats of the 1930s* (London: JCARP Publications, 1985), pp. 46–60; and Elaine R. Smith, 'Jewish Responses to Political Antisemitism and Fascism in the East End of London, 1920–1939', pp. 63–7.
22. See the various letters written by Neville Laski, the Board's president, and A. G. Brotman, its secretary, in file 15/13, Parkes archive. Laski wrote to Dr Redcliffe N. Salaman, 8 Dec. 1936, that the JPC had 'certain elements associated with them which I suspected to have communistic influence'. The Zionists involved were also criticized by members of the executive of the Zionist Federation of Great Britain and Ireland. Gideon Shimoni, 'The Non-Zionists in Anglo-Jewry, 1937–1948', *Jewish Journal of Sociology* 28 (Dec. 1986): 93.
23. Piratin, *Our Flag Stays Red*, p. 28.
24. Interview, Phil Piratin, London, 30 Nov. 1978.
25. *Jewish Chronicle*, 6 Nov. 1936, p. 29.
26. *Jewish Chronicle*, 30 July 1937, p. 13.
27. Sokoloff, *Edith and Stepney*, p. 81.
28. Piratin, *Our Flag Stays Red*, p. 27; *Jewish Chronicle*, 2 June 1939, p. 20. The *Chronicle* article included an interview with Tubby Rosen, who claimed the rent strikes, by creating alliances between Jews and non-Jews, had major repercussions for the Fascist movement: according to Rosen, the tenants had overcome 'artificially imported differences'.
29. *Daily Worker*, 22 June 1939, p. 3.

30. *Jewish Chronicle*, 21 July 1939, p. 18.
31. This pamphlet is included in the Julius Jacobs Collection.
32. *Jewish Chronicle*, 13 Oct. 1939, p. 12. See also 3 Nov. 1939, p. 22, for further examples of Fascist propaganda along these lines.
33. *A Stepney to be Proud of: Plan and Proposals*, p. [13].
34. Tony Kushner's work has gone far in detailing this: 'in many ways', he notes, 'the years 1939–45 witnessed a climax of the forms of anti-Semitism that had existed in Britain in the inter-war period'. Tony Kushner, 'The Impact of British Anti-Semitism, 1918–1945', in David Cesarani (ed.), *The Making of Modern Anglo-Jewry*, pp. 192–3.
35. 'Special Branch Report of Fascist and anti-Fascist Meetings Held During August 1939', 15 Sept. 1939, PRO MEPOL 2/3127/29A.
36. 'Special Branch Report . . . During September 1939', 10 Oct. 1939, PRO MEPOL 2/3127/33A.
37. 'Special Branch Report . . . During November 1939', 8 Dec. 1939, PRO MEPOL 2/3127/41A. For more detail on BUF activities during this period, see Tony Kushner, *The Persistence of Prejudice*, pp. 16–23.
38. *Jewish Chronicle*, 19 Jan. 1940, p. 16.
39. *Jewish Chronicle*, 19 January 1940, p. 10.
40. Letter from Peter Valentine on behalf of the Grand Order Sons of Jacob, *Jewish Chronicle*, 23 Feb. 1940, p. 11; Valentine was later a member of the National Jewish Committee of the CPGB. File C15/3/19 of the Board of Deputies Archives includes letters from a number of other groups.
41. Quoted by *Di Tsayt*, 22 Feb. 1940, p. 4 [English section].
42. Benewick, *The Fascist Movement in Britain*, p. 294. For more on the legislation enabling the authorities to detain BUF members, see Lewis, *Illusions of Grandeur*, pp. 231–3, and Thurlow, *Fascism in Britain*, pp. 188–93. See also Neil Stammers, *Civil Liberties in Britain During the 2nd World War: A Political Study* (London: Croom Helm, 1983).
43. *Jewish Chronicle*, 12 July 1940, p. 14, and 19 July 1940, p. 14.
44. Cross, *The Fascists in Britain*, p. 196.
45. Tony Kushner, 'The Paradox of Prejudice: The Impact of Organised Antisemitism in Britain During an Anti-Nazi War', in Kushner and Lunn (eds), *Traditions of Intolerance: Historical Perspectives on Fascism and Race Discourse in Britain*, p. 75.
46. *Jewish Chronicle*, 28 June 1940, p. 6.
47. *Daily Worker*, 29 Dec. 1942, p. 4.
48. *Jewish Chronicle*, 27 June 1941, p. 5, and 26 Sept. 1941, pp. 17–18.
49. Jessica Mitford, *A Fine Old Conflict* (London: Michael Joseph, 1977; reprint ed., Quartet Books, 1978), p. 55.
50. *Jewish Chronicle*, 18 Dec. 1942, p. 13.
51. *Daily Worker*, 18 March 1943, p. 1.
52. *Daily Worker*, 29 Oct. 1942, p. 2. Though the Duke (then the Marquis of Tavistock) was the main force behind the British People's Party, a Fascist group founded in 1939, and had met with German officials in Dublin in January 1940 in an attempt to negotiate peace terms, he was not detained under regulation 18B.
53. *Daily Worker*, 8 Dec. 1942, p. 4.
54. 'Draft PB [Political Bureau] Letter to London District', 10 Jan. 1943; R. Palme Dutt archives, British Library, CUP 1262k4.
55. *Daily Worker*, 17 Dec. 1942, p. 4.
56. *Daily Worker*, 13 Feb. 1943, p. 2.

NOTES TO CHAPTER 4

57. *Daily Worker*, 17 Feb. 1943, p. 3, and 19 Feb. 1943, p. 3.
58. *Daily Worker*, 22 Feb. 1943, p. 4.
59. *Daily Worker*, 25 Feb. 1943, p. 4.
60. *Daily Worker*, 10 April 1943, p. 3, and 15 April 1943, p. 3.
61. William Gallacher, *Anti-Semitism: What it Means to You* (London: CPGB, April 1943), p. 21.
62. *Daily Worker*, 9 Aug. 1943, p. 3.
63. *Daily Worker*, 6 Aug. 1943, p. 3, and 11 Nov. 1943, p. 1.
64. 'The Release of Sir Oswald and Lady Mosley', *Civil Liberty* 4 (Dec. 1943): 1–2.
65. *Daily Worker*, 20 Nov. 1943, p. 4.
66. *Daily Worker*, 19 Nov. 1943, p. 2.
67. *Daily Worker*, 19 Nov. 1943, p. 2.
68. *Daily Worker*, 20 Nov. 1943, p. 4.
69. *Keep Mosley in Prison* ([London]: CPGB, 1943), p. 2.
70. *Parliamentary Debates (Hansard) House of Commons*, Fifth Series, Vol. 393, 23 Nov. 1943, cols. 1427–36.
71. *Jewish Chronicle*, 26 Nov. 1943, p. 1.
72. *Jewish Chronicle*, 26 Nov. 1943, p. 10.
73. *Daily Worker*, 27 Nov. 1943, p. 1.
74. *Put Mosley Back in Prison* (London: CPGB, 1943), pp. 3–4.
75. *Parliamentary Debates (Hansard) House of Commons*, Fifth Series, Vol. 395, 1 Dec. 1943, col. 395.
76. Ibid., cols 475–8.
77. *Parliamentary Debates (Hansard) House of Commons*, Fifth Series, Vol. 395, 9 Dec. 1943, col. 1114.
78. Angus Calder, *The People's War*, p. 636, refers to the disillusionment with Labour.
79. *East London Advertiser*, 26 Nov. 1943, p. 1.
80. *Daily Worker*, 7 Dec. 1943, p. 4; *East London Advertiser*, 10 Dec. 1943, p. 4.
81. See Bernard Donoughue and G.W. Jones, *Herbert Morrison: Portrait of a Politician* (London: Weidenfeld and Nicolson, 1973), p. 225. Morrison was secretary of the London Labour Party from 1915 to 1947.
82. 'Party Work Amongst the Jews in Britain', TS, National Jewish Committee, Communist Party, 8 Dec. 1943; the Zaidman Collection.
83. Letter to the editor from C[himen] Abramsky, *Jewish Chronicle*, 24 Dec. 1943, p. 15.
84. 'The Eleventh Convention', the *Circle* 11 (April 1945): 4.
85. *Jewish Chronicle*, 21 Jan. 1944, p. 5.
86. *Daily Worker*, 27 Sept. 1944, p. 1.
87. *Daily Worker*, 27 Sept. 1944, p. 4, and 28 Sept. 1944, p. 2.
88. *The Case of Captain Ramsay* (London: Daily Worker Defence League, 1944).
89. Central committee minutes, Workers' Circle, 1 Oct. 1944; the Zaidman Collection.
90. L[azar] Zeidman [sic], 'Jewish Board of Deputies in London Discusses Post-war Policy', the *Review: A Jewish Monthly* (Feb. 1945), p. 12.
91. *Daily Worker*, 6 Nov. 1944, p. 1; *Jewish Chronicle*, 10 Nov. 1944, p. 16.
92. *Daily Worker*, 13 Nov. 1944, p. 4.
93. *Jewish Chronicle*, 17 Nov. 1944, p. 5.
94. *Jewish Chronicle*, 17 Nov. 1944, p. 10.
95. 'Commentary', *Jewish Opinion* (Feb. 1945), p. 9.
96. *Daily Worker*, 5 May 1945, p. 2.
97. *Daily Worker*, 11 May 1945, p. 4.
98. Austin Stevens, *The Dispossessed: German Refugees in Britain* (London: Barrie &

Jenkins, 1975), p. 173. For more on this subject, see Peter Gillman and Leni Gillman, *'Collar the Lot!': How Britain Interned and Expelled Its Wartime Refugees* (London: Quartet Books, 1980); Miriam Kochan, *Britain's Internees in the Second World War* (London: Macmillan, 1983); and Ronald Stent, *A Bespattered Page? The Internment of His Majesty's 'most loyal enemy aliens'* (London: André Deutsch, 1980).

99. Selig Brodetsky, *Memoirs: From Ghetto to Israel* (London: Weidenfeld & Nicolson, 1960), p. 200.
100. *Daily Worker*, July 19, 1940, p. 7; NAFTA took up the cause of these workers.
101. Kochan, *Britain's Internees in the Second World War*, p. 124.
102. Ivor Montagu, *The Traitor Class* (London: Lawrence & Wishart, 1940), pp. 89–91. There were also complaints about anti-Semitism in the Canadian camps. Mark Lilly, *The National Council for Civil Liberties: The First Fifty Years* (London: Macmillan, 1984), p. 51.
103. Richard Collier, *1940: The World in Flames* (London: Hamish Hamilton, 1979; reprint ed., Harmondsworth: Penguin, 1980), p. 168.
104. 'The Forgotten Refugees', *New Statesman and Nation* 20 (5 Oct. 1940): 326. See also 'For They Know Not What They Do', *New Statesman and Nation* 20 (3 Aug. 1940): 104–5, which made the point that the government was interning the very people 'for whom a Nazi victory means the concentration camp or death'.
105. *Jewish Chronicle*, 28 Feb. 1941, p. 19.
106. *Jewish Chronicle*, 25 April 1941, p. 5.
107. *Parliamentary Debates (Hansard) House of Commons*, Fifth Series, Vol. 364, 22 Aug. 1940, cols 1434–5. His statement drew criticism from Communist MP Willie Gallacher.
108. *The Times*, 16 Aug. 1940, p. 2.
109. F[rançois] Lafitte, *The Internment of Aliens* (Harmondsworth: Penguin Books, 1940). Lafitte had been a Communist organizer in East London.
110. *Daily Worker*, 24 July 1940, p. 7.
111. *Jewish Chronicle*, 26 July 1940, p. 10.
112. Michael Seyfert, '"His Majesty's Most Loyal Internees"', in Gerhard Hirshfeld (ed.), *Exile in Great Britain: Refugees from Hitler's Germany* (Leamington Spa: Berg, 1984), p. 177.
113. 'The Eleventh Convention', the *Circle* 11 (April 1945): 2. Although 23 members of the Circle were detained, all had been released by July 1941, according to [Nathan Weiner], 'General Secretary's Report', the *Circle-Arbeter Ring* 8 (July 1941): 3 [English section].
114. See the letter of Andrew Conley, NUTGW general secretary, to J. L. Fine, secretary of the branch, 11 Nov. 1940, in the NUTGW papers, London; and the *Report of the Committee for a Christmas to Interned Refugees* (London: March 1941), pp. [2–3].
115. *Daily Worker*, 26 July 1940, p. 4; see also Stevens, *The Dispossessed*, pp. 184, 189.
116. Holmes, *John Bull's Island*, p. 192.
117. Tony Kushner, 'All Quiet on the Home Front?', *Jewish Quarterly* 36 (autumn 1989): 12. See also 'The Impact of British Anti-Semitism, 1918–1945', p. 199, and *The Persistence of Prejudice*, pp. 114–19, 143–50, 174–5. Kushner criticizes the Board of Deputies for not attempting to do more to help aliens during this crisis.
118. *Daily Worker*, 5 Dec. 1940, p. 2.
119. *Daily Worker*, 30 Nov. 1940, p. 4.
120. *Jewish Chronicle*, 15 May 1942, p. 17.
121. 'War-time Diary: 1940', in Sonia Orwell and Ian Angus (eds), *The Collected Essays, Journalism and Letters of George Orwell*, Vol. II: *My Country Right or Left 1940–1943*

NOTES TO CHAPTER 4

(London: Secker & Warburg, 1968; reprint ed., Harmondsworth: Penguin, 1970), p. 428.
122. Letter from Sidney Salomon to T. H. Hutchinson, 19 Dec. 1940; file C15/3/19, Board of Deputies archives.
123. Angus Calder, *The Myth of the Blitz*, p. 126; Walter Laqueur, *The Terrible Secret: An Investigation into the Suppression of Information About Hitler's 'Final Solution'* (London: Weidenfeld & Nicolson, 1980), p. 92; Ian McLaine, *Ministry of Morale: Home Front Morale and the Ministry of Information in World War II* (London: George Allen & Unwin, 1979), pp. 116, 167.
124. Kushner, *The Persistence of Prejudice*, p. 122.
125. *Jewish Chronicle*, 4 May 1979, p. 23, obituary of Maurice Orbach; for more on the TAC, see N[oah] Barou, *The Jews in Work and Trade* (London: Trades Advisory Council, 1946). The documents concerning the TAC in the Board of Deputies archives have been closed to researchers.
126. *Jewish Chronicle*, 23 Jan. 1942, p. 19.
127. See Bernard Wasserstein, *Britain and the Jews of Europe 1939–1945* (Oxford: Clarendon Press, 1979), p. 119; Wasserstein also quotes 'a gleeful diary comment from Dr Goebbels' concerning the statements made in the British House of Commons. Even the Home Secretary, Herbert Morrison, had launched an inquiry into Jewish involvement in the black market. Tony Kushner, 'The Impact of British Anti-Semitism, 1918–1945', p. 206, and *The Persistence of Prejudice*, p. 139.
128. *Jewish Chronicle*, 13 March 1942, p. 10.
129. *Jewish Chronicle*, 13 March 1942, p. 17.
130. *Jewish Chronicle*, 17 July 1942, p. 8.
131. *Jewish Chronicle*, 24 July 1942, pp. 1, 8.
132. Maurice Orbach, 'Noah Barou and the Trades Advisory Council', in Henrik F. Infield (ed.), *Essays in Jewish Sociology, Labour and Co-operation in Memory of Dr Noah Barou 1889–1955* (London: Thomas Yoseloff, 1962), p. 31.
133. *East London Advertiser*, 1 Aug. 1942, p. 4.
134. *Jewish Chronicle*, 31 July 1942, p. 1.
135. *East London Advertiser*, 23 Jan. 1943, p. 7.
136. William Rust, 'Foreword' to *13 Years of Anti-Fascist Struggle* (Manchester: CPGB [1943]), p. 1.
137. Gallacher, *Anti-Semitism: What It Means to You*, p. 8.
138. Notice from J. E. Arnold James, town clerk, for an 'Extraordinary Meeting, Metropolitan Borough of Stepney', 23 Feb. 1943; file C15/3/19, Board of Deputies archives.
139. *Daily Worker*, 26 Feb. 1943, p. 4.
140. *Daily Worker*, 3 March 1943, p. 4; *East London Advertiser*, 6 March 1943, p. 5.
141. Sam Alexander, 'Antisemitism – the Powerful Weapon of the Fifth Column', the *Circle-Arbeter Ring* 10 (April 1943): 1 [English section].
142. *Daily Herald*, 6 March 1943, p. 3. For more on this disaster, see Kushner, *The Persistence of Prejudice*, pp. 60–1, 125–6.
143. *Jewish Chronicle*, 18 Sept. 1942, pp. 1, 8.
144. Quoted in Ernest Hearst, 'The British and the Slaughter of the Jews – (II)', *Wiener Library Bulletin* 21 (spring 1967): 39.
145. *Daily Worker*, 29 March 1943, p. 3.
146. Elizabeth A. Allen, *It Shall Not Happen Here: Anti-Semitism, Fascists and Civil Liberty* (London: Walthamstow Press, 1943), p. 31.
147. *Daily Worker*, 19 April 1943, pp. 1, 4.
148. Transcript of the meeting, file C10/2/8, Board of Deputies archives. See also file

C13/1/12 for evidence of reluctance on the part of the Board's Law and Parliamentary Committee to work with the CP on this issue.
149. 'Committee on Community Libel – December 6, 1943', file C4/1, Board of Deputies archives.
150. *Jewish Chronicle*, 31 Dec. 1943, p. 8. Tony Kushner, however, notes in *The Persistence of Prejudice*, p. 101, that the campaign to make anti-Semitism an offence was not very popular with the public at large.
151. Central committee minutes, Workers' Circle, 1 Oct. 1944; in the Zaidman Collection.
152. Nathan Weiner to A. G. Brotman, 12 Oct. 1944; file E3/247, Board of Deputies archives.
153. Notice of motion from H. Lubbock; file E3/247, Board of Deputies archives.
154. Letter from A. G. Brotman to Harry Lubbock, 11 Oct. 1944; file E3/247, Board of Deputies archives.
155. Central committee minutes, Workers' Circle, 2 Dec. 1944; in the Zaidman Collection.
156. *Jewish Chronicle*, 3 November 1944, p. 8.
157. Joseph Heller, 'Anglo-Zionist Relations, 1939–1947', *Wiener Library Bulletin* 31 (1978): 70.
158. *Jewish Chronicle*, 29 Dec. 1944, p. 8.
159. Issie Panner ['I. Rennap'], *Anti-Semitism and the Jewish Question* (London: Lawrence & Wishart, 1942), p. 114.
160. Ibid., p. 116.
161. Gallacher, *Anti-Semitism: What it Means to You*, p. 17.
162. John Gollan, 'Anti-Semitism', *Labour Monthly* 25 (June 1943): 179.
163. *13 Years of Anti-Fascist Struggle*, p. 1.
164. Interview, Morry Lebow, London, 21 Nov. 1978.
165. For the founding of the National Jewish Committee, see the 'Report of National Jewish Committee to International Affairs Committee'; TS in the Zaidman Collection. Abramsky arrived in England with his father, the Lithuanian-born Talmudic scholar Dayan Yehezkel Abramsky, who became one of Anglo-Jewry's most eminent religious figures. Dayan Abramsky became rabbi of the extremely Orthodox *Machzikei Hadath* congregation in London's East End and from 1935 to 1951 was the head of the Chief Rabbi's ecclesiastical court, the *Beth Din*. Yet, by his own account, Chimen Abramsky became the 'right hand man' of R. Palme Dutt, the CP's chief ideologue, particularly concerning Jewish matters; interview, Chimen Abramsky, London, 26 May 1978. Lazar Zaidman was born in England but as a young man had returned with his family to their country of origin, Romania. Becoming involved in Communist politics there, he was arrested and tortured by the political police. He became owner of the Amhurst Valet Service in Hackney after being deported back to England. For more detail on Zaidman's life and work, see Tony Kushner, 'Jewish Communists in Twentieth-century Britain: the Zaidman Collection', *Labour History Review* 55 (autumn 1990): 66–75.
166. Sidney Salomon to Frank Renton, 28 July 1944; file C/15/3/9, Board of Deputies archives. See also, in the same file, the exchange of letters between Salomon and J. W. Morgan, librarian of Marx House; and between Salomon and Jack Knife, secretary of Marx House.
167. 'Details of the Week-End School for Jewish Party Members To Be Held at Marx House, 1 Doughty St., W.C. 1 on 22nd. & 23rd. April 1944'; TS in the Zaidman Collection.
168. The transcript of this meeting, in TS, is in the Zaidman Collection; see also the

NOTES TO CHAPTER 4

summary in the *Daily Worker*, 12 May 1944, p. 2.
169. *The Jewish Question: Statement by the National Jewish Committee of the Communist Party* (London: Communist Party, [1944], pp. 6, 13, 17–18.
170. 'The Communist Party. National Jewish Committee. Third Annual Enlarged Meeting. 13th. 14th. January 1945', TS, pp. 1, 4; the Zaidman Collection.
171. 'The Election Campaign & the Jewish People. Statement by the National Jewish Committee'; TS, pp. 1, 3–4, in the Zaidman Collection.
172. 'Jews and the General Election'; draft TS [1945] in the Zaidman Collection.
173. 'Commentary', *Jewish Forum* (May–June 1945), p. 12.
174. Letter from Lazar Zaidman to Isaac Gust, London, 31 May 1945, in the Zaidman Collection.
175. *Fascist Murderers: Pictures of the Concentration Camps You Must Never Forget* (London: CPGB, April 1945), p. [8].
176. R. Palme Dutt, *Truth About the Tories* (London: CPGB, June 1945), pp. 11–14.
177. *News Chronicle*, 9 June 1945, p. 4.
178. *A Stepney to Be Proud of: Plan and Proposals*, p. [5].
179. 'Commentary', *Jewish Forum* (May–June 1945), pp. 11–12.
180. 'Yidn Un Di Vahlen' ['Jews and the Elections'], *Di Tsayt*, 29 June 1945, p. 2.
181. Phil Piratin, 'Appeal to the Jewish Electors'; TS in the Zaidman Collection.
182. Phil Piratin, 'The Communist Party and the Jewish People. Every Jew Must Vote Progressive!', *Jewish Forum* (May–June 1945), p. 1; Ramsay's motion had no seconder. See also the flier, *Mile End Election Special! Vote Piratin*, p. [2]. Even in detention Ramsay had remained the elected representative of his Scottish contituency and managed to indulge his anti-Semitic views: in March 1944 he sent a written question to Oliver Stanley, the Colonial Secretary, regarding the 'terrorist activities' of the 'Stern Gang' in Palestine. *Jewish Chronicle*, 10 March 1944, p. 5.
183. *Vote for Piratin. A Fighter Against Fascism*; in the Zaidman Collection.
184. 'Notes for Canvassers and Speakers: The Communist Party and the Jewish People'; undated mimeo in the Zaidman Collection.
185. Piratin, *Our Flag Stays Red*, p. 60.
186. At one such rally, Pat Gold, a Stepney Communist, so impressed a group of Mile End women with the need for action that they took a bus to No. 10 Downing Street, where they demanded to see Chamberlain; see Piratin, *Our Flag Stays Red*, p. 63.
187. *East London Observer*, 18 Oct. 1941, p. 1.
188. *East London Advertiser*, 7 Feb. 1942, p. 10.
189. *East London Advertiser*, 16 May 1942, p. 7; and 23 May 1942, p. 5.
190. *East London Advertiser*, 6 June 1942, p. 7.
191. *East London Advertiser*, 10 Oct. 1942, p. 6.
192. *East London Advertiser*, 7 Nov. 1942, p. 7.
193. Morrison is quoted in Aaron Goldman, 'Germans and Nazis: The Controversy over "Vansittartism" in Britain During the Second World War', *Journal of Contemporary History* 14 (Jan. 1979): 180.
194. Andrew Sharf, *The British Press and Jews Under Nazi Rule*, pp. 133–4.
195. *Daily Worker*, 14 Dec. 1942, p. 4.
196. *Daily Worker*, 19 Dec. 1942, p. 2.
197. *Daily Worker*, 7 Jan. 1943, p. 2. Some scholars have attributed Morrison's procrastinations, delays and obfuscations regarding the entry of Jewish victims of Nazism to his persistent fear of large-scale underlying domestic anti-Semitic feeling in Britain during the war – and, perhaps, his own antipathy towards Jews. See also Tony Kushner, 'The Impact of British Anti-Semitism, 1918–1945', pp. 204–5, and *The*

LONDON JEWS AND BRITISH COMMUNISM

Persistence of Prejudice, pp. 153-6.
198. 'Jewish Information: Digest of News and Views', TS, 24 Feb. 1943, p. 2; the Waterman collection.
199. 'News Summary & Comment', National Jewish Committee, CPGB, 27 Feb. 1943, p. [1]; the Waterman Collection.
200. *Daily Worker*, 1 March 1943, p. 3.
201. *Daily Worker*, 7 April 1943, p. 1. The Bermuda Conference is discussed in Wasserstein, *Britain and the Jews of Europe 1939-1945*, pp. 188-205 and *passim*. See also Kushner, *The Persistence of Prejudice*, pp. 178-80, for the 'impotent' part played by the Board of Deputies during this period.
202. H[yman] Levy, *Soviet Jews at War* (London: Russia Today Society, April 1943), pp. 12, 31.
203. Quoted in *This is the Enemy: A Book of Facts, Figures and Pictures About Fascism* (London: CPGB, July 1943), p. 13.
204. Ilya Ehrenburg, 'I Cannot Remain Silent', mimeo (London: Jewish Fund for Soviet Russia, [1943]), pp. 2, 4; the Zaidman Collection.
205. 'Finance as a Weapon', *Organising for Victory in 1943* (London: CPGB, May 1943), pp. 18-19.
206. *Daily Worker*, 7 Sept. 1943, pp. 1, 4.
207. 'Fraction of Workers' Circle', TS report to the NJC; the Zaidman Collection.
208. L. Gollhard, 'How East London Organised a Record Rally', *Tune Up Our Organisation* (London: CPGB, Jan. 1944), p. 3.
209. *Daily Worker*, 28 April 1944, p. 1.
210. R. B. McCallum and Alison Readman, *The British General Election of 1945* (London: Oxford University Press, 1947), p. 95.
211. *A Stepney to be Proud Of*, p. [13].
212. 'Commentary', *Jewish Opinion* (Feb. 1945), p. 9.
213. Academician Komarov, 'Jew Baiting Must Be Wiped Out', *Jewish Opinion* (Feb. 1945), pp. 7, 12.
214. Minutes, central committee, Workers' Circle, 13 May 1945; the Zaidman Collection.
215. *Daily Worker*, 15 May 1945, p. 1; 18 May 1945, p. 1; and 29 May 1945, p. 1.
216. *Daily Worker*, 30 June 1945, p. 1.
217. *Communist Election Policy* (London: CPGB, June 1945), p. 5.
218. *Peace and World Security. Communist Party Leaflet 12* (London: CPGB, [1945]), p. [2].
219. 'No Softness to Fascist Beasts', *Jewish Forum* (May-June 1945), pp. 6-7.
220. *General Election - July 5, 1945. Parliamentary Division of Mile End. Election Address. A Personal Letter from the Communist Candidate Phil Piratin*, p. [3].

CHAPTER 5

1. Interview, Mick Mindel, London, 5 Nov. 1978. See also on this, Sharman Kadish, *Bolsheviks and British Jews: The Anglo-Jewish Community, Britain and the Russian Revolution* (London: Frank Cass, 1992).
2. Andrew Rothstein ['R. F. Andrews'] (ed.), *What Lenin Said About the Jews: Extracts from His Writings* (London: CPGB, [c. 1935]), p.1.
3. *The Communist Solar System* (London: Labour Party, Sept. 1933), pp. 9-10.
4. 'Autobiographical Sketch of Alec Waterman', TS dated 22 Feb. 1952; the Waterman Collection.
5. Interview, Solly Kaye, London, 31 Oct. 1978.
6. *An Urgent Warning on a Most Important Matter: Jews and Fascism* (London: Coordinating Committee Against Fascism, [1935]), p. 14.

NOTES TO CHAPTER 5

7. See the articles by Hymie Lee, one of the CP's nationality experts, appearing periodically in the *Daily Worker*. The Jews in the Soviet Union were 'living peacefully together' with other nationalities; 'there is no Palestine problem of "partition" here'. *Daily Worker*, 20 Aug. 1937, p. 7; 6 Aug. 1937, p. 7.
8. *Daily Worker*, 29 Jan. 1935, p. 2; *Jewish Chronicle*, 1 Feb. 1935, p. 24. Such debates were frequent occurrences; for example, Issie Panner debated with a Zionist spokesman on 'Zionism and the Problem of the Jews' at Circle House on 9 December 1938; see the *East London Advertiser*, 17 Dec. 1938, p. 8. Many Zionists despaired of their inability to successfully counter Communist propaganda concerning Birobidzhan. See David Cesarani, 'The East London of Simon Blumenfeld's *Jew Boy*', p. 50. On Poale Zion's ideological quarrels with Jewish Communists, see Shimoni, 'Poale Zion', pp. 251–3.
9. I. Panner, 'The Soviet Government's Decree of May 7th, 1934 and Its Lesson', the *Circle-Arbeter Ring* 1 (Oct. 1934): 5–6 [English section].
10. A Yiddish film at a cinema in Charing Cross Road was greeted with 'a tremendous burst of clapping' when footage of Birobidzhan appeared on-screen. *Daily Worker*, 19 March 1935, p. 4. There is a substantial amount of literature on the Birobidzhan enterprise and its supporters. For a brief summary of the scheme, see Chimen Abramsky, 'The Biro-Bidzhan Project, 1927–1959', in Lionel Kochan (ed.), *The Jews in Soviet Russia Since 1917* (New York: Oxford University Press, 1970), pp. 64–77.
11. A[lec] Waterman, 'Baruch Weinberg Un "ICOS"' ['Baruch Weinberg and "ICOS"'], the *Circle-Arbeter Ring* 8 (Oct. 1941): 5–6 [Yiddish section]. 'ICOS' was the English transliteration of the acronym for the group.
12. *Daily Worker*, 7 April 1936, p. 4.
13. *Daily Worker*, 10 May 1935, p. 4, and 14 May 1935, p. 4.
14. *Daily Worker*, 31 Aug. 1935, p. 7, and 13 Sept. 1935, p. 4.
15. *Jewish Chronicle*, 13 March 1936, p. 13.
16. *Jewish Chronicle*, 3 April 1936, pp. 23–24.
17. *Daily Worker*, 7 May 1936, p. 4.
18. *Daily Worker*, 16 May 1936, pp. 4, 6; and 20 May 1936, p. 5. Alf Holland has also made note of ICOS's connections with like-minded pro-Soviet organizations elsewhere: the American Communist activist Gina Medem, a correspondent for the New York daily *Morgn Freiheit*, 'helped us a lot with ICOS; she came through London quite a bit speaking on behalf of ICOR,' the Organization for Jewish Colonization in the Soviet Union, the American counterpart to ICOS. Interview, Alf Holland, London, 16 June 1978.
19. Issie Panner ['I. Rennap'], *Anti-Semitism and the Jewish Question*, pp. 34–65.
20. *Jewish Chronicle*, 14 April 1944, p. 4; Levy may have been referring to Palestine.
21. *Jewish Chronicle*, 20 Oct. 1944, p. 9.
22. Victor Gollancz, 'The New Situation', the *Left News*, No. 61 (July 1941), p. 1788.
23. Interview, Jacob Sonntag, London, 8 May 1980.
24. *London–Veitchepl [London–Whitechapel]*, special issue entitled *Sovyet-Rusland [Soviet Russia]*, No. 13 (July 1941).
25. See *Jews Against Hitler: Appeal and Report of International Conference of Jews held in Moscow August 24th, 1941* (London: Anglo-Russian Parliamentary Committee, Nov. 1941). Many accounts have been written about the history of the JAFC. See, for instance, Shimon Redlich, *Propaganda and Nationalism in Wartime Russia: The Jewish Antifascist Committee in the USSR, 1941–1948*, East European Monographs, No. 108 (Boulder, CO: East European Quarterly, 1982).
26. *East London Advertiser*, 27 Sept. 1941, p. 1.

27. *East London Advertiser*, 27 Sept. 1941, p. 1.
28. The *Circle-Arbeter Ring* 8 (July 1941): 1 [English section].
29. The *Circle-Arbeter Ring* 9 (Jan. 1942): 1 [English section].
30. *Jewish Chronicle*, 28 Nov. 1941, p. 21; see also Sam Alexander, 'Britain Greets 24th Anniversary of Russian Revolution', the *Circle-Arbeter Ring* 9 (Jan. 1942): 4–5 [English section], and I[ssie] Pushkin, 'On Winning the War', the *Circle-Arbeter Ring* 9 (Jan. 1942): 5 [English section].
31. *East London Observer*, 18 Oct. 1941, p. 1.
32. *East London Advertiser*, 27 Dec. 1941, p. 3.
33. A[be] Gilbert, 'The Workers' Circle and Soviet Jewry', the *Circle* 11 (April 1945): 10.
34. *Jewish Chronicle*, 9 Oct. 1942, p. 13.
35. Letter to the editor from A. Silverman, *East London Advertiser*, 21 March 1942, p. 4.
36. *East London Advertiser*, 28 March 1942, p. 2.
37. *East London Advertiser*, 25 April 1942, p. 1.
38. *East London Advertiser*, 6 June 1942, p. 1. Maisky's messages even appeared on theatre posters, such as the one advertising the play *Tsvay Khaverim [Two Comrades]* being staged at the Grand Palais on 25 June 1942 to raise money for the Soviet war effort. The poster was on display at the 'Yiddish Theatre in London 1880–1987' exhibition in the National Theatre, London, 30 June to 8 Aug. 1987.
39. *East London Advertiser*, 20 June 1942, p. 6; 27 June 1942, p. 1.
40. Letter to the editor from Simon Blumenfeld, *Jewish Chronicle*, 19 June 1942, p. 13.
41. 'Declaration of Aims' and 'Resolution' of the Jewish 1942 Committee; file C11/12/27, Board of Deputies archives.
42. *Jewish Chronicle*, 26 June 1942, p. 8.
43. *Jewish Chronicle*, 3 July 1942, p. 11.
44. *Jewish Chronicle*, 10 July 1942, p. 15.
45. *Jewish Chronicle*, 10 July 1942, p. 1.
46. For this exchange, see the memo in file C11/12/127, Board of Deputies archives.
47. *Jewish Chronicle*, 14 Aug. 1942, p. 15.
48. Letter from Simon Blumenfeld, 17 Aug. 1942; file C/11/12/127, Board of Deputies archives.
49. *Jewish Chronicle*, 4 Sept. 1942, p. 1; the *East London Advertiser* of 5 Sept. 1942, p. 7, devoted two columns to this meeting.
50. Selig Brodetsky to Simon Blumenfeld, 25 Aug. 1942; file C11/12/127, Board of Deputies archives.
51. Letter to the editor of the *Jewish Chronicle* from Joseph Leftwich, 16 Oct. 1942, p. 6.
52. Interview, Mrs Ray Waterman, London, 30 Oct. 1978.
53. Interview with Chimen Abramsky by Dr Shimon Redlich, in Hebrew, Jerusalem, 20 Aug. 1972; Institute of Contemporary Jewry, Oral History Division, Hebrew University of Jerusalem.
54. Interview, Jacob Sonntag, London, 15 May 1980.
55. See, for example, *Ruf Tsu Einheit Un Kamf [Call to Unity and Battle]* (London: Jewish Cultural Club, May 1942).
56. *Yidn In'm Kamf Kegn Hitlerism* (London: Jewish Cultural Club, May 1942).
57. Asher Frucht (ed.), *25 Yor Sovyetn Farband* (London: Jewish Cultural Club, Nov. 1942).
58. *Daily Worker*, 1 March 1943, p. 3; *East London Advertiser*, 6 March 1943, p. 2.
59. *Jewish Chronicle*, 16 Oct. 1942, p. 13.
60. Letter from Selig Brodetsky to I[van] Greenberg, 28 Oct. 1942; file C11/12/127,

NOTES TO CHAPTER 5

Board of Deputies archives.
61. *Daily Worker*, 6 Nov. 1942, p. 4; *Jewish Chronicle*, 13 Nov. 1942, p. 7.
62. Draft memo for formal registration of the JFSR, hand dated 18 Nov. 1942; the Waterman Collection.
63. Interview, Jacob Sonntag, London, 15 May 1980.
64. Interview with Chimen Abramsky by Dr Shimon Redlich, Jerusalem, 20 Aug. 1972.
65. 'News Summary and Comment', TS, 27 Feb. 1943; the Waterman Collection. The JFSR was on the agenda for 12 of the 35 meetings of the National Jewish Committee between 9 April 1943 and 23 June 1944, according to an 'Analysis of Discussions at Meetings of National Jewish Committee', TS in the Zaidman Collection; no other topic was included on the agenda so many times.
66. Minutes, undated, of the National Jewish Committee of the CPGB; Zaidman Collection.
67. 'Message to the Jewish Fund for Soviet Russia from M. Maisky', in *The Russian Jews in the War* (London: Jewish Fund for Soviet Russia, [late 1943]), p. 105.
68. Press Department, Soviet Embassy, London, *New Soviet Documents on Nazi Atrocities* London: Hutchinson & Co., Ltd, [1943]).
69. *Jews of Britain! Soviet Russia Needs Your Help!. Admiration is Not Enough* (London: Jewish Fund for Soviet Russia, Jan. 1943), p. 19.
70. [Chimen Abramsky (ed.)], *Calling All Jews to Action!* (London: Jewish Fund for Soviet Russia, May 1943), p. 24.
71. Ibid., p. 26.
72. Ibid., p. 1.
73. See messages from the Federation of Zionist Youth, 26 Sept. 1941, and from the Federation of Women Zionists of Great Britain and Ireland, 16 Oct. 1941; both are in file C11/12/127, Board of Deputies archives.
74. Ivor Montagu spoke to the Anglo-Palestinian Club in December 1941 about the 'total ban on anti-Semitism' in the Soviet Union. *Jewish Chronicle*, 12 Dec. 1941, p. 19.
75. See, for instance, Schneier Levenberg's impassioned plea for aid to the Soviets in 'Farvos Shvaygt Veitchepl?' ['Why is Whitechapel Silent?'], the *Circle-Arbeter Ring* 9 (Jan. 1942): 4–5 [Yiddish section].
76. '£10,000 Cheque From Palestine Jewish Labour for Russian Red Cross', in *The Russian Jews in the War*, pp. 97–8; *Jewish Chronicle*, 28 Aug. 1942, p. 6.
77. Letter, Joseph Leftwich to Selig Brodetsky, 12 Feb. 1943; file C11/12/127, Board of Deputies archives. Levenberg later served as the Poale Zion representative on the JFSR executive.
78. The resolutions, which differed slightly from those passed by the general convention, are in the Zaidman Collection.
79. Ilya Ehrenburg, 'Let the Blood of the Children Call to the Conscience of the World!', *Zionist Review* 8 New Series (13 Aug. 1943): 4.
80. Herzl Berger, 'Soviet Jewry in the Front Line', *Zionist Review* 8 New Series (17 Sept. 1943): 4.
81. *Jews of Britain! Soviet Russia Needs Your Help*, pp. 14–16; Feffer's poem was translated into English by Joseph Leftwich. It was republished in *The Russian Jews in the War*, p. 9, and in many other places.
82. 'Report of National Jewish Committee to International Affairs Committee', minutes of the 9 April 1943 NJC meeting; TS in the Zaidman Collection.
83. See, for example, a letter from Nathan Weiner, general secretary of the Workers' Circle, to B. A. Bagnari, general chairman, London, 7 Sept. 1943, regarding the

activities of Maurice Essex in arranging for Circle and tailors' union members to get involved. Document 47–1991/4, Pushkin/Rayner archive.

84. See *National Reception Committee in Honour of the Visit of Colonel Itzik Feffer and Professor Solomons Mikhoels* (London: Jewish Fund for Soviet Russia, [1943]); in the Waterman Collection. Included among the celebrities were actors John Gielgud, Michael Redgrave and Sybil Thorndike; and authors H. G. Wells, Julian Huxley and Sean O'Casey.
85. *Daily Worker*, 25 Sept. 1943, p. 2.
86. 'Di Gest Mikhoels Un Feffer' ['The Guests Mikhoels and Feffer'], *London–Veitchepl [London–Whitechapel]*, 15 Sept. 1943, p. 12.
87. The two articles on Mikhoels were by A. N. Stencl, 'Der "Folks-Artist", Anfirer Fun Moskver Yiddish Kunst-Teater – Professor Sh. Mikhoels' ['The "People's Artist", Founder of the Moscow Yiddish Art Theatre – Professor Sh. Mikhoels'], and by Mark Markov (director of the London Yiddish Theatre), 'Prof. Sh. M. Mikhoels'; see *London–Veitchepl [London–Whitechapel]*, 15 Nov. 1943, pp. 1–2 and 2–4.
88. *East London Advertiser*, 8 Oct. 1943, p. 5, and 15 Oct. 1943, p. 1.
89. *Daily Worker*, 11 Oct. 1943, p. 4.
90. *Daily Worker*, 18 Oct. 1943, p. 4. 'A Rosh Hashanah Message' from the chief rabbi, in the *Jewish Bulletin* No. 26 (Oct. 1943), p. [1], spoke of 'Russia's marvellous stand against the hordes of tyranny'.
91. *Daily Worker*, 30 Oct. 1943, p. 3.
92. *Daily Worker*, 1 Nov. 1943, p. 4.
93. *Daily Worker*, 6 Nov. 1943, p. 4.
94. *Daily Worker*, 8 Nov. 1943, p. 4.
95. *East London Advertiser*, 19 Nov. 1943, p. 5. The figure of 5 million Jews in the Soviet armies was, of course, a gross exaggeration. The usual number given is 'almost half a million'; see Reuben Ainsztein, 'Soviet Jewry in the Second World War', in Lionel Kochan (ed.), *The Jews in Soviet Russia Since 1917*, p. 275.
96. Transcript of the various speeches made at the People's Palace meeting, Sunday, 14 Nov. 1943; file C11/12/127, Board of Deputies archives.
97. *Daily Worker*, 15 Nov. 1943, p. 4.
98. Interview with Chimen Abramsky, by Dr Shimon Redlich, Jerusalem, 20 Aug. 1972.
99. Interview, Alf Holland, London, 16 June 1978.
100. 'The Eleventh Convention', the *Circle* 11 (April 1945): 2.
101. Interview with Chimen Abramsky, by Dr Shimon Redlich, Jerusalem, 20 Aug. 1972.
102. *Jewish Chronicle*, 26 Nov. 1943, p. 6.
103. Transcript of the meeting of the Board of Deputies, Sunday, 21 November, and of the reception given to Professor Mikhoels and Colonel Feffer; file C11/12/127, Board of Deputies archives.
104. Interview with Chimen Abramsky, by Dr Shimon Redlich, Jerusalem, 20 Aug. 1972.
105. Interview, Mick Mindel, London, 5 Nov. 1978.
106. Interview, Mrs Ray Waterman, London, 30 Oct. 1978.
107. See the 'Message to Jews in Soviet Russia', dated 1 Dec. 1943, and written by Councillor M. H. Davis, who was president of the Federation. This letter is reproduced in a compilation of *Greetings and Goodwill Messages from Anglo-Jewry to Soviet Jewry in commemoration of the visit to Great Britain of Prof. Solomon Mikhoels and Col. Itzik Feffer, November, 1943* [London, 1944]; it can be found in file C11/12/127, Board of Deputies archives. Another message came from the Anglo-Palestinian Club.
108. Interview, J. W. Bentley, London, 13 Nov. 1979.

NOTES TO CHAPTER 5

109. *Zionist Review* 8 New Series (5 Nov. 1943): 1. See also the letter of 24 Nov. 1943, from Paul Goodman, chairman of the Political Department of the Zionist Federation, writing about his 'fraternal affection' for Mikhoels and Feffer; it is in the collection of *Greetings and Goodwill Messages from Anglo-Jewry to Soviet Jewry* . . ., p. 12; file C11/12/127, Board of Deputies archives. Weizmann did, however, paint a less rosy picture of Soviet Jewry in an address to the Board of Deputies a few months later, forcing Walter Holmes of the *Daily Worker* to rush into print claiming that Soviet Jews enjoyed the 'fullest social, religious and cultural development'. *Daily Worker*, 27 June 1944, p. 2.
110. 'The Eleventh Convention', the *Circle* 11 (April 1945): 4.
111. A. N. Stencl, 'Unzere Brider in Sovyet Rusland', *London–Veitchepl*, No. 54 (July 1944), pp. 1–3; 'Vilna Yerushalayim D'Lita', *London–Veitchepl*, No. 55 (Aug. 1944), p. 1; and 'Tsu der Roiter Fon', *London–Veitchepl*, No. 58 (Nov. 1944), p. 1.
112. Lazar Zaidman, 'Tsum Zibetn November' ['To the Seventh of November'], *London–Veitchepl*, No. 58 (Nov. 1944), pp. 4–6; and Chimen Abramsky, 'Unzere Brider in Rusland' ['Our Brothers in Russia'], ibid., pp. 7–9.
113. Alec Waterman, 'Tsen Yor Birobidzhan' ['Ten Years of Birobidzhan'], *London–Veitchepl*, No. 54 (July 1944), pp. 3–6; and 'Yiddish-Sovyetishe Poezye in der Periode fun der Groiser Faterlandishe Milchome' ['Yiddish Soviet Poetry in the Period of the Great Fatherland War'], *London–Veitchepl*, No. 63 (April 1945), pp. 33–6, and No. 65 (June 1945), p. 45.
114. Minutes, branch meeting of NAFTA 15, 15 Oct. 1944; East London United Office, London.
115. *Jewish Fund for Soviet Russia, Beaver Hall Conference* (London, [1944]), pp. 3, 4, 11, 15.
116. 'Statement on the Jewish Question' of the National Jewish Committee (London, 1944), TS, pp. 9–10; in the Zaidman Collection.
117. *Jewish Chronicle*, 10 Nov. 1944, p. 10.
118. *Jewish Chronicle*, 23 Feb. 1945, p. 7.
119. 'Anglo-Jewry and European Relief', *Jewish Bulletin* No. 44 (April 1945), p. [3].
120. *Jewish Clarion* (April 1945), p. 9. Some £2,500 of this had been contributed by the Workers' Circle. *Diamond Jubilee: The Workers' Circle Friendly Society 1909–1969* (London: Workers' Circle, 1969), p. 8.
121. 'Party Work Amongst the Jews in Britain', draft TS prepared by the National Jewish Committee (London, [Dec. 1943]), p. 1; in the Zaidman Collection.
122. 'Statement on the Jewish Question', p. 8.
123. *The Jewish Question: Statement by the National Jewish Committee of the Communist Party* (London: Communist Party, [1944]) p. 16.
124. 'Anglo-Soviet Jewish Relations. Collaboration is Vital', *Jewish Clarion* (April 1945), p. 3.
125. 'The Meaning of Unity', *Jewish Opinion* (Feb. 1945), pp. 8–9.
126. David Zaslavsky, 'Jew-Baiters Will Perish', *Jewish Forum* (May–June 1945), p. 2.
127. 'Birobidjan's Progress', *Russia Today* (March 1945), p. 7.
128. Interview, William Carver, Old Colwyn, Colwyn Bay, Wales, 31 Aug. 1976.
129. Phil Piratin, 'The Communist Party and the Jewish People. Every Jew Must Vote Progressive', pp. 4–5.
130. Phil Piratin, 'Appeal to the Jewish Electors'.
131. *General Election – July 5th 1945. Parliamentary Division of Mile End. Election Address. A Personal Letter from the Communist Candidate Phil Piratin*, pp. [2–3].
132. 'Notes for Canvassers and Speakers: The Communist Party and the Jewish People.'

CHAPTER 6

1. Interview, Morry Lebow, London, 21 Nov. 1978.
2. *East London Advertiser*, 12 Sept. 1936, p. 5.
3. S[am] Alexander, 'Help to Defeat the "Butchers of Badajoz"', the *Circle-Arbeter Ring* 3 (Oct. 1936): 1–2 [English section].
4. A[lec] Waterman, 'Vu iz der Kinstler?' ['Where is the Artist?'], in I. A. Lisky *et al.*, *Yiddish London*, Vol. 2, pp. 126–7.
5. Bill Alexander estimates the number of British volunteers who fought in Spain at about 2,200, of whom perhaps 180 to 200 were Jews. Bill Alexander, *British Volunteers for Liberty: Spain, 1936–1939* (London: Lawrence & Wishart, 1982), pp. 29–30, 32. Albert Prago, *Jews in the International Brigades in Spain* (New York: Jewish Currents, 1979), p. 6, maintains that over 10 per cent of the British volunteers were Jewish, while David Diamant, *Combattants juifs dans l'armée républicaine espagnol* (Paris: Editions Renouveau, 1974), p. 390, puts the figure at slightly below ten per cent. However, Tom Wintringham, one of the military commanders of the British Battalion, in his book *English Captain* (London: Faber & Faber, 1939), p. 329, stated that the Jewish component of the battalion was about 3 per cent. His estimate, which was made at the end of the war, may have been intentionally low in order to counteract anti-Semitic charges made by some on the right wing that the battalion had been 'overrun' by Jews.
6. The Waterman Collection included papers relating to these committees.
7. *East London Advertiser*, 12 Sept. 1936, p. 5.
8. See the pamphlet advertising a Hackney meeting for 25 Feb. 1937, issued by the North London Branch of the JPC, in the Julius Jacobs collection. JPC propaganda often referred to the Spanish struggle; two typical pamphlets, 'Hitler Pays the Piper – What Tune Does He Call?' and 'Boycott', both printed in 1939, are in the Jacobs Collection.
9. K. W. Watkins, *Britain Divided: The Effect of the Spanish Civil War on British Political Opinion* (London: Nelson, 1963), p. 159.
10. S[am] Alexander, 'Help to Defeat the "Butchers of Badajoz"', p. 1 [English section].
11. [Nathan Weiner], 'General Secretary's Report', the *Circle-Arbeter Ring* 3 (Oct. 1936): 7 [English section].
12. B. A. Bagnari, 'May Day 1937', the *Circle-Arbeter Ring* 5 (May 1937): 1 [English section].
13. A. L. Cohen, 'How Workers' Circle Members Have Helped Spain', the *Circle-Arbeter Ring* 5 (May 1937): 7 [English section]; and *The Circle Golden Jubilee 1909–1959* (London: Workers' Circle Central Committee, 1959), p. 10.
14. 'Extracts from Minutes', the *Circle-Arbeter Ring* 5 (May 1937): [English section].
15. [George Kenneth Tate], *London Trades Council 1860–1950: A History* (London: Lawrence & Wishart, 1950), pp. 143–4.
16. *Daily Worker*, 12 Sept. 1936, p. 1.
17. *Daily Worker*, 13 Jan. 1937, p. 5.
18. [Alex Gossip], 'General Secretary's Opening Remarks and State of Trade', *NAFTA Monthly Report* 36 (March 1937): 2.
19. 'Summary of Business Transacted by E.C.', *NAFTA Monthly Report* 36 (Sept. 1937): 9. Altogether, over a two-year period, NAFTA 15 members subscribed £500 for Spain. Hew Reid, *The Furniture Makers: A History of Trade Unionism in the Furniture Trade 1865–1972* (Oxford: Malthouse Press, 1986), p. 149.
20. [Alex Gossip], 'General Secretary's Opening Remarks and State of Trade', *NAFTA Monthly Report* 36 (Feb. 1937): 2.

NOTES TO CHAPTER 6

21. *Daily Worker*, 30 April 1938, p. 1 of the May Day supplement.
22. A[lex] Donaldson, 'Britons in Spain', *The Volunteer for Liberty: Organ of the International Brigades* 1 (20 Sept. 1937): 3 [Madrid]. On the death of Sam Masters, see 'Notes of the Month', *Tailor and Garment Worker* 7 (Jan. 1938): 1.
23. *East London Observer*, 30 April 1938, pp. 1, 7.
24. A[ndrew] Conley, 'Events at Home and Abroad', *Tailor and Garment Worker* 7 (July 1938); 1, 9.
25. *Daily Worker*, 17 Dec. 1938, p. 6.
26. See the union's 'Fraternal Greetings to our Members at home and to our comrades of the International Brigade in Spain', signed by Fine, the secretary, and by Mick Mindel, the chairman, in the *Daily Worker*, 30 April 1938, p. 1 of the May Day supplement.
27. NUTGW Papers, London.
28. NUTGW Papers, London.
29. For the events leading up to the formation of the company, see Joshua Rothenberg, 'The Jewish Naftali Botwin Company (An Episode from Recent History)', *Jewish Frontier* 47 (April 1980): 15; Albert Prago, 'The Botwin Company in Spain, 1937–1939', *Jewish Currents* 46 (March 1992): 8–9; and David Diamant, *Combattants juifs dans l'armée républicaine espagnol*, pp. 148–9. Prago estimates that, altogether, some 6,000 to 7,000 Jews fought in the International Brigades, about 15–16 per cent of the total number of volunteers (p. 7).
30. S[am] Alexander, 'Anti-Semitism on the Increase . . .', the *Circle-Arbeter Ring* 5 (Aug. 1938): 1–2 [English section]; 'The Workers' Circle Renews its Aid for Spain', the *Circle-Arbeter Ring* 5 (Aug. 1938): 3 [English section]; and the 'Extracts from Minutes' of the central committee, the *Circle-Arbeter Ring* 5 (Aug. 1938): 7 [English section] and 9 [English and Yiddish section].
31. Alf Holland [writing under the pseudonym 'Avreyml'], 'Di "Botvin" Kompanye un Unzer Khoyv' ['The "Botwin" Company and Our Debt'], the *Circle-Arbeter Ring* 5 (Aug. 1938): 5 [Yiddish section].
32. Gina Medem, 'A Glorious Chapter in Jewish History: The Botwin Company', the *Circle-Arbeter Ring* 5 (Nov. 1938): 10 [English section], and 10 [Yiddish section]. Medem also wrote a pamphlet, *Los Judios Voluntarios de la Libertad (Un ano de lucha en las Brigadas Internacionales) [Jewish Volunteers for Liberty (A Year of Fighting in the International Brigades)]* (Madrid: Ediciones del Comisariado de las Brigadas Internacionales, 1937).
33. See Rothenberg, 'The Jewish Naftali Botwin Company', *passim*.
34. Piratin, *Our Flag Stays Red*, p. 51. Altogether, 526 British volunteers were killed. Bill Alexander, *British Volunteers for Liberty*, p. 259.
35. *Daily Worker*, 3 Dec. 1938, p. 6.
36. *East London Advertiser*, 17 Dec. 1938, p. 8.
37. *East London Advertiser*, 25 Feb. 1939, p. 8.
38. *Daily Worker*, 25 Feb. 1939, p. 6.
39. Minutes, ULTTU executive committee meeting, 30 March 1939; NUTGW Papers, London.
40. The letter is reprinted in the *Circle-Arbeter Ring* 6 (May 1939): 9 [English section].
41. 'Extracts from Minutes', central committee, the *Circle-Arbeter Ring* 6 (May 1939): 7 [English section].
42. The *Circle* 11 (April 1945): 1.
43. Alec Waterman, 'Salud di Heldn!' ['Hail the Heroes!'], the *Circle-Arbeter Ring* 6 (May 1939): 8 [Yiddish section].
44. J[ulius] Pilchik, 'A Brief Survey', the *Circle-Arbeter Ring* (May 1939): 1 [English

section].
45. *Daily Worker*, 20 Aug. 1937, p. 2.
46. See the advertisement in the *Daily Worker*, 6 Jan. 1938, p. 7.
47. *East London Advertiser*, 8 Jan. 1938, p. 5.
48. Piratin, *Our Flag Stays Red*, p. 51.
49. Interview, Solly Kaye, London, 31 Oct. 1978.
50. 'The Eleventh Convention', the *Circle* 11 (April 1945): 1.
51. [Nathan Weiner], 'General Secretary's Report', the *Circle* 11 (April 1945): 7.
52. Hyman Levy, 'The Problem of Assimilation', in J. J. Lynx, (ed.), *The Future of the Jews* (London: Lindsay Drummond, 1945), pp. 60–1.
53. Morris Myer, 'Di Itstike Internatsionale Lage in Historishn Perspektiv' ['The Current International Situation in Historical Perspective'], in I. A. Lisky *et al.* (eds), *Yiddish London*, Vol. 2, p. 24.
54. 'Yidn un di Vahlen' ['Jews and the Elections'], *Di Tsayt*, 29 June 1945, p. 2.
55. 'Jews and the General Election', draft TS [1945], p. [2]; the Zaidman Collection.
56. Piratin, *Communist Candidate for Mile End. Popular Stepney Fighter and Leader*; the Zaidman Collection.
57. *General Election – July 5th, 1945. Parliamentary Division of Mile End, Election Address. A Personal Letter from the Communist candidate, Phil Piratin*, p. [3]; the Zaidman Collection.
58. *Mile End Has a Memory*; the Zaidman Collection.
59. *Jewish Chronicle*, 22 Feb. 1935, p. 7.
60. *Jewish Chronicle*, 10 May 1935, p. 9.
61. N[oah] Barou, 'The Economic and Social Position of Polish Jewry', the *Circle-Arbeter Ring* 5 (May 1937): 6 [English section].
62. *Diamond Jubilee: The Workers' Circle Friendly Society, 1909–1969*, p. 9.
63. Joe Jacobs, *Out of the Ghetto*, p. 203.
64. 'Medem Sanatorium', the *Circle-Arbeter Ring* 3 (June 1936): 7 [English section].
65. S[am] A[lexander], 'Save the Jewish Children in Poland', the *Circle-Arbeter Ring* 4 (Feb. 1937): 3–4 [English section]. Alexander had already mentioned the 'apathy' of the Anglo-Jewish establishment in 'The Menace of Anti-Semitism!', the *Circle-Arbeter Ring* 3 (June 1936): 2 [English section].
66. 'The Jewish Children in Poland Appeal to You', the *Circle-Arbeter Ring* 5 (May 1937): 6 [English section].
67. *Jewish Chronicle*, 28 Jan. 1938, p. 29.
68. 'Resolution' of Circle House Conference, 3 April 1938; NUTGW Papers, London.
69. Letter from the Jewish Protest Committee, 28 July 1937; NUTGW Papers, London.
70. *Daily Worker*, 5 Feb. 1938, p. 6.
71. *Jewish Chronicle*, 8 March 1940, p. 14.
72. *Jewish Chronicle*, 16 Aug. 1940, p. 9.
73. *Parliamentary Debates (Hansard) House of Commons*, Fifth Series, Vol. 364, 22 Aug. 1940, col. 1493.
74. *Daily Herald*, 28 April 1943, p. 2.
75. All three of these articles appeared in the *Daily Worker*, 3 May 1943, p. 4. Perhaps in response to these activities, the *Catholic Herald* claimed that complaints about anti-Semitism in the Polish army were part of a 'conspiracy' to discredit the 'London Poles'. R[euben] Ainsztein, 'The Enemy Within: Antisemitism among Polish Soldiers in War-Time Britain', p. 58.
76. A. L. Easterman to Selig Brodetsky, 23 Dec. 1943; file C11/10/6, Board of Deputies archives.

NOTES TO CHAPTER 6

77. Tom Driberg, *Ruling Passions: The Autobiography of Tom Driberg* (London: Jonathan Cape, 1977; reprint ed., Quartet Books, 1978), p. 202.
78. Bernard Wasserstein, *Britain and the Jews of Europe 1939-1945*, pp. 126-7.
79. Tom Driberg, *Absentees for Freedom: The Case of the Jews in the Polish Forces* (London: National Council for Civil Liberties, May 1944), p. [2].
80. Driberg, *Ruling Passions*, pp. 202-3.
81. *Daily Worker*, 6 April 1944, p. 3.
82. *Daily Worker*, 8 April 1944, p. 3.
83. Driberg, *Absentees for Freedom*, p. [2].
84. 'An Appeal to Members of the Board of Deputies of British Jews', TS [London, April 1944]; the Zaidman Collection.
85. The resolution was included in a letter of 21 April 1944 signed by Harry Frankel, the branch secretary; among the recipients of the letter were the Prime Minister, the World Jewish Congress, the Board of Deputies, Driberg, and seven newspapers. The National Jewish Committee discussed the Polish Jewish soldiers at its meeting of 28 April, according to the 'Analysis of Discussions at Meetings of National Jewish Committee' included in the Zaidman Collection.
86. *Daily Worker*, 25 April 1944, p. 1; and 26 April 1944, p. 3.
87. Zvi Avital, 'The Polish Government in Exile and the Jewish Question', *Wiener Library Bulletin* 28 New Series (1975): 47.
88. Wasserstein, *Britain and the Jews of Europe, 1939-1945*, p. 129.
89. *Daily Worker*, 26 April 1944, p. 3.
90. *Daily Worker*, 27 April 1944, p. 3.
91. *Daily Worker*, 11 May 1944, p. 3.
92. A total of 210 telegrams were received from shop stewards representing 12,000 workers, according to Leon Samuels, 'The Jewish Labour Movement', p. 36.
93. *Daily Worker*, 12 May 1944, p. 4.
94. *Daily Worker*, 15 May 1944, p. 4.
95. *Daily Worker*, 13 May 1944, p. 1.
96. Letter from Harry Frankel to the Board of Deputies, 7 June 1944; the Zaidman Collection.
97. *The Jewish Question: Statement by the National Jewish Committee of the Communist Party*, p. 18.
98. *Jewish Chronicle*, 28 March 1941, p. 12.
99. *Jewish Chronicle*, 1 March 1940, p. 14.
100. A. R. Rollin, 'Jewish Labour Notes', the *Circle-Arbeter Ring* 9 (Jan. 1942): 3 [English section].
101. *Stop Them Now. German Mass Murder of Jews in Poland* (London: Federation of Polish Jews in Great Britain, [1943]).
102. 'The Eleventh Convention', the *Circle-Arbeter Ring* 11 (April 1945): 2.
103. *Remember the Warsaw Ghetto: In Tribute to the Heroes* (London: Narod Press, [April 1944]).
104. Pamphlet announcing the meeting; the Zaidman Collection.
105. See *London-Veitchepl*, No. 52 (May 1944), subtitled 'Unsere Kiddushim un Heldn' ['Our Martyrs and Heroes'].
106. A. N. Stencl, 'Dos Poylishe Yidntum' ['Polish Jewry'], *London-Veitchepl*, No. 61 (Feb. 1945), subtitled 'Dos Bafrayte Poyln' ['Liberated Poland'], pp. 2, 4.
107. Yosef Hillel Levy, 'Zay Gebentsht Du Marshal Stalin' ['Bless You Marshal Stalin'], *London-Veitchepl*, No. 62 (March 1945), p. 31.
108. This document is in the Zaidman Collection.

109. Minutes, National Jewish Committee of the Communist Party, 11 Feb. 1945; the Zaidman Collection.
110. L[azar] Zaidman, 'Jews in Liberated Europe', *World News and Views* 25 (27 Jan. 1945): 27.
111. *Victory Peace Security: Report of the 17th National Congress of the Communist Party, Shoreditch Town Hall, London, E.C.1 October 28-30, 1944* (London: Communist Party, Nov. 1944), pp. 24-25.
112. Communist Party, Political Committee, *Political Letter to All Members: The Communist Party and the Crimea Conference*, London, 21 Feb. 1945, p. [2]; the Zaidman Collection.
113. R. Howard, *Poland Liberated* (London: CPGB, Feb. 1945), pp. 3-4, 7-8, 10. This pamphlet also extolled the virtues of the new government in Poland and discussed the controversy concerning the Curzon line.
114. Academician Komarov, 'Jew Baiting Must Be Wiped Out', *Jewish Opinion* (Feb. 1945), p. 12.
115. 'Polish Government Honours Dr Sommerstein', *Jewish Opinion* (Feb. 1945), p. 4.
116. 'Polish Jewry Rebuilds', *Jewish Clarion* (April 1945), p. 8.
117. '"We Rose in the Ghetto Against the Fascist Beast"', *Jewish Clarion* (April 1945), p. 5. The same page also carried a declaration from the Polish government restoring Polish citizenship to any Jews who had been denaturalized by previous Polish administrations.
118. 'Where Anti-Semitism is Dying Out', *Jewish Forum* (May-June 1945), p. 3.
119. Minutes, National Jewish Committee of the Communist Party, 11 Feb. 1945; the Zaidman Collection.
120. Minutes, LJC Meeting [of the National Jewish Committee], 26 April 1945; the Zaidman Collection.
121. 'Unity Theatre Presents "The Yellow Star"', *Jewish Forum* (May-June 1945), p. 4; Minutes, LJC Meeting [of the National Jewish Committee], 26 April 1945, in the Zaidman Collection.
122. J. L. Fine, 'Two Successful Experiments', *Garment Worker* 14 (July 1945): 139.
123. *Challenge* 11 (16 June 1945), p. 8. This was the publication of the Young Communist League.
124. 'Who Are These Tories?', *Educational Commentary on Current Affairs*, sixth series (London: Marx House, June 1945), p. 4.
125. 'Commentary', *Jewish Forum* (May-June 1945), p. 11.
126. *Daily Worker*, 29 June 1945, p. 1.
127. Piratin, 'The Communist Party and the Jewish People', p. 1.
128. For the details, see three articles by Gideon Shimoni: 'Selig Brodetsky and the Ascendancy of Zionism in Anglo-Jewry (1939-1945)', *Jewish Journal of Sociology* 22 (Dec. 1980): 125-61; 'From Anti-Zionism to Non-Zionism in Anglo-Jewry, 1917-1937', *Jewish Journal of Sociology* 28 (June 1986): 19-47; and 'The Non-Zionists in Anglo-Jewry, 1937-1948', *Jewish Journal of Sociology* 28 (Dec. 1986): 89-115.
129. See, typically, *Palestine*, a pamphlet published in London in 1936 by the International Secretariat of the League Against Imperialism, a CP-controlled front organization. After citing all of the arguments against Jewish colonization in Palestine, it describes in some detail (pp. 22-4) the Jewish Autonomous Region in Birobidzhan.
130. *Daily Worker*, 28 July 1936, p. 2.
131. See the following issues of *Discussion*: 4 (May 1936); 8 (Sept. 1936); 10 (Dec. 1936); 12 (Feb. 1937); 13 (March 1937); and 14 (April 1937). The quotes are from pp. 22-3 of the April 1937 issue.

NOTES TO CHAPTER 6

132. Letter from Chimen Abramsky to Shloime Perel, London, 7 Dec. 1978. Mr Perel, whose research has concentrated on the Jewish Communist movement in Canada, kindly allowed me to read this letter.
133. *Zionist Review* 8 New Series (8 Oct. 1943): 2.
134. Letter from Joseph Leftwich to Selig Brodetsky, London, 8 Oct. 1943; file C11/12/127, Board of Deputies archives.
135. Arnold Krammer, 'Soviet Motives in the Partition of Palestine, 1947–48', *Journal of Palestine Studies* 2 (winter 1973): 109.
136. *Jewish Chronicle*, 8 Sept. 1944, p. 8.
137. *Jewish Chronicle*, 23 Feb. 1945, p. 6.
138. Interview, Chimen Abramsky, London, 26 May 1978. Abramsky said that the inner secretariat of the International Affairs Committee, to which the NJC reported, consisted of himself and two non-Jews, Dutt and Idris Cox. Mick Mindel has noted that Abramsky was able to read Russian, so could also interpret Soviet changes of policy to other British Communists; interview, London, 5 Nov. 1978.
139. Letter from Lazar Zaidman to Isaac Gust, London, 31 May 1945; in the Zaidman Collection.
140. 'Report of National Jewish Committee to International Affairs Committee', 9 April 1943, pp. 2–3; Zaidman Collection.
141. 'Party Work Amongst the Jews in Britain', [Dec. 1943], draft TS prepared by the NJC, p. 2. The covering letter was addressed to Ben Bradley of the International Affairs Committee and, among others, NJC members Chimen Abramsky, Maurice Essex, Hyman Levy, Harry Lubbock, Mick Mindel, Jack Perry, Alf Silverman and Alec Waterman. Mr Mindel kindly made his copy available.
142. Issie Panner ['I. Rennap'], 'The Middle East', *Labour Monthly* 26 (Jan. 1944): 24, 27.
143. 'Statement on the Jewish Question' of the National Jewish Committee (London, 1944), TS, pp. 3–4; in the Zaidman Collection. Of course, the Jewish Communists continued to oppose the Zionist movements on the right wing. When Lord Moyne, the British minister resident in the Middle East, was assassinated by the Lehi or 'Stern Gang' in Cairo in November 1944, a Stepney Communist Party rally held two weeks later was instructed by Hyman Levy, Alec Waterman and Lazar Zaidman to eschew support for such organizations. *East End News*, 24 Nov. 1944, p. 3. *Jewish Opinion* (Feb. 1945), p. 3, called the murder a 'treacherous act' which had caused 'considerable harm to the Jews'.
144. Schneier Levenberg, *The Board and Zion: An Historical Survey* (Hull: Rare Times, 1985), p. 62. Board member Harry Lubbock, an NJC member, hoped that Arab–Jewish agreement could be reached first (p. 144).
145. Gorny, *The British Labour Movement and Zionism 1917– 1948*, pp. 178–9.
146. 'The Communist Party. National Jewish Committee. Third Annual Enlarged Meeting. 13th. 14th. January 1945', TS, pp. 3–4; the Zaidman Collection.
147. 'Information Document for International Affairs Committee: Palestine', TS, 16 March 1945, pp. 1–3; the Zaidman Collection.
148. 'Statement to International Affairs Committee from National Jewish Committee: Palestine', TS, [April 1945], pp. 2, 4; the Zaidman Collection.
149. 'Minutes of L.J.C. [London Jewish Committee of the NJC] Meeting', TS, 26 April 1945; the Zaidman Collection. The Communists supported the Zionists in their quarrel with the non-Zionist Anglo-Jewish Association. See 'The Board of Deputies and the Anglo-Jewish Association', *Jewish Opinion* (Feb. 1945), p. 11.
150. [R. Palme Dutt], 'Information Document: Palestine and the Middle East', International Affairs Committee, 26 April [1945], pp. 1, 5–10; the Zaidman Collection.

151. 'The Election Campaign & the Jewish People. Statement by the National Jewish Committee', TS, p. 3; the Zaidman Collection.
152. 'Notes for Canvassers and Speakers: The Communist Party and the Jewish People'; undated mimeo in the Zaidman Collection.
153. Phil Piratin, 'The Communist Party and the Jewish People. Every Jew Must Vote Progressive!', p. 1.
154. Phil Piratin, 'Appeal to the Jewish Electors'; TS in the Zaidman Collection.
155. *Vote for Piratin. A Fighter Against Fascism*; the Zaidman Collection.

CHAPTER 7

1. George Lansbury, 'Anti-Semitism in the East End', *Spectator* (24 July 1936), p. 133. According to Nicholas Deakin, 'The Vitality of a Tradition', p. 166, the population of Stepney was about 45 per cent Jewish in the 1930s.
2. 'The Election Campaign & The Jewish People. Statement by the National Jewish Committee', TS, p. 2; the Zaidman Collection.
3. The Stepney Reconstruction Group estimated in 1945 that 'just under half the population is Jewish'; see *Living in Stepney: Past Present and Future*, p. 44. See also A. B. Levy, *East End Story*, pp. 16, 98.
4. *London Statistics*, Vol. I, New Series, *1945-1954*, p. 11.
5. The 1945 electoral register for Stepney is in the Tower Hamlets Local History Library and Archives, Bancroft Library, Bancroft Road, Mile End. My calculations are based upon the surnames of voters.
6. Interview, Tom Rampling, Banbury, Oxfordshire, 20 Jan. 1979.
7. Ibid.; and Interview, Phil Piratin, London, 30 Nov. 1978.
8. *London District Bulletin*, Jan. 1943, no pagination.
9. Douglas Hyde, *I Believed: The Autobiography of a Former British Communist* (London: Heinemann, 1951; reprint ed., The Reprint Society, 1952), p. 178.
10. *East London Advertiser*, 25 May 1945, p. 2.
11. *The Times*, 17 June 1943, p. 8.
12. Harry Pollitt, *How to Win the Peace* (London: CPGB, Sept. 1944), pp. 79, 81-3.
13. *Victory Peace Security: Report of the 17th National Congress of the Communist Party*, Shoreditch Town Hall, London, E.C. 1 October 28-30, 1944, pp. 27, 31-2.
14. Ibid., p. 37.
15. Communist Party Political Committee, *Political Letter to all Members: The Communist Party and the Crimea Conference*, p. [3].
16. CP Executive Committee, 'Political Letter to All Members: Results of Party Discussion', 21 March 1945, p. 4; R. Palme Dutt archives, British Library, CUP 1262k3.
17. *Daily Worker*, 7 May 1945, p. 3. Jacobs held the position until 1953.
18. *Your Vote. How Will You Use It?* (London: London District Communist Party, 1945), p. [3].
19. Minutes, London Jewish Committee of the NJC, 6 Nov. 1944; the Zaidman Collection.
20. Letter to the editor from Bertha Sokoloff, *East London Advertiser*, 8 Sept. 1944, p. 6.
21. *East London Advertiser*, 1 Dec. 1944, p. 1. This incident was also reported in the national press; see *The Times*, 25 Nov. 1944, p. 2. Geoffrey Alderman feels that Davis's transgressions 'repelled many non-Jews and Jews alike' and were partly responsible for Communist strength in Stepney during this period. Alderman, 'M. H. Davis: The Rise and Fall of a Communal Upstart', p. 264. Davis did not, of course, contest either his borough or LCC seats in 1945 and 1946.
22. Bertha Sokoloff, letter to the author, Bromley, Kent, 29 Jan. 1979.

NOTES TO CHAPTER 7

23. *East London Advertiser*, 1 June 1945, p. 4; 15 June 1945, p. 4.
24. *East London Advertiser*, 29 Dec. 1944, p. 2.
25. *Your Vote. How Will You Use It?*, p. 8.
26. 'Is the Communist Party Splitting the Working-Class Vote?', undated pamphlet; the Zaidman Collection.
27. *Mile End Election Special! Vote Piratin*, p. [2].
28. *General Election – July 5th, 1945. Parliamentary Division of Mile End. Election Address. A Personal Letter from the Communist Candidate Phil Piratin*, p. [3].
29. Interview, I. A. Lisky, London, 10 Aug. 1978.
30. Letter from H[arry] Frankel, branch secretary, to Willie Gallacher, London, 7 June 1944; the Zaidman Collection.
31. Circular letter from the Propaganda Committee, Workers' Circle, 15 March 1945; the Zaidman Collection.
32. This undated pamphlet, entitled '1945 General Election', is included in the Zaidman Collection.
33. Interview, Chimen Abramsky, London, 26 May 1978.
34. The declaration of the STC is reproduced in the *Mile End Election Special! Vote Piratin*, p. [3].
35. Minutes, special branch committee, Mantle & Costume branch, NUTGW, 12 June 1945; NUTGW papers, London.
36. *East London Advertiser*, 22 June 1945, p. 5.
37. Douglas Hyde recalled how 'subscriptions from East End clothing and furniture manufacturers sky-rocketed' during the war; they saw the CP and its press as 'an insurance premium against Fascism'. Douglas Hyde, *I Believed*, pp. 132, 137. Many Jews preferred to donate money to left-wing anti-Fascist groups rather than to the Board of Deputies Defence Committee; file C6/7/5/1, Board of Deputies archives. See also in this regard a letter from a Manchester Jew to Selig Brodetsky describing a meeting between Harry Politt; Pat Devine, a former CP organizer in East London; and what the writer called a group of about 75 wealthy Jews, at which 'no less than £1,059 was subscribed in hard cash'. L. Harris to Selig Brodetsky, Manchester, 27 March 1942; file B4/RV12, Board of Deputies archives.
38. Interview, Morry Lebow, London, 21 Nov. 1978.
39. Interview, Tom Rampling, Banbury, Oxfordshire, 20 Jan. 1979.
40. Interview, J. W. Bentley, London, 13 Nov. 1979. Bentley, an insurance broker, became a member of the Trades Advisory Council.
41. Interview, Bill Carver, Old Colwyn, Colwyn Bay, Wales, 31 Aug. 1976.
42. Interview, Phil Piratin, London, 30 Nov. 1978.
43. Interview, Mick Mindel, London, 5 Nov. 1978.
44. Perry was mentioned by J. W. Bentley (interview, London, 13 Nov. 1979), and by Bertha Sokoloff (interview, London, 11 Sept. 1979).
45. Essex was mentioned by Bertha Sokoloff (interview, London, 11 Sept. 1979), and by Chimen Abramsky (interview, in Hebrew, with Chimen Abramsky by Dr Shimon Redlich, Jerusalem, 20 Aug. 1972). A typewritten profile of Essex, written by Abramsky and dated 23 Jan. 1943, is included in the Zaidman Collection.
46. Minutes, London Jewish Committee of the NJC, 6 Nov. 1944; the Zaidman Collection. NJC members Essex and Perry were elected to the national executive of the Trades Advisory Committee in 1946 – an indication of how acceptable Communist businessmen had become. Commented the *Jewish Clarion* of May 1946, 'Amongst Jewish traders there are many progressive people'; the TAC, it added, was 'a useful place' to fight anti-Semitism (p. 4).

47. *East London Advertiser*, 20 April 1945, p. 4.
48. *East London Advertiser*, 8 June 1945, p. 1.
49. *Daily Worker*, 28 June 1945, p. 4; *East London Advertiser*, 29 June 1945, p. 5.
50. Interview, Bill Carver, Old Colwyn, Colwyn Bay, Wales, 31 Aug. 1976.
51. Interviews, Alf Holland, London, 5 and 16 June 1978.
52. Undated circular letter from Phil Piratin in the Zaidman Collection; the special meeting was to be held on June 19.
53. Interview, Hymie Fagan, London, 10 May 1978.
54. Interview, Mick Mindel, London, 2 Aug. 1976.
55. Phil Piratin, 'The Communist Party and the Jewish People. Every Jew Must Vote Progressive!', p. 4.
56. 'Notes for Canvassers and Speakers. The Communist Party and the Jewish People'; mimeo in the Zaidman Collection.
57. Interview, Joseph Leftwich, London, 12 March 1978.
58. Interview, Hetty Donnelly, Hove, Brighton, Sussex, 11 June 1978.
59. Phil Piratin, 'Appeal to the Jewish Electors', TS, p. 1; the Zaidman Collection.
60. *Daily Worker*, 7 June 1945, p. 3.
61. *East London Advertiser*, 8 June 1945, p. 4.
62. *East London Advertiser*, 22 June 1945, p. 6; the offending article, entitled 'What the Cook Told Premier', appeared in the *Evening Standard*, 11 June 1945, p. 6.
63. *East London Advertiser*, 29 June 1945, p. 5.
64. *Mile End Has a Memory*; the Zaidman Collection.
65. George Orwell, 'Morrison and Bracken Face Stiff Fights: Heavy Poll Expected', *Observer*, 24 June 1945, p. 5.
66. *Daily Worker*, 5 July 1945, p. 4.
67. Interview, Hetty Donnelly, Hove, Brighton, Sussex, 11 June 1978.
68. *Daily Worker*, 6 July 1945, p. 4.
69. David Butler and Jennie Freeman, *British Political Facts 1900–1968* (London: Macmillan, 1969), p. 143.
70. Colin Ravden explains the high level of Communist support in these areas by remarking that the miners in Fifeshire and in South Wales, as well as the East London Jews, were 'outside the influence of English dominant values'; see Ravden, 'The Electoral Big Dipper, 1920–1974', *Comment: Communist Fortnightly Review* 16 (11 Nov. 1978): 360. William Rust, editor of the *Daily Worker*, came third behind Labour and National Liberal candidates in Hackney South, but gained a respectable 4,891 votes (24.2 per cent); [Colin Ravden], *Parliamentary Elections and the British Communist Party: A Historical Analysis 1920–1978* (London: CPGB, June 1978), p. [14]. This had been Herbert Morrison's seat, but in January 1945 the London Labour leader decided to stand for East Lewisham, prompting Churchill to taunt him with having 'run away' from a confrontation with Rust. McCallum and Readman, *The British General Election of 1945*, p. 176. Although Harry Pollitt gained 45.5 per cent of the vote in the Rhondda East constituency in South Wales, it was not enough to win the seat. [Ravden], *Parliamentary Elections and the British Communist Party*, pp. [21–2].
71. Ibid., p. [16].
72. Documents box 321.5, Tower Hamlets Local History Library and Archives, Bancroft Library, Bancroft Road, London E1 4DQ. The fact that only two-thirds of the eligible voters went to the polls probably helped the Communists, whose supporters would have been more likely to turn out than those of the Labour party.
73. Interview, Bill Carver, Old Colwyn, Colwyn Bay, Wales, 31 Aug. 1976.
74. *East London Advertiser*, 27 July 1945, p. 1.

NOTES TO CHAPTER 7

75. About 1,000 Mile End Communists and supporters gathered at the People's Palace on September 1, for example; see the *East London Advertiser*, 7 Sept. 1945, p. 2.
76. *Daily Worker*, 28 July 1945, p. 4.
77. *Daily Worker*, 25 Aug. 1945, p. 2.
78. Interview, Phil Piratin, London, 30 Nov. 1978.
79. Interview, Phil Piratin, London, 3 Aug. 1976.
80. Interview, Maurice 'Tubby' Rosen, London, 13 Nov. 1978.
81. Interview, Phil Piratin, London, 3 Aug. 1976.
82. Interview, Bill Carver, Old Colwyn, Colwyn Bay, Wales, 31 Aug. 1976.
83. Minutes, London Jewish Committee of the National Jewish Committee, 6 Nov. 1944.
84. R. P. [Dutt], 'Notes of the Month', *Labour Monthly* 27 (Aug. 1945): 230.
85. 'Communist Executive Meeting', *World News and Views* 25 (25 Aug. 1945): 263.
86. *Daily Worker*, 2 Oct. 1945, p. 2.
87. *East London Advertiser*, 12 Oct. 1945, p. 1.
88. *East London Advertiser*, 26 Oct. 1945, p. 1.
89. The Communists did not run in predominantly Irish wards such as Mile End Centre, which included the Duckett, Lydia and Ocean Street neighbourhoods that had been BUF strongholds before the war.
90. Piratin, *Our Flag Stays Red*, p. 85.
91. Solly Kaye, 'The East End and the Left in the 1930s', lecture at Limehouse Town Hall, London, 5 Feb. 1978.
92. Sokoloff, *Edith and Stepney*, p. 122.
93. *East London Advertiser*, 19 Oct. 1945, p. 5.
94. Phil Piratin, 'Jobs and Houses', *World News and Views* 25 (25 Aug. 1945): 259.
95. *Daily Worker*, 12 Oct. 1945, p. 2.
96. *East London Advertiser*, 26 Oct. 1945, p. 4.
97. *East London Advertiser*, 26 Oct. 1945, p. 9.
98. Letter to the editor from Bertha Sokoloff, *East London Advertiser*, 26 Oct. 1945, p. 2.
99. *Daily Worker*, 20 Sept. 1945, p. 1.
100. *Daily Worker*, 17 Oct. 1945, p. 2.
101. See, for instance, 'Belsen Beast Taken Back to Death Camp', *Daily Worker*, 22 Sept. 1945, p. 1; and '"I Escaped from the Gas Chamber". Young Polish Jewess Tells Her Story', *Daily Worker*, 25 Sept. 1945, p. 4.
102. See *The Times*, 9 Oct. 1945, p. 3. Tom Bower has written about this episode in *Blind Eye to Murder: Britain, America and the Purging of Nazi Germany – a Pledge Betrayed* (London: André Deutsch, 1981), pp. 197–202.
103. *Daily Worker*, 25 Oct. 1945, p. 1. On November 4, the Central Committee of the Workers' Circle moved an emergency resolution protesting against Winwood's statements; see the Minutes, Central Committee, Workers' Circle, 4 Nov. 1945, in the Zaidman Collection.
104. For full details of the 1945 municipal elections, see *The Times*, 3 Nov. 1945, p. 2.
105. Interview, Tom Rampling, Banbury, Oxfordshire, 20 Jan. 1979.
106. *East London Advertiser*, 9 Nov. 1945, pp. 1, 5. In the five wards in which Communists stood, the number of votes polled by each of the three winning candidates was as follows:

Mile End North:	W. Carver (Comm.)	667
	F. Goldberg (Comm.)	620
	A. Kershaw (Lab.)	520
Mile End West:	M. Rosen (Comm.)	1,046

	B. Sokoloff (Comm.)	1,001
	A. Goodman (Lab.)	588
St. George's North-West:	E. Kirby (Comm.)	769
	M. Shapiro (Comm.)	751
	J. Sambrook (Lab.)	559
Spitalfields East:	P. Piratin (Comm.)	713
	T. Rampling (Comm.)	632
	M. Barst (Lab.)	457
Whitechapel East:	M. Levitas (Comm.)	539
	Q. Weinberg (Comm.)	520
	J. Fine (Lab.)	357

107. *Daily Worker*, 3 Nov. 1945, p. 1.
108. Harry Hopkins, 'Painting the East End Red', *John Bull* (11 Jan. 1947), p. 16.

CHAPTER 8

1. Paul F. Lazarsfeld, Bernard Berelson and Hazel Gaudet, *The People's Choice: How the Voter Makes Up His Mind in a Presidential Campaign* (New York: Duell, Sloane & Pearce, 1944), p. 137. David Butler and Donald Stokes, in their *Political Change in Britain: The Evolution of Electoral Choice* (London: Macmillan, 1969; 2nd ed., 1974), p. 107, feel that neighbourhood 'probably has more to do with defining the subcultures of social class' which give rise to local political norms than does almost any other variable.
2. Jean Blondel, *Thinking Politically* (London: Wildwood House, 1976), p. 118.
3. Bernard R. Berelson and Gary A. Steiner, *Human Behavior: An Inventory of Scientific Findings* (New York: Harcourt, Brace & World, 1964), pp. 331–9, 558.
4. Gabriel A. Almond, 'Introduction: A Functional Approach to Comparative Politics', in Gabriel A. Almond and James S. Coleman (eds), *The Politics of the Developing Areas* (Princeton, NJ: Princeton University Press, 1960), pp. 33–8.
5. David B. Truman, *The Governmental Process: Political Interests and Public Opinion* (New York: Knopf, 1951), p. 45.
6. Raymond E. Wolfinger, 'The Development and Persistence of Ethnic Voting', *American Political Science Review* 59 (Dec. 1965): 896.
7. Robin M. Williams, Jr, 'Competing Models of Multiethnic and Multiracial Societies: An Appraisal of Possibilities', in J. Milton Yinger and Stephen J. Cutler (eds), *Major Social Issues: A Multidisciplinary View* (New York: Free Press, 1978), pp. 51–2, 54.
8. Martin Plax, 'Towards a Redefinition of Ethnic Politics', *Ethnicity* 3 (March 1976): 26.
9. Kasfir, 'Explaining Ethnic Political Participation', p. 366; Hechter, *Internal Colonialism*, p. 340; Rothschild, *Ethnopolitics*, pp. 1–2. In such political organizations, 'ethnic substructures and identification [are] highly accessible and responsive', according to Michael Parenti, 'Ethnic Politics and the Persistence of Ethnic Identification', *American Political Science Review* 61 (Sept. 1967): 725.
10. Hechter, *Internal Colonialism*, p. 328.
11. Foltz, 'Ethnicity, Status, and Conflict', p. 107.
12. See Milton M. Gordon, *Assimilation in American Life: The Role of Race, Religion and National Origins* (New York: Oxford University Press, 1964), pp. 51–4. Crawford Young, in *The Politics of Cultural Pluralism*, p. 39, agrees that 'in many instances, social strata and cultural segment may offer simultaneously relevant role definition'. Clearly, 'in the Jewish working class there were both ethnic and class solidarities'. David Feldman, 'There was an Englishman, an Irishman and a Jew . . .: Immigrants and Minorities in Britain', *Historical Journal* 26 (March 1983): 193.

NOTES TO CHAPTER 8

13. Van den Berghe, *The Ethnic Phenomenon*, p. 242.
14. A. W. Wright, 'Socialism and Nationalism', in Leonard Tivey (ed.), *The Nation-State: The Formation of Modern Politics* (Oxford: Martin Robertson, 1981), p. 166.
15. Hechter, *Internal Colonialism*, p. 42.
16. Daniel Bell, 'Ethnicity and Social Change', in Glazer and Moynihan (eds), *Ethnicity*, p. 169.
17. Rothschild, *Ethnopolitics*, p. 130.
18. Katherine O'Sullivan See, *First World Nationalisms: Class and Ethnic Politics in Northern Ireland and Quebec* (Chicago: University of Chicago Press, 1986), p. 31.
19. L[azar] Zaidman, 'The Demand for Legislation in Great Britain Against Anti-semitism', *Voice: A Jewish Monthly* (Nov. 1945), p. 11. This was a magazine published by Jewish Communists in Melbourne, Australia.
20. Letter from Lazar Zaidman to Isaac Gust, London, 19 July 1945; the Zaidman Collection.
21. Geoffrey Alderman, in *The Jewish Vote in Great Britain Since 1945*, Studies in Public Policy No. 72 (Glasgow: Centre for the Study of Public Policy, University of Strathclyde, 1980), p. 6, points out that 'Jews were well to the fore in Communist strongholds such as Stepney' and views Piratin's election as 'testimony to Jewish support for his party'. Alderman suggests that Jews made up about one-third of the Mile End electorate but accounted for about half of Piratin's vote in 1945; *The Jewish Community in British Politics*, pp. 118 and 196 note 46. Although he followed the same procedure, his estimate of the size of the Jewish electorate is lower than mine.
22. Jews totally dominated the Stepney CP: during the Second World War the party had six secretaries – Phil Piratin, Sid Greenberg, Morry Lebow, Bertha Sokoloff (twice), Alf Silverman, and Alf Rockman. All were Jewish. Arnold Posner, also a Jew, replaced Sokoloff after the war. He and Max Levitas tried to uphold the Jewish CP 'tradition' in Stepney. *Morning Star* [formerly the *Daily Worker*], 17 April 1968, p. 2; letter to the author from Arnold H. Posner, London, 2 Aug. 1976.
23. Ofira Seliktar, 'The Political Attitudes and Behaviour of British Jews', in *Jewish Political Behaviour: Two Studies by Herschel Katz and Ofira Seliktar*, Survey Research Centre, Occasional Paper No. 12 (Glasgow: University of Strathclyde Press, 1974), p. 42.
24. See Davies, *Social Mobility and Political Change*, p. 109; and Gerhard Lenski, 'Status Crystallization: A Non-Vertical Dimension of Social Status', *American Sociological Review* 19 (Aug. 1954): 405–13.
25. N. Gorty, 'The Nazi Liberal', the *Circle-Arbeter Ring* 3 (Oct. 1936): 8 [English section].
26. *Jewish Chronicle*, 21 Oct. 1938, p. 11.
27. *Jewish Chronicle*, 3 Aug. 1945, p. 10. Matters had not been helped by the fact that Lloyd George had been advocating a negotiated settlement with Germany earlier in the war. See Angus Calder, *The People's War*, pp. 66, 93; Kenneth O. Morgan, *The Age of Lloyd George* (London: George Allen & Unwin, 1971), pp. 105–6.
28. Brodetsky, *Memoirs*, pp. 139–40.
29. *East London Advertiser*, 5 Sept. 1936, p. 5. Janner became president of the Board of Deputies in 1955.
30. Two other Jews were elected to the House: D. Leslie Lipson, the independent Conservative from Cheltenham, and, of course, Piratin. No Jews were elected from the Tory or Liberal lists.
31. The Liberals did not nominate a candidate in Mile End in 1945. In neighbouring Whitechapel-St George's, their candidate was a poor third, behind the Conservative

and W. J. Edwards, the Labour incumbent who had succeeded J. H. Hall; Edwards won the seat with a massive majority. Documents Box 321.5, Tower Hamlets Local History Library and Archives, Bancroft Library, Bancroft Road, London E1 4DQ.

32. See Sokoloff, *Edith and Stepney*, pp. 121, 124, 218–19. On the national level Labour was compromised by its participation in the wartime government coalition; and even the local Labour Party was identified by some 'with the prewar establishment', according to Nicholas Deakin, 'The Vitality of a Tradition', p. 172.
33. See Rex, *Race, Colonialism and the City*, p. 40.
34. Clifford Geertz, 'Ideology as a Cultural System', in David E. Apter (ed.), *Ideology and Discontent*, International Yearbook of Political Behavior Research 5 (New York: Free Press, 1964), p. 65.
35. See Jeffrey C. Alexander, 'Core Solidarity, Ethnic Outgroup, and Social Differentiation', pp. 10–11, 14–15, 20–3.
36. Raphael Samuel, 'The Lost World of British Communism', *New Left Review* 154 (Nov./Dec. 1985): 53. See also Todd M. Endelman, *Radical Assimilation in English Jewish History 1656–1945* (Bloomington, IN: Indiana University Press, 1990), pp. 189–90.
37. Michael Lipsky, 'Protest as a Political Resource', in Donald E. Gelfand and Russell D. Lee (eds), *Ethnic Conflicts and Power: A Cross-National Perspective* (New York: Wiley, 1973), p. 277.
38. Oberschall, *Social Conflict and Social Movements*, p. 292.
39. Bruce Fireman and William A. Gamson, 'Utilitarian Logic in the Resource Mobilization Perspective', in Zald and McCarthy (eds), *The Dynamics of Social Movements*, p. 31.
40. On this point see Oberschall, *Social Conflict and Social Movements*, p. 28.
41. Enloe, *Ethnic Conflict and Political Development*, p. 40.
42. Tamotsu Shibutani and Kian M. Kwan, *Ethnic Stratification* (New York: Macmillan, 1965), p. 403.
43. See Alderman, 'The Political Impact of Zionism in the East End of London Before 1940', pp. 37–8; and Cesarani, 'The East London of Simon Blumenfeld's *Jew Boy*', pp. 47, 49–50. Zionists complained that the CP 'was draining off much of the potential local support' (p. 49).
44. See, for example, Phil Piratin's own brief account of the Mile End election in the Communist Party monthly *News and Views*. He completely ignores any Jewish aspect of the victory. Phil Piratin, '1945 Victories', *News and Views*, (July 1987), p. 3.
45. Interview, Della Saltiel, London, 26 Nov. 1978.
46. Robert Turner, 'Communism in England: A Suggestion to the Party', *Discussion* 2 (March 1936): 30.
47. R. P. D[utt], 'Notes of the Month', *Labour Monthly* 27 (Aug. 1945): 227.
48. Leo Kuper, 'Race, Class and Power: Some Comments on Revolutionary Change in Plural Societies', in Kuper (ed.), *Race, Class and Power*, p. 205.
49. Kasfir, 'Explaining Ethnic Political Participation', p. 369.
50. Rothschild, *Ethnopolitics*, pp. 241, 243.
51. David Easton, 'A Re-Assessment of the Concept of Political Support', *British Journal of Political Science* 5 (Oct. 1975): 435–57.
52. For these 'diffuse' supporters of the CP, party preference was similar to religious identification and was often spoken of 'in terms of the language of faith'; see Richard Rose, *People in Politics: Observations Across the Atlantic* (London: Faber & Faber, 1970), p. 73.
53. Research has shown that typically there is heterogeneity and even discrepancies within a movement, and that leaders and followers may differ in beliefs and motivation; see

NOTES TO CHAPTER 8

Marx and Wood, 'Strands of Theory and Research in Collective Behavior', pp. 382–3.
54. Gabriel Almond has also pointed out that, in general, middle-class members of Communist parties were more troubled by Soviet direction of their movement than were working-class members, who tended to be more locally oriented in their perspectives and goals; see Gabriel Almond, *The Appeals of Communism* (Princeton, NJ: Princeton University Press, 1954), pp. 326–7. In this context, it is interesting to note that, when the London District Committee of the CP was asked to endorse the Hitler–Stalin Pact, the only one of 28 members to vote against it was the solicitor Jack Gaster. Branson, *History of the Communist Party of Great Britain*, p. 271.
55. *The Times*, 9 March 1946, p. 2. Gaster was then chairman of the National Jewish Committee; see 'Points for Canvassers' (mimeo), in the Zaidman Collection; and *Jewish Clarion* (March 1946), p. 1. The NJC's *Jewish Clarion* of July 1946 attributed their victory to the 'proud tradition' of the Jewish working class (p. 3). But a well-known observer of Anglo-Jewish life reported a year later that 'Comrade Gaster gallantly refuses to believe that the Jews are a nation'. C. C. Aronsfeld, 'Communists in British Jewry: A Zionist Socialist Analysis', *Jewish Monthly* 1 (Nov. 1947): 34. One of the defeated Labour candidates was Elsie Janner, wife of Barnett Janner. Communists Michael Shapiro and Bill Carver stood in neighbouring Whitechapel-St George's, but lost to Labour; Phil Piratin, *Our Flag Stays Red*, p. 86, attributed their defeat in part to Irish Catholic anti-Semitism.
56. *Local Government News Letter* (London: Local Government Department, London Communist Party, 1947), p. 2; *East London Advertiser*, 12 Dec. 1947, p. 1; 27 Feb. 1948, p. 1; *Jewish Clarion* (March 1948), p. 4.
57. Many of these reforms had their genesis in the 1942 Beveridge Report, which had the support of the Communist Party. See the *Daily Worker*, 2 Dec. 1942, p. 1. The issue of 17 Dec. 1942, p. 2, carried an interview with Sir William Beveridge. See R. Palme Dutt's comments in CP Political Bureau, 'Guiding Lines on Questions of Post-War Reconstruction', [Dec. 1942], p. 6, in the R. Palme Dutt archives, British Library, CUP1262k3; and also in *Britain To-Day and To-Morrow* (London: CPGB, July 1943), pp. 5–7. The NJC also approved the report's recommendations; see *The Jewish Question: Statement by the National Jewish Committee of the Communist Party*, p. 15.
58. William Fishman, 'Zangwill's East End and Its Relevance Today', a lecture delivered at Woburn House, London, 13 March 1980.
59. See Stewart and Hunter, *The Needle is Threaded*, pp. 213–14, 218.
60. Karl Mannheim, 'The Problem of a Sociology of Knowledge', in Karl Mannheim, *Essays on the Sociology of Knowledge* (London: Routledge & Kegan Paul, 1952), p. 138; Karl Mannheim, *Ideology and Utopia*, p. 86.
61. As David Cesarani has noted, 'a secular Jewish identity drawn from the Jewish socialist, autonomist tradition of Eastern Europe could have little purchase on an upwardly mobile middle-class Jewish population'; Zionism would now make a much better vehicle for Jewish ethnic identity. David Cesarani, 'The Transformation of Communal Authority in Anglo-Jewry, 1914–1940', p. 140.
62. Interviews, Solly Kaye, London, 31 Oct. 1978; Tom Rampling, Banbury, Oxfordshire, 20 Jan. 1979.
63. Barnet Litvinoff, 'Zangwill's Ghetto is No More: The Passing of Whitechapel', *Commentary* 10 (Oct. 1950): 360. See also Pollins, *Economic History of the Jews in England*, pp. 209–35. By the mid-1980s there were fewer than 7,500 Jews in the entire Borough of Tower Hamlets (5.4 per cent of the total population), out of a London Jewish population of 201,000. Stanley Waterman and Barry Kosmin, *British*

Jewry in the Eighties: A Statistical and Geographical Study (London: Board of Deputies of British Jews, 1986), pp. 21–3.

64. Bertha Sokoloff, who herself moved from Stepney to South London in 1950, makes this point in *Edith and Stepney*, pp. 128, 133: 'the young, the active, the "cadres", the indigenous strength of Stepney had moved on'. According to Piratin, those Jews left behind were elderly and more Orthodox, hence less likely to vote Communist. Interview, Phil Piratin, London, 30 Nov. 1978.
65. Geoffrey Alderman, *The Jewish Vote in Great Britain Since 1945*, p. 6.
66. *Report of the Stepney Borough Executive Committee Communist Party May 1948 to June 1949* (London: Stepney Borough Communist Party, July 1949), p. 10. The CP, now with three candidates in each ward, retained Mile End West and Whitechapel East, and gained the three seats in Whitechapel Middle, which they had not contested in 1945, for a total of nine seats. They lost their three seats in Spitalfields East, their two seats each in Mile End North and St George's North-West, and their Spitalfields West seat. The Communists had also failed to win a Mile End South seat in a by-election in September 1948.
67. Documents Box 321.5, Tower Hamlets Local History Library and Archives, Bancroft Library, Bancroft Road, London E1 4DQ. The Liberal candidate came last, with 2,105 votes. Nationally the CP stood in 100 constituencies across Britain, gathering only 91,812 votes (0.3 per cent of the total) and losing both their seats in the House of Commons; see Michael Kinnear, *The British Voter: An Atlas and Survey Since 1885* (Ithaca, NY: Cornell University Press, 1968), p. 58.
68. Tom Rampling felt that the Mile End area was amalgamated within a larger Stepney constituency in order to give a Catholic 'a fairly safe anti-Communist majority'; interview, Tom Rampling, Banbury, Oxfordshire, 20 Jan. 1979. Maurice Essex explained that 'they altered the boundaries, so that the part of the vote which was Jewish became less important'; interview, Maurice Essex, London, 3 May 1978.
69. Interview, Phil Piratin, London, 3 Aug. 1976.
70. See, for example, Phil Piratin's attempt to refute these charges in 'Anti-Semitism and Anti-Sovietism', *Zionist Review* New Series 10 (14 Oct. 1949): 18. He called the charges 'oft-exposed falsehoods and slanders' and insisted they were nothing but myth. None the less, Jewish Communists were placed on the defensive; *New Life*, the magazine extolling the virtues of Jewish life in the USSR, ceased publication in October 1948. Interview, Jacob Sonntag, London, 15 May 1980.
71. Interview, Maurice 'Tubby' Rosen, London, 13 Nov. 1978. See also Sokoloff, *Edith and Stepney*, p. 133.
72. Interview, Julius Jacobs, Leigh-on-Sea, Essex, 20 May 1978.
73. A plea by Piratin to avoid an excessively sectarian approach was ignored. Phil Piratin, 'The Parliamentary Struggle and the Coming General Election', *Communist Review* 4 (Oct. 1949): 682–7. For more on this period, see David Childs, 'The Cold War and the "British Road", 1946–53', *Journal of Contemporary History* 23 (Oct. 1988): 551–72.
74. The invitation came from Mick Mindel, then secretary of the Mantle & Costume branch of the NUTGW. See the letter from W. J. Edwards to Mick Mindel, London, 28 Jan. 1950; NUTGW Papers, London. Edwards, an Irish Catholic, was able to mobilize Catholic supporters, especially in the aftermath of the 1949 treason trial of Joszef Cardinal Mindszenty by the Hungarian Communist regime. Some Catholic priests preached sermons against Piratin. Interviews, Phil Piratin, London, 3 Aug. 1976, 30 Nov. 1978; Tom Rampling, Banbury, Oxfordshire, 20 Jan. 1979.
75. Along with Dutt, they all contributed articles to the February 1950 *Jewish Clarion*,

emphasizing the party's support for the creation of Israel in 1948 in the face of Labour Party hostility; the CP's continued opposition to Mosley and Fascism; and Communist resistance to the formation of a West German state where, it was asserted, the Nazis would make a political comeback. In 1950 Piratin was one of nine Jews standing for the CP; all lost.

76. See *The Times*, 2 Nov. 1950, p. 3, and 5 Dec. 1950, p. 2. Although Piratin remained a Communist, he was never a public figure again. He became a director of a merchant bank in the City. Interview, Phil Piratin, London, 30 Nov. 1978.

77. In the May 1956 borough elections, the party made a partial comeback: four Jewish Communists, including Solly Kaye and Max Levitas, were elected to the Stepney Council. But by this time Jewish matters were of little concern in Stepney elections. Deakin, 'The Vitality of a Tradition', pp. 174–5. Kaye and Levitas retained their seats (in what in 1965 became the Borough of Tower Hamlets) for over a decade. But in the 1971 elections, Labour won all 70 council seats, and there was no further Communist representation on the council.

78. L[azar] Zaidman, 'On the Jewish Problem', *Marxism Today* 3 (May 1959): 159. Zaidman became a member of the London District Committee of the CP, but failed to get elected to the party's executive committee in 1945. See the account of Zaidman's funeral in the *Daily Worker*, 23 Dec. 1963, p. 3. Many leading Communist officials attended, including R. Palme Dutt on behalf of the executive committee of the CPGB, and John Mahon, the London district secretary.

79. Rebecca West, *The New Meaning of Treason* (New York: Viking Press, 1964), p. 249; *East London Advertiser*, 5 April 1968, p. 4; 16 April 1971, p. 32; 2 Feb. 1973, p. 44. Hymie Fagan, who was the CP's national election agent at the time, said that it was he who suggested that Shapiro take up the Chinese offer. Interview, Hymie Fagan, London, 10 May 1978.

80. Mindel remained a Communist 'because of a very deep sense of loyalty' to the USSR, but 'never recovered politically from 1956'. Interviews, Mick Mindel, London, 26 July 1976 and 5 Nov. 1978. Sarah Wesker's nephew, the playwright Arnold Wesker, said 'the events of 1956 broke her heart. She never officially renounced her belief in Communism, although she suffered disillusionment privately.' Interview, Arnold Wesker, London, 26 Nov. 1978.

81. Interview, Mrs Ray Waterman, London, 23 Oct. 1978.

82. A[lec] Waterman, 'On the Jewish Question', *Marxism Today* 3 (April 1959): 123–4.

83. Geoffrey Sinclair, 'The Jews in Russia', *Tribune* 30 (1 July 1966): 12.

84. Among his many popular works were *Thinking* (London: Newnes, 1936), *A Philosophy for Modern Man* (London: Gollancz, 1938), and *Social Thinking* (London: Cobbett Press, 1945).

85. Interview, Bertha Sokoloff, London, 11 Sept. 1979. Active in the JFSR and the NJC, Levy was also on the national council of the World Jewish Congress (British Section) at the end of the war. See 'Portrait of a Jewish Professor', *Jewish Clarion*, April 1945, pp. 6–7, 12.

86. See the exchange of letters between Levy and Victor Gollancz in the *New Statesman and Nation* 20 (13 July 1940): 39; 20 (27 July 1940): 89–90; 20 (3 Aug. 1940): 112; 20 (17 Aug. 1940): 160.

87. Jacob Sonntag felt that Levy had his doubts about Stalin's accusations but 'found it necessary to defend the USSR'; interview, London, 15 May 1980. Chimen Abramsky maintained that Levy 'privately refused to accept the Soviet explanation of the "plot"'; interview, London, 26 May 1978.

88. Hyman Levy, 'Blot on the History of Socialism', *Jewish Clarion* (July–Aug. 1956), pp. 2, 4.

89. Pelling, *The British Communist Party*, pp. 179–80. See also John Saville, 'The Twentieth Congress and the British Communist Party', in Ralph Miliband and John Saville (eds), *Socialist Register 1976* (London: Merlin Press, 1976), p. 16.
90. Hyman Levy, 'A Marxist Party?', *New Statesman and Nation* 53 (27 April 1957): 535–6.
91. *Jewish Chronicle*, 27 Sept. 1957, p. 8. Dutt and Solly Kaye had also visited Israel that summer as guests of the Israeli Communist Party. *Daily Worker*, 1 June 1957, p. 3; 3 June 1957, p. 3; 8 June 1957, p. 1; *Jerusalem Post* 3 June 1957, p. 3; 6 June 1957, p. 3.
92. Hyman Levy, *Jews and the National Question* (London: Hillway Publishing, 1958), p. 93. The book was in fact published by Chimen Abramsky, Hillway being the name of the street where he lived. Julius Jacobs and Ray Zaidman, Lazar's widow, both insisted that Abramsky led Levy to break with the Communist Party. Interviews, Julius Jacobs, Leigh-on-Sea, Essex, 20 May 1978; Mrs Ray Zaidman, London, 18 Aug. 1978.
93. *Labour Israel* 122 (April 1958), p. 6. Dan Leon, in 'Prof. Levy and the Jewish Problem', *Labour Israel* 123 (May–June 1958), p. 3, compared Levy to the socialist-Zionist theoretician Ber Borochov.
94. *Jewish Chronicle*, 21 Feb. 1958, p. 17.
95. R. Palme Dutt, 'An Anti-Marxist Book on the Jewish Question', *World News* 5 (8 March 1958): 156–7, 160.
96. Communist Party Executive Committee, 'The Expulsion of Hyman Levy', 'Weekly Letter No. 13 (Incorporating the Central Bulletin)', TS, 11 April 1958, pp. 4–5; the Zaidman Collection.
97. *Socialist Leader* 50 (24 May 1958), p. 5.
98. Jonathan Ree, *Proletarian Philosophers: Problems in Socialist Culture in Britain, 1900–1940* (Oxford: Clarendon Press, 1984), p. 100.
99. Hyman Levy to Lazar Zaidman, London, 10 April 1959; the Zaidman Collection. Levy died in 1975, still politically heartbroken. Gary Werskey, *The Visible College* (London: Allen Lane, 1978), p. 313.
100. For the concept of cognitive dissonance, see Leon Festinger, *A Theory of Cognitive Dissonance* (Evanston, IL: Row, Peterson, 1957), pp. 3, 12–15, 18–24.
101. Interview, Maurice Essex, London, 3 May 1978.
102. Interview, Maurice 'Tubby' Rosen, London, 13 Nov. 1978.
103. Interview, Bertha Sokoloff, London, 11 Sept. 1979.
104. See Maurice Duverger, *Political Parties*, pp. 124–32; and Rudolf Heberle, *Social Movements*, pp. 350–4. For a particularly arresting account of Communism as an ersatz religious belief-system, see Samuel, 'The Lost World of British Communism', pp. 36–47. The disillusionment that followed, understandably, left in its wake 'demoralization and cynicism. Hopes perpetually raised and dashed take their toll'. Russell Jacoby, *Dialectic of Defeat: Contours of Western Marxism* (Cambridge: Cambridge University Press, 1981), p. 15.
105. Many of Abramsky's detractors emphasized his sudden and extreme political turnabout after 1956. Interviews, Alf Holland, London, 16 June 1978; Hymie Fagan, London, 10 May 1978; Julius Jacobs, Leigh-on-Sea, Essex, 20 May 1978; Phil Piratin, London, 30 Nov. 1978; Mrs Ray Waterman, London, 19 Jan. 1979. However, after he left the party Abramsky maintained that 'members of my former [CP] branch are boycotting me as an untouchable. . . . Personally I want to remain on very friendly terms with all party members.' Letter from Chimen Abramsky to Lazar Zaidman, London, 28 March 1959; the Zaidman Collection.

106. While Jewish Communism as an ideology had crumbled, a number of individual Jews still remained in the CPGB. In 1965 the *Jewish Chronicle* estimated that perhaps 10 per cent of the party's membership were still Jewish. Barnet Litvinoff, *A Peculiar People* (London: Weidenfeld & Nicolson, 1969), p. 158. There was yet another precipitous decline after the 1967 Middle East war.

Select Bibliography

Though numerous other works have been consulted, this bibliography lists mainly material cited in the text or Notes.

I. UNPUBLISHED SOURCES

Archives, Public Records, and Private Collections

Archives of the Board of Deputies of British Jews, London. Files concerning anti-Fascist activities in the East End of London; community libel; Polish refugees in Great Britain; wartime evacuations; wartime rescue work; pro-Soviet activities; formation of the Jewish Fund for Soviet Russia; visit of Mikhoels and Feffer.
R. Palme Dutt Archives, British Library, London. Correspondence, internal documents of the Communist Party of Great Britain, articles in typescript, printed material concerning the CPGB.
Julius Jacobs Collection (private), Leigh-on-Sea, Essex. Papers and pamphlets concerning the Jewish People's Council Against Fascism and Anti-Semitism and the agitation against the British Union of Fascists.
Marx Memorial Library Archives, London. Documents concerning the British Battalion of the International Brigades; numerous miscellaneous files relating to the activities of the CPGB.
Papers of the National Amalgamated Furnishing Trades Association, East London United Branch, London. Minutes, pamphlets and other material documenting the involvement of the Branch in East London politics.
Papers of the National Union of Tailors and Garment Workers, London & Southern Divisional Office, London. Minutes and papers of the ULTTU and its successor, the Mantle & Costume Branch of the NUTGW. This collection has now been deposited in the Hackney Borough Local History Archive.
James Parkes Archive, University of Southampton Library, Southampton. Documents and correspondence concerning the Board of Deputies of British Jews, the Jewish People's Council Against Fascism and Anti-Semitism, and the struggle against Fascism in the East End of London.

BIBLIOGRAPHY

Public Record Office, Kew, London. Metropolitan Police files concerning Fascist and anti-Fascist activities in East London, anti-Semitism in East London, Communist Party meetings and political marches; Home Office files concerning the use of the London Underground stations as air raid shelters.
Pushkin/Rayner, Workers' Circle Friendly Society, and Political History Archives, London Museum of Jewish Life, Sternberg Centre for Judaism, London. Pamphlets, letters and records, some originally in the possession of Isaac 'Issie' Pushkin and Martin D. Rayner, and mainly concerned with the activities of the Workers' Circle, the Jewish Fund for Soviet Russia and other East End groups.
Maurice 'Tubby' Rosen Collection (private), London. Papers and newspaper cuttings concerning the Stepney Tenants' Defence League.
Tower Hamlets Local History Archives, Bancroft Library, London. Newspaper cuttings, manuscripts, and other material dealing with the history of Stepney.
Alec Waterman Collection (private), London. Documents, letters and other material concerning Anglo-Jewish involvement in the Spanish Civil War; 'Autobiographical Sketch of Alec Waterman' in typescript. This collection has recently been accidentally destroyed.
Lazar Zaidman Collection, University of Sheffield, Sheffield. Pamphlets, documents, correspondence, minutes of Communist organizations, and other material; this collection is particularly strong in regard to the activities of the National Jewish Committee of the CPGB and the Workers' Circle, and the involvement of the Stepney Communist Party in the election of 1945.

Interviews and Personal Correspondence

Abramsky, Chimen. Interview, London, 26 May 1978. I have also made use of an interview with Professor Abramsky conducted in Hebrew by Dr Shimon Redlich, 20 August 1972; the transcript of this interview is deposited at the Institute of Contemporary Jewry, Oral History Division, Hebrew University of Jerusalem.
Bentley, J. W. Interview, London, 13 November 1979.
Carver, William (Bill). Interview, Old Colwyn, Colwyn Bay, Wales, 31 August 1976.
Cohen, Hymie. Interview, London, 12 November 1978.
Donnelly, Hetty. Interview, Hove, Brighton, Sussex, 11 June 1978.
Einhorn, Dora. Interview, London, 10 December 1978.
Einhorn, Montagu (Monty). Interview, London, 10 December 1978.
Essex, Maurice. Interview, London, 3 May 1978.
Fagan, Hymie. Interview, London, 10 May 1978.
Findlay, Charles. Interview, London, 15 September 1987.

Findlay, Gloria Devine. Interview, London, 15 September 1987.
Goldsmith, Maurice. Interview, London, 31 May 1978.
Holland, Alf. Interviews, London, 5 and 16 June 1978.
Jacobs, Julius (Julie). Interview, Leigh-on-Sea, Essex, 20 May 1978.
Kaye, Solly. Interview, London, 31 October 1978.
Lebow, Morris (Morry). Interviews, London, 21 November and 10 December 1978.
Leftwich, Joseph. Interview, London, 12 March 1978.
Lisky, I. A. Interview, in Yiddish, London, 10 August 1978.
Maitlis, Dr Yaacov. Interview, London, 14 November 1978.
Mindel, Mick. Interviews, London, 26 July and 2 August 1976 and 5 and 19 November 1978.
Pilchick, Julius. Interviews, London, 18 and 22 August 1978.
Piratin, Phil. Interviews, London, 3 August 1976 and 30 November 1978.
Posner, Arnold. Letter to the author, London, 2 August 1976.
Rampling, Tom. Interview, Banbury, Oxfordshire, 20 January 1979.
Reid, Betty. Letter to the author, London, 7 June 1978; interview, London, 1 November 1978.
Rosen, Maurice ('Tubby'). Interview, London, 13 November 1978.
Saltiel, Della. Interview, London, 26 November 1978.
Saltiel, Ralph. Interview, London, 26 November 1978.
Seedo, N. M. Interview, in Yiddish, London, 10 August 1978.
Sokoloff, Bertha. Letters to the author, Bromley, Kent, 9 December 1978 and 29 January 1979; interview, London, 11 September 1979.
Sonntag, Jacob. Interviews, London, 8 and 15 May 1980.
Sorrin, Sid. Interviews, London, 15 and 24 November 1978.
Stencl, A. N. Interview, in Yiddish, London, 8 August 1978.
Waterman, Ray. Interviews, London, 23, 30 October and 1 November 1978, 19 January 1979 and 5 August 1991.
Wesker, Arnold. Interview, London, 26 November 1978.
Zaidman, Ray. Interviews, in Yiddish, London, 18 August and 25 October 1978.

A number of other individuals were approached but declined to be interviewed.

II. PUBLISHED PRIMARY SOURCES

Official Publications

Administrative County of London. London County Council. *County of London Plan*, by J. H. Forshaw and Patrick Abercrombie. London: Macmillan, 1943.

BIBLIOGRAPHY

—. *London Statistics 1935–37*, Vol. 40. London: London County Council, December 1937.
—. *London Statistics 1936–38*, Vol. 41. London: London County Council, June 1939.
—. *London Statistics*, Vol. 1 New Series, *1945–1954*. London: London County Council, 1957.
—. *Metropolitan Borough Council Elections, 1937*. London: London County Council, 1937.
—. *Metropolitan Borough Council Elections, 1945*. London: London County Council, 1945.
—. *Statistics of Metropolitan Boroughs 1936–37* (Eighth Year of Issue). London: London County Council, October 1937.
—. *Statistics of Metropolitan Boroughs 1937–38* (Ninth Year of Issue). London: London County Council, October 1938.
Great Britain. Census Office. *Census, 1931: Classification of Occupations*. London: HMSO, 1934.
—. *Census of England and Wales 1931, County of London*. London: HMSO, 1932.
—. *Census of England and Wales 1931: General Report*. London: HMSO, 1950.
Great Britain. Department of Employment and Productivity. *British Labour Statistics: Historical Abstract 1886–1968*. London, HMSO, 1971.
Great Britain. Parliament. *Parliamentary Debates (Hansard) House of Commons*, 5th series, Vols 297–417 (1935–1945).
Great Britain. Registrar-General. *The Registrar-General's Statistical Review of England and Wales for the Year 1935* (New Annual Series, No. 15), *Text*. London: HMSO, 1938.
—. *The Registrar-General's Statistical Review of England and Wales for the Year 1936* (New Annual Series, No. 16), *Text*. London: HMSO, 1938.
—. *The Registrar-General's Statistical Review of England and Wales for the Year 1937* (New Annual Series, No. 17), *Text*. London: HMSO, 1940.
—. *The Registrar-General's Statistical Review of England and Wales for the Years 1938 and 1939* (New Annual Series, Nos 18 and 19), *Text*. London: HMSO, 1947.
—. *The Registrar-General's Statistical Review of England and Wales for the Six Years 1940–1945, Text*, Vol. 1, *Medical*. London: HMSO, 1949.
Stepney Borough Council. *Industries of Stepney*. London: Stepney Borough Council, 1946.
—. *Stepney: The Associations and Features of this Interesting Borough, [Metropolitan Borough of Stepney, Official Guide]*. London: Stepney Borough Council, 1934.

Newspapers and Periodicals

Circle-Arbeter Ring (Workers' Circle, London), 1935–45
Civil Liberty (National Council for Civil Liberties, London) 1937–45
Daily Worker (CPGB, London), 1935–45
Discussion: A Journal for Political Controversy (CPGB, London), 1936–39
Di Tsayt–Jewish Times (Morris Myer, ed., London), 1935–45
East End News, 1935–45
East London Advertiser, 1935–45
East London Observer, 1935–45
International Press Correspondence (later *World News and Views*; CPGB, London), 1935–45
Jewish Bulletin (Office of the Chief Rabbi), 1941–45
Jewish Chronicle, 1935–45
Jewish Clarion (National Jewish Committee, CPGB, London), 1945
Jewish Forum (Workers' Circle, Branch 9, London), 1945
Jewish Opinion (National Jewish Committee, CPGB, London), 1945
Jewish Review (later *Voice: A Jewish Monthly*; Isaac Gust, ed., Melbourne, Australia), 1935–45
Labour Monthly (R. Palme Dutt, ed., London), 1935–45
Left News (Left Book Club, London), 1936–45
London–Veitchepl [London–Whitechapel] (A. N. Stencl, ed., London), 1941–45
NAFTA Monthly Report (later *NAFTA Record*), 1935–45
New Statesman and Nation, 1935–45
News Chronicle, 1935–45
Party Organiser (CPGB, London), 1939–40
Reynolds News, 1935–45
Spectator, 1935–45
Tailor and Garment Worker (later *Garment Worker*), 1935–45
Tribune, 1937–45
Zionist Review (Zionist Federation of Great Britain and Ireland, London), 1935–45

Publications and Pamphlets

[Abramsky, Chimen] (ed.). *Calling All Jews to Action!*. London: Jewish Fund for Soviet Russia, May 1943.
Adler, Henrietta. 'Jewish Life and Labour in East London'. In London School of Economics and Political Science. *The New Survey of London Life and Labour*, Vol. 6: *Survey of Social Conditions (2) The Western Area (Text)*. London: P. S. King & Son, 1934.
Allen, Elizabeth A. *It Shall Not Happen Here: Anti-Semitism, Fascists and Civil Liberty*. London: Walthamstow Press, 1943.

BIBLIOGRAPHY

Anglo-Russian Parliamentary Committee. *Jews Against Hitler: Appeal and Report of International Conference of Jews held in Moscow August 24th, 1941*. London: Anglo-Russian Parliamentary Committee, November 1941.
Aronsfeld, C. C. 'Communists in British Jewry: A Zionist Socialist Analysis'. *Jewish Monthly* 1 (November 1947).
Barou, N[oah]. *The Jews in Work and Trade*. London: Trades Advisory Council, 1946.
Bell, Tom. *The British Communist Party: A Short History*. London: Lawrence & Wishart, 1937.
Bentwich, Norman. 'England and the Aliens'. *Political Quarterly* 12 (January–March 1941).
Board of Deputies of British Jews. *The Jews – Are They Hated?*. London: Woburn Press, 1939.
—. *The Jews. Some Plain Facts*. London: Woburn Press, 1941.
—. *The Refugees: Some Facts and Figures*. London: Woburn Press, 1945.
Bramley, Ted. *The Battle for Homes*. Light on London Series, No. 1. Watford: Farleigh Press, [1945].
—. *Bombers Over London*. London: CPGB, October 1940.
—. *New London*. London: Workers' Bookshop, 1936.
Burns, Emile. *Spain*. London: CPGB, [1936].
Calder, Ritchie. *The Lesson of London*. Searchlight Book, No. 3. London: Secker & Warburg, 1941.
Cameron, William. 'Whitechapel'. *Picture Post* 1 (15 October 1938).
Cloud, Yvonne. *The Basque Children in England. An Account of their Life at North Stoneham Camp*. London: Gollancz, 1937.
Clunn, Harold P. *The Face of London: The Record of a Century's Changes and Development*. London: Simpkin Marshall, 1937.
Coates, W. P., and Coates, Zelda K. *A History of Anglo-Soviet Relations*. London: Lawrence & Wishart/Pilot Press, 1944.
Cole, Margaret. *The General Election 1945 and After*. Fabian Research Series, No. 102. London: Gollancz, October 1945.
Committee for a Christmas to Interned Refugees. *Report of the Committee for a Christmas to Interned Refugees*. London: Committee for a Christmas to Interned Refugees, March 1941.
Communist Party of Great Britain. *ARP – Act Now!* London: CPGB, September 1938.
—. *The Case for the Second Front and the Arguments Against It*. London: CPGB, June 1942.
—. *Communist Election Policy*. London: CPGB, June 1945.
—. *Fascist Murderers: Pictures of the Concentration Camps You Must Never Forget*. London: CPGB, April 1945.
—. *Keep Mosley in Prison*. [London]: CPGB, 1943.
—. *Mobilising the Party for the Second Front*. London: CPGB, October 1942.

—. *Organising for Victory in 1943*. London: CPGB, May 1943.
—. *Peace and World Security*. Communist Party Leaflet 12. London: CPGB, [1945].
—. *Put Mosley Back in Prison*. London: CPGB, 1943.
—. *Report of the Central Committee to the 14th National Congress, Communist Party of Great Britain*. London: CPGB, 1937.
—. *Save Peace! Aid Spain*. London: CPGB, May 1937.
—. *The Siege of Stalingrad*. London: CPGB, 1943.
—. *'The Stench of Nazism'*. London: CPGB, April 29, 1943.
—. *13 Years of Anti-Fascist Struggle*. Manchester: CPGB, [1943].
—. *This Is the Enemy: A Book of Facts, Figures and Pictures About Fascism*. London: CPGB, July 1943.
—. *Tune Up Our Organisation*. London: CPGB, January 1944.
—. *Victory Peace Security: Report of the 17th National Congress of the Communist Party, Shoreditch Town Hall, London, E.C.1, October 28–30, 1944*. London: CPGB, November 1944.
—. *The Voice of Free Poland*. London: CPGB. May 1943.
Communist Party of Great Britain, London Communist Party, Local Government Department. *Local Government News Letter*. London: London Communist Party, December 1947.
Communist Party of Great Britain, London District Committee. *A.R.P. for Londoners*. London: London District Communist Party, [1938].
—. *Ban the Fascists: Britain's Enemies Within*. London: London District Communist Party, 1945.
—. *Examination of the County of London Plan*. London: London District Communist Party, [1943].
—. *Where's That Fact?*. London: London District Communist Party, 1945.
—. *Your Vote. How Will You Use It?*. London: London District Communist Party, 1945.
Communist Party of Great Britain, National Jewish Committee. *The Jewish Question: Statement by the National Jewish Committee of the Communist Party*. London: CPGB, [1944].
Communist Party of Great Britain, Political Committee. *Political Letter to all Members: The Communist Party and the Crimea Conference*. London: CPGB, 21 February 1945.
Communist Party of Great Britain, Stepney Communist Party. *Communist Plan for Life in Stepney*. London: Stepney Communist Party, [1937].
—. *General Election – July 5th, 1945. Parliamentary Division of Mile End. Election Address. A Personal Letter from the Communist Candidate Phil Piratin*. London: Stepney Communist Party, [1945].
—. *Mile End Election Special! Vote Piratin*. London: Stepney Communist Party, [1945].
—. *Mile End Has a Memory*. London: Stepney Communist Party, [1945].

BIBLIOGRAPHY

—. *Piratin, Communist Candidate for Mile End. Popular Stepney Fighter and Leader.* London: Stepney Communist Party, [1945].
—. *Prepare Now! Prevent Panic Later. Air Raid Precautions for Stepney.* London: Stepney Communist Party, October 1938.
—. *Report of the Stepney Borough Executive Committee Communist Party May 1948 to June 1949.* London: Stepney Borough Communist Party, July 1949.
—. *A Stepney to Be Proud Of: Plans and Proposals.* London: Stepney Communist Party, [winter 1944–45].
—. *Vote for Piratin. A Fighter Against Fascism.* London: Stepney Communist Party, [1945].
Co-ordinating Committee Against Fascism, *An Urgent Warning on a Most Important Matter: Jews and Fascism.* London: Co-ordinating Committee Against Fascism, [1935].
Creditor, L. S. 'Yiddishe Literatur In London Biz 1948' ['Yiddish Literature In London Up to 1948']. *Fraye Yiddishe Tribune [Free Jewish Tribune]* No. 6 (January–March 1948).
Daily Worker Defence League. *The Case of Captain Ramsay.* London: Daily Worker Defence League, 1944.
Driberg, Tom. *Absentees for Freedom: The Case of the Jews in the Polish Forces.* London: National Council for Civil Liberties, May 1944.
Dutt, R. Palme. *Britain in the World Front.* London: Lawrence & Wishart, 1942.
—. *Britain To-Day and To-Morrow.* London: CPGB, July 1943.
—. *The Political and Social Doctrine of Communism.* London: Hogarth Press, 1938.
—. *Truth About the Tories.* London: CPGB, June 1945.
Ehrenburg, Ilya. *The Fate of Europe.* London: CPGB, April 1943.
Evans-Gordon, William Eden. *The Alien Immigrant.* London: William Heinemann, 1903.
Farson, Negley. *Bomber's Moon.* London: Gollancz, 1941.
Federation of Polish Jews in Great Britain. *Remember the Warsaw Ghetto: In Tribute to the Heroes.* London: Narod Press, [April, 1944].
—. *Stop Them Now. German Mass Murder of Jews in Poland.* London: Federation of Polish Jews in Great Britain, [1943].
Fine, J. L. 'The Jewish Trade Unions'. *Jewish Vanguard* No. 123 (31 July 1953).
Folk House (Beth Am). *Cultural Topics: Review of the Activities of the Folk House and Jewish Cultural Centre – Kultur Yidies. Fun Folks-Hoyz Un Yiddishn-Kultur-Tsenter.* London: Folk House (Beth Am), summer 1944.
Frucht, Asher (ed.). *25 Yor Sovyetn Farband [25 Years of the Soviet Union].* London: Jewish Cultural Club, November 1942.
Gallacher, William. *Anti-Semitism: What It Means to You.* London: CPGB,

April 1943.
—. *Mighty Russia: The First Socialist State Celebrates Its 25th Birthday.* London: CPGB, October 1942.
Gollancz, Victor. *Russia and Ourselves.* London: Gollancz, 1941.
Haldane, J. B. S. *A.R.P.* London: Gollancz, 1938.
Hopkins, Harry. 'Painting the East End Red'. *John Bull* (11 January 1947).
Howard, R. *Poland Liberated.* London: CPGB, February 1945.
Jewish Cultural Club. *Ruf Tsu Einheit Un Kamf [Call to Unity and Battle].* London: Jewish Cultural Club, May 1942.
—. *Yidn In'm Kamf Kegn Hitlerism [Jews in the Struggle Against Hitlerism].* London: Jewish Cultural Club, May 1942.
Jewish Fund for Soviet Russia. *Jews of Britain! Soviet Russia Needs Your Help. Admiration Is Not Enough.* London: JFSR, January 1943.
—. *The Russian Jews in the War.* London: JFSR, [late 1943].
Jewish People's Council Against Fascism and Anti-Semitism. *The Jewish People and the Borough Council Elections.* London: JPC, [1937].
Joseph, S. 'Kampf Un Kultur' ['Battle and Culture']. In *Yiddish London.* 2 vols. Edited by I. A. Lisky, N. M. Seedo, and A. N. Stencl. London: YKUF [Society for Yiddish Culture], 1938–39.
Labour Party. *The Communist Solar System.* London: Labour Party, September 1933.
Labour Research Department. *Houses for the People.* London: Labour Research Department, [May 1945].
—. *Mosley Fascism: The Man, His Policy and Methods.* London: Labour Research Department, August 1935.
Lafitte, F[rançois]. *The Internment of Aliens.* Harmondsworth: Penguin, 1940.
[Leftwich, Joseph] (ed.). *Jews Must Answer!.* London: United Jewish Committee, 1942.
Levy, Hyman. *Jews and the National Question.* London: Hillway Publishing Company, 1958.
—. 'The Problem of Assimilation'. In J. J. Lynx (ed.), *The Future of the Jews.* London: Lindsay Drummond, 1945.
—. *Soviet Jews At War.* London: Russia Today Society, April 1943.
Lewey, Frank R. *Cockney Campaign.* London: Stanley Paul, [1944].
—. 'Front-Line London Closes Ranks Again', *Jewish Bulletin* 37 (September 1944).
Lisky, I. A. 'A Yor YKUF Arbet in London' ['A Year of YKUF Work in London']. In *Yiddish London.* 2 vols. Edited by I. A. Lisky, N. M. Seedo, and A. N. Stencl. London: YKUF [Society for Yiddish Culture], 1938–39.
Litvinoff, Barnet. 'Zangwill's Ghetto Is No More: The Passing of Whitechapel'. *Commentary* 10 (October 1950).
London Trades Council. *Protection of Civil Population In Case of Air Raids:*

BIBLIOGRAPHY

The Most Vital Aspect of Air Raid Precautions. London: London Trades Council, February 1938.
Marx House. *Anti-Semitism — A Nazi Weapon*. London: Marx House, [1944].
—. *Educational Commentary on Current Affairs*, sixth series. London: Marx House, June 1945.
Medem, Gina. *Los Judios Voluntarios de la Libertad (Un año de lucha en las Brigadas Internacionales) [Jewish Volunteers for Liberty (A Year of Fighting in the International Brigades)]*. Madrid: Ediciones Del Comisariado de Las Brigadas Internacionales, 1937.
Montagu, Ivor. *The Traitor Class*. London: Lawrence & Wishart, 1940.
Munby, D. L., for the Stepney Reconstruction Group, Toynbee Hall. *Industry and Planning in Stepney*. London: Oxford University Press, 1951.
Myer, Morris. 'Di Itstike Internatsionale Lage in Historishn Perspektiv' ['The Current International Situation in Historical Perspective']. In *Yiddish London*. 2 vols. Edited by I. A. Lisky, N. M. Seedo, and A. N. Stencl. London: YKUF [Society for Yiddish Culture], 1938–39.
National Council for British-Soviet Unity. *Alliance for Victory*. London: National Council for British–Soviet Unity, [1942].
Orwell, George. 'The British General Election'. *Commentary* 1 (November 1945).
—. *The Collected Essays, Journalism and Letters of George Orwell*. 4 vols. Edited by Sonia Orwell and Ian Angus. London: Secker and Warburg, 1968; reprint ed., Harmondsworth: Penguin, 1970.
Panner, Issie ['I. Rennap']. *Anti-Semitism and the Jewish Question*. London: Lawrence & Wishart, 1942.
Pollitt, Harry. *How to Win the Peace*. London: CPGB, September 1944.
—. *Smash Hitler Now!*. London: CPGB, June 26, 1941.
—. *Spain: What Next?* London: CPGB, March 1939.
Rathbone, Eleanor F. *Falsehoods and Facts About the Jews*. London: Gollancz, 1944.
—. *Rescue the Perishing*. [London]: National Committee for Rescue from Nazi Terror, May 1943.
Rothstein, Andrew ['R. F. Andrews'] (ed.). *What Lenin said about the Jews: Extracts from His Writings*. [London: CPGB, c. 1935].
Rust, William. *Britons in Spain: The History of the British Battalion of the XVth International Brigade*. London: Lawrence & Wishart, 1939.
—. *The Story of the Daily Worker*. Edited and completed by Allen Hutt. London: People's Press Printing Society, 1949.
Shapiro, Michael ['Michael Best']. *Heartbreak Homes: An Indictment of the National Government's Housing Policy*. London: CPGB, [1935].
—. *How to Speed Up the Repairs*. London: CPGB, [1944].
—. ['Michael Best']. *The Tenant's Guide*. London: Labour Research

Department, [1938].
Soviet Embassy, London, Press Department. *New Soviet Documents on Nazi Atrocities*. London: Hutchinson, [1943].
Stepney Reconstruction Group, Toynbee Hall. *Living in Stepney: Past Present and Future*. London: Pilot Press, 1945.
[Tate, George Kenneth]. *London Trades Council 1860–1950: A History*. London: Lawrence & Wishart, 1950.
Trades Union Congress. *Report of Proceedings*. 67th–77th Annual Trades Union Congresses. 10 vols. London: TUC, 1935–45.
United Ladies Tailors' Trade Union. *Twenty-Eighth Annual Balance Sheet and Report for 12 Months ended 31st December, 1935*. [London: ULTTU, 1936].
Waterman, A[lec]. 'Vu Is Der Kinstler?' ['Where Is the Artist?'] In *Yiddish London*. 2 vols. Edited by I. A. Lisky, N. M. Seedo, and A. N. Stencl. London: YKUF [Society for Yiddish Culture], 1938–39.
Wintringham, Tom. *English Captain*. London: Faber & Faber, 1939.
Workers' Circle. *The Circle Golden Jubilee 1909–1959*. London: Workers' Circle Central Committee, 1959.
—. *Diamond Jubilee: The Workers' Circle Friendly Society, 1909–1969*. London: Workers' Circle, 1969.

Memoirs and Fiction

Blumenfeld, Simon. *Doctor of the Lost*. London: Jonathan Cape, 1938.
—. *Jew Boy*. London: Jonathan Cape, 1935; reprint ed., Lawrence & Wishart, 1986.
—. *Phineas Kahn, Portrait of an Immigrant*. London: Jonathan Cape, 1937.
—. *They Won't Let You Live*. London: Nicholson and Watson, 1939.
Brodetsky, Selig. *Memoirs: From Ghetto to Israel*. London: Weidenfeld & Nicolson, 1960.
Driberg, Tom. *Ruling Passions: The Autobiography of Tom Driberg*. London: Jonathan Cape, 1977; reprint ed., Quintet Books, 1978.
Gallacher, William. *The Last Memoirs of William Gallacher*. London: Lawrence & Wishart, 1966.
Groser, St John B. *Politics and Persons*. London: SCM Press, 1949.
Henriques, Basil L. Q. *The Indiscretions of a Warden*. London: Methuen, 1937.
Hyde, Douglas. *I Believed: The Autobiography of a Former British Communist*. London: Heinemann, 1951; reprint ed., The Reprint Society, 1952.
Jacobs, Joe. *Out of the Ghetto: My Youth in the East End. Communism and Fascism, 1913–1939*. London: Janet Simon, 1978.
Kops, Bernard. *The World is a Wedding*. London: MacGibbon & Kee, 1963.
Litvinoff, Emanuel. *Journey Through a Small Planet*. Harmondsworth:

Penguin, 1976.
Maisky, Ivan. *Memoirs of a Soviet Ambassador. The War: 1939–43*. Translated by Andrew Rothstein. New York: Scribners', 1968.
Mitford, Jessica. *A Fine Old Conflict*. London: Michael Joseph, 1977; reprint ed., Quartet Books, 1978.
Montagu, Ivor. *The Youngest Son: Autobiographical Sketches*. London: Lawrence & Wishart, 1970.
Piratin, Phil. *Our Flag Stays Red*. London: Thames Publications, 1948.
Rocker, Rudolf. *The London Years*. Translated by Joseph Leftwich. London: Robert Anscombe, 1956.
Seedo, N. M. *In the Beginning Was Fear*. London: Narod Press, 1964.
Waterman, Ray. *A Family of Shopkeepers*. London: W. H. Allen, 1973.
—. ['Ruth Adler']. *Beginning Again*. London: Hodder & Stoughton, 1983.
Wesker, Arnold. *The Wesker Trilogy* ['Chicken Soup With Barley'; 'Roots'; 'I'm Talking About Jerusalem']. London: Jonathan Cape, 1960.

III. PUBLISHED SECONDARY SOURCES

Abramsky, Chimen. 'The Biro-Bidzhan Project, 1927–1959'. In Lionel Kochan (ed.), *The Jews in Soviet Russia Since 1917*. New York: Oxford University Press, 1970.
—. 'The Jewish Labour Movement: Some Historiographical Problems'. *Soviet Jewish Affairs* 1 (June 1971).
Addison, Paul. *The Road to 1945: British Politics and the Second World War*. London: Jonathan Cape, 1975.
Ainsztein, R[euben]. 'The Enemy Within: Antisemitism among Polish Soldiers in War-Time Britain'. *Wiener Library Bulletin* 13 (1959).
—. 'Soviet Jewry in the Second World War'. In Lionel Kochan (ed.), *The Jews in Soviet Russia Since 1917*. New York: Oxford University Press, 1970.
Alderman, Geoffrey. *British Elections: Myth and Reality*. London: B. T. Batsford, 1978.
—. *The Jewish Community in British Politics*. Oxford: Clarendon Press, 1983.
—. *The Jewish Vote in Great Britain Since 1945*. Studies in Public Policy No. 72. Glasgow: Centre for the Study of Public Policy, University of Strathclyde, 1980.
—. *London Jewry and London Politics 1889–1986*. London: Routledge, 1989.
—. 'M. H. Davis: The Rise and Fall of a Communal Upstart'. *Jewish Historical Studies: Transactions of the Jewish Historical Society of England* 31 (1988–90).
—. *Modern British Jewry*. Oxford: Clarendon Press, 1992.

—. 'Not Quite British: The Political Attitudes of Anglo-Jewry'. In Ivor Crewe (ed.), *British Political Sociology Yearbook*, Vol. 2: *The Politics of Race*. London: Croom Helm, 1975.

—. 'The Political Impact of Zionism in the East End of London Before 1940'. *London Journal* 9 (summer 1983).

Alexander, Bill. *British Volunteers for Liberty: Spain 1936–1939*. London: Lawrence & Wishart, 1982.

Alexander, Jeffrey C. 'Core Solidarity, Ethnic Outgroup, and Social Differentiation: A Multidimensional Model of Inclusion in Modern Societies'. In Jacques Dofny and Akinsola Akiwowo (eds), *National and Ethnic Movements*. Sage Studies in International Sociology No. 19. Beverly Hills, CA: Sage Publications, 1980.

Almond, Gabriel. *The Appeals of Communism*. Princeton, NJ: Princeton University Press, 1954.

—. 'Introduction: A Functional Approach to Comparative Politics'. In Gabriel A. Almond and James S. Coleman (eds), *The Politics of the Developing Areas*. Princeton, NJ: Princeton University Press, 1960.

Almond, Gabriel A., and Verba, Sidney. *The Civic Culture: Political Attitudes and Democracy in Five Nations*. Princeton, NJ: Princeton University Press, 1963.

Anderson, Gerald D. *Fascists, Communists, and the National Government: Civil Liberties in Great Britain, 1931–1937*. Columbia, MO: University of Missouri Press, 1983.

Apter, David E. *Choice and the Politics of Allocation: A Developmental Theory*. New Haven, CT: Yale University Press, 1971.

—. 'Radicalization and Embourgeoisement: Hypotheses for a Comparative Study of History'. In David E. Apter, *Political Change: Collected Essays*. London: Frank Cass, 1973.

Ash, Roberta. *Social Movements in America*. Chicago: Markham, 1972.

Attfield, John, and Williams, Stephen (eds), *1939: The Communist Party of Great Britain and the War*. Proceedings of a Conference Held on 21 April 1979, Organised by the Communist Party History Group. London: Lawrence & Wishart, 1984.

Avineri, Shlomo. 'Marx and Jewish Emancipation'. *Journal of the History of Ideas* 25 (July–September 1964).

Avital, Zvi. 'The Polish Government in Exile and the Jewish Question'. *Wiener Library Bulletin* 28 New Series (1975).

Ballard, Roger. 'Ethnicity: Theory and Experience (A Review Article)'. *New Community* 5 (autumn 1976).

Banks, J. A. *The Sociology of Social Movements*. London: Macmillan, 1972.

Barry, Brian. 'Political Accommodation and Consociational Democracy'. *British Journal of Political Science* 5 (October 1975).

Barth, Fredrik. 'Introduction'. In Fredrik Barth (ed.), *Ethnic Groups and Boundaries: The Social Organization of Cultural Difference*. Boston:

Little, Brown, 1969.
Bell, Daniel. 'Ethnicity and Social Change'. In Nathan Glazer and Daniel P. Moynihan (eds), *Ethnicity: Theory and Experience*. Cambridge, MA: Harvard University Press, 1975.
Bellamy, Joyce M., and Saville, John (eds), *Dictionary of Labour Biography*, 8 vols. London: Macmillan, 1972–87.
Beloff, Max. 'Anglo-Jewry Revisited'. *Jewish Journal of Sociology* 33 (June 1991).
Benewick, Robert. *The Fascist Movement in Britain*. London: Allen Lane, 1972.
Berelson, Bernard and Steiner, Gary A. *Human Behavior: An Inventory of Scientific Findings*. New York: Harcourt, Brace & World, 1964.
Berger, Peter L., and Luckmann, Thomas. *The Social Construction of Reality: A Treatise in the Sociology of Knowledge*. Garden City, NY: Doubleday, 1966; reprint ed., Anchor Books, 1967.
Bermant, Chaim. *The Cousinhood: The Anglo-Jewish Gentry*. London: Eyre & Spottiswoode, 1971.
—. *Point of Arrival: A Study of London's East End*. London: Eyre Methuen, 1975.
Birnbaum, Norman. *The Crisis of Industrial Society*. New York: Oxford University Press, 1969.
—. *Toward a Critical Sociology*. New York: Oxford University Press, 1971.
Black, Eugene C. *The Social Politics of Anglo-Jewry 1880–1920*. Oxford: Basil Blackwell, 1988.
Blondel, Jean. *Political Parties: A Genuine Case for Discontent?* London: Wildwood House, 1978.
—. *Thinking Politically*. London: Wildwood House, 1976.
Blumer, Herbert. 'Collective Behavior'. In Alfred M. Lee (ed.), *Principles of Sociology*. New York: Barnes & Noble, 1951.
—. 'Social Movements'. In R. Serge Denisoff (ed.), *The Sociology of Dissent*. New York: Harcourt Brace Jovanovich, 1974.
Bornstein, Sam, and Richardson, Al. *Two Steps Back: Communists and the Wider Labour Movement, 1939–1945. A Study in the Relations Between 'Vanguard' and Class*. Ilford, Essex: Socialist Platform, [1982].
Bottomore, Tom. *Political Sociology*. New York: Harper & Row, 1979.
Bower, Tom. *Blind Eye to Murder: Britain, America and the Purging of Nazi Germany – A Pledge Betrayed*. London: André Deutsch, 1981.
Branson, Noreen. *History of the Communist Party of Great Britain 1927–1941*. London: Lawrence & Wishart, 1985.
Branson, Noreen, and Heinemann, Margot. *Britain in the Nineteen Thirties*. London: Weidenfeld & Nicolson, 1971; reprint ed., Panther, 1973.
Brewer, John D. 'The British Union of Fascists: Some Tentative Conclusions on its Membership'. In Stein Ugelvik Larsen *et al.* (eds), *Who Were the Fascists: Social Roots of European Fascism*. Bergen, Norway:

Universitetsforlaget, 1980.
Briggs, Asa, and Macartney, Anne. *Toynbee Hall: The First Hundred Years*. London: Routledge & Kegan Paul, 1984.
Brill, Kenneth. 'The World His Parish'. In Kenneth Brill (ed.), *John Groser, East London Priest*. London: Mowbrays, 1971.
Buchanan, Tom. *The Spanish Civil War and the British Labour Movement*. Cambridge: Cambridge University Press, 1991.
Burnett, John et al. (eds), *The Autobiography of the Working Class. An Annotated Critical Bibliography. Vol. II: 1900-1945*. Brighton: Harvester Press, 1987.
Butler, David, and Freeman, Jennie. *British Political Facts 1900-1968*. London: Macmillan, 1969.
Butler, David, and Stokes, Donald. *Political Change in Britain: The Evolution of Electoral Choice*. London: Macmillan, 1969; 2nd ed., 1974.
Calder, Angus. *The Myth of the Blitz*. London: Jonathan Cape, 1991.
—. *The People's War: Britain 1939-45*. London: Jonathan Cape, 1969; reprint ed., Panther, 1971.
Cameron, William B. *Modern Social Movements: A Sociological Outline*. New York: Random House, 1966.
Campbell, Angus, Gurin, Gerald E., and Miller, Warren E. *The Voter Decides*. Evanston, IL: Row, Peterson, 1954.
Carlebach, Julius. *Karl Marx and the Radical Critique of Judaism*. London: Routledge & Kegan Paul, 1978.
Cesarani, David. 'The East London of Simon Blumenfeld's *Jew Boy*'. *London Journal* 13 (1987-88).
—. 'Introduction'. In David Cesarani (ed.), *The Making of Modern Anglo-Jewry*. Oxford: Basil Blackwell, 1990.
—. 'The Transformation of Communal Authority in Anglo-Jewry, 1914-1940'. Ibid.
Childs, David. 'The Cold War and the "British Road", 1946-53'. *Journal of Contemporary History* 23 (October 1988).
Cohen, Abner. 'The Lesson of Ethnicity'. In Abner Cohen (ed.), *Urban Ethnicity*. London: Tavistock Publications, 1974.
Cohen, Stuart A. 'Anglo-Jewish Responses to Antisemitism: Suggestions for a Framework of Analysis'. In Jehuda Reinharz (ed.), *Living With Antisemitism: Modern Jewish Responses*. Hanover, NH: University Press of New England, 1987.
—. *English Zionists and British Jews: The Communal Politics of Anglo-Jewry, 1895-1920*. Princeton, NJ: Princeton University Press, 1982.
Collier, Richard. *1940: The World in Flames*. London: Hamish Hamilton, 1979; reprint ed., Harmondsworth: Penguin, 1980.
Coser, Lewis A. *The Functions of Social Conflict*. Glencoe, IL: Free Press, 1956.
Cross, Colin. *The Fascists in Britain*. London: Barrie and Rockliff, 1961.

BIBLIOGRAPHY

Dahl, Robert A. 'Some Explanations'. In Robert A. Dahl (ed.), *Political Oppositions in Western Democracies*. New Haven, CT: Yale University Press, 1966.
Davies, Ioan. *Social Mobility and Political Change*. New York: Praeger, 1970.
Deakin, Nicholas. 'The Vitality of a Tradition'. In Colin Holmes (ed.), *Immigrants and Minorities in British Society*. London: Allen & Unwin, 1978.
Denver, D. T., and Bochel, J. M. 'The Political Socialization of Activists in the British Communist Party'. *British Journal of Political Science* 3 (January 1973).
Deutsch, Karl. *Nationalism and Social Communication: An Inquiry into the Foundations of Nationality*. Cambridge, MA: MIT Press, 1953; 2nd ed., 1966.
—. 'Social Mobilization and Political Development'. *American Political Science Review* 55 (September 1961).
De Vos, George. 'Ethnic Pluralism: Conflict and Accommodation'. In George De Vos and Lola Romanucci-Ross (eds), *Ethnic Identity: Cultural Continuities and Change*. Palo Alto, CA: Mayfield, 1975.
Dewar, Hugo. *Communist Politics in Britain: The CPGB From Its Origins to the Second World War*. London: Pluto Press, 1976.
Diamant, David. *Combattants Juifs Dans l'armée Républicaine Espagnole, 1936–1939*. Paris: Editions Renouveau, 1979.
Donoughue, Bernard, and Jones, G.W. *Herbert Morrison: Portrait of a Politician*. London: Weidenfeld & Nicolson, 1973.
Duverger, Maurice. *Party Politics and Pressure Groups: A Comparative Introduction*. Translated by David Wagoner. New York: Crowell, 1972.
—. *Political Parties: Their Organization and Activity in the Modern State*. Translated by Barbara North and Robert North. New York: Wiley, 1954; 3rd ed., 1965.
Easton, David. *The Political System: An Inquiry into the State of Political Science*. New York: Knopf, 1953.
—. 'A Re-Assessment of the Concept of Political Support'. *British Journal of Political Science* 5 (October 1975).
—. *A Systems Analysis of Political Life*. New York: Wiley, 1965.
Edwards, Jill. *The British Government and the Spanish Civil War, 1936–1939*. London: Macmillan, 1979.
Elazar, Daniel J. (ed.). 'Federalism and Consociationalism: A Symposium'. *Publius: The Journal of Federalism* 15 (spring 1985).
Endelman, Todd M. 'Communal Solidarity Among the Jewish Elite of Victorian London'. *Victorian Studies* 28 (spring 1985).
—. *Radical Assimilation in English Jewish History 1656–1945*. Bloomington, IN: Indiana University Press, 1990.
Enloe, Cynthia H. *Ethnic Conflict and Political Development*. Boston: Little,

Brown, 1973.
Esman, Milton J. 'Introduction'. In Milton J. Esman (ed.), *Ethnic Conflict in the Western World*. Ithaca, NY: Cornell University Press, 1977.
Etzioni, Amitai. 'Toward a Theory of Societal Guidance'. *American Journal of Sociology* 73 (September 1967).
Feldman, David. 'Jews in London, 1880–1914'. In Raphael Samuel (ed.), *Patriotism: The Making and Unmaking of British National Identity*. Vol. II: *Minorities and Outsiders*. London: Routledge, 1989.
—. 'There was an Englishman, an Irishman and a Jew . . .: Immigrants and Minorities in Britain'. *Historical Journal* 26 (March 1983).
Festinger, Leon. *A Theory of Cognitive Dissonance*. Evanston, IL: Row, Peterson, 1957.
Field, Geoffrey G. 'Anti-Semitism with the Boots Off'. *Wiener Library Bulletin* Special Issue [1983].
Fireman, Bruce, and Gamson, William A. 'Utilitarian Logic in the Resource Mobilization Perspective'. In Mayer N. Zald and John D. McCarthy (eds), *The Dynamics of Social Movements: Resource Mobilization, Social Control, and Tactics*. Cambridge, MA: Winthrop Publishers, 1979.
Fishman, William J. *East End Jewish Radicals 1875–1914*. London: Duckworth, 1975.
—. 'A People's Journée: The Battle of Cable Street (October 4th 1936)'. In Frederick Krantz (ed.), *History from Below: Studies in Popular Protest and Popular Ideology in Honour of George Rudé*. Montreal: Concordia University Press, 1985.
—. *The Streets of East London*. London: Duckworth, 1979.
Flood, Lawrence G. 'Ethnic Politics and Political Science: A Survey of Leading Journals'. *Ethnicity* 7 (March 1980).
Foltz, William J. 'Ethnicity, Status, and Conflict'. In Wendell Bell and Walter E. Freeman (eds), *Ethnicity and Nation-Building: Comparative, International and Historical Perspectives*. Beverly Hills, CA: Sage, 1974.
Francis, E.K. *Interethnic Relations: An Essay in Sociological Theory*. New York: Elsevier, 1976.
Freeman, Walter E. 'Functions of Ethnic Conflict and Their Contributions to National Growth'. In Wendell Bell and Walter E. Freeman (eds), *Ethnicity and Nation-Building: Comparative, International, and Historical Perspectives*. Beverly Hills, CA: Sage, 1974.
Fyrth, Jim. *The Signal Was Spain: The Spanish Aid Movement in Britain, 1936–39*. London: Lawrence & Wishart, 1986.
Gainer, Bernard. *The Alien Invasion: The Origins of the Alien Act of 1905*. London: Heinemann, 1972.
Gamson, William A. *Power and Discontent*. Homewood, IL: Dorsey, 1968.
—. 'Rancorous Conflict in Community Politics'. *American Sociological Review* 31 (February 1966).
—. *The Strategy of Social Protest*. Homewood, IL: Dorsey, 1975.

BIBLIOGRAPHY

Gardner, Llew. 'The Fringe Left'. In Gerald Kaufman (ed.), *The Left: A Symposium*. London: Anthony Blond, 1966.
Garrard, John A. *The English and Immigration, 1880–1910: A Comparative Study of the Jewish Influx*. London: Oxford University Press, 1971.
— . 'Trade Unionism and the Jewish Immigrant'. *Wiener Library Bulletin* 24 New Series (1970).
Gartner, Lloyd P. *The Jewish Immigrant in England, 1870–1914*. London: Allen & Unwin, 1960; 2nd ed., Simon Publications, 1973.
Geertz, Clifford. 'After the Revolution: The Fate of Nationalism'. In Clifford Geertz, *The Interpretation of Cultures: Selected Essays*. New York: Basic Books, 1973.
— . 'Ideology as a Cultural System'. In David E. Apter (ed.), *Ideology and Discontent*. International Yearbook of Political Behavior Research, Vol. 5. New York: Free Press, 1964.
Gerlach, Luther P., and Hine, Virginia H. *People, Power, Change: Movements of Social Transformation*. Indianapolis: Bobbs-Merrill, 1970.
Gillman, Peter, and Gillman, Leni. *'Collar the Lot!': How Britain Interned and Expelled Its Wartime Refugees*. London: Quartet Books, 1980.
Glazer, Nathan, and Moynihan, Daniel P. 'Introduction'. In Nathan Glazer and Daniel P. Moynihan (eds), *Ethnicity: Theory and Experience*. Cambridge, MA: Harvard University Press, 1975.
Goldman, Aaron. 'Germans and Nazis: The Controversy over "Vansittartism" in Britain During the Second World War'. *Journal of Contemporary History* 14 (January 1979).
— . 'The Resurgence of Antisemitism in Britain During World War II'. *Jewish Social Studies* 46 (winter 1984).
Goldsmith, S. J. 'Yiddish Laureate of Whitechapel'. *Jewish Observer and Middle East Review* 21 (June 2, 1972).
Gordon, Milton M. *Assimilation in American Life: The Role of Race, Religion and National Origins*. New York: Oxford University Press, 1964.
Gorny, Joseph. *The British Labour Movement and Zionism 1917–1948*. London: Frank Cass, 1983.
Gramsci, Antonio. *Selections from the Prison Notebooks*. Translated and edited by Quintin Hoare and G. Nowell Smith. London: Lawrence & Wishart, 1971.
Griffiths, Richard. *Fellow Travellers of the Right: British Enthusiasts for Nazi Germany 1933–39*. London: Constable, 1980.
Gross, Feliks. 'Dynamics of a Political Party'. In Feliks Gross, *The Revolutionary Party: Essays in the Sociology of Politics*. Contributions in Sociology No. 12. Westport, CT: Greenwood Press, 1974.
Gurr, Ted Robert. *Why Men Rebel*. Princeton, NJ: Princeton University Press, 1970.
Gurr, Ted Robert, and Duvall, Raymond D. 'Introduction to a Formal Theory of Political Conflict'. In Lewis A. Coser and Otto N. Larsen

(eds), *The Uses of Controversy in Sociology*. New York: Free Press, 1976.
Gusfield, Joseph R. 'Introduction: A Definition of the Subject'. In Joseph R. Gusfield (ed.), *Protest, Reform and Revolt: A Reader in Social Movements*. New York: Wiley, 1970.
—. 'Mass Society and Extremist Politics'. *American Sociological Review* 27 (February 1962).
Guttsman, W. L. *The British Political Elite*. London: MacGibbon & Kee, 1963.
Halebsky, Sandor. *Mass Society and Political Conflict: Toward a Reconstruction of Theory*. Cambridge: Cambridge University Press, 1976.
Halpern, Ben, and Reinharz, Jehuda. 'Nationalism and Jewish Socialism: The Early Years'. *Modern Judaism* 8 (October 1988).
Halsey, A. H. 'Ethnicity: A Primordial Social Bond?' *Ethnic and Racial Studies* 1 (January 1978).
Harrisson, Tom. *Living Through the Blitz*. London: Collins, 1976; reprint ed., Harmondsworth: Penguin, 1978.
Harsanyi, John C. 'Explanation and Comparative Dynamics in Social Science'. *Behavioral Science* 5 (April 1960).
Hartz, Louis (ed.), *The Founding of New Societies: Studies in the History of the United States, Latin America, South Africa, Canada and Australia*. New York: Harcourt, Brace & World, 1964.
—. *The Liberal Tradition in America: An Interpretation of American Political Thought Since the Revolution*. New York: Harcourt, Brace & World, 1955.
Hearst, Ernest. 'The British and the Slaughter of the Jews – (1) and (2)'. *Wiener Library Bulletin* 21, No. 6 N.S. (winter 1966–67) and No. 7 N.S. (spring 1967).
Heberle, Rudolf. *Social Movements: An Introduction to Political Sociology*. New York: Appleton-Century-Crofts, 1951.
Hechter, Michael. *Internal Colonialism: The Celtic Fringe in British National Development, 1536–1966*. Berkeley, CA: University of California Press, 1975.
—. 'Towards a Theory of Ethnic Change'. *Politics and Society* 2 (fall 1971).
Heller, Joseph. 'Anglo-Zionist Relations, 1939–1947'. *Wiener Library Bulletin* 31, Nos 45/46 New Series (1978).
Hill, Douglas (ed.), *Tribune 40: The First Forty Years of a Socialist Newspaper*. London: Quartet Books, 1977.
Holmes, Colin. 'Anti-Semitism and the BUF'. In Kenneth Lunn and Richard C. Thurlow (eds), *British Fascism: Essays on the Radical Right in Inter-War Britain*. London: Croom Helm, 1980.
—. *Anti-Semitism in British Society 1876–1939*. London: Edward Arnold, 1979.
—. 'East End Anti-Semitism, 1936'. *Bulletin of the Society for the Study of Labour History* No. 32 (spring 1976).
—. 'Introduction: Immigrants and Minorities in Britain'. In Colin Holmes

(ed.), *Immigrants and Minorities in British Society*. London: Allen & Unwin, 1978.
—. *John Bull's Island: Immigration and British Society, 1871–1971*. London: Macmillan, 1988.
—. *A Tolerant Country? Immigrants, Refugees and Minorities in Britain*. London: Faber & Faber, 1991.
Horowitz, Donald L. *Ethnic Groups in Conflict*. Berkeley, CA: University of California Press, 1985.
—. 'Three Dimensions of Ethnic Politics'. *World Politics* 23 (January 1971).
Husbands, Christopher T. 'East End Racism 1900–1980: Geographical Continuities in Vigilantist and Extreme Right-wing Political Behaviour'. *London Journal* 8 (summer 1982).
Jackson, John A. 'The Irish'. In Ruth Glass *et al.* (eds), *London: Aspects of Change*. London: MacGibbon & Kee, 1964.
—. *The Irish in Britain*. London: Routledge & Kegan Paul, 1963.
—. 'The Irish in East London'. *East London Papers* 6 (December 1963).
Jacoby, Russell. *Dialectic of Defeat: Contours of Western Marxism*. Cambridge: Cambridge University Press, 1981.
Jaeger, Gertrude and Selznick, Philip. 'A Normative Theory of Culture'. *American Sociological Review* 29 (October 1964).
Jenkins, J. Craig. 'Sociopolitical Movements'. In Samuel L. Long (ed.), *The Handbook of Political Behavior*, Vol. 4. New York: Plenum Press, 1981.
Jessop, Bob. *Traditionalism, Conservatism and British Political Culture*. London: Allen & Unwin, 1974.
Johnpoll, Bernard K. *The Politics of Futility: The General Jewish Workers Bund of Poland, 1917–1943*. Ithaca, NY: Cornell University Press, 1967.
Jones, Catherine. *Immigration and Social Policy in Britain*. London: Tavistock Publications, 1977.
Jupp, James. *Political Parties*. London: Routledge & Kegan Paul, 1968.
—. *The Radical Left in Britain, 1931–1941*. London: Frank Cass, 1982.
Kadish, Sharman. *Bolsheviks and British Jews: The Anglo-Jewish Community, Britain and the Russian Revolution*. London: Frank Cass, 1992.
Kaplan, Stanley, 'The Anglicization of the East European Jewish Immigrant as seen by the London *Jewish Chronicle*, 1870–1897'. *YIVO Annual of Jewish Social Science* 10 (1955).
Kasfir, Nelson. 'Explaining Ethnic Political Participation'. *World Politics* 31 (April 1979).
Kavanagh, Dennis. *Political Culture*. London: Macmillan, 1972.
Kendall, Walter. 'The Communist Party of Great Britain'. *Survey* 20 (winter 1974).
Kershen, Anne J. *Trade Unionism Amongst the Jewish Tailoring Workers of*

London 1872–1915. London: London Museum of Jewish Life, 1991.
King, Francis, and Matthews, George. 'The Communist Party Library', *Labour History Review* 56 (winter 1991).
Kinnear, Michael. *The British Voter: An Atlas and Survey Since 1885*. Ithaca, NY: Cornell University Press, 1968.
Kochan, Miriam. *Britain's Internees in the Second World War*. London: Macmillan, 1983.
[Kolinsky, Martin]. 'Introduction'. In Martin Kolinsky and William E. Paterson (eds), *Social and Political Movements in Western Europe*. New York: St Martin's Press, 1976.
Krammer, Arnold. 'Soviet Motives in the Partition of Palestine, 1947–48'. *Journal of Palestine Studies* 2 (winter 1973).
Krausz, Ernest. *Ethnic Minorities in Britain*. London: MacGibbon & Kee, 1971.
Kriesberg, Louis. *The Sociology of Social Conflicts*. Englewood Cliffs, NJ: Prentice-Hall, 1973.
Kuper, Leo. 'On Theories of Race Relations'. In Wendell Bell and Walter E. Freeman (eds), *Ethnicity and Nation-Building: Comparativ, International, and Historical Perspectives*. Beverly Hills, CA: Sage, 1974.
—. 'Political Change in Plural Societies: Problems in Racial Pluralism'. In Leo Kuper, *Race, Class and Power: Ideology and Revolutionary Change in Plural Societies*. London: Duckworth, 1974.
—. 'Race, Class, and Power: Some Comments on Revolutionary Change'. Ibid.
Kushner, Tony. 'All Quiet on the Home Front?'. *Jewish Quarterly* 36 (autumn 1989).
—. 'The British and the Shoah'. *Patterns of Prejudice* 23 (autumn 1989).
—. 'The Impact of British Anti-Semitism, 1918–1945'. In David Cesarani (ed.), *The Making of Modern Anglo-Jewry*. Oxford: Basil Blackwell, 1990.
—. 'Jewish Communists in Twentieth-century Britain: the Zaidman Collection'. *Labour History Review* 55 (autumn 1990).
—. 'The Paradox of Prejudice: The Impact of Organized Anti-semitism in Britain During an Anti-Nazi War'. In Tony Kushner and Kenneth Lunn (eds), *Traditions of Intolerance: Historical Perspectives on Fascism and Race Discourse in Britain*. Manchester: Manchester University Press, 1989.
—. *The Persistence of Prejudice: Antisemitism in British Society During the Second World War*. Manchester: Manchester University Press, 1989.
Kushner, Tony, and Lunn, Kenneth (eds), *The Politics of Marginality: Race, the Radical Right and Minorities in Twentieth Century Britain*. London: Frank Cass, 1990.
Laqueur, Walter. *The Terrible Secret: An Investigation into the Suppression of Information About Hitler's 'Final Solution'*. London: Weidenfeld &

Nicolson, 1980.
Lasswell, Harold. *Politics: Who Gets What, When, How*. New York: McGraw-Hill, 1936.
Lauer, Robert H. 'Introduction: Social Movements and Social Change: The Interrelationships'. In Robert H. Lauer (ed.), *Social Movements and Social Change*. Carbondale, IL: Southern Illinois University Press, 1976.
Lazarsfeld, Paul F., Berelson, Bernard, and Gaudet, Hazel. *The People's Choice: How the Voter Makes Up His Mind in a Presidential Campaign*. New York: Duell, Sloane & Pearce, 1944.
Lebzelter, Gisela C. *Political Anti-Semitism in England 1918–1939*. London: Macmillan, 1978.
Leech, K[enneth]. 'The Decay of Spitalfields'. *East London Papers* 7 (December 1964).
Leeson, R. A. *Strike: A Live History 1887-1971*. London: Allen & Unwin, 1973.
Leftwich, Joseph. 'Abram Stenzel'. *East London Papers* 1 (October 1958).
Lenski, Gerhard. 'Status Crystallization: A Non-Vertical Dimension of Social Status'. *American Sociological Review* 19 (August 1954).
Lerner, Shirley W. *Breakaway Unions and the Small Trade Union*. London: Allen & Unwin, 1961.
Levenberg, Schneier. *The Board and Zion: An Historical Survey*. Hull: Rare Times, 1985.
Levine, Norman. 'Lenin on Jewish Nationalism'. *Wiener Library Bulletin* 31 New Series (1980).
LeVine, Robert A., and Campbell, Donald T. *Ethnocentrism: Theories of Conflict, Ethnic Attitudes, and Group Behavior*. New York: Wiley, 1972.
Levy, A. B. *East End Story*. London: Constellation Books, 1951.
—. 'The Jewish Theatre'. *East London Papers* 6 (July 1963).
Lewis, D. S. *Illusions of Grandeur: Mosley, Fascism and British Society, 1931–81*. Manchester: Manchester University Press, 1987.
Liebman, Arthur. *Jews and the Left*. New York: Wiley, 1979.
Lijphart, Arend. 'Consociational Democracy'. *World Politics* 21 (January 1969).
—. *Democracy in Plural Societies: A Comparative Exploration*. New Haven, CT: Yale University Press, 1977.
Lilly, Mark. *The National Council for Civil Liberties: The First Fifty Years*. London: Macmillan, 1984.
Lipman, V. D. *A History of the Jews in Britain Since 1858*. Leicester: Leicester University Press, 1990.
—. 'Jewish Settlement in the East End of London 1840–1940: The Topographical and Statistical Background'. In Aubrey Newman (ed.), *The Jewish East End 1840–1939*. Proceedings of the Conference held on 22 October 1980 jointly by the Jewish Historical Society of England and the Jewish East End Project of the Association for Jewish Youth.

London: Jewish Historical Society of England, 1981.
—. *Social History of the Jews in England 1850–1950*. London: Watts, 1954.
Lipset, Seymour Martin. *Political Man: The Social Bases of Politics*. Garden City, NY: Doubleday, 1960.
Lipsky, Michael. 'Protest as a Political Resource'. In Donald E. Gelfand and Russell D. Lee (eds), *Ethnic Conflicts and Power: A Cross-National Perspective*. New York: Wiley, 1973.
Litvinoff, Barnet. *A Peculiar People*. London: Weidenfeld & Nicolson, 1969.
—. *Journey Through a Small Planet*. London: Michael Joseph, 1972.
Loewe, L. L. *Basil Henriques A Portrait: Based on His Diaries, Letters and Speeches as Collected by His Widow, Rose Henriques*. London: Routledge & Kegan Paul, 1976.
Lorwin, Val R. 'Segmented Pluralism: Ideological Cleavages and Political Cohesion in the Smaller European Democracies'. *Comparative Politics* 3 (January 1971).
Lunn, Kenneth. 'Parliamentary Politics and the "Jewish Vote" in Whitechapel, 1906–1914'. In Aubrey Newman (ed.), *The Jewish East End 1840–1939*. Proceedings of the Conference held on 22 October 1980 jointly by the Jewish Historical Society of England and the Jewish East End Project of the Association for Jewish Youth. London: Jewish Historical Society of England, 1981.
Lunn, Kenneth, and Thurlow, Richard C. (eds). *British Fascism: Essays on the Radical Right in Inter-War Britain*. London: Croom Helm, 1980.
Lustick, Ian. 'Stability in Deeply Divided Societies: Consociationalism versus Control'. *World Politics* 31 (April 1979).
Macintyre, Stuart. *Little Moscows: Communism and Working-class Militancy in Inter-war Britain*. London: Croom Helm, 1980.
Mack, Joanna, and Humphries, Steve. *The Making of Modern London 1939–1945: London at War*. London: Sidgwick and Jackson, 1985.
Macridis, Roy. 'Interest Groups in Comparative Analysis'. *Journal of Politics* 23 (February 1961).
Mahon, John. *Harry Pollitt: A Biography*. London: Lawrence & Wishart, 1976.
Mandle, W. F. *Anti-Semitism and the British Union of Fascists*. London: Longmans, 1968.
Mannheim, Karl. *Ideology and Utopia. An Introduction to the Sociology of Knowledge*. Translated by Louis Wirth and Edward Shils. New York: Harcourt, Brace, 1936; reprint ed., Harvest Books, [1955?].
—. 'The Problem of a Sociology of Knowledge'. In Karl Mannheim, *Essays on the Sociology of Knowledge*. London: Routledge & Kegan Paul, 1952.
Martin, Roderick. *Communism and the British Trade Unions, 1924–1933: A Study of the National Minority Movement*. Oxford: Clarendon Press, 1969.

Marx, Gary T., and Wood, James L. 'Strands of Theory and Research in Collective Behavior'. In Alex Inkeles (ed.), *Annual Review of Sociology* 1. Palo Alto, CA: Annual Reviews, 1975.
Marx, Karl. *The Poverty of Philosophy: A Translation of the Misère de la Philosophie (A Reply to 'La Philosophie de la Misère' of M. Proudhon)*. Translated by H[arry] Quelch. Chicago: Kerr, 1910.
McCallum, R. B., and Readman, Alison. *The British General Election of 1945*. London: Oxford University Press, 1947.
McCarthy, John D., and Zald, Mayer N. 'Resource Mobilization and Social Movements: A Partial Theory'. *American Journal of Sociology* 82 (May 1977).
McCreery, Kathleen. 'Proltet: Yiddish theatre in the 1930s'. *Race & Class* 20 (winter 1979).
McKay, James, and Lewins, Frank. 'Ethnicity and Ethnic Group: A Conceptual Analysis and Reformulation'. *Ethnic and Racial Studies* 1 (October 1978).
McLaine, Ian. *Ministry of Morale: Home Front Morale and the Ministry of Information in World War II*. London: Allen & Unwin, 1979.
McRae, Kenneth (ed.). *Consociational Democracy: Political Accommodation in Segmented Societies*. Toronto: McClelland & Stewart, 1974.
Medding, Peter Y. 'Towards a General Theory of Jewish Political Interests and Behaviour'. *Jewish Journal of Sociology* 19 (December 1977).
Merton, Robert K. *Social Theory and Social Structure*. Glencoe, IL: Free Press, 1949; revised and enlarged ed., 1957.
Milbrath, Lester W. *Political Participation: How and Why Do People Get Involved in Politics?* Chicago: Rand McNally, 1965.
Mills, C. Wright. *The Sociological Imagination*. New York: Oxford University Press, 1959; reprint ed., Harmondsworth: Penguin, 1978.
Milne, R. S. *Politics in Ethnically Bipolar States: Guyana, Malaysia, Fiji*. Vancouver: University of British Columbia Press, 1981.
Mindel, Mick. 'Socialist Eastenders'. *Jewish Socialist* 6/7 (summer/autumn 1986).
Montgomery, David. 'To Study the People: The American Working Class'. *Labor History* 21 (fall 1980).
Morgan, Kenneth O. *The Age of Lloyd George*. London: Allen & Unwin, 1971.
Munby, Denys. 'The Social Order'. In Kenneth Brill (ed.), *John Groser, East London Priest*. London: Mowbrays, 1971.
Naylor, John F. *Labour's International Policy: The Labour Party in the 1930s*. London: Weidenfeld and Nicolson, 1969.
Nelson, Dale C. 'Ethnicity and Socioeconomic Status as Sources of Participation: The Case for Ethnic Political Culture'. *American Political Science Review* 73 (December 1979).
Nettl, J. P. *Political Mobilization: A Sociological Analysis of Methods and*

Concepts. London: Faber & Faber, 1967.
Neumann, Sigmund. *Modern Political Parties: Approaches to Comparative Politics*. Chicago: University of Chicago Press, 1956.
Newton, Kenneth. *The Sociology of British Communism*. London: Allen Lane/Penguin, 1969.
Nordlinger, Eric A. *Conflict Regulation in Divided Societies*. Occasional Papers in International Affairs No. 29. Cambridge, MA: Center for International Affairs, Harvard University, January 1972.
—. *The Working Class Tories*. London: MacGibbon & Kee, 1967.
Oberschall, Anthony. *Social Conflict and Social Movements*. Englewood Cliffs, NJ: Prentice-Hall, 1973.
O'Connor, Kevin. *The Irish in Britain*. Dublin: Torc Books, 1974.
Oliver, J. Leonard. 'The East London Furniture Industry'. *East London Papers* 4 (October 1961).
Orbach, Maurice. 'Noah Barou and the Trades Advisory Council'. In Henrik F. Infield (ed.), *Essays in Jewish Sociology, Labour and Co-operation in Memory of Dr Noah Barou 1889–1955*. London: Thomas Yoseloff, 1962.
Parenti, Michael. 'Ethnic Politics and the Persistence of Ethnic Identification'. *American Political Science Review* 61 (September 1967).
Pelling, Henry. *The British Communist Party: A Historical Profile*. London: A. & C. Black, 1958; reprint ed., 1975.
—. 'The 1945 General Election Reconsidered'. *Historical Journal* 23 (June 1980).
Pimlott, Ben. *Labour and the Left in the 1930s*. Cambridge: Cambridge University Press, 1977.
Piratin, Phil. '1945 Victories'. *News and Views* (July 1987).
Plax, Martin. 'Towards a Redefinition of Ethnic Politics'. *Ethnicity* 3 (March 1976).
Pollins, Harold. *Economic History of the Jews in England*. Rutherford, NJ: Fairleigh Dickinson University Press, 1982.
Polonsky, Anthony, and Drukier, Boleslaw. *The Beginnings of Communist Rule in Poland*. London: Routledge & Kegan Paul, 1980.
Prager, Leonard. 'A Bibliography of Yiddish Periodicals in Great Britain (1867–1967)'. *Studies in Bibliography and Booklore* 9 (1969–1971).
Prago, Albert. 'The Botwin Company in Spain, 1937–1939'. *Jewish Currents* 46 (March 1992).
—. *Jews in the International Brigades*. New York: Jewish Currents, 1979.
Prawer, S. S. *A. N. Stencl: Poet of Whitechapel*. Oxford: Oxford Centre for Postgraduate Hebrew Studies, 1984.
Ramirez, Bruno. 'Ethnic Studies and Working-Class History'. *Labour/le Travail: Journal of Canadian Labour Studies* 19 (spring 1987).
Ravden, Colin. 'The Electoral Big Dipper, 1920–1974'. *Comment: Communist Fortnightly Review* 16 (November 11, 1978).

—. *Parliamentary Elections and the British Communist Party: A Historical Analysis*. London: CPGB, June 1978.
Rawnsley, Stuart. 'The Membership of the British Union of Fascists'. In Kenneth Lunn and Richard C. Thurlow (eds), *British Fascism: Essays on the Radical Right in Inter-War Britain*. London: Croom Helm, 1980.
Redlich, Shimon. *Propaganda and Nationalism in Wartime Russia: The Jewish Antifascist Committee in the USSR, 1941–1948*. East European Monographs, No. 108. Boulder, CO: East European Quarterly, 1982.
Ree, Jonathan. *Proletarian Philosophers*. Oxford: Clarendon Press, 1984.
Reid, Betty. 'Communist Party Archive'. *Our History Journal* 12 (January 1988).
Reid, Hew. *The Furniture Makers: A History of Trade Unionism in the Furniture Trade 1865–1972*. Oxford: Malthouse Press, 1986.
Rex, John. *Race, Colonialism and the City*. London: Routledge & Kegan Paul, 1973.
—. *Social Conflict: A Conceptual and Theoretical Analysis*. London: Longman, 1981.
—. 'The Sociology of a Zone in Transition'. In R. E. Pahl (ed.), *Readings in Urban Sociology*. Oxford: Pergamon, 1968.
Roberts, Ron E., and Kloss, Robert Marsh. *Social Movements: Between the Balcony and the Barricade*. St Louis: Mosby, 1974.
Rose, Arnold M., and Rose, Caroline B. 'Introduction: Some Definitions'. In Arnold M. Rose and Caroline B. Rose (eds), *Minority Problems*. New York: Harper & Row, 1965; 2nd ed., 1972.
Rose, Richard. *People in Politics: Observations Across the Atlantic*. London: Faber & Faber, 1970.
Rosenberg, David. *Facing up to Antisemitism: How Jews in Britain Countered the Threats of the 1930s*. London: JCARP Publications, 1985.
Rosenhead, Louis. *Professor Selig Brodetsky: Scholar, Dreamer, Man of Action*. Leeds: Leeds University Press, 1963.
Roth, Cecil. 'The Anglo-Jewish Community in the Context of World Jewry'. In Julius Gould and Shaul Esh (eds), *Jewish Life in Modern Britain*. London: Routledge & Kegan Paul, 1964.
Rothenberg, Joshua. 'The Jewish Naftali Botwin Company (An Episode From Recent History)'. *Jewish Frontier* 47 (April 1980).
Rothschild, Joseph. *Ethnopolitics: A Conceptual Framework*. New York: Columbia University Press, 1981.
Samuel, Raphael. 'The Lost World of British Communism'. *New Left Review* 154 (November/December 1985).
Samuels, Leon. 'The Jewish Labour Movement'. *Jewish Quarterly* 3 (winter 1956).
Saville, John. 'The Twentieth Congress and the British Communist Party'. In Ralph Miliband and John Saville (eds), *Socialist Register 1976*. London: Merlin Press, 1976.

Schermerhorn, R. A. *Comparative Ethnic Relations: A Framework for Theory and Research.* New York: Random House, 1970.
—. 'Toward a General Theory of Minority Groups'. *Phylon* 25 (fall 1964).
See, Katherine O'Sullivan. *First World Nationalisms: Class and Ethnic Politics in Northern Ireland and Quebec.* Chicago: University of Chicago Press, 1986.
Seliktar, Ofira. 'The Political Attitudes and Behaviour of British Jews'. In *Jewish Political Behaviour: Two Studies by Herschel Katz and Ofira Seliktar.* Survey Research Centre, Occasional Paper No. 12. Glasgow: University of Strathclyde, 1974.
Seyfert, Michael. '"His Majesty's Most Loyal Internees"'. In Gerhard Hirschfeld (ed.), *Exile in Great Britain: Refugees from Hitler's Germany.* Leamington Spa: Berg, 1984.
Sharf, Andrew. *The British Press and Jews Under Nazi Rule.* London: Oxford University Press, 1964.
Sherman, A. V. 'Epitaph for the East End'. *Commentary* 30 (November 1960).
Shibutani, Tamotsu, and Kwan, Kian M. *Ethnic Stratification: A Comparative Approach.* New York: Macmillan, 1965.
Shils, Edward. 'Center and Periphery'. In Edward Shils, *Center and Periphery: Essays in Macrosociology.* Chicago: University of Chicago Press, 1975.
Shimoni, Gideon. 'From Anti-Zionism to Non-Zionism in Anglo-Jewry, 1917–1937'. *Jewish Journal of Sociology* 28 (June 1986).
—. 'The Non-Zionists in Anglo-Jewry, 1937–1948'. *Jewish Journal of Sociology* 28 (December 1986).
—. 'Poale Zion: A Zionist Transplant in Britain (1905–1945)'. In Peter Y. Medding (ed.), *Studies in Contemporary Jewry*, Vol. II. Bloomington, IN: Indiana University Press, 1986.
—. 'Selig Brodetsky and the Ascendency of Zionism in Anglo-Jewry (1939–1945)'. *Jewish Journal of Sociology* 22 (December 1980).
Silberner, Edmund. 'British Socialism and the Jews'. *Historica Judaica* 14 (April 1952).
Simpson, George E., and Yinger, J. Milton. *Racial and Cultural Minorities: An Analysis of Prejudice and Discrimination.* New York: Harper, 1953; 4th ed., 1972.
Skidelsky, Robert. *Oswald Mosley.* London: Macmillan, 1975.
Skocpol, Theda. 'Explaining Revolutions: In Quest of a Social-Structural Approach'. In Lewis A. Coser and Otto N. Larsen (eds), *The Uses of Controversy in Sociology.* New York: Free Press, 1976.
Smelser, Neil J. *Theory of Collective Behavior.* New York: Free Press, 1962.
Smith, Anthony D. *The Ethnic Revival.* Cambridge: Cambridge University Press, 1981.
Smith, Elaine R. 'East End Tailors, 1918–1939: An Aspect of the Jewish

Workers' Struggle'. *Jewish Quarterly* 34 (summer 1987).
—. 'Jewish Responses to Political Antisemitism and Fascism in the East End of London, 1920–1939'. In Tony Kushner and Kenneth Lunn (eds), *Traditions of Intolerance: Historical Perspectives on Fascism and Race Discourse in Britain*. Manchester: Manchester University Press, 1989.
—. 'Jews and Politics in the East End of London, 1918–1939'. In David Cesarani (ed.), *The Making of Modern Anglo-Jewry*. Oxford: Basil Blackwell, 1990.
Smith, M. G. *The Plural Society in the British West Indies*. Berkeley, CA: University of California Press, 1965.
—. 'Social and Cultural Pluralism'. *Annals of the New York Academy of Sciences* 83 (January 20, 1960).
Smythe, Tony. 'The Role of the National Council for Civil Liberties'. In Robert Benewick and Trevor Smith (eds), *Direct Action and Democratic Politics*. London: Allen & Unwin, 1972.
Sokoloff, Bertha. *Edith and Stepney: The Life of Edith Ramsay*. London: Stepney Books, 1987.
Soref, Harold. 'Portrait of Anglo-Jewry'. *Menorah Journal* 41 (spring 1953).
Srebrnik, Henry F. 'The British Communist Party's National Jewish Committee and the Fight Against Anti-Semitism During the Second World War'. In Tony Kushner and Kenneth Lunn (eds), *The Politics of Marginality: Race, the Radical Right and Minorities in Twentieth Century Britain*. London: Frank Cass, 1990.
—. 'Communism and Pro-Soviet Feeling Among the Jews of East London, 1935–45'. *Immigrants and Minorities* 5 (November 1986).
—. '"Salud di Heldn!": Jewish Communist Activity in London on Behalf of the Spanish Republic'. *Michigan Academician* 16 (spring 1984).
Stammers, Neil. *Civil Liberties in Britain During the 2nd World War: A Political Study*. London: Croom Helm, 1983.
Stent, Ronald. *A Bespattered Page? The Internment of His Majesty's 'most loyal enemy aliens'*. London: André Deutsch, 1980.
Stevens, Austin. *The Dispossessed: German Refugees in Britain*. London: Barrie & Jenkins, 1975.
Stevenson, John, and Cook, Chris. *The Slump: Society and Politics During the Depression*. London: Jonathan Cape, 1977.
Stewart, Margaret, and Hunter, Leslie. *The Needle is Threaded: The History of an Industry*. London: Heinemann/Newman Neame, 1964.
Thompson, Paul. *Socialists, Liberals and Labour: The Struggle for London*. London: Routledge & Kegan Paul, 1967.
Thompson, Willie. *The Good Old Cause: British Communism 1920–1991*. London: Pluto Press, 1992.
Thurlow, Richard. *Fascism in Britain: A History, 1918–1985*. Oxford:

Basil Blackwell, 1987.
—. 'The Mosley Papers and the Secret History of British Fascism, 1918–1926'. In Tony Kushner and Kenneth Lunn (eds), *Traditions of Intolerance: Historical Perspectives on Fascism and Race Discourse in Britain*. Manchester: Manchester University Press, 1989.
Tilly, Charles. *From Mobilization to Revolution*. Reading, MA: Addison-Wesley, 1978.
Toch, Hans. *The Social Psychology of Social Movements*. Indianapolis: Bobbs-Merrill, 1965.
Truman, David B. *The Governmental Process: Political Interests and Public Opinion*. New York: Knopf, 1951.
Turner, Ralph H. 'The Theme of Contemporary Social Movements'. *British Journal of Sociology* 20 (December 1969).
van den Berghe, Pierre L. *The Ethnic Phenomenon*. New York: Elsevier, 1981.
Vlavianos, Basil J., and Gross, Feliks (eds), *Struggle for Tomorrow: Political Ideologies of the Jewish People*. New York: Arts, Inc., 1954.
Wasserstein, Bernard. *Britain and the Jews of Europe 1939–1945*. Oxford: Clarendon Press, 1979.
Waterman, Ray. 'Memories of Proltet'. In Raphael Samuel *et al.* (eds), *Theatres of the Left 1880–1935: Workers' Theatre Movements in Britain and America*. London: Routledge & Kegan Paul, 1985.
—. 'Proltet: The Yiddish-speaking Group of the Workers' Theatre Movement'. *History Workshop* 5 (spring 1978).
Waterman, Stanley and Kosmin, Barry. *British Jewry in the Eighties: A Statistical and Geographical Study*. London: Board of Deputies of British Jews, 1986.
Watkins, K. W. *Britain Divided: The Effect of the Spanish Civil War on British Political Opinion*. London: Nelson, 1963.
Webber, G. C. *The Ideology of the British Right 1918–1939*. London: Croom Helm, 1986.
—. 'Patterns of Membership and Support for the British Union of Fascists'. *Journal of Contemporary History* 19 (October 1984).
Werskey, Gary. *The Visible College*. London: Allen Lane, 1978.
West, Rebecca. *The New Meaning of Treason*. New York: Viking, 1964.
White, Jerry. *Rothschild Buildings: Life in an East End Tenement Block 1887–1920*. London: Routledge & Kegan Paul, 1980.
Whitfield, Stephen J. 'After Strange Gods: Radical Jews in Modern America'. *Forum* 56 (summer 1985).
Wilcher, Robert. *Understanding Arnold Wesker*. Columbia, SC: University of South Carolina Press, 1991.
Wilkinson, Paul. *Social Movement*. London: Pall Mall, 1971.
Williams, Robin M., Jr. 'Competing Models of Multiethnic and Multiracial Societies: An Appraisal of Possibilities'. In J. Milton Yinger and

Stephen J. Cutler (eds), *Major Social Issues: A Multi-disciplinary View*. New York: Free Press, 1978.
Wilson, John. *Introduction to Social Movements*. New York: Basic Books, 1973.
Wilson, Trevor. *The Downfall of the Liberal Party 1914–1935*. London: Collins, 1976.
Wistrich, Robert S. 'Marxism and Jewish Nationalism: the theoretical roots of confrontation'. In Robert S. Wistrich (ed.), *The Left Against Zion: Communism, Israel and the Middle East*. London: Vallentine Mitchell, 1979.
—. *Revolutionary Jews from Marx to Trotsky*. London: Harrap, 1976.
Wolfinger, Raymond E. 'The Development and Persistence of Ethnic Voting'. *American Political Science Review* 59 (December 1965).
Wood, Neal. *Communism and British Intellectuals*. London: Gollancz, 1959.
Worpole, Ken. *Dockers and Detectives. Popular Reading. Popular Writing*. London: Verso, 1983.
Wright, A. W. 'Socialism and Nationalism'. In Leonard Tivey (ed.), *The Nation-State: The Formation of Modern Politics*. Oxford: Martin Robertson, 1981.
Young, Crawford. *The Politics of Cultural Pluralism*. Madison, WI: University of Wisconsin Press, 1976.
Yuval-Davis, Nira. 'Marxism and Jewish Nationalism'. *History Workshop* 24 (autumn 1987).
Zald, Mayer N., and Ash, Roberta. 'Social Movement Organizations: Growth, Decay annd Change'. *Social Forces* 44 (March 1966).
Zald, Mayer N., and McCarthy, John D. 'Introduction'. In Mayer N. Zald and John D. McCarthy (eds), *The Dynamics of Social Movements: Resource Mobilization, Social Control, and Tactics*. Cambridge, MA: Winthrop Publishers, 1979.

Index

Abramsky, Chimen 62–3, 72, 91, 93, 97, 99, 122, 123, 136, 164, 194 n165, 218 n105
Abyssinia 54
Acworth, Captain Bernard 59
Adams, W. Eric 45
Aid Spain committees 107, 108–9
Aid to Spain 105
air raid precautions 9, 36, 43–9, 57, 129, 142, 157
Alderman, Geoffrey 166 n11, 213, n21
Alexander, Sam 69, 104, 160
Aliens Act, 1905 2
Alveltlekher Yiddisher Kultur Farband 14, 26–7, 91
Amin el-Husseini, Haj, Mufti of Jerusalem 122
anarchism 13
Anderson shelters 45
Anderson, Sir John 45, 46, 66
Anglo-German Fellowship 53
Anglo-Jewish Association 6
Anglo-Jewry, established 6–7, 113, 128, 168 n39
Anski, S. 27
anti-Semitism 32, 48, 53, 55–64, 92, 145, 152, 153, 159; British 78–9, 129–30, 157; National Jewish Committee response 71–6; Polish 112, 113–16, 119, 130; Soviet 160, 161; wartime 66–71
Arabs 122, 123, 124, 157, 160
Ashkenazi 13
Association of Jewish Friendly Societies 87
Association of Jewish Writers and Journalists 27, 89
Attlee, Clement 30, 53, 62, 87, 89, 135

Bagnari, B. A. 24, 70, 81–2, 105, 111, 117
Baldwin, Stanley 44
Balfour Declaration 6, 121
Ballard, Robert 1
Bar Kochba, Simon 73, 104
Barou, Noah 24, 26, 67, 88, 89, 93, 111

Barry, Brian 8
Baxter, Beverley 67
Beamish, Henry Hamilton 53
Beaverbrook, Lord 140
Beckett, John 53, 58
Bedford, H. W. S. Russell, 12th Duke 59, 64
Beitler, N. 27
Bell, Daniel 149
Bell, Tom 83
Belsen 145, 146
Benabo, Mr 39
Bentley, J. W. 137
Bentwich, Norman 89
Bergelson, David 87, 162
Berger, Peter 13
Berling, Colonel Zygmunt 116
Berman, Adolph 120
Bethnal Green Underground Station disaster 68–9
Bevin, Ernest 136–7, 157
Birnbaum, Shliome 26
Birobidzhan, Jewish autonomous region 14, 24, 83, 84, 85–6, 99, 102, 122, 130, 157, 197 n10
black market 66–8, 130
Blatt, Alan 158
blitz 144; Stepney 42–9
Blumenfeld, Simon 40, 89–90, 184 n20
Board of Deputies of British Jews 6, 81–2, 90, 115, 121, 125; attitude to Fascism 56, 58, 63; discourages talk of 'Jewish vote' 2; and legislation against anti-Semitism 70; Palestine as Jewish state 124; Trades Advisory Council 67
Botwin Company 107–9
Botwin, Naftali 107
Bradley, Ben 92
Bramley, Ted 40–1, 46, 47, 50, 59, 143, 157, 158, 159
Bridgeman, Reginald 122
British Battalion 107
British Council for Christian Settlement in Europe 58

251

British National Party 59–60, 64
British People's Party 64
British Red Cross 88
British Union of Fascists 10, 33, 53–7, 129, 145, 153, 181 n126, 182 n130
Brodetsky, Selig 90, 91, 92, 95, 97, 114, 115, 125, 152
Brotman, A. G. 70
Brown, Isabel 85
Burke, Owen 33

Cable Street, 'Battle of' 17, 32, 54, 56, 61, 78, 81, 103, 188 n5
Calder, Ritchie 45, 48
Canada 25, 94, 142
Carver, Bill 101, 137, 138, 141, 143, 145, 146
Catholic Herald 33
Chamberlain, George 88
China 162
Churchill, Clementine 88, 92, 97, 100
Churchill, Winston 6, 46, 59, 63, 78, 110, 121, 126, 140
Circle-Arbeter Ring 107, 109, 111, 116, 129
Clarke, E. G., 'Mick' 33
class 2; ethnicity and 149
Cockburn, Claude 45
Cohen, Nat 106
Cold War 160
Cole, Margaret 1
Comintern, Seventh Congress 13–14
Communism, Jewish *see* Jewish Communism
Communist Party, Soviet (CPSU) 123, 161; Stepney *see* Stepney Communist Party
Communist Party of Great Britain 3, 42–3, 46, 54–5, 59–60, 83, 114, 118, 119, 129–30, 133–4, 138, 154, 156, 163; National Jewish Committee 14, 16–17, 23, 62–3, 64, 69, 71–6, 79, 88, 92, 95, 97, 98–9, 100–1, 110, 116, 118, 120, 123, 124–6, 129, 130, 134, 136, 161, 164, 194 n165
Conley, Andrew 136
Conn, Harry 39
Conservative Party 151; attempts to discredit 75–6
County of London Plan 49
Cracow 118
Creditor, L. S. 26
Cultural Revolution 162
Curzon Line 119

Dahl, Robert 5
Daily Herald 114
Daily Mail 64
Daily Worker 46–7, 50, 52, 57, 58, 59–60, 63, 66, 68, 78–9, 81, 82, 85, 95, 97, 109, 112, 115, 121, 122, 133, 141, 142, 143, 145, 146
Davies, Ioan 11
Davis, M. H. 31, 35, 43, 44, 45, 48, 55, 62, 87, 134, 153
defence regulation 18B 58–9
Devine, Pat 46, 109
Diaspora 15, 23
Discussion 122
'Doctors' Plot' 161, 162, 164
Doenitz, Admiral Karl 82
Domville, Sir Barry 58, 60
Donnelly, Hetty 139, 141
Donovan, Ella 39
Dreen, Sam 70, 111
Driberg, Tom 61, 114–16
Dutt, R. Palme 72, 74, 75, 92, 123, 125–6, 129, 143, 156, 162, 163

East London Advertiser 54, 67, 77, 87, 88, 95, 109, 133, 134, 138, 142, 144, 145
East London Observer 77
East London Spanish Medical Aid Committee 105
Easterman, A. L. 88, 114
Easton, David 8, 156
Ede, James Chuter 157
Eden, Anthony 78, 79, 81, 115
Edwards, W. J. 49, 62, 91, 135, 153, 159–60
Ehrenburg, Ilya 80, 81, 87, 94
Einhorn, Montagu 32
Eisenstein, Sergei 87
Elliot, Walter 41
Epstein, Jacob 89
Epstein, Shakhno 87, 91, 125
Essex, Maurice 73, 92, 137–8, 163–4, 209 n45
ethnic animosity, Stepney 29–37
ethnicity, and party preference 148–51, 156; political problems 1–2
Evans, Admiral Sir Edward R. 48

Fagan, Hymie 139
Fascism 3, 6, 9–10, 13, 18, 48, 53–7, 134, 139, 145, 152, 153, 157; Jewish concern over 31–5; wartime 57–64

INDEX

Feather, Victor 88
Federation of Jewish Relief Societies 97
Federation of Polish Jews in Great Britain 117
Feffer, Itzik 91, 94–102, 131, 162
Fine, J. L. 28, 62, 68, 87, 88, 89, 96, 106, 136–7, 146
Fineman, Sid 23
Finkelstein, Alf 55
Finsbury 146
Folk House 27
Foltz, William 7
Foot, Michael 116
France 125
Franco, Francisco 33, 103, 107, 110
Frankel, Dan 31, 35, 44, 49, 51, 53, 54, 61, 62, 89, 91, 108, 134, 136–7, 140–1, 144, 146, 153
Friends of the Soviet Union 83
Frucht, Asher 73
Fuchs, A. M. 26, 89, 91
Fyfe, Hamilton 41

Gallacher, Willie 60, 61, 68, 72, 73, 84, 91, 113, 139, 141
Gamson, William 8
Gaster, Dr Moses 85
Gaster, Jack 85, 157, 158, 159, 160, 162, 215 n55
General Election 1945 76, 82, 101–2, 110–11, 131, 138–42
genocide 78–9, 93
Gilbert, Abe 85
Gilbert, Simon 85
Gold, Mike 26
Goldberg, Fannie 143, 146
Gollan, John 72
Gordon, H. H. 18, 36, 39, 57
Gordon-Canning, Captain Robert 58, 60
Graham, Captain Alan 65
Greenberg, Sid 56
Greenblatt, 'Ginger' 55
Groser, Reverend St John B. 29, 39, 41, 42, 52, 184 n9
Gross, Harry 106
Gusev, Feodor 96
Gusfield, Joseph 12

Hackney 146
Halebsky, Sandor 10
Haldane, J. B. S. 42–3, 44, 47, 106, 140
Hall, George 115
Hall, J. H. 30, 41, 44, 53, 62, 87

Halsey, A. H. 2
Hamm, Jeffrey 63
Harris, Sir Percy 41
Hartz, Louis 172 n94
Hashomer Hatzair 124
Haskalah 13
Heberle, Rudolf 12
Hechter, Michael 5, 149
Henriques, Basil 25, 48, 87, 88
Hertz, J. H., Chief Rabbi 78, 91, 92, 95–6, 97, 98
Hinchingbrooke, Viscount 44
Histadrut 93, 94
Hitler, Adolf 6, 54, 60, 75, 79, 80, 98, 103, 110, 159
Hitler–Stalin Pact 157
Holland, Alf 23–4, 26, 72, 73, 84, 85, 89, 92, 107, 138
Holmes, Walter 59, 60, 79, 95
Holocaust 76, 78–9, 118, 131, 153, 159
Horowitz, Donald 9
housing 143, 157; Stepney 9, 28, 29, 144–5; wartime 49-52
Hungarian revolution 161
Hungary 86
Hyde, Douglas 60, 64, 133, 209 n37
Hyndman, H. M. 21

Ibbetson, Harry 92, 125, 137
ideology, and social movements 12–13
Imperial Fascist League 53, 58
Independent Jewish Cabinet Makers Association 23
International Brigades 108
International Press Correspondence 129
internment, Jews in wartime 64–6
Ireland, neutrality 32
Irish, relations with Jews 7, 128–9, 153, 179 n96; Stepney 3, 29–30, 132, 155; Stepney Labour Party 8–9, 10, 30–2, 36–7, 152
Iron Curtain 160
Israel 160, 163

Jabotinsky Revisionist Zionists 85
Jacobs, Joe 53, 54, 55
Jacobs, Julius 23, 31, 104, 106, 109, 134, 160
Jacobs, Morris 23, 99, 109
James, J. E. Arnold 45
Janner, Barnett 30, 87, 88, 92, 96, 97, 99, 152
Jestem Polakiem 113

253

Jewish 1942 Committee 89, 90
Jewish Agency 93
Jewish Anti-Fascist Committee (JAFC) 87, 91, 94, 100, 102, 125, 130, 161
Jewish Autonomous Region 84, 85–6, 130
Jewish Board of Guardians 6
Jewish Charter of Freedom 73, 74, 130
Jewish Chronicle 30, 45, 47, 56, 57–8, 61, 63, 64, 65, 67, 70–1, 85, 86, 89, 100, 111, 112, 113, 116, 123, 129, 151, 163
Jewish Clarion 101, 119, 120, 129, 162, 164
Jewish Communism 11–19, 151–6; and anti-Semitism 71–6; campaign against Mosley 53–7; decline 156–64; defence of Jewish community in wartime 64–71; opposition to Nazi Germany 76–82; opposition to wartime Fascism 57–64; and Palestine 121–7; and Poland 111–21; pro-Soviet activities 86–94; and Soviet nationality policy 83–6; and Spanish Civil War 103–11; visit of Mikhoels and Fefer 94–102; world-wide 14
Jewish community, Stepney 20–7
Jewish Cultural Club 16, 18, 73, 91, 114, 120, 130, 131
Jewish Enlightenment 13
Jewish Forum 75, 101, 120, 121, 126, 129
Jewish Fund for Soviet Russia (JFSR) 16, 18, 92, 93, 94, 95, 97, 98, 99, 100, 130–1, 152
Jewish Labour Bund 13, 14, 24
Jewish National Theatre 26
Jewish Opinion 81, 101, 119, 129
Jewish People's Council Against Fascism and Anti-Semitism (JPC) 16, 17, 18, 24, 35, 55–7, 98, 105, 130, 137
Jewish Protest Committee 112
Jewish Quarterly 86
Jewish soldiers, in Polish army 114–16
Jews, displaced, Germany 145; East London 4–11; Polish 111–21; in wartime 64–71
Johnson, Hewlett, Dean of Canterbury 96
Johnson, Joseph 36
Joyce, William 53, 61, 145

Kaiser, A. M. 27, 116
Kanter, Hymie 136–7
Katyn massacre 113
Kaye, Solly 83, 110
Kershaw, A. 146

Khruschev, Nikita 161, 162
Kiev 96
Kirby, Edward 143
Koenig, Leo 26, 89, 91
Kramer, Joseph 145–6

Labour Israel 163
Labour Monthly 129
Labour Party 3, 8, 24, 113–14, 124, 133, 146; attitude to Fascism 53–4, 55, 61–2; Irish influence 8–9, 10, 30–7, 128–9; Jewish support 151–2; Stepney 134–5, 144, 152
Lansbury, George 132
Laski, Harold 91
Lawder, J. C. 31, 147
League Against Imperialism 122
League of Ex-Servicemen and Women 63–4
Lebow, Morry 34, 137
Leese, Arnold 53, 58, 63
Left Book Club Theatre Guild 26
Leftwich, Joseph 26, 90, 91, 95, 96, 123
Lenin, V. I. 71, 83
Levenberg, Schneier 93, 94
Lever, Solomon 27
Levitas, Max 143
Levy, Hyman 26, 72, 73, 74, 80, 86, 89–90, 91, 96, 97, 110, 141, 162–3
Levy, Joseph Hillel 117–18
Lewey, Frank 44–5, 88
Liberal Party, Anglo-Jewish adherence 2–3, 151; Stepney 30–1
Lieberman, Aaron 21
Limehouse 29
'Link', pro-German organization 53, 58, 76
Lipsky, Michael 154
Lisky, I. A. 26, 27, 90, 91, 136
literature, Yiddish 24–7
Litvinoff, Emanuel 21
Lloyd George, David 151
Locker, Berl 92, 93–4
Locker-Lampson, Commander Oliver 62
London Botwin Aid Committee 107
London Committee of the Medem Sanatorium 111
London Poles 112–16, 119, 130
London Trades Council 104, 106, 134
London Yiddish Theatre 27
London–Veitchepl 86, 95, 98–9, 117, 118, 129
Long, J. J. 32–3, 35, 36
Loyalists, Spanish Civil War 6, 32

INDEX

Lubbock, Harry 70, 72
Lublin 119
Lublin Poles 116
Luckmann, Thomas 13
Lyons, A. J. 77
Lyons, Lewis 21

Maisky, Ivan 48, 89, 90, 91, 92, 94, 122–3
Mallon, J. J. 49, 65, 87, 88, 95
Manger, Itzik 26
Mannheim, Karl 13, 158, 172 n90
Markish, Peretz 87, 162
Markov, Mark 27
Martin, Kingsley 45
Marx, Karl 71
Marxism 14–15
Marxism Today 162
Masters, Sam 106
Matthew, C. J. 30
Medem, Gina 26, 108
Mexico 94
Mikhoels, Shloime 87, 94–102, 131
Mikolajczyk, Stanislaw 115
Mile End 19, 31, 132; general election 76, 82, 101–2, 110–11, 131, 138–42, 150; preparation for election campaign 133–8
Militant Christian Patriots 53
Milne, R. S. 13
Mindel, Mick 72, 83, 87, 88, 89, 96, 98, 108, 136–7, 140, 162, 172 n95, 181 n122
Mindel, Morris 117
Ministry of Information 66
Mitford, Jessica 59
Mola, Emilio 103, 107
Montagu, Ivor 145
Morgn Freiheit 108, 125
Morrison, Herbert 30, 45, 59, 60, 61, 63, 64, 66, 69, 71, 78, 79
Moscow Yiddish State Theatre 94, 95, 102
Moses, Miriam 96
Mosley, Diana 59, 62
Mosley, Sir Oswald 9, 18, 32, 33, 35, 74, 75, 81, 98, 103, 106, 139, 145, 151, 157; campaign against 53–7, 130; detention 58–62
Motion, Squadron Leader Vernon 135, 141
Moyne, Lord 207 n143
Murray, Stephen 42
Mussolini, Benito 33, 53–4, 75, 103, 110
Myer, Morris 25, 26, 27, 87, 89, 90, 96, 110, 112

Nathan of Churt, Lord 92
Nathani, Itzhak 27, 70, 163
National Amalgamated Furnishing Trades Association (NAFTA) 16, 21–2, 28, 46, 80, 99, 105–6, 108, 109, 128, 136
National Council for Civil Liberties 60, 69–70, 114, 116, 130
National Council of Labour 105–6
National Joint Committee for Spanish Relief 105
National Socialist League 53, 58
National Union of Tailors and Garment Workers (NUTGW) 16, 21, 30, 65–6, 78, 87, 106–7, 109, 128, 136, 146
Nationalists, Spanish Civil War 32
Nazism 13, 33; opposition to 76–82
Nelson, Dale 10
New Life 158
New Life–Neilebn 84
New Statesman 45
newspapers, Yiddish 25–6
North Atlantic Treaty 160
North Korea 162

O'Brien, Edward 62
Opatoshu, Joseph 26
Orbach, Maurice 60, 67
Organization for Jewish Colonization in Soviet Russia (ICOS) 84–5, 130, 197 n18
Orwell, George 1, 66, 141
O'Shiel, F. R. 29
Oved, Moshe 26, 89, 90, 91
overcrowding, Stepney 27–8

Palestine 6, 18, 84, 85, 93, 96, 97, 98, 118, 121–7, 131, 153, 157
Palestine Communist Party 122
Panner, Issie 48, 56, 71–2, 84, 85–6, 123–4, 130
Parker, John 61
Pearce, Jack 56
Pelling, Henry 165 n2
Perlzweig, Reverend M. L. 84
Perry, Jack 137–8, 160
Phillips, Morgan 32, 55
Phillips, Percy 89
Pilchik, Julius 109
Piratin, Phil 19, 68, 88, 109, 121, 132, 143, 144, 145, 146; on ARP 43, 44, 46, 47, 48–9; bankruptcy 161; borough council election winner 35–6, 39, 143; defeat in Stepney 159–60; electoral victory 1, 4,

255

148–51; on Fascism 55, 56, 60, 62; general election campaign 76, 82, 101–2, 110–11, 131, 138–42; housing 38, 42, 49, 51–2; on Palestine 126–7; Savoy Hotel occupation 47; selected for Mile End 135–8; on Stepney Communist Party 34; on Stepney as slum 29
'Pitcairn, Frank' 45
Poale Zion 26, 88, 93–4, 120
Poland 6, 18, 20, 86, 97, 128, 152
Polish Committee of National Liberation 116, 117
Polish government-in-exile 112–16, 119
Polish Jews 111–21, 159
Polish National Council 112–13
Pollitt, Harry 30, 35, 60–1, 118, 133, 163
Port of London Authority 47
poverty, Stepney 28, 29
Priestley, J. B. 96
Pritchard, John 67, 88
Pritt, D. N. 64, 69, 85, 116
Proltet 26
Pushkin, Issie 56, 72, 85, 137

Raczkiewicz, Wladyslaw 116
Rampling, Tom 29, 34, 75, 132, 143, 145, 146
Ramsay, Captain Archibald 53, 58, 63, 70, 76, 195 n182
Ramsay, Edith 32
Rathbone, Eleanor 66, 116
Rawidowicz, Simon 92
Rawnsley, Stuart 33
Red Cross Aid-to-Russia Fund 88, 92, 97
refugees 79; Jewish, internment 64–6
rent control 36, 39, 41
rent strikes 17, 29, 39–42, 189 n28
Ribbentrop, Joachim von 76
Right Club 53
Roberts, Helena 31, 36, 43, 55
Rockman, Alf 77
Roeder, H. C. 95
Rollin, A. R. 89, 106, 109, 116
Roman Catholicism, Stepney Irish 31–3
Rosen, Tubby 34, 39, 40, 41, 42, 44, 47, 142, 143, 145, 157, 164
Roth, Cecil 89
Rothermere, Harold Harmsworth, 1st Viscount 64
Rothschild, Joseph 2
Russia 20; Pale of Settlement 13, 14, *see also* Soviet Union
Russia Today 101

Russia Today Society 79–80, 83, 114, 130
Russian Revolution 33, 83

Salaman, Redcliffe 92, 93
Samuel, Herbert 3
Samuel, Raphael 154
Savoy Hotel, occupation 46–7
Schwartzbart, Ignacy 113
Second Front 77, 80–2
Seedo, N. M. 27
Segal, 'Chick' 55
Segal, Morrie 55
Seliktar, Ofira 151
Sevareid, Eric 46
Shapiro, Michael 38, 39, 40, 42, 50, 143, 144–5, 159, 161–2
shelters, Anderson 45; deep (Haldane shelters) 43, 44, 47; London Underground 46, 140, 186 n72
Shils, Edward 5
Shinwell, Emanuel 61
Sieff, Mrs Israel M. 92
Silkin, Lewis 49
Silkoff, Ruby 55, 181 n122
Silverman, Alf 72, 88, 106
Silverman, Sydney 61, 93
Simon, Sir John 54
Simpson, George 7
Skidelsky, Robert 33
Sloves, Chaim 26
slum landlords 9, 18, 145
Smith, M. G. 8
Social Democratic Federation 21
social movement, Jewish Communism as 11–19
socialism 13
Sokoloff, Bertha 50, 73, 134, 138, 143, 145, 164, 183 n157, 216 n64
Solomons, Henry 18
Sommerstein, Emil 119
Sonntag, Jacob 86, 89, 91, 97, 158
South Africa 125, 142
Soviet Union 6, 14, 18, 59, 70–1, 74, 125, 126–7, 136, 152, 160; Jewish Communist support for 76–82, 86–94; Jewish criticism 160, 161, 162–3; nationality policy 83–6, 130; Soviet–Polish split 113–14
Spain 152, 159
Spanish Civil War 6, 10, 32, 103–11, 128, 131, 202 n5
Spanish Relief Committee (Jewish Section) 105

INDEX

Spanish Relief Fund 105
Spitalfields 21
Springhall, D. F. 109
Stalin, J. V. 71, 86, 95, 99, 119, 161
Stalingrad 92, 97
Stein, Leonard J. 92
Steinberg, A. L., 'Chirps' 56, 158
Stencl, A. N. 26, 86, 91, 95, 98–9, 117, 129, 177 n60
Stepney 4; blitz 43–9; Committee for Air Raid Precautions 43; demography 132; ethnic animosity 29–37; housing 28, 29; Jewish community 20–7; problems in 1930s 27–9
Stepney Aid to Russia Committee 88, 99
Stepney Communist Party 1, 34–6, 45–7, 49–50, 68, 154–5, 156; borough elections 1945 142–7; campaign against Mosley 53–7; general election 76, 82, 101–2, 110–11, 131, 138–42; Jewish phenomenon 3–4; political base 128–31; preparation for general election 133–8; support for Soviet Union 77–8
Stepney Council for Peace and Democracy 32, 43
Stepney Reconstruction Group 49
Stepney Shelters Co-ordinating Committee 47
Stepney Tenants' Defence League (STDL) 16, 18, 36, 38–42, 44, 45, 47, 49, 51–2, 56, 57, 130, 144, 152, 157
Stepney Trades Council 55, 136, 137
Strabolgi, Lord 69
Strauss, G. R. 116
sweatshops 21

Temple, William, Archbishop of Canterbury 69
theatre, Yiddish 26, 27
Tilbury shelter 33, 47–8, 186 n75
Tillett, Ben 88
The Times 65
trade unions 8; Jewish 21–3
Trades Union Congress, 88, 105; resolutions against 'pauper aliens' 21
Truman, David 148
Di Tsayt 25–6, 76, 87, 110, 129
Turner, Robert 156

unemployment, Stepney 28–9
United Clothing Workers' Union (UCWU) 10
United Jewish Committee 90, 91–2

United Jewish Workers' Committee for the Relief of the Jewish Children in Poland 111, 112
United Ladies Tailors' Trade Union (ULTTU) 16, 22, 28–9, 30, 106–7, 108, 128
United States 25, 94, 118, 125, 142, 159
United Synagogue 6
USSR *see* Soviet Union

V-1/V-2 rockets 49, 50
Valentine, Peter 72, 123
Versailles Treaty 78
Vichy France 79
Vogler, I. M. 18, 31, 32, 34, 36–7, 43, 44, 45, 68, 105

Wapping 29
war crimes 82, 93
Warner, Sylvia Townsend 122
Warsaw 118
Warsaw ghetto, uprising 116–17
Wasilewska, Wanda 117
Waterman, Alec 26, 70, 72, 73, 83, 84, 89, 91, 97, 99, 104, 109, 162
Waterman, Mrs Ray 98
Wedgwood, Lord 69
Weinberg, Barnett 84, 111
Weinberg, Queenie 143
Weiner, Nathan 70, 110
Weizmann, Chaim 98
Wesker, Sarah 55, 108, 162
Westminster 146
Whitechapel 21, 29
Williams, Robin 148
Willis, Ted 120–1
Winchevsky, Morris 21
Winwood, Major Thomas 146
Woods, George 61
Workers' Circle 7, 16, 17, 23–5, 26, 27, 63, 65, 69, 70, 81, 83, 87, 88, 97, 98, 104–5, 107, 108–9, 110, 111–12, 115, 116, 117, 120, 126, 128, 129, 130, 131, 136; Yiddish Drama Group 26
Workers' Theatre Movement 26
World Congress Against Racialism and Anti-Semitism 24
World Jewish Congress 88, 114, 115; first 24
World Jewish Cultural Union 14, 26–7, 91
World News and Views 129
Wright, A. W. 149

Yalta Conference 74, 118–19
Yiddish, language and literature 24–7
Yiddish Folks Theatre 26, 27
Yiddish London 26
Yinger, Milton 7
Yishuv 122, 124, 125
YKUF 14, 26–7, 91
Young, Crawford 9

Zaidman, Lazar 15, 63, 70, 72, 74–5, 97, 99, 118, 150, 161, 163, 194 n65
Zak, William 46
Zangwill, Mrs Israel 92
Zionism 6, 13, 24, 71, 85, 93–4, 98, 121–2, 123, 124, 128, 131, 155, 159, 160, 163
Zionist Federation of Great Britain 87, 90, 99
Zionist Review 94, 98
Zygielbojm, Shmuel 113, 117